SPEAK THE SPEECH

❧ SPEAK THE SPEECH

The Shakespeare Quotation Book

Louis Marder, *Editor*

The Shakespeare Data Bank
COMPILED BY KATHY WAGNER
PRODUCED BY THE PHILIP LIEF GROUP, INC.

 HarperPerennial
A Division of HarperCollinsPublishers

A hardcover edition of this book was published in 1994 by HarperCollins Publishers, Inc.

"Speak the Speech" from *Hamlet*, III.ii.1.
Published by arrangement with
    The Philip Lief Group, Inc.
    6 West 20th Street
    New York, NY 10011

First HarperPerennial edition published 1995.

Designed by Janet Tingey

The Library of Congress has catalogued the hardcover edition as follows:

Shakespeare, William, 1564–1616.
    Speak the speech : the Shakespeare quotation book / Louis Marder, editor ;
compiled by Kathy Wagner ; produced by the Philip Lief Group, Inc. — 1st ed.
        p. cm.
    Includes indexes.
    ISBN 0-06-270070-7
    1. Shakespeare, William, 1564–1616—Quotations. 2. Quotations, English.
I. Marder, Louis, 1915–   . II. Wagner, Kathy. III. Philip Lief Group. IV. Title.
PR2892.M285 1993
822.3'3—dc20   93-4842

ISBN 0-06-272063-5 (pbk.)

95 96 97 98 99 ❖/RRD 10 9 8 7 6 5 4 3 2 1

❧ CONTENTS

❧ PREFACE

Words are but words, but when they say something with universal signif-
icance, they become quotations in a form that Alexander Pope described
as "What oft was said, but ne'er so well expressed." The practice of anthol-
ogizing Shakespearean quotations celebrates the power of words to express
human thought in a succinct and memorable manner, even outside the
context in which the words originally appeared. The most carefully
extracted quotations are universally applicable. They offer writers and
speakers a feeling of quiet contentment, agreement, identification, and
kinship with the author. They add the breadth of Shakespeare's mind to
that of the user, and affords her or him the tang of classic utterance. In
short, an anthology of Shakespearean quotations constitutes a currency
which can be used anywhere in the world.

William Shakespeare's genius and quotability were recognized early in
his career. In 1598, when Shakespeare was only thirty-four years old, Francis Meres wrote in his *Palladis Tamia* or "Wit's Treasury" that "the Muses
would speak with Shakespeare's fine-filed phrases if they would speak
English." In 1601, the students at St. John's College in Cambridge performed a play in which Shakespeare is praised and quoted as a poet several
times. A few years later, William Camden, the Herald/historian to whom
Shakespeare applied for his coat-of-arms, wrote in his *Remaines...Concerning
Britain* (1605) that Shakespeare was among the "pregnant wits of these
our times," and, prophetically, among those "whom succeeding ages may
justly admire." In John Bodenham's *Belvedere*, or *The Garden of the Muses*
(1600), an anthology of quotations from contemporaries, Shakespeare is
quoted (not always correctly) no less than 213 times, spanning six plays

and the long poems "Venus and Adonis," and "The Rape of Lucrece." The first anthologies devoted to Shakespearean quotations appeared in 1752 when William Dodd (1729–1777), Chaplain to King George III, published *The Beauties from Shakespeare*, which was reprinted forty times and has become a classic.

When we realize that Shakespeare wrote 118,406 lines consisting of 884,647 words in 31,959 speeches, we can understand what a remarkable resource in quantity, quality, and variety *Speak the Speech* is, considering the quotability of the author. It is no wonder that, through the centuries, imaginative writers, speakers, theater artists, politicians, editors, educators, students, legal professionals, businesspeople, policymakers, and more have turned to him to illustrate and enhance their ideas.

When you peruse this book, you may notice that some of Shakespeare's quotable material is proverbial. Quite remarkably, Shakespeare used over 3000 proverbs in his plays, and this figure does not include the thousands of original quotations his works have made proverbial. When Shakespeare uses a proverb, it is a valuable thought. When Shakespeare writes something original that becomes widely applicable, these quotations become almost proverbial in their widespread use. That Shakespeare was able to hold this wealth of proverb lore in his mind and insert them so casually into his plays and poems makes us wonder about the kind of mind he had.

Because he knew the limits of his formal education and was not one of the "University wits"—those dramatists who had attended Oxford and Cambridge—Shakespeare had to strive harder to pick up all the knowledge and lore he knew he could eventually use. It is important to know that Shakespeare had a vocabulary of about 20,000 different words. Scholars have written hundreds of books and articles about Shakespeare's knowledge of law, music, botany, animals, the Bible, medicine, insects, printing, sports, flowers, heraldry, etc. It has been aptly said that if all the religious material in the world disappeared, we would be able to reconstruct a new ethical system from the works of Shakespeare.

How did Shakespeare achieve such admiration? We must accept the fact that Shakespeare was a Genius. No one else in his period or since has achieved his eminence. He is the most quoted author in the world, and has been translated into over a hundred languages. If we add the generic term "genius" to Shakespeare's mind, it does help to explain his great talent for describing characters and events as they have never been described before or since. The fact remains that Shakespeare had a brain like a sponge. It is the only way we can account for his knowledge. He absorbed everything from the people he spoke with, he listened intently, and when he was writing, he could squeeze that sponge for anything he had ever seen, read, or heard. In the spirit of this compilation, I leave it to the Bard himself to offer the quintessential description of his own creative and intellectual capacities:

> What a piece of work is man! How noble in reason! How infinite in faculty!...in apprehension how like a God! The beauty of the world! The paragon of animals.—Hamlet, *Hamlet*, II.ii.303

LOUIS MARDER, PH.D.
EDITOR
The Shakespeare Data Bank

❋ INTRODUCTION

"How long a time lies in one little word!" Bullingbrook says in *Richard II*. "These words will cost ten thousand lives this day," says Edward Prince of Wales in *Henry VI Part III*. "Good words are better than bad strokes," exclaims Hamlet in *Hamlet*. Shakespeare's genius was that he understood the power of words; he also knew that words are stubborn, that often words don't seem to match what it is we are trying to say. Words express the known, and the unknown, or the ineffable. This is why we always come back to them. They are our curse and our salvation.

The quotations from Shakespeare's plays and poems in *Speak the Speech* are here to guide you to the right word, the right expression, the right glimmer of truth. This book is for everybody—students, businesspeople, gardeners, writers and actors, lawyers, doctors, teachers and more. All of the quotations have been organized into categories that reflect meaning, use, and application, ranging from the philosophical ("idealism") to the political and social ("civil rights") to the practical ("snoring"). *Speak the Speech* is not a concordance or an index, but a book created for people interested in thoughts and ideas.

SHAKESPEARE IN TODAY'S WORLD

In this book, you'll find over 3,000 quotations distributed across approximately 500 categories—reflecting an eclectic mix of the traditional and the contemporary. Many of the quotes and categories echo such age-old themes as love ("So are you to my thoughts as food to life,/ Or as sweet-season'd showers are to the ground." Sonnet 75, 1-2), death ("We were born to die." Capulet, *Romeo and Juliet*, III.iv.4), and knowledge ("And seeing ignorance is the curse of God,/ Knowledge the wing wherewith we fly to heaven." Lord Say, *2 Henry VI*, IV.VII.73). But many of the categories have a distinctly modern ring and are included in the book to provide you with a sense of the relevance of Shakespeare's plays and poems to the world today, especially as we enter the new century.

You will discover, for example, several categories which relate to issues of gender, including "men," "women," "misogyny," "gender," "feminism," "singlehood," and "marriage." The inclusion of "feminism" and "misogyny" reflects contemporary interest in both the treatment of women in Shakespeare and the rise to legitimacy of Women's Studies in general. The more traditional categories of "men" and "women" encompass a wide range of quotations about the nature of both men and women from a variety of male and female perspectives ("I had rather hear my dog bark at a crow than a man swear he loves me." Beatrice, *Much Ado About Nothing*, I.I.131; or "A woman is a dish for the gods, if the devil dress her not." Clown, *Love's Labor's Lost*, IV.III.298.) The category "gender" includes quotes that look at manhood and womanhood as fluid constructs, i.e. "Thy beauty hat made me effeminate/ And in my temper soft'ned valor's steel" Romeo, *Romeo and Juliet*, III.I.113).

Some of the other unusual categories attesting to the range of Shakespeare's thinking and its contemporary appeal include "vegetarianism," "cosmetics," "fads and fashion," "drugs and medication," and "environmentalism." You may be surprised to discover, through this book, Shakespeare's sensitivity to the power of drugs to alter human behavior ("I do know her spirit/ And will not trust one of her malice with/ A drug of such damned nature. Those she has will stupefy and dull the sense awhile,/ Which first (perchance) she'll prove on cats and dogs,/ Then afterward up higher." Cornelius, *Cymbeline*, I.v.34). Or you may find a quote which suggests Shakespeare's sensitivity to environmental concerns ("Nature's bequest gives nothing, but doth lend,/ And being frank she lends to those are free." (Sonnet 4, 3).

Some of the quotations in *Speak the Speech* will be easily recognized. Richard's moving "Now is the winter of our discontent" speech (Richard Duke of Gloucester, Richard III, I.I.1) can be easily found in the "winter" category and also under "Character-Richard III.") "By the pricking of my thumbs/ Something wicked this way comes." (Witch #2, *Macbeth*, IV.I.44) awaits under the header "supernatural." And to find "Shall I compare thee to a summer's day?/ Thou art more lovely and more temperate: / Rough winds to shake the darling buds of May,/ And summer's lease hath all too short a date." (Sonnet 6, 1-3), you need only look under "summer."

In addition to the famous lines and speeches *Speak the Speech* includes many quotations chosen for their pith or their ability to say a great deal in a few words. "They do not love that do not show their love," says Julia in

The Two Gentlemen of Verona. "He that dies pays all debts," declares Stephano in *The Tempest*. "Nature must obey necessity," warns Brutus in *Julius Caesar*. Many of these pungently spare quotations, and others chosen for their vibrancy, color, humor, style, and wit are from the lesser known works.

A whole section of "character" quotes offers over twenty-five descriptions of many of the major characters in Shakespeare's plays. Browse through here to study the complexity of a master craftsperson, gingerly weaving together the many layers that comprise Hamlet, Cleopatra, or Coriolanus. Many of these quotes depict one character describing another. Others sound the subject character's voice itself. Here, characters reveal themselves overtly or by expressing their opinions of their world.

Another distinctive feature of *Speak the Speech* is the inclusion of quotations from Shakespeare's sonnets and poems. Lines from many of the famous sonnets are found in such categories as "love" and "beauty" ("Let me not to the marriage of true minds/ Admit impediments; love is not love/ Which alters when it alteration finds,/ Or bends with the remover to the remove." Sonnet 116, 1-4). Shakespeare's longer poems are also represented in this book; you'll find quotes from "Venus and Adonis," "The Rape of Lucrece," "A Lover's Complaint," and "The Phoenix and the Turtle."

IN SEARCH OF THE PERFECT QUOTE

All quotations are followed by the name of the speaker, the play from which the quotation comes, the act, the scene, and the specific line. This will allow you quick access to the exact spot in the original text from which the quote has been extracted, further elucidating the quote's meaning. By referring back to the text, you will not only glean the importance of a specific quotation in the context of an individual act or scene, but can also begin a more thorough study of a character or theme.

Several features will expedite your search for perfect quotes. Many of the categories are cross-referenced. If you can't find a quote under "dreams" that expresses exactly what you'd like to say, you can follow any of the other routes suggested, including "daydreaming," "imagination," and "sleep."

The indexes at the back of the book are arranged by work and by speaker. If, for example, you need to find a quote from *All's Well That Ends Well*, you need only look for that title in the alphabetically arranged "By-Work" index. Every page within *Speak the Speech* featuring a quote from this play is listed in this index, along with the subject headers categorizing these quotes. The "By-Speaker" index encompasses all the plays and is organized by the name (or names) of the character (or characters) to whom quotes are attributed. As Shakespeare often uses the same name in several plays (i.e.

Portia appears both in *Julius Caesar* and *The Merchant of Venice*), the "By-Speaker" index lists the title of the play along with the character's name.

Speak the Speech's glossary will give you definitions for antiquated, idiomatic, or cryptic words and terms. This glossary will help cure "logophobia," which students and readers of Shakespeare often feel, mitigating the fear that might prevent one from quoting Feste's observation in *Twelfth Night*: "Thus the whirligig of time brings in his revenges. (V.i.376). Upon stumbling over this rare word, you can simply turn to the glossary and discover that a *whirligig* is nothing more than a "spinning top," thus enabling you to use this quote with confidence.

SHAKESPEARE FOR EVERY OCCASION

The quotes in *Speak the Speech* are categorized not necessarily by intent of the original speaker, but with an ear for their most effective use out of context, in a wide range of contemporary situations. Don't be surprised to stumble upon category headers that would have certainly been anachronistic to Shakespeare's England, like "artificial respiration," "plastic surgery," or "baseball." The point here is that Shakespeare's language lives today, and can be joyously perpetuated through active use.

A student in a Shakespeare class, for example, might look up the subject header of "madness and mental illness." After finding several quotations from the great tragedies—*Macbeth*, *Hamlet*, and *King Lear*—he or she might be inspired to develop a comparative analysis of madness in two or three of the plays, or search further by heeding the cross-references included under the category header. By doing so, relevant quotes might be found under "depression," for example.

Lawyers, physicians, businesspeople, and politicians writing letters and giving speeches will find many of the categories in *Speak the Speech* germane to their particular fields. There are categories on "law" and "lawyers" ("We must not make a scarecrow of the law," says Angelo in *Measure for Measure*.) Physicians express their humility with a quote from *Cymbeline* ("By med'cine life may be prolong'd, yet death/ Will seize the doctor too.") Executives and politicians addressing the public may find several categories of interest and inspiration; there are quotations about "public opinion," "persuasion," "bigotry and intolerance," "business," "complaints," "disorder," "hunger," and "homelessness."

In the same way that William Faulkner took inspiration for his book *The Sound and the Fury* from *Macbeth*, a budding novelist or poet may find a line or two which will bring into focus her vision of the world. Actors may find several quotations a perfect springboard to an audition passage. Gardeners faced with the task of pruning back their beautiful plants may take some comfort in the gardener's lines from *Richard II*, "Superfluous branches/ We lop away, that bearing boughs may live." And those kept awake by snoring mates may finally know what to say to the well-rested perpetrator in the morning: "Thou dost snore distinctly,/ There's meaning in thy snores." (Sebastian, *The Tempest*, II.i.217).

Many quotations have been pruned for easier use. Where possible, excess lines have been deleted and the quote stripped down to its essence. Although great care has been given to getting at the essence of a specific quote, you should feel free to pare the quotes even further. The quotes are for your use—be flexible with the language.

THE BEAUTY OF LANGUAGE

The right quote can clarify one's own perceptions and foster the expression of one's thoughts. A comparative glance at Shakespeare can offer you not only a sense of the genius of one of the world's greatest writers, but also a sense of the range and flexibility of the English language.

It is the poetry and texture of the words in Shakespeare's plays and poems, coupled with his enduring wisdom, which is the meat of *Speak the Speech*. Within this book, you'll encounter a distillation of the remarkable intelligence and wit that distinguishes the Shakespeare canon. His voice, his "spirit all compact," remains with us today. "He speaks plain cannon—fire, and smoke, and bounce" says Philip the Bastard in *King John*. We only need to be gently reminded that his is a voice for all people and for all times.

Kathy Wagner
Washington College

ABSENCE

How like a winter hath my absence been
From thee, the pleasure of the fleeting year!
What freezings I have felt, what dark days I have seen!
What old December's bareness every where!

SONNET 97, 1–4

Noblest of men, woo't die?
Hast thou no care of me? Shall I abide
In this dull world, which in thy absence is
No better than a sty?

CLEOPATRA, *Antony and Cleopatra*, IV.XV.59

Here may his head lie on my throbbing breast;
But where's the body that I should embrace?

QUEEN MARGARET, *2 Henry VI*, IV.IV.5

I have been long a sleeper; but I trust
My absence doth neglect no great design,
Which by my presence might have been concluded.

RICHARD, DUKE OF GLOUCESTER, *Richard III*, III.IV.23

O thou that dost inhabit in my breast,
Leave not the mansion so long tenantless,
Lest growing ruinous, the building fall
And leave no memory of what it was!

VALENTINE, *The Two Gentlemen of Verona*, V.IV.7

You would be another Penelope: yet they
say, all the yarn she spun in Ulysses' absence did but
fill Ithaca full of moths.

VALERIA, *Coriolanus*, I.III.82

ABSTINENCE
see also CHASTITY; SELF-RESTRAINT

To fast, to study, and to see no women—
Flat treason 'gainst the kingly state of youth.
Say, can you fast? Your stomachs are too young,
And abstinence engenders maladies.

BEROWNE, *Love's Labor's Lost*, IV.III.288

O, these are barren tasks, too hard to keep,
Not to see ladies, study, fast, not sleep.

BEROWNE, *Love's Labor's Lost*, I.I.47

Not to-night, good Iago, I have very poor
and unhappy brains for drinking. I could well wish
courtesy would invent some other custom of entertainment.

CASSIO, *Othello*, II.III.34

Brave conquerors—for so you are,
That war against your own affections
And the huge army of the world's desires.

FERDINAND, KING OF NAVARRE, *Love's Labor's Lost*, I.I.8

Refrain to-night,
And that shall lend a kind of easiness
To the next abstinence, the next more easy;
For use almost can change the stamp of nature.

HAMLET, *Hamlet*, III.IV.165

Yet I think
Did I not by th' abstaining of my joy,
Which breeds a deeper longing, cure their surfeit
That craves a present med'cine, I should pluck
All ladies' scandal on me.

HIPPOLYTA, *The Two Noble Kinsmen*, I.I.188

The mind shall banquet, though the body pine;
Fat paunches have lean pates; and dainty bits
Make rich the ribs, but bankrout quite the wits.

LONGAVILLE, *Love's Labor's Lost*, I.I.25

Good faith, this same young sober-
blooded boy doth not love me, nor a man cannot make
him laugh, but that's no marvel, he drinks no wine.

SIR JOHN FALSTAFF, *2 Henry IV*, IV.III.87

He doth with holy abstinence subdue
That in himself which he spurs on his pow'r
To qualify in others.

VINCENTIO, DUKE OF VIENNA, *Measure for Measure*, IV.II.81

ACCUSATION
see also GUILT

Wrong hath but wrong, and blame the due of blame.

BUCKINGHAM, *Richard III*, V.I.29

But beseech your Grace
Be plainer with me, let me know my trespass
By its own visage.

CAMILLO, *The Winter's Tale*, I.II.264

Then call them to our presence; face to face,
And frowning brow to brow, ourselves will hear
The accuser and the accused freely speak.

KING RICHARD, *Richard II*, I.I.15

I was provokèd by her sland'rous tongue,
That laid their guilt upon my guiltless shoulders.

RICHARD, DUKE OF GLOUCESTER, *Richard III*, I.II.97

I do the wrong, and first begin to brawl.
The secret mischiefs that I set abroach
I lay unto the grievous charge of others.
RICHARD, DUKE OF GLOUCESTER, Richard III, I.III.324

ACHIEVEMENT
see also ACTION, SUCCESS

What you cannot as you would achieve,
You must perforce accomplish as you may.
AARON, Titus Andronicus, II.I.106

He hath borne himself beyond the promise of his age, doing
in the figure of a lamb the feats of a lion. He hath
indeed better bett'red expectation.
MESSENGER, Much Ado About Nothing, I.I.13

ACTION
see also ACHIEVEMENT; BEHAVIOR

Let my deeds be witness of my worth.
AARON, Titus Andronicus, V.I.103

What I will, I will, and there an end.
ANTONIO, The Two Gentlemen of Verona, I.III.65

'Tis deeds must win the prize.
BAPTISTA, The Taming of the Shrew, II.I.342

Between the acting of a dreadful thing
And the first motion, all the interim is
Like a phantasma or a hideous dream.
BRUTUS, Julius Caesar, II.I.63

We must not stint
Our necessary actions in the fear
To cope malicious censurers, which ever,
As rav'nous fishes, do a vessel follow
That is new trimm'd, but benefit no further
Than vainly longing.
CARDINAL WOLSEY, Henry VIII, I.II.76

When good will is show'd, though't come too short,
The actor may plead pardon.
CLEOPATRA, Antony and Cleopatra, II.v.8

I cannot give due action to my words,
Except a sword or sceptre balance it.
DUKE OF YORK, 2 Henry VI, V.I.8

That we would do,
We should do when we would; for this "would" changes,
And hath abatements and delays as many

As there are tongues, are hands, are accidents,
And then this "should" is like a spendthrift's sigh,
And the huge army of the world's desires.
FERDINAND, KING OF NAVARRE, Love's Labor's Lost, I.I.8

Suit the action to the word, the word to the action.
HAMLET, Hamlet, III.II.17

O, the blood more stirs
To rouse a lion than to start a hare.
HOTSPUR, 1 Henry IV, I.III.197

Then pause not; for the present time's so sick,
That present med'cine must be minist'red,
Or overthrow incurable ensues.
KING JOHN, King John, V.I.14

Your actions are my dreams.
LEONTES, The Winter's Tale, III.II.82

Strange things I have in head that will to hand,
Which must be acted ere they may be scann'd.
MACBETH, Macbeth, III.IV.138

From this moment
The very firstlings of my heart shall be
The firstlings of my hand.
MACBETH, Macbeth, IV.I.145

Talkers are no good doers. Be assur'd;
We got to use our hands, and not our tongues.
MURDERERS, Richard III, I.III.350

Words pay no debts, give her deeds.
PANDARUS, Troilus and Cressida, III.II.55

Thoughts speculative their unsure hopes relate,
But certain issue strokes must arbitrate.
SIWARD, Macbeth, V.IV.19

Things in motion sooner catch the eye
Than what stirs not.
ULYSSES, Troilus and Cressida, III.III.83

Action is eloquence, and the eyes of the ignorant
More learned than the ears.
VOLUMNIA, Coriolanus, III.II.76

ACTORS AND ACTING
see also ART; SPEAKING AND SPEECH; THEATER

Let me play the lion too. I will roar, that I will do any
man's heart good to hear me. I will roar, that I will make

the Duke say, "Let him roar again; let him roar again."

BOTTOM, A Midsummer Night's Dream, I.II.70

Let not him that plays the lion pare his nails, for they
shall hang out for the lion's claws. And, most dear actors,
eat no onions nor garlic, for we are to utter sweet breath;
and I do not doubt but to hear them say, it is a sweet
comedy.

BOTTOM, A Midsummer Night's Dream, IV.II.40

As in a theatre the eyes of men,
After a well-graced actor leaves the stage,
Are idly bent on him that enters next,
Thinking his prattle to be tedious,
Even so, or with much more contempt, men's eyes
Did scowl on gentle Richard.

DUKE OF YORK, Richard II, V.II.23

Let me not play a woman; I have a beard coming.

FLUTE, A Midsummer Night's Dream, I.II.47

Is it not monstrous that this player here,
But in a fiction, in a dream of passion,
Could force his soul so to his own conceit
That from her working all the visage wann'd,
Tears in his eyes, distraction in his aspect,
A broken voice, an' his whole function suiting
With forms to his conceit? And all for nothing,
For Hecuba!
What's Hecuba to him, or he to Hecuba,
That he should weep for her? What would he do
Had he the motive and the cue for passion
That I have? He would drown the stage with tears,
And cleave the general ear with horrid speech,
Make mad the guilty, and appall the free,
Confound the ignorant, and amaze indeed
The very faculties of eyes and ears.

HAMLET, Hamlet, II.II.551

They are the abstract and brief chronicles of the time.
After your death you were better have a bad epitaph than
their ill report while you live.

HAMLET, Hamlet, II.II.524

Speak the speech, I pray you, as I pronounc'd it to you,
trippingly on the tongue, but if you mouth it, as many of
our players do, I had as live the town-crier spoke my lines.
Nor do not saw the air too much with your hand, thus, but
use all gently, for in the very torrent, tempest, and, as I

may say, whirlwind of your passion, you must acquire and
beget a temperance that may give it smoothness.

HAMLET, Hamlet, III.II.1

Let those that play your clowns speak no more than is set
down for them, for there be of them that will themselves
laugh to set on some quantity of barren spectators to laugh
too, though in the mean time some necessary question of the
play be then to be consider'd.

HAMLET, Hamlet, III.II.38

O, there be players that I have seen play—and heard others
praise, and that highly—not to speak it profanely, that,
neither having th' accent of Christians nor the gait of
Christian, pagan, nor man, have so strutted and bellow'd
that I have thought some of Nature's journeymen had made
men, and not made them well, they imitated humanity so
abominably.

HAMLET, Hamlet, III.II.28

To be paddling palms and pinching fingers
As now they are, and making practic'd smiles,
As in a looking-glass; and then to sign, as 'twere
The mort o' th' deer—O, that is entertainment
My bosom likes not, nor my brows!

LEONTES, The Winter's Tale, I.II.115

And if the boy have not a woman's gift
To rain a shower of commanded tears,
An onion will do well for such a shift,
Which in a napkin (being close convey'd)
Shall in despite enforce a watery eye.

LORD, The Taming of the Shrew, IND.I.124

Come, cousin, canst thou quake and change thy color,
Murder thy breath in middle of a word,
And then again begin, and stop again,
As if thou were distraught and mad with terror?

RICHARD, DUKE OF GLOUCESTER, Richard III, III.V.1

ADULTERY
see also BETRAYAL; INFIDELITY

By long and vehement suit I was seduc'd
To make room for him in my husband's bed.
Heaven! lay not my transgression to my charge,
That art the issue of my dear offense,
Which was so strongly urg'd past my defense.

LADY FAULCONRIDGE, King John, I.I.254

Thou shalt not die. Die for adultery? No,
The wren goes to't, and the small guilded fly
Does lecher in my sight.
Let copulation thrive.

LEAR, *King Lear*, IV.VI.110

Praise her but for this her without-door form
(Which on my faith deserves high speech) and straight
The shrug, the hum or ha (these petty brands
That calumny doth use—O, I am out—
That mercy does, for calumny will sear
Virtue itself), these shrugs, these hums and ha's,
When you have said she's goodly, come between
Ere you can say she's honest: but be't known
(From him that has most cause to grieve it should be)
She's an adult'ress.

LEONTES, *The Winter's Tale*, II.1.69

Naked in bed, Iago, and not mean harm?
It is hypocrisy against the devil.
They that mean it virtuously, and yet do so,
The devil their virtue tempts, and they tempt heaven.

OTHELLO, *Othello*, IV.1.5

What committed?
Heaven stops the nose at it, and the moon winks;
The bawdy wind, that kisses all it meets,
Is hush'd within the hollow mine of earth
And will not hear't. What committed?

OTHELLO, *Othello*, IV.II.76

ADVERSITY
see also MISERY; SUFFERING

O how full of briers is this working-day world!

ROSALIND, *As You Like It*, I.III.12

ADVICE

Counsel may stop a while what will not stay;
For when we rage, advice is often seen
By blunting us to make our wits more keen.

A Lover's Complaint, 159

Love thyself last, cherish those hearts that hate thee:
Corruption wins not more than honest.

CARDINAL WOLSEY, *Henry VIII*, III.II.443

Love all, trust a few,
Do wrong to none. Be able for thine enemy
Rather in power than use, and keep thy friend
Under thy own life's key.

COUNTESS OF ROSSILLION, *All's Well That Ends Well*, I.1.64

Obey thy parents,
keep thy word's justice, swear not, commit not
with man's sworn spouse, set not thy sweet heart on
proud array.

EDGAR, King Lear, III.IV.80

I pray thee cease thy counsel,
Which falls into mine ears as profitless
As water in a sieve. Give not me counsel,
Nor let no comforter delight mine ear
But such a one whose wrongs do suit with mine.

LEONATO, Much Ado About Nothing, V.I.3

Do not, as some ungracious pastors do,
Show me the steep and thorny way to heaven,
Whiles, like a puff'd and reckless libertine,
Himself the primrose path of dalliance treads,
And recks not his own rede.

OPHELIA, Hamlet, I.III.47

Live a little, comfort a little, cheer thyself a little.

ORLANDO, As You Like It, II.VI.5

These few precepts in thy memory
Look thou character. Give thy thoughts no tongue,
Nor any unproportion'd thought his act.
Be thou familiar, but by no means vulgar:
Those friends thou hast, and their adoption tried,
Grapple them unto thy soul with hoops of steel,
But do not dull thy palm with entertainment
Of each new-hatch'd, unfledg'd courage. Beware
Of entrance to a quarrel, but being in,
Bear't that th' opposèd may beware of thee.
Give every man thy ear, but few thy voice,
Take each man's censure, but reserve thy judgment.
Costly thy habit as thy purse can buy,
But not express'd in fancy, rich, not gaudy,
For the apparel oft proclaims the man,
And they in France of the best rank and station
Are of a most select and generous chief in that.
Neither a borrower nor a lender be,
For loan oft loses both itself and friend,
And borrowing dulleth th' edge of husbandry.
This above all: to thine own self be true,
And it must follow, as the night the day,
Thou canst not then be falst to any man.

POLONIUS, Hamlet, I.III.58

It is a good divine that follows his own instructions; I can
easier teach twenty what were good to be done, than to be
one of the twenty to follow mine own teaching.

PORTIA, *The Merchant of Venice*, I.II.12

Our good old friend,
Lay comforts to your bosom, and bestow
Your needful counsel to our businesses,
Which craves the instant use.

REGAN, *King Lear*, II.I.125

AFFECTION
see also KISS; LOVE—GENERAL

Affection faints not like a pale-fac'd coward,
But then woos best when most his choice is froward.

Venus and Adonis, 569

Affection is a coal that must be cool'd,
Else suffer'd it will set the heart on fire.

Venus and Adonis, 387

They do not love that do not show their love.

JULIA, *The Two Gentlemen of Verona*, I.II.31

AFTERLIFE
see also DEATH; GHOSTS; HEAVEN; HELL; SUPERNATURAL

And after death our spirits shall be led
To those that love eternally.

ARCITE, *The Two Noble Kinsmen*, II.II.116

No, no, my dream was lengthen'd after life.
O then began the tempest to my soul!
I pass'd (methought) the melancholy flood,
With that sour ferryman which poets write of,
Unto the kingdom of perpetual night.

CLARENCE, *Richard III*, I.IV.43

But that I am forbid
To tell the secrets of my prison-house,
I could a tale unfold whose lightest word
Would harrow up thy soul, freeze thy young blood,
Make thy two eyes like stars start from their spheres,
Thy knotted and combined locks to part,
And each particular hair to stand an end,
Like quills upon the fearful porpentine.

GHOST, *Hamlet*, I.V.13

The dread of something after death,
The undiscover'd country, from whose bourn
No traveller returns.

HAMLET, *Hamlet*, III.I.77

Sir, fare you well.
Hereafter, in a better world than this,
I shall desire more love and knowledge of you.
> LE BEAU, *As You Like It*, I.II.283

That life is better life, past fearing death,
Than that which lives to fear.
> VINCENTIO, DUKE OF VIENNA, *Measure for Measure*, V.I.397

AGING
see also GROWING UP; MATURITY; OLD AGE

For such a time do I now fortify
Against a confounding age's cruel knife,
That he shall never cut from memory
My sweet love's beauty, though my lover's life.
> SONNET 63, 9–12

Though grey
Do something mingle with our younger brown, yet ha' we
A brain that nourishes our nerves, and can
Get goal for goal of youth.
> ANTONY, *Antony and Cleopatra*, IV.VIII.19

I have seen the day
That I have worn a visor and could tell
A whispering tale in a fair lady's ear,
Such as would please; 'tis gone, 'tis gone, 'tis gone.
> CAPULET, *Romeo and Juliet*, I.V.21

You'll find a difference,
As we his subjects have in wonder found,
Between the promise of his greener days
And these he masters now.
> DUKE OF EXETER, *Henry V*, II.IV.134

Careful hours with time's deformed hand
Have written strange defeatures in my face.
> EGEON, *The Comedy of Errors*, V.I.299

Age cannot wither her, nor custom stale
Her infinite variety.
> ENOBARBUS, *Antony and Cleopatra*, II.II.234

Shorten my days thou canst with sullen sorrow,
And pluck nights from me, but not lend a morrow;
Thou canst help time to furrow me with age,
But stop no wrinkle in his pilgrimage.
> JOHN OF GAUNT, *Richard II*, I.III.227

O uncle, would some part of my young years
Might but redeem the passage of your age!
> RICHARD PLANTAGENET, *1 Henry VI*, II.V.107

Your lordship,
though not clean past your youth, have yet some smack
of an ague in you, some relish of the saltness of time
in you, and I most humbly beseech your lordship to
have a reverend care of your health.

SIR JOHN FALSTAFF, *2 Henry IV*, I.II.96

AGRICULTURE
see also GARDENING; NATURE

Ceres, most bounteous lady, thy rich leas
Of wheat, rye, barley, fetches, oats, and pease;
Thy turfy mountains, where live nibbling sheep,
And flat meads thatch'd with stover, them to keep;
Thy banks with poinèd and twillèd brims,
Which spungy April at thy hest betrims,
To make cold nymphs chaste crowns; and thy broomgroves,
Whose shadow the dismissèd bachelor loves,
Being lass-lorn; thy pole-clipt vineyard,
And thy sea-marge, sterile and rocky-hard,
Where thou thyself dost air.

IRIS, *The Tempest*, IV.I.60

Here's a farmer, that hanged himself on the expectation of
plenty.

PORTER, *Macbeth*, II.III.4

AIR
see also ELEMENTS

The air breathes upon us here most sweetly.

ADRIAN, *The Tempest*, II.I.46

Welcome then,
Thou unsubstantial air that I embrace:
The wretch that thou hast blown unto the worst
Owes nothing to thy blasts.

EDGAR, *King Lear*, IV.I.6

ALCOHOL
see also ALCOHOLISM; BARS AND RESTAURANTS; DRUNKENNESS; TOASTS

Come, let's all take hands,
Till that the conquering wine hath steep'd our sense
In soft and delicate Lethe.

ANTONY, *Antony and Cleopatra*, II.VII.106

O thou invisible spirit of
wine, if thou hast no name to be known by, let us call
thee devil!

CASSIO, *Othello*, II.III.281

Come, come; good wine is a good familiar
creature, if it be well us'd.

IAGO, *Othello*, II.III.308

That which hath made them drunk hath made me bold;
What hath quench'd them hath given me fire.

LADY MACBETH, *Macbeth*, II.II.1

Macd. What three things does drink especially provoke?
Port. Marry, sir, nose-painting, sleep, and urine.
Lechery, sir, it provokes, and unprovokes: it provokes
the desire, but it takes away the performance. Therefore
much drink maybe said to be an equivocator
with lechery: it makes him, and it mars him; it sets him
on, and it takes him off; it persuades him, and disheartens
him; makes him stand to, and not stand to; in conclusion,
equivocates him in a sleep, and giving him the lie, leaves
him.

PORTER, MACDUFF, *Macbeth*, II.III.26

A good sherris-sack hath a twofold
operation in it. It ascends me into the brain, dries me
there all the foolish and dull and crudy vapors which
environ it, makes it apprehensive, quick, forgetive, full
of nimble, fiery, and delectable shapes, which deliver'd o'er to the voice, the tongue, which is the birth,
becomes excellent wit.

SIR JOHN FALSTAFF, *2 Henry IV*, IV.III.96

Come, thou monarch of the vine,
Plumpy Bacchus with pink eyne!
In thy fats our cares be drown'd,
With thy grapes our hairs be crown'd!
Cup us till the world go round,
Cup us till the world go round!

SONG, *Antony and Cleopatra*, II.VII.113

He shall taste of my bottle; if he have never
drunk wine afore, it will go near to remove his fit.

STEPHANO, *The Tempest*, II.II.74

ALCOHOLISM
see also ALCOHOL; DRUNKENNESS

We are merely cheated of our lives by
drunkards.

ANTONIO, *The Tempest*, I.I.56

One drunkard loves another of the name.

BEROWNE, *Love's Labor's Lost*, IV.III.48

That quaffing and drinking will undo you.
> MARIA, *Twelfth Night*, I.III.14

Thou art so fat-witted with drinking of old
sack, and unbuttoning thee after supper, and sleeping
upon benches after noon, that thou hast forgotten to
demand that truly which thou wouldest truly know.
> PRINCE HENRY, *1 Henry IV*, I.II.2

He has a sin that often
Drowns him and takes his valor prisoner.
> SENATOR, *Timon of Athens*, III.V.67

ALIENATION
see also SOLITUDE

He that commends me to mine own content,
Commends me to the thing I cannot get:
I to the world am like a drop of water,
That in the ocean seeks another drop,
Who, falling there to find his fellow forth
(Unseen, inquisitive), confounds himself.
> ANTIPHOLUS OF SYRACUSE, *The Comedy of Errors*, I.II.33

Now my soul's palace is become a prison.
> PRINCE EDWARD, *3 Henry VI*, II.I.74

I shall do my friends no wrong, for I have none to lament
me; the world no injury, for in it I have nothing.
Only in the world I fill up a place, which may be better
supplied when I have made it empty.
> ORLANDO, *As You Like It*, I.II.185

AMBITION
see also POLITICS AND POWER

The noble Brutus
Hath told you Caesar was ambitious;
If it were so, it was a grievous fault,
And grievously hath Caesar answer'd it.
> ANTONY, *Julius Caesar*, III.II.77

There is tears for his love; joy for his fortune; honor for
his valor; and death for his ambition.
> BRUTUS, *Julius Caesar*, III.II.24

Cromwell, I charge thee, fling away ambition!
By that sin fell the angels; how can man then
(The image of his Maker) hope to win by it?
> CARDINAL WOLSEY, *Henry VIII*, III.II.440

Go forward, and be chok'd with thy ambition!
                    EARL OF SUFFOLK, *1 Henry VI*, II.IV.112

Ham. O God, I could be bounded in a nutshell, and
count myself a king of infinite space—were it not that I
have bad dreams.
Guil. Which dreams are indeed ambition, for the
very substance of the ambitious is merely the shadow
of a dream.
Ham. A dream itself is but a shadow.
Ros. Truly, and I hold ambition of so airy and light
a quality that it is but a shadow's shadow.
         HAMLET, ROSENCRANTZ, GUILDENSTERN, *Hamlet*, II.II.254

Who doth ambition shun,
And loves to live i' th' sun,
Seeking the food he eats,
And pleas'd with what he gets,
Come hither, come hither, come hither!
Here shall he see
No enemy
But winter and rough weather.
                    JAQUES, *As You Like It*, II.V.38

I fear thy nature,
It is too full o' th' milk of human kindness
To catch the nearest way. Thou wouldst be great,
Art not without ambition, but without
The illness should attend it. What thou wouldst highly,
That wouldst thou holily; wouldst not play false,
And yet wouldst wrongly win.
                    LADY MACBETH, *Macbeth*, I.V.16

I dare do all that may become a man;
Who dares do more is none.
                    MACBETH, *Macbeth*, I.VII.46

I have no spur
To prick the sides of my intent, but only
Vaulting ambition, which o'erleaps itself,
And falls on th' other.
                    MACBETH, *Macbeth*, I.VII.25

Ill-weav'd ambition, how much art thou shrunk!
When that this body did contain a spirit,
A kingdom for it was too small a bound,
But now two paces of the vilest earth
Is room enough.
                    PRINCE HENRY, *1 Henry IV*, V.IV.88

Urge them while their souls
Are capable of this ambition,
Lest zeal, now melted by the windy breath
Of soft petitions, pity, and remorse,
Cool and congeal again to what it was.

QUEEN ELINOR, *King John*, II.I.475

Thriftless ambition, that will ravin up
Thine own live's means!

ROSSE, *Macbeth*, II.IV.28

Who does i' th' wars more than his captain can
Becomes his captain's captain; and ambition
(The soldier's virtue) rather makes choice of loss
Than gain which darkens him.

VENTIDIUS, *Antony and Cleopatra*, III.I.21

ANARCHY AND CHAOS
see also DISORDER; REBELLION; RIOT

O judgment! thou art fled to brutish beasts,
And men have lost their reason.

ANTONY, *Julius Caesar*, III.II.104

That is the way to lay the city flat,
To bring the roof to the foundation,
And bury all, which yet distinctly ranges,
In heaps and piles of ruin.

COMINIUS, *Coriolanus*, III.I.203

And all our vineyards, fallows, meads, and hedges,
Defective in their natures, grow to wildness.
Even so our houses, and ourselves, and children,
Have lost, or do not learn for want of time,
The sciences that should become our country,
But grow like savages.

DUKE OF BURGUNDY, *Henry V*, V.II.54

'Tis the time's plague, when madmen lead the blind.

EARL OF GLOUCESTER, *King Lear*, IV.I.46

The times are wild, contention, like a horse
Full of high feeding, madly hath broke loose,
And bears down all before him.

EARL OF NORTHUMBERLAND, *2 Henry IV*, I.I.9

Obedience, fail in children! Slaves and fools,
Pluck the grave wrinkled Senate from the bench,
And minister in their steads! To general filths
Convert o' th' instant, green virginity!
Do't in your parents' eyes! Bankrupts, hold fast;

Rather than render bank, out with your knives,
And cut your trusters' throats! Bound servants, steal;
Large-handed robbers your grave masters are,
And pill by law.

TIMON, *Timon of Athens*, IV.i.4

When the planets
In evil mixture to disorder wander,
What plagues and what portents, what mutiny!
What raging of the sea, shaking of earth!
Commotion in the winds! frights, changes, horrors
Divert and crack, rend and deracinate
The unity and married calm of states
Quite from their fixure! O, when degree is shak'd,
Which is the ladder of all high designs,
The enterprise is sick. How could communities,
Degrees in schools, and brotherhoods in cities,
Peaceful commerce from dividable shores,
The primogeneity and due of birth,
Prerogative of age, crowns, sceptres, laurels,
But by degree stand in authentic place?
Take but degree away, untune that string,
And hark what discord follows. Each thing meets
In mere oppugnancy: the bounded waters
Should lift their bosoms higher than the shores,
And make a sop of all this solid globe;
Strength should be lord of imbecility,
And the rude son should strike his father dead;
Force should be right, or rather, right and wrong
(Between whose endless jar justice resides)
Should lose their names, and so should justice too!
Then every thing include itself in power,
Power into will, will into appetite,
And appetite, an universal wolf
(So doubly seconded with will and power),
Must make perforce an universal prey,
And last eat up himself.

ULYSSES, *Troilus and Cressida*, I.iii.94

Fair is foul, and foul is fair.

WITCHES (ALL), *Macbeth*, I.i.11

ANGELS
see also HEAVEN; HIGHER POWER; SPIRITUALITY AND RELIGION

To win my soon to hell, my female evil
Tempteth my better angel from my side,
And would corrupt my saint to be a devil,
Wooing his purity with her foul pride.

And whether that my angel be turn'd fiend
Suspect I may, yet not directly tell.

SONNET 144, 5–10

Thou hast the sweetest face I ever look'd on.
Sir, as I have a soul, she is an angel.

SECOND GENTLEMAN, *Henry VIII*, IV.I.43

Go with me like good angels to my end,
And as the long divorce of steel falls on me,
Make of your prayers one sweet sacrifice,
And lift my soul to heaven.

DUKE OF BUCKINGHAM, *Henry VIII*, II.I.75

Then if angels fight,
Weak men must fall, for heaven still guards the right.

KING RICHARD, *Richard II*, III.II.61

Angels are bright still, though the brightest fell.

MALCOLM, *Macbeth*, IV.III.22

And those musicians that shall play to you
Hang in the air a thousand leagues from hence,
And straight they shall be here.

OWEN GLENDOWER, *1 Henry IV*, III.I.223

O, speak again, bright angel, for thou art
As glorious to this night, being o'er my head,
As is a winged messenger of heaven
Unto the white-upturned wond'ring eyes
Of mortals that fall back to gaze on him,
When he bestrides the lazy puffing clouds,
And sails upon the bosom of the air.

ROMEO, *Romeo and Juliet*, II.II.26

ANGER
see also CURSES; REVENGE; THREATS

To be in anger is impiety;
But who is man that is not angry?

ALCIBIADES, *Timon of Athens*, III.v.56

I have savage cause,
And to proclaim it civilly were like
A halter'd neck which does the hangman thank
For being yare about him.

ANTONY, *Antony and Cleopatra*, III.XIII.128

Seek, seek for him,
Lest his ungovern'd rage dissolve the life
That wants the means to lead it.

CORDELIA, *King Lear*, IV.III.17

Anger is like
A full hot horse, who being allow'd his way,
Self-mettle tires him.

DUKE OF NORFOLK, *Henry VIII*, I.i.132

Mad ire and wrathful fury makes we weep,
That thus we die, while remiss traitors sleep.

DUKE OF YORK, *1 Henry VI*, IV.iii.28

To be furious
Is to be frighted out of fear, and in that mood
The dove will peck the estridge.

ENOBARBUS, *Antony and Cleopatra*, III.xiii.194

How low am I? I am not yet so low
But that my nails can reach unto thine eyes.

HERMIA, *A Midsummer Night's Dream*, III.ii.297

I have seen the cannon
When it hath blown his ranks into the air,
And like the devil from his very arm
Puff'd his own brother—and is he angry?

IAGO, *Othello*, III.iv.134

My tongue will tell the anger of my heart,
Or else my heart concealing it will break,
And rather than it shall, I will be free,
Even to the uttermost, as I please, in words.

KATE, *The Taming of the Shrew*, IV.iii.75

I should be angry with you, if the time were convenient.

KING HENRY, *Henry V*, IV.i.203

Yet notwithstanding, being incens'd, he is flint,
As humorous as winter, and as sudden
As flaws congealed in the spring of day.
His temper therefore must be well observ'd.

KING HENRY IV, *2 Henry IV*, IV.iv.33

Thy rage shall burn thee up, and thou shalt turn
To ashes, ere our blood shall quench that fire.

KING PHILIP, *King John*, III.i.345

Rage must be withstood,
Give me his gage. Lions make leopards tame.

KING RICHARD, *Richard II*, I.i.173

No, if I digg'd up thy forefathers' graves
And hung their rotten coffins up in chains,
It could not slake mine ire nor ease my heart.

LORD CLIFFORD, *3 Henry VI*, I.iii.27

And like a hungry lion did commence
Rough deeds of rage and stern impatience.

> LORD TALBOT, *1 Henry VI*, IV.VII.7

Never anger made good guard for itself.

> MAECENAS, *Antony and Cleopatra*, IV.I.9

The brain may devise laws for the blood, but a hot temper
leaps o'er a cold decree.

> PORTIA, *The Merchant of Venice*, I.II.18

The lion dying thrusteth forth his paw,
And wounds the earth, if nothing else, with rage
To be o'erpow'r'd, and wilt thou, pupil-like,
Take the correction, mildly kiss the rod,
And fawn on rage with base humility,
Which art a lion and the king of beasts?

> QUEEN, *Richard II*, V.I.29

Witness my son, now in the shade of death,
Whose bright out-shining beams thy cloudy wrath
Hath in eternal darkness folded up.

> QUEEN MARGARET, *Richard III*, I.III.266

O, were mine eyeballs into bullets turn'd,
That I in rage might shoot them at your faces!

> SIR WILLIAM LUCY, *1 Henry VI*, IV.VII.79

Anger's my meat; I sup upon myself,
And so shall starve with feeding.

> VOLUMNIA, *Coriolanus*, IV.II.50

ANTICIPATION

Against ill chances men are ever merry,
But heaviness foreruns the good event.

> ARCHBISHOP, *2 Henry IV*, IV.II.81

Lo, as at the English feasts, so I regreet
The daintiest last, to make the end most sweet.

> BULLINGBROOK, *Richard II*, I.III.67

The setting sun, and music at the close,
As the last taste of sweets, is sweetest last.

> JOHN OF GAUNT, *Richard II*, II.I.12

APPEARANCE
see also DISGUISE; FACE; PRESENCE

O place, O form,
How often dost thou with thy case, thy habit,
Wrench awe from fools, and tie the wiser souls
To thy false seeming!

> ANGELO, *Measure for Measure*, II.IV.12

So may the outward shows be least themselves—
The world is still deceiv'd with ornament.

> BASSANIO, *The Merchant of Venice*, III.II.73

My heart is ten times lighter than my looks.

> EARL OF SURREY, *Richard III*, V.III.3

Seems, madam? nay, it is, I know not "seems."
'Tis not alone my inky cloak, good mother,
Nor customary suits of solemn black,
Nor windy suspiration of forc'd breath,
No, nor the fruitful river in the eye,
Nor the dejected havior of the visage,
Together with all forms, moods, shapes of grief,
That can denote me truly. These indeed seem,
For thy are actions that a man might play,
But I have that within which passes show,
These but the trappings and the suits of woe.

> HAMLET, *Hamlet*, I.II.76

I' faith, sweet heart, methinks now you are in
an excellent good temperality. Your pulsidge beats as
extraordinarily as heart would desire, and your color,
I warrant you, is as red as any rose.

> HOSTESS QUICKLY, *2 Henry IV*, II.IV.22

Things sweet to taste prove in digestion sour.

> JOHN OF GAUNT, *Richard II*, I.III.236

How courtesy would seem to cover sin,
When what is done is like an hypocrite,
The which is good in nothing but in sight!

> PERICLES, *Pericles*, I.I.121

To shame the guise o' th' world, I will begin
The fashion: less without and more within.

> POSTHUMUS, *Cymbeline*, V.I.32

Now I think on't,
They should be good men, their affairs as righteous.
But all hoods make not monks.

> QUEEN KATHERINE, *Henry VIII*, III.I.21

There is a fair behavior in thee, captain,
And though that nature with a beauteous wall
Doth oft close in pollution, yet of thee
I will believe thou hast a mind that suits
With this thy fair and outward character.

> VIOLA, *Twelfth Night*, I.II.47

ARGUMENT
see also QUARRELS

There has been much throwing around of brains.

GUILDENSTERN, *Hamlet*, II.II.358

Rightly to be great
Is not to stir without great argument,
But greatly to find quarrel in a straw
When honor's at the stake.

HAMLET, *Hamlet*, IV.IV.53

Falling in, after falling out, may make them three.

HELEN, *Troilus and Cressida*, III.I.103

A fine volley of words, gentlemen, and quickly shot off.

SILVIA, *The Two Gentlemen of Verona*, II.IV.33

I cannot fight upon this argument;
It is too starv'd a subject for my sword.

TROILUS, *Troilus and Cressida*, I.I.92

ARROGANCE
see also BOASTING; CONFIDENCE; PRIDE

Your wisdom is consum'd in confidence.

CALPHURNIA, *Julius Caesar*, II.II.49

Contemplation makes a rare turkey-cock of him. How he jets
under his advanc'd plumes!

FABIAN, *Twelfth Night*, II.V.30

There are a sort of men whose visages
Do cream and mantle like a standing pond,
And do a willful stillness entertain,
With purpose to be dress'd in an opinion
Of wisdom, gravity, profound conceit,
As who should say, "I am Sir Oracle,
And when I ope my lips let no dog bark!"
O my Antonio, I do know of these
That therefore only are reputed wise
For saying nothing; when I am very sure
If they should speak, would almost damn those ears
Which hearing them would call their brothers fools.

GRATIANO, *The Merchant of Venice*, I.I.88

Security
Is mortals' chiefest enemy.

HECAT, *Macbeth*, III.V.32

Possess'd he is with greatness,
And speaks not to himself but with a pride
That quarrels at self-breath. Imagin'd worth

Holds in his blood such swoll'n and hot discourse
That 'twixt his mental and his active parts
Kingdom'd Achilles in commotion rages,
And batters down himself.

ULYSSES, *Troilus and Cressida*, II.III.170

Pride hath no other glass
To show itself but pride; for supple knees
Feed arrogance and are the proud man's fees.

ULYSSES, *Troilus and Cressida*, III.III.47

ART
see also DANCING; MUSIC; PAINTING; POETRY; THEATER; WRITING

A thousand lamentable objects there,
In scorn of nature, art gave liveless life.

The Rape of Lucrece, 1373

The fixture of her eye has motion in't,
As we are mock'd with art.

LEONTES, *The Winter's Tale*, V.III.67

If this be magic, let it be an art
Lawful as eating.

LEONTES, *The Winter's Tale*, V.III.110

Arm. How hast thou purchas'd this experience?
Moth. By my penny of observation.

MOTH, ARMADO, *Love's Labor's Lost*, III.1.26

In framing an artist, art hath thus decreed,
To make some good, but others to exceed
And you are her labor'd scholar.

SIMONIDES, *Pericles*, II.III.15

ARTIFICIAL RESPIRATION
see also BREATH

For on the grass she lies as she were slain,
Till his breath breatheth life in her again.

Venus and Adonis, 473

ATTRACTION
see also BEAUTY; COURTING; DESIRE; INFATUATION; LOVE; LUST; SEX

Ben. Be rul'd by me, forget to think of her.
Rom. O, teach me how I should forget to think.
Ben. By giving liberty to thine eyes:
Examine other beauties.

BENVOLIO, ROMEO, *Romeo and Juliet*, I.1.225

A maiden, never bold;
Of spirit so still and quiet that her motion

Blush'd at herself; and she, in spite of nature,
Of years, of country, credit, every thing,
To fall in love with what she fear'd to look on!

BRABANTIO, Othello, I.III.94

Rom. Is love a tender thing? It is too rough,
Too rude, too boist'rous, and it pricks like thorn.
Mer. If love be rough with you, be rough with love;
Prick love for pricking, and you beat love down.

MERCUTIO, ROMEO, Romeo and Juliet, I.IV.25

Love goes toward love as schoolboys from their books,
But love from love, toward school with heavy looks.

ROMEO, Romeo and Juliet, II.II.156

Did my heart love till now? Forswear it, sight!
For I ne'er saw true beauty till this night.

ROMEO, Romeo and Juliet, I.V.52

AUTHORITY
see also LEADERSHIP; POLITICS AND POWER

Authority melts from me. Of late, when I cried "Ho!"
Like boys unto a muss, kings would start forth
And cry, "Your will?"

ANTONY, Antony and Cleopatra, III.XIII.90

Though authority be a
stubborn bear, yet he is oft led by the nose with gold.

CLOWN, The Winter's Tale, IV.IV.801

Could great men thunder
As Jove himself does, Jove would never be quiet,
For every pelting, petty officer
Would use his heaven for thunder,
Nothing but thunder! Merciful heaven,
Thou rather with thy sharp and sulphurous bolt
Splits the unwedgeable and gnarled oak
Than the soft myrtle; but man, proud man,
Dress'd in a little brief authority,
Most ignorant of what he's most asssur'd
(His glassy essence), like an angry ape
Plays such fantastic tricks before high heaven
As makes the angels weep; who, with our spleens,
Would all themselves laugh mortal.

ISABELLA, Measure for Measure, II.II.110

Authority, though it err like others,
Hath yet a kind of medicine in itself,
That skins the vice o' th' top.

ISABELLA, Measure for Measure, II.II.134

AUTUMN
see also SEASONS

> That time of year thou mayst in me behold
> When yellow leaves, or none, or few, do hang
> Upon those boughs which shake against the cold,
> Bare ruin'd choirs, where late the sweet birds sang.
>
> SONNET 73, 1–4

> You sunburn'd sicklemen, of August weary,
> Come hither from the furrow and be merry,
> Make holiday; your rye straw hats put on,
> And these fresh nymphs encounter every one
> In country footing.
>
> IRIS, *The Tempest*, IV.i.134

BABIES
see also BIRTH; CHILDREN

> Come on, poor babe.
> Some powerful spirit instruct the kites and ravens
> To be thy nurses!
>
> ANTIGONUS, *The Winter's Tale*, II.iii.185

> A daughter, and a goodly babe,
> Lusty and like to live. The Queen receives
> Much comfort in't; says, "My poor prisoner,
> I am as innocent as you."
>
> EMILIA, *The Winter's Tale*, II.ii.24

> Holy writ in babes hath judgment shown,
> When judges have been babes.
>
> HELENA, *All's Well That Ends Well*, II.i.138

> Thou wast the prettiest babe that e'er I nurs'd.
>
> NURSE, *Romeo and Juliet*, I.iii.60

> Ah, my poor princes! ah, my tender babes!
> My unblown flow'rs, new-appearing sweets!
> If yet your gentle souls fly in the air
> And be not fix'd in doom perpetual,
> Hover about me with your airy wings
> And hear your mother's lamentation!
>
> QUEEN ELIZABETH, *Richard III*, IV.iv.9

BALDNESS

> What he [time] hath scanted men in hair he hath given them
> in wit.
>
> DROMIO OF SYRACUSE, *The Comedy of Errors*, II.ii.80

> Time himself is bald, and therefore, to world's end, will I
> have bald followers.
>
> DROMIO OF SYRACUSE, *The Comedy of Errors*, II.ii.106

There's no time for a man to recover his hair that grows
bald by nature.
DROMIO OF SYRACUSE, The Comedy of Errors, II.II.72

BANKRUPTCY
see also DOWNFALL; POVERTY

Such a house broke?
So noble a master fall'n, all gone, and nor
One friend to take his fortune by the arm,
And go along with him.
FIRST SERVANT, Timon of Athens, IV.II.5

BARS AND RESTAURANTS
see also ALCOHOL; FOOD

Small cheer and great welcome makes a merry feast.
BALTHAZAR, The Comedy of Errors, III.I.26

Epicurism and lust
Makes it more like a tavern or a brothel
Than a grac'd palace.
GONERIL, King Lear, I.IV.244

I reckon this always, that a man is never undone till he be
hang'd, nor never welcome to a place till some certain shot
be paid and the hostess say "Welcome."
LAUNCE, The Two Gentlemen of Verona, II.v.4

BASEBALL

Make him fly an ordinary pitch.
FLAVIUS, Julius Caesar, I.I.73

She would be as swift in motion as a ball.
JULIET, Romeo and Juliet, II.v.13

Fair is foul and foul is fair.
WITCHES, Macbeth, I.I.11

It was a black ill-favor'd fly.
MARCUS, Titus Andronicus, III.II.66

The good humor is to steal at a minute's rest.
NYM, The Merry Wives of Windsor, I.III.27

A hit, a very palpable hit.
OSRIC, Hamlet, V.II.281

Thou canst not hit it, hit it, hit it,
Thou canst not hit it, my good man.
ROSALINE, Love's Labor's Lost, IV.I.125

BATTLE
see also COMPETITION; ENEMY; SOLDIERS; WAR; WEAPONS

I will be treble-sinew'd, hearted, breath'd,
And fight maliciously; for when mine hours
Were nice and lucky, men did ransom lives
Of me for jests; but now I'll set my teeth,
And send to darkness all that stop me.

ANTONY, *Antony and Cleopatra*, III.XIII.177

Now put your shields before your hearts, and fight
With hearts more proof than shields.

CAIUS MARTIUS, *Coriolanus*, I.IV.24

No, good my lord, let's fight with gentle words,
Till time lend friends, and friends their helpful swords.

DUKE OF AUMERLE, *Richard II*, III.III.131

My liege, the wound that bred this meeting here
Cannot be cur'd by words; therefore be still.

LORD CLIFFORD, *3 Henry VI*, II.II.121

I am afeared there are few die
well that die in a battle; for how can they charitably
dispose of any thing, when blood is their argument?

MICHAEL WILLIAMS, *Henry V*, IV.I.141

There was excellent command—to charge in with our horse
upon our own wings, and to rend our own soldiers!

PAROLLES, *All's Well That Ends Well*, III.VI.48

BEAUTY
see also ATTRACTION; COSMETICS; LOVE; PLASTIC SURGERY

O how much more doth beauty beauteous seem
By that sweet ornament which truth doth give!

SONNET 54, 1–2

Look in mine eyeballs, there thy beauty lies;
Then why not lips on lips, since eyes in eyes?

Venus and Adonis, 119

Had I no eyes but ears, my ears would love
That inward beauty and invisible,
Or were I deaf, thy outward parts would move
Each part in me that were but sensible.

Venus and Adonis, 433

All orators are dumb when beauty pleadeth.

The Rape of Lucrece, 268

Since that my beauty cannot please his eye,
I'll weep what's left away, and weeping die.

ADRIANA, The Comedy of Errors, II.i.114

A wither'd hermit, fivescore winters worn,
Might shake off fifty, looking in her eye:
Beauty doth varnish age, as if new born,
And gives the crutch the cradle's infancy.
O, 'tis the sun that maketh all things shine!

BEROWNE, Love's Labor's Lost, IV.iii.238

Where is any author in the world
Teaches such beauty as a woman's eye?

BEROWNE, Love's Labor's Lost, IV.iii.308

I have no power to let her pass,
My hand would free her, but my heart says no.
As plays the sun upon the glassy streams,
Twinkling another counterfeited beam,
So seems this gorgeous beauty to mine eyes.
Fain would I woo her, yet I dare not speak.

EARL OF SUFFOLK, 1 Henry VI, V.iii.60

The power of beauty will
sooner transform honesty from what it is to a bawd
than the force of honesty can translate beauty into
his likeness.

HAMLET, Hamlet, III.i.110

Your eyes are lodestars, and your tongue's sweet air
More tuneable than lark to shepherd's ear
When wheat is green, when hawthorn buds appear.

HELENA, A Midsummer Night's Dream, I.i.182

My beauty, though but mean,
Needs not the painted flourish of your praise:
Beauty is bought by judgment of the eye,
Not utt'red by base sale of chapmen's tongues.

PRINCESS OF FRANCE, Love's Labor's Lost, II.i.13

Your beauty, that did haunt me in my sleep
To undertake the death of all the world,
So I might live one hour in your sweet bosom.

RICHARD, DUKE OF GLOUCESTER, Richard III, I.ii.124

These eyes could not endure that beauty's wrack;
You should not blemish it, if I stood by:
As all the world is cheerèd by the sun,
So I by that; it is my day, my life.

RICHARD, DUKE OF GLOUCESTER, Richard III, I.ii.130

One fairer than my love! The all-seeing sun
Ne'er saw her match since first the world begun.

ROMEO, *Romeo and Juliet*, I.II.92

O, she doth teach the torches to burn bright!
It seems she hangs upon the cheek of night
As a rich jewel in an Ethiop's ear—
Beauty too rich for use, for earth too dear.

ROMEO, *Romeo and Juliet*, I.V.44

Beauty provoketh thieves sooner than gold.

ROSALIND, *As You Like It*, I.III.110

BEGGING
see also NEED AND NECESSITY; POVERTY

What, wouldst thou have me go and beg my food?
Or with a base and boist'rous sword enforce
A thievish living on the common road?
This I must do, or know not what to do;
Yet this I will not do, do how I can.

ORLANDO, *As You Like It*, II.III.31

His poor self,
A dedicated beggar to the air,
With his disease of all-shunn'd poverty,
Walks, like contempt, alone.

SECOND SERVANT, *Timon of Athens*, IV.II.12

BEGINNING

Those that with haste will make a mighty fire
Begin it with weak straws.

CASSIUS, *Julius Caesar*, I.III.107

Bad begins and worse remains behind.

HAMLET, *Hamlet*, III.IV.179

BEHAVIOR
see also ACTION

If I do not put on a sober habit,
Talk with respect, and swear but now and then,
Wear prayer-books in my pocket, look demurely,
Nay more, while grace is saying hood mine eyes
Thus with my hat, and sigh and say amen,
Use all the observance of civility,
Like one well studied in a sad ostent
To please his grandam, never trust me more.

GRATIANO, *The Merchant of Venice*, II.II.190

Who can be wise, amaz'd, temp'rate, and furious,
Loyal, and neutral, in a moment? No man.

MACBETH, *Macbeth*, II.III.108

He has been yonder i' the sun practicing behavior to his own
shadow this half hour.

MARIA, *Twelfth Night*, II.v.16

'Tis in our power
(Unless we fear that apes can tutor's) to
Be masters of our manners.

PALAMON, *The Two Noble Kinsmen*, I.II.43

Nature hath fram'd strange fellows in her time:
Some that will evermore peep through their eyes,
And laugh like parrots at a bagpiper;
And other of such vinegar aspect
That they'll not show their teeth in way of smile
Though Nestor swear the jest be laughable.

SOLANIO, *The Merchant of Venice*, I.I.51

There is a fair behavior in thee, captain,
And though that nature with a beauteous wall
Doth oft close in pollution, yet of thee
I will believe thou hast a mind that suits
With this thy fair and outward character.

VIOLA, *Twelfth Night*, I.II.47

BETRAYAL
see also ENEMY; INFIDELITY; TREASON

If we two be one, and thou play false,
I do digest the poison of thy flesh,
Being strumpeted by the contagion.

ADRIANA, *The Comedy of Errors*, II.II.142

Freeze, freeze, thou bitter sky,
That doth not bite so nigh
As benefits forgot:
Though thou the waters warp,
Thy sting is not so sharp
As friend rememb'red not.

AMIENS (SONG), *As You Like It*, II.VII.184

Friendship is constant in all other things
Save in the office and affairs of love;
Therefore all hearts in love use their own tongues.
Let every eye negotiate for itself,
And trust no agent; for beauty is a witch
Against whose charms faith melteth into blood.

CLAUDIO, *Much Ado About Nothing*, II.I.175

Never was there queen
So mightily betrayed! yet at the first
I saw the treasons planted.

CLEOPATRA, *Antony and Cleopatra*, I.III.24

O monstrous treachery! can this be so?
That in alliance, amity, and oaths,
There should be found such false dissembling guile?

DUKE OF GLOUCESTER, *1 Henry VI*, IV.I.61

This is most strange,
That she, whom even but now was your best object,
The argument of your praise, balm of your age,
The best, the dearest, should in this trice of time
Commit a thing so monstrous, to dismantle
So many folds of favor.

KING OF FRANCE, *King Lear*, I.I.213

O time most accurst!
'Mongst all foes that a friend should be the worst!

VALENTINE, *The Two Gentlemen of Verona*, V.IV.71

BEWILDERMENT
see also CONFUSION; WONDER

I am mop'd:
Food took I none these two days—
Sipp'd some water. I have not clos'd mine eyes
Save when my lids scour'd of their brine.

DAUGHTER, *The Two Noble Kinsmen*, III.II.25

Go, bear him in thine arms.
I am amaz'd, methinks, and lose my way
Among the thorns and dangers of the world.

PHILIP THE BASTARD, *King John*, IV.III.139

I have lost myself, I am not here:
This is not Romeo, he's some other where.

ROMEO, *Romeo and Juliet*, I.I.197

BIGOTRY AND INTOLERANCE
see also CHILDREN OF UNMARRIED PARENTS; HATRED; IGNORANCE; MISANTHROPY;
MISOGYNY

In time we hate that which we often fear.

CHARMIAN, *Antony and Cleopatra*, I.III.12

Mislike me not for my complexion,
The shadowed livery of the burnish'd sun,
To whom I am a neighbor and near bred.

PRINCE OF MOROCCO, *The Merchant of Venice*, II.I.1

There is more difference. . . between thy flesh and hers than
between jet and ivory, more between your bloods than there
is between red wine and Rhenish.

SALERIO, The Merchant of Venice, III.I.39

Hath not a Jew eyes? Hath not a Jew hands, organs,
dimensions, sense, affections, passions; fed with
the same food, hurt with the same weapons, subject
to the same diseases, heal'd by the same means,
warm'd and cool'd by the same winter and summer,
as a Christian is? If you prick us, do we not bleed?
If you tickle us, do we not laugh? If you
poison us, do we not die? And if you wrong us, shall
we not revenge? If we are like you in the rest, we
Will resemble you in that. If a Jew wrong a Christian,
what is his humility? Revenge. If a Christian wrong
a Jew, what should his sufferance be by Christian
example? Why, revenge.

SHYLOCK, The Merchant of Venice, III.I.59

BIRDS

This guest of summer,
The temple-haunting marlet, does approve,
By his lov'd mansionry, that the heaven's breath
Smells wooingly here; no jutty, frieze,
Buttress, nor coign of vantage, but this bird
Hath made his pendant bed and procreant cradle.
Where they most breed and haunt, I have observ'd
The air is delicate.

BANQUO, Macbeth, I.VI.3

Go home to bed, and like the owl by day,
If he arise, be mock'd and wond'red at.

DUKE OF SOMERSET, 3 Henry VI, V.IV.56

We bodg'd again, as I have seen a swan
With bootless labor swim against the tide,
And spend her strength with overmatching waves.

DUKE OF YORK, 3 Henry VI, I.IV.19

Bring forth that fatal screech-owl to our house
That nothing sung by death to us and ours.
Now death shall stop his dismal threat'ning sound,
And his ill-bodying tongue no more shall speak.

PRINCE EDWARD, 3 Henry VI, II.V.56

I have heard
The cock, that is the trumpet to the morn,
Doth with his lofty and shrill-sounding throat

Awake the god of day, and at his warning,
Whether in sea or fire, in earth or air,
Th' extravagant and erring spirit hies
To his confine.

HORATIO, *Hamlet*, I.I.149

It is the lark that sings so out of tune,
Straining harsh discords and unpleasing sharps.
Some say the lark makes sweet division;
This doth not so, for she divideth us.

JULIET, *Romeo and Juliet*, III.V.27

A wanton's bird
That lets it hop a little from his hand,
Like a poor prisoner in his twisted gyves,
And with a silken thread plucks it back again,
So loving-jealous of his liberty.

JULIET, *Romeo and Juliet*, II.II.177

O Westmerland, thou art a summer bird,
Which ever in the haunch of winter sings
The lifting up of day.

KING HENRY IV, *2 Henry IV*, IV.IV.91

The owl shriek'd at thy birth, an evil sign;
The night-crow cried, aboding luckless time.

KING HENRY, *3 Henry VI*, V.VI.44

Came he right now to sing a raven's note,
Whose dismal tune bereft my vital pow'rs.

KING HENRY, *2 Henry VI*, III.II.40

BIRTH

see also BABIES; HUMAN CONDITION; PREGNANCY

There was a star danc'd, and under that I was born.

BEATRICE, *Much Ado About Nothing*, II.I.335

But thou art fair, and at thy birth, dear boy,
Nature and Fortune join'd to make thee great.
Of nature's gifts thou mayst with lilies boast,
And with the half-blown rose.

CONSTANCE, *King John*, III.I.51

Why railest thou on thy birth? the heaven and earth?
Since birth, and heaven, and earth, all three do meet
In thee at once, which thou at once wouldst lose.

FRIAR LAWRENCE, *Romeo and Juliet*, III.III.119

You were born under a charitable star.

HELENA, *All's Well That Ends Well*, I.I.190

Her life is safest only in her birth.

> KING RICHARD, *Richard III*, IV.IV.214

At my nativity
The front of heaven was full of fiery shapes
Of burning cressets, and at my birth
The frame and huge foundation of the earth
Shak'd like a coward.

> OWEN GLENDOWER, *1 Henry IV*, III.I.13

This child was prisoner to the womb, and is
By law and process of great Nature thence
Freed and enfranchis'd.

> PAULINA, *The Winter's Tale*, II.II.58

BLACKNESS

Coal-black is better than another hue,
In that it scorns to bear another hue;
For all the water in the ocean
Can never turn the swan's black legs to white,
Although she lave them hourly in the flood.

> AARON, *Titus Andronicus*, IV.II.99

BLESSING

see also GRATITUDE; PRAYER; SPIRITUALITY AND RELIGION

Lend me a heart replete with thankfulness!
For thou hast given me in this beauteous face
A world of earthly blessings to my soul,
If sympathy of love unite our thoughts.

> KING HENRY, *2 Henry VI*, I.I.20

A double blessing is a double grace.

> LAERTES, *Hamlet*, I.III.53

BLINDNESS

see also DISABILITY; EYES AND SIGHT; SENSUALITY

Fortune
is painted blind, with a muffler afore his eyes, to signify
to you that Fortune is blind.

> FLUELLEN, *Henry V*, III.VI.30

A man may see how this
world goes with no eyes. Look with thine ears; see
how yond justice rails upon yond simple thief. Hark
in thine ear: change places, and handy-dandy, which is
the justice, which is the thief? Thou hast seen a
farmer's dog bark at a beggar?

> LEAR, *King Lear*, IV.VI.150

He that is strooken blind cannot forget
The precious treasure of his eyesight lost.

ROMEO, *Romeo and Juliet*, I.I.232

BOASTING
see also ARROGANCE

Scambling, outfacing, fashion-monging boys,
That lie and cog and flout, deprave and slander,
Go anticly, and show outward hideousness,
And speak off half a dozen dang'rous words,
How they might hurt their enemies—if they durst—
And this is all.

ANTHONY, *Much Ado About Nothing*, V.I.94

Who knows himself a braggart,
Let him fear this; for it will come to pass
That every braggart shall be found an ass.

PAROLLES, *All's Well That Ends Well*, IV.III.334

BODY

What is thy body but a swallowing grave,
Seeming to bury that posterity
Which by the rights of time thou needs must have,
If thou destroy them not in dark obscurity?

Venus and Adonis, 757

My body or my soul, which was the dearer,
When the one pure, the other made divine?

The Rape of Lucrece, 1163

I never knew so young a body with so old a head.

DUKE OF VENICE (READING), *The Merchant of Venice*, IV.I.63

Virtue? a fig! 'tis in ourselves that we are
thus or thus. Our bodies are our gardens, to the
which our wills are gardeners; so that if we will plant
nettles or sow lettuce, set hyssop and weed up tine,
supply it with one gender of herbs or distract it with
many, either to have it sterile with idleness or manur'd
with industry—why, the power and corrigible
authority of this lies in our wills.

IAGO, *Othello*, I.III.319

No, no, I am but shadow of myself.
You are deceiv'd my substance is not here;
For what you see is but the smallest part
And least proportion of humanity.
I tell you, madam, were whole frame here,

It is of such a spacious lofty pitch,
Your roof were not sufficient to contain't.

LORD TALBOT, *1 Henry VI*, II.III.50

What, old acquaintance! could not all this flesh
Keep in a little life?

PRINCE HENRY, *1 Henry IV*, V.IV.102

'Tis known I am a pretty piece of flesh.

SAMPSON, *Romeo and Juliet*, I.I.29

BOOKS
see also LITERACY; READING; WRITING

Remember
First to possess his books; for without them
He's but a sot, as I am; nor hath not
One spirit to command: they all do hate him
As rootedly as I. Burn but his books.

CALIBAN, *The Tempest*, III.II.91

A beggar's book
Outworths a noble's blood.

DUKE OF BUCKINGHAM, *Henry VIII*, I.I.122

And now I will unclasp a secret book,
And to your quick-conceiving discontents
I'll read you matter deep and dangerous,
As full of peril and adventurous spirit
As to o'erwalk a current roaring loud
On the unsteadfast footing of a spear.

EARL OF WORCESTER, *1 Henry IV*, I.III.189

Thou hast most traitorously
corrupted the youth of the realm in erecting a grammar
school; and whereas, before, our forefathers had no
other books but the score and the tally, thou hast
caus'd printing to be us'd, and, contrary to the King,
his crown, and dignity, thou has built a paper-mill.

JACK CADE, *2 Henry VI*, IV.VII.32

A book? O rare one,
Be not, as is our fangled world, a garment
Nobler than that it covers! Let thy effects
So follow, to be most unlike our courtiers,
As good as promise!

POSTHUMUS, *Cymbeline*, V.IV.133

So of his gentleness,
Knowing I lov'd my books, he furnish'd me

From mine own library with volumes that
I prize above my dukedom.

PROSPERO, *The Tempest*, I.II.109

I had rather than forty shillings I had my Book of Songs and
Sonnets here.

SLENDER, *The Merry Wives of Windsor*, I.I.198

Come and take choice of all my library,
And so beguile thy sorrow.

TITUS, *Titus Andronicus*, IV.I.34

BOREDOM
see also INACTION

Quietness, grown sick of rest, would purge
By any desperate change.

ANTONY, *Antony and Cleopatra*, I.III.53

O, he is as tedious
As a tired horse, a railing wife,
Worse than a smoky house.

HOTSPUR, *1 Henry IV*, III.I.157

Life is as tedious as a twice-told tale
Vexing the dull ear of a drowsy man.

LEWIS, *King John*, III.IV.108

BORROWING
see also POSSESSION

Albeit I neither lend nor borrow
By taking nor by giving of excess,
Yet to supply the ripe wants of my friend,
I'll break a custom.

ANTONIO, *The Merchant of Venice*, I.III.61

Neither a borrower nor a lender be,
For loan oft loses both itself and friend,
And borrowing dulleth th' edge of husbandry.

POLONIUS, *Hamlet*, I.III.75

BOXING

Thou hast hit it; for there's no better sign
of a brave mind than a hard hand.

GEORGE BEVIS, *2 Henry VI*, IV.II.19

BRAVADO
see also COURAGE; FEARLESSNESS

You must not think
That we are made of stuff so flat and dull
That we can let our beard be shook with danger

And think it pastime.
CLAUDIUS, Hamlet, IV.VII.30

Hath no man's dagger here a point for me?
LEONATO, Much Ado About Nothing, IV.I.109

BREATH
see also ARTIFICIAL RESPIRATION

If her breath were as terrible as her terminations, there
were no living near her, she would infect to the north star.
BENEDICK, Much Ado About Nothing, II.I.248

Lend me a looking-glass,
If that her breath will mist or stain the stone,
Why then she lives.
LEAR, King Lear, V.III.262

I saw her coral lips to move,
And with her breath she did perfume the air.
LUCENTIO, The Taming of the Shrew, I.I.174

Nurse. Do you not see I am out of breath?
Jul. How art thou out of breath, when thou hast breath
To say to me that thou art out of breath?
NURSE, JULIET, Romeo and Juliet, II.V.31

Speed. "Item, She is not to be kissed fasting, in
respect of her breath."
Launce. Well, that fault may be mended with a breakfast.
Read on.
Speed. "Item, she hath a sweet mouth."
Launce. That makes amends for her sour breath.
SPEED, LAUNCE, The Two Gentlemen of Verona, III.I.323

BRIBERY
see also CORRUPTION; CRIME

I thank you, general;
But cannot make my heart consent to take
A bribe to apy my sword. I do refuse it,
And stand upon my common part with those
That have beheld the doing.
CAIUS MARTIUS, Coriolanus, I.IV.37

Though you and all the kings of Christiandom
Are led so grossly by this meddling priest,
Dreading the curse that money may buy out,
And by the merit of vild gold, dross, dust,
Purchase corrupted pardon of a man
Who in that sale sells pardon from himself.
KING JOHN, King John, III.I.162

BUSINESS
see also WORK

> When rich villains have need of poor ones, poor ones may
> make what price they will.
>> BORACHIO, *Much Ado About Nothing*, III.III.113

> Affairs that walk
> (As they say spirits do) at midnight, have
> In them a wilder nature than the business
> That seeks dispatch by day.
>> GARDINER, *Henry VIII*, V.I.13

> Every man hath business and desire,
> Such as it is.
>> HAMLET, *Hamlet*, I.V.130

> Our hands are full of business, let's away,
> Advantage feeds him fat while men delay.
>> KING HENRY, *1 Henry IV*, III.II.179

> Yet such extenuation let me beg
> As in reproof of many tales devis'd,
> Which oft the ear of greatness needs must hear
> By smiling pick-thanks and base newsmongers,
> I may for some things true, wherein my youth
> Hath faulty wand'red and irregular,
> Find pardon on my true submission.
>> PRINCE HENRY, *1 Henry IV*, III.II.22

> 'Tis not sleepy business,
> But must be look'd to speedily and strongly.
>> QUEEN, *Cymbeline*, III.V.26

> I will buy with you, sell with you, talk with you, walk with
> you, and so following; but I will not eat with you, drink
> with you, nor pray with you.
>> SHYLOCK, *The Merchant of Venice*, I.III.35

> Let us like merchants first show foul wares,
> And think perchance they'll sell; if not,
> The lustre of the better shall exceed
> By showing the worse first.
>> ULYSSES, *Trolius and Cressida*, I.III.358

CARE AND CONCERN
see also FEAR; SECURITY; WORRY

> What though care killed a cat, thou hast mettle enough to
> kill care.
>> CLAUDIO, *Much Ado About Nothing*, V.I.132

Care is no cure, but rather corrosive,
For things that are not to be remedied.
JOAN DE PUCELLE, 1 Henry VI, III.III.3

Things done well
And with a care exempt themselves from fear.
KING HENRY, Henry VIII, I.II.88

Past care is still past cure.
ROSALINE, Love's Labor's Lost, V.II.28

Care's an enemy to life.
SIR TOBY, Twelfth Night, I.III.3

CATS

I could endure anything before but a cat, and now he's a
cat to me.
BERTRAM, All's Well That Ends Well, IV.III.237

The cat, with eyne of burning coal
Now crouches fore the mouse's hole.
GOWER, Pericles, III.CHO.5

I am as vigilant as a cat to steal cream.
SIR JOHN FALSTAFF, 1 Henry IV, IV.II.58

CELEBRATION
see also PARTIES

Feasts are too proud to give thanks to the gods.
APEMANTUS, Timon of Athens, I.II.61

O, rejoice
Beyond a common joy, and set it down
With gold on lasting pillars.
GONZALO, The Tempest, V.I.206

This day, no man think
H'as business at his house; for all shall stay:
This little one shall make it Holy-day.
KING HENRY, Henry VIII, V.IV.74

'Tis true, fair daughter, and this blessed day
Ever in France shall be kept festival.
To solemnize this day the glorious sun
Stays in his course and plays the alchymist,
Turning with splendor of his precious eye
The meagre cloddy earth to glittering gold.
The yearly course that brings this day about
Shall never see it but a holy day.
KING PHILIP, King John, III.I.75

Feast here awhile,
Until our stars that frown lend us a smile.

PERICLES, *Pericles*, I.iv.107

Why ring not out the bells aloud throughout the town?
Dolphin, command the citizens make bonfires,
And feast and banquet in the open streets,
To celebrate the joy that God hath given us.

REIGNER, *1 Henry VI*, I.vi.11

Prepare for mirth, for mirth becomes a feast.

SIMONIDES, *Pericles*, II.iii.7

CHANCE
see also FATE; FORTUNE; GAMBLING

But as th' unthought-on accident is guilty
To what we wildly do, so we profess
Ourselves to be the slaves of chance, and flies
Of every wind that blows.

FLORIZEL, *The Winter's Tale*, IV.iv.538

O God, that one might read the book of Fate,
And see the revolution of the times
Make mountains level, and the continent,
Weary of solid firmness, melt itself
Into the sea, and other times to see
The beachy girdle of the ocean
Too wide for Neptune's hips; how chance's mocks
And changes fill the cup of alteration
With divers liquors!

KING HENRY IV, *2 Henry IV*, III.i.45

CHANGE
see also INCONSTANCY; REFORM; TIME; TRANSIENCE

But reckoning Time, whose million'd accidents
Creep in 'twixt vows, and change decrees of kings,
Tan sacred beauty, blunt the sharp'st intents,
Divert strong minds to th' course of alt'ring things.

SONNET 115, 5–8

O world, thy slippery turns! Friends now fast sworn,
Whose double bosoms seems to wear one heart,
Whose hours, whose bed, whose meal and exercise
Are still together, who twin, as 'twere, in love
Unseparable, shall within this hour,
On a dissension of a doit, break out
To bitterest enmity; so, fellest foes,
Whose passions and whose plots have broke their sleep
To take the one the other, by some chance,

Some trick not worth an egg, shall grow dear friends
And interjoin their issues.

CORIOLANUS, *Coriolanus*, IV.IV.12

Presume not that I am the thing I was,
For God doth know, so shall the world perceive,
That I have turn'd away my former self.

KING HENRY V, *2 Henry IV*, V.v.56

I do not shame
To tell you what I was, since my conversion
So sweetly tastes, being the thing I am.

OLIVER, *As You Like It*, IV.III.135

Good Camillo,
Your chang'd complexions are to me a mirror
Which shows me mine chang'd too; for I must be
A party in this alteration, finding
Myself thus alter'd with't.

POLIXENES, *The Winter's Tale*, I.II.380

CHARACTER—ANTONIO

The dearest friend to me, the kindest man,
The best-condition'd and unwearied spirit
In doing courtesies, and one in whom
The ancient Roman honor more appears
Than any that draws breath in Italy.

BASSANIO, *The Merchant of Venice*, III.II.292

CHARACTER—ARMADO

His humor is lofty, his discourse peremptory, his tongue
filled, his eye ambitious, his gait
majestical, and his general behavior vain, ridiculous, and
thrasonical. He is too picked, too
spruce, too affected, too odd at it were, too peregrinate,
as I may call it.

HOLOFERNES, *Love's Labor's Lost*, V.I.9

CHARACTER—BEATRICE

Nature never fram'd a woman's heart
Of prouder stuff than that of Beatrice.

HERO, *Much Ado About Nothing*, III.I.49

CHARACTER—BOYET

This fellow pecks up wit as pigeons pease,
And utters it again when God doth please.
He is wit's pedlar, and retails his wares
At wakes and wassails, meetings, markets, fairs:

And we that sell by gross, the Lord doth know,
Have not the grace to grace it with such show.
This gallant pins the wenches on his sleeve;
Had he been Adam, he had tempted Eve.
'A can carve too, and lisp; why, this is he
That kissed his hand away in courtesy;
This is the ape of form, monsieur the nice,
That when he plays at tables chides the dice
In honorable terms; nay, he can sing
A mean most meanly, and in hushering
Mend him who can. The ladies call him sweet,
The stirs as he treads on them kiss his feet.
This is the flow'r that smiles on every one,
To show his teeth as white as whale's bone;
And consciences that will not die in debt
Pay him the due of honey-tongued Boyet.

BEROWNE, *Love's Labor's Lost*, V.II.315

CHARACTER—BRUTUS

This was the noblest Roman of them all:
All the conspirators, save only he,
Did that they did in envy of great Caesar;
He, only in a general honest thought
And common good to all, made one of them.
His life was gentle, and the elements
So mix'd in him that Nature might stand up
And say to all the world, "This was a man!"

ANTONY, *Julius Caesar*, V.v.68

CHARACTER—CASSIUS

He reads much,
He is a great observer, and he looks
Quite through the deeds of men. He loves no plays,
As thou dost, Antony; he hears no music;
Seldom he smiles, and smiles in such a sort
As if he mock'd himself, and scorn'd his spirit
That could be mov'd to smile at any thing.
Such men as he be never at heart's ease
Whiles they behold a greater than themselves,
And therefore are they very dangerous.
Is dearly bought as mine, and I will have it.

CAESAR, *Julius Caesar*, I.II.201

CHARACTER—CLEOPATRA

Her passions are made of nothing but the finest part of pure
love. We cannot call her winds and waters sighs and tears;
they are greater storms and tempests than almanacs can

report. This cannot be cunning to her; if it be, she makes
a show'r of rain as well as Jove.

ENOBARBUS, Antony and Cleopatra, I.II.146

CHARACTER—CORIOLANUS

2. Off. Three, they say; but 'tis thought of every one
Coriolanus will carry it.
1. Off. That's a brave fellow; but he's vengeance proud,
and loves not the common people.
2. Off. Faith, there hath been many great men that have
flatter'd the people, who ne'er lov'd them; and there be
many that they have lov'd, they know not wherefore; so that,
if they love they know not why, they hate upon no better a
ground. Therefore, for Coriolanus neither to care whether
they love or hate him manifests the true knowledge he has in
their disposition, and out of his noble carelessness lets
them plainly see't.
1. Off. If he did not care whether he had their love or no,
he wav'd indifferently 'twixt doing them neither good nor
harm; but he seeks their hat with greater devotion than they
can render it him, and leaves nothing undone that may fully
discover him their opposite. Now, to seem to affect the
malice and displeasure of the people is as bad as that which
he dislikes, to flatter them for their love.
2. Off. He hath deserv'd worthily of his country, and his
ascent is not by such easy degrees as those who, having
been supple and courteous to the people, bonneted, without
any further deed to have them at all into their estimation
and report. But he hath so planted his honors in their eyes
and his actions in their hearts that for their tongues to
be silent and not confess so much were a kind of ingrateful
injury; to report otherwise were a malice that, giving
itself the lie, would pluck reproof and rebuke from every
ear that heard it.

OFFICERS, Coriolanus, II.II.3

CHARACTER—FALSTAFF

Men of all sorts take a pride to gird at me.
The brain of this foolish-compounded clay, man, is not
able to invent any thing that intends to laughter more
than I invent or is invented on me: I am not only witty
in myself, but the cause that wit is in other men.
I do here walk before thee like a sow that hath overwhelm'd all her litter but one.

SIR JOHN FALSTAFF, 2 Henry IV, I.II.6

CHARACTER—LORD OF GLOUCESTER

Can you not see? or will ye not observe
The strangeness of his alter'd countenance?
With what a majesty he bears himself,
How insolent of late he is become,
How proud, how peremptory, and unlike himself?
We know the time since he has mild and affable,
And if we did but glance a far-off look,
Immediately he was upon his knee,
That all the court admir'd him for submission;
But meet him now, and, be it in the morn,
When every one will give the time of day,
He knits his brow and shows an angry eye,
And passeth by with stiff unbowed knee,
Disdaining duty that to us belongs.
Small curs are not regarded when they grin,
But great men tremble when the lion roars,
And Humphrey is no little man in England.
First note that he is near you in descent,
And should you fall, he is the next will mount.
Me seemth then it is no policy,
Respecting what a rancorous mind he bears
And his advantage following your decease,
That he should come about your royal person,
Or be admitted to your Highness' Council.
By flattery hath he won the commons' hearts;
And when he please to make commotion,
'Tis to be fear'd they all will follow him.
Now 'tis the spring, and weeds are shallow-rooted;
Suffer them now, and they'll o'ergrown the garden
And choke the herbs for want of husbandry.
The reverent care I bear unto my lord
Made me collect these dangers in the Duke.
If it be fond, call it a woman's fear;
Which fear, if better reasons can supplant.

QUEEN MARGARET, 2 *Henry VI*, III.1.4

CHARACTER—HENRY IV

God knows, my son,
By what by-paths and indirect crook'd ways
I met this crown, and I myself know well
How troublesome it sat upon my head.
To thee it shall descend with better quiet,
Better opinion, better confirmation,
For all the soil of the achievement goes
With me into the earth. It seem'd in me
But as an honor snatch'd with boist'rous hand,

And I had many living to upbraid
My gain of it by their assistances,
Which daily grew to quarrel and to bloodshed,
Wounding supposèd peace. All these bold fears
Thou seest with peril I have answered;
For all my reign hath been but as a scene
Acting that argument. And now my death
Changes the mood, for what in me was purchas'd
Falls upon thee in a more fairer sort;
So thou the garland wear'st successively.
Yet though thou stand'st more sure than I could so,
Thou art not firm enough, since griefs are green,
And all my friends, which thou must make thy friends,
Have but their stings and teeth newly ta'en out;
By whose fell working I was first advanc'd,
And by whose power I well might lodge a fear
To be again displac'd; which to avoid,
I cut them off, and had a purpose now
To lead out many to the Holy Land,
Lest rest and lying still might make them look
Too near unto my state. Therefore, my Harry,
Be it thy course to busy giddy minds
With foreign quarrels, that action, hence borne out,
May waste the memory of the former days.
More would I, but my lungs are wasted so
That strength of speech is utterly denied me.
How I came by the crown, O God forgive,
And grant it may with thee in true peace live!

> KING HENRY IV, *2 Henry IV*, IV.v.183

CHARACTER—HENRY V

The King's a bawcock, and a heart of gold,
A lad of life, an imp of fame,
Of parents good, of fist most valiant.
I kiss his dirty shoe, and from heart-string
I love the lovely bully.

> PISTOL, *Henry V*, IV.i.44

CHARACTER—HENRY VI

O God! methinks it were a happy life
To be no better than a homely swain,
To sit upon a hill, as I do now,
To carve out dials quaintly, point by point,
Thereby to see the minutes how they run:
How many makes the hour full complete,
How many hours brings about the day,
How many days will finish up the year,

How many years a mortal man may live.
When this is known, then to divide the times:
So many hours must I tend my flock,
So many hours must I take my rest,
So many hours must I contemplate,
So many hours must I sport myself,
So many days my ewes have been with young,
So many weeks ere the poor fools will ean,
So many years ere I shall shear the fleece:
So minutes, hours, days, months, and years,
Pass'd over to the end thy were created,
Would bring white hairs unto a quiet grave.
Ah! what a life were this! how sweet! how lovely!
Gives not the hawthorn bush a sweeter shade
To shepherds looking on their silly sheep
Than doth a rich embroider'd canopy
To kings that fear their subjects' treachery?
O yes, it doth; a thousandfold it doth.
And to conclude, the shepherd's homely curds,
His cold thin drink out of his leather bottle,
His wonted sleep under a fresh tree's shade,
All which secure and sweetly he enjoys,
Is far beyond a prince's delicates—
His viands sparkling in a golden cup,
His body crouched in a curious bed,
When care, mistrust, and treason waits on him.

KING HENRY, *3 Henry VI*, II.v.21

CHARACTER—HENRY VIII

My conscience first receiv'd a tenderness,
Scruple, and prick, on certain speeches utter'd
By th' Bishop of Bayonne, then French ambassador,
Who had been hither sent on the debating
A marriage 'twixt the Duke of Orleans and
Our daughter Mary. I' th' progress of this business,
Ere a determine resolution, he
(I mean the Bishop) did require a respite,
Wherein he might the King his lord advertise
Whether our daughter were legitimate,
Respecting this our marriage with the dowager,
Sometimes our brother's wife. This respite shook
The bosom of my conscience, enter'd me,
Yea, with a spitting power, and made to tremble
The region of my breast, which forc'd such way,
That many maz'd considerings did throng
And press'd in with this caution. First, methought

I stood not in the smile of heaven, who had
Commanded nature, that my lady's womb,
If it conceiv'd a male-child by me, should
Do no more offices of life to't than
The grave does to th' dead; for her male issue
Or died where they were made, or shortly after
This world had air'd them. Hence I took a thought
This was a judgment on me, that my kingdom
(Well worthy the best heir o' th' world) should not
Be gladded in't by me. Then follows, that
I weigh'd the danger which my realms stood in
By this my issue's fail, and that gave to me
Many a groaning throe. Thus hulling in
The wild sea of my conscience, I did steer
Toward this remedy, whereupon we are
Now present here together: that's to say,
I meant to rectify my conscience—which
I then did feel full sick, and yet not well—
By all the reverend fathers of the land
And doctors learn'd. First I began in private
With you, my Lord of Lincoln. You remember
How under my oppression I did reek
When I first mov'd you.

KING HENRY, *Henry VIII*, II.iv.171

CHARACTER—HERMIONE

But thus, if pow'rs divine
Behold our human actions (as they do),
I doubt not then but innocence shall make
False accusation blush, and tyranny
Tremble at patience. You, my lord, best know
(Who least will seem to do so) my past life
Hath been as continent, as chaste, as true,
As I am now unhappy; which is more
Than history can pattern, though devis'd
And play'd to take spectators. For behold me,
A fellow of the royal bed, which owe
A moi'ty of the throne, a great king's daughter,
The mother to a hopeful prince, here standing
To prate and talk for life and honor 'fore
Who please to come and hear. For life, I prize it
As I weigh grief, which I would spare; for honor,
'Tis a derivative from me to mine,
And only that I stand for.

HERMIONE, *The Winter's Tale*, III.ii.28

CHARACTER—KING JOHN

When I spake darkly what I purposed,
Or turn's an eye of doubt upon my face,
As bid me tell my tale in express words,
Deep shame had struck me dumb, made me break off,
And those thy fears might have wrought fears in me.
But thou didst understand me by my signs,
And didst in signs again parley with sin,
Yea, without stop, didst let thy heart consent,
And consequently thy rude hand to act
The deed, which both our tongues held vild to name.
Out of my sight, and never see me more!
My nobles leave me, and my state is braved,
Even at my gates, with ranks of foreign pow'rs;
Nay in the body of this fleshly land,
This kingdom, this confine of blood and breath,
Hostility and civil tumult reigns
Between my conscience and my cousin's death.

KING JOHN, *King John*, IV.II.232

CHARACTER—KING LEAR

Pray do not mock me.
I am a very foolish fond old man,
Fourscore and upward, not an hour more nor less;
And to deal plainly,
I fear I am not in my perfect mind.
Methinks I should know you, and know this man,
Yet I am doubtful; for I am mainly ignorant
What place this is, and all the skill I have
Remembers not these garments; nor I know not
Where I did lodge last night. Do not laugh at me,
For (as I am a man) I think this lady
To be my child Cordelia.

LEAR, *King Lear*, IV.VII.59

CHARACTER—LEONTES

What studies torments, tyrant, hast for me?
What wheels? rack? fires? What flaying? boiling
In leads or oils? What old or newer torture
Must I receive, whose every word deserves
To taste of thy most worst? Thy tyranny,
Together working with thy jealousies
(Fancies too weak for boys, too green and idle
For girls of nine), O think what they have done,
And then run mad indeed—stark mad! for all
Thy by-gone fooleries were but spices of it.

That thou betrayedst Polixenes, 'twas nothing—
That did but show thee, of a fool, inconstant,
And damnable ingrateful; nor was't much
Thou wouldst have poison'd good Camillo's honor,
To have him kill a king—poor trespasses,
More monstrous standing by; whereof I reckon
The casting forth to crows the baby daughter
To be or none or little—though a devil
Would have shed water out of fire ere done't;
Nor is't directly laid to thee, the death
Of the young Prince, whose honorable thoughts
(Thoughts high for one so tender) cleft the heart
That could conceive a gross and foolish sire
Blemish'd his gracious dam; this is not, no,
Laid to thy answer: but the last—O lords,
When I have said, cry "Woe!"—the Queen, the Queen,
The sweet'st, dear'st creature's dead, and vengeance for't
Not dropp'd down yet.

> PAULINA, *The Winter's Tale*, III.II.175

CHARACTER—MACBETH

I grant him bloody,
Luxurious, avaricious, false, deceitful,
Sudden, malicious, smacking of every sin
That has a name.

> MALCOLM, *Macbeth*, IV.III.57

CHARACTER—ORSINO

I suppose him virtuous, know him noble,
Of great estate, of fresh and stainless youth;
In voices well-divulg'd, free, learn'd, and valiant,
And in dimension, and the shape of nature,
A gracious person.

> OLIVIA, *Twelfth Night*, I.v.258

CHARACTER—OTHELLO

Soft you; a word or two before you go.
I have done the state some service, and they know't—
No more of that. I pray you, in your letters,
When you shall these unlucky deeds relate,
Speak of me as I am; nothing extenuate,
Nor set down aught in malice. Then must you speak
Of one that lov'd not wisely but too well;
Of one not easily jealous, but being wrought,
Perplexed in the extreme; of one whose hand
(Like the base Indian threw a pearl away

Richer than all his tribe; of one whose subdu'd eyes,
Albeit unused to the melting mood,
Drops tears as fast as the Arabian trees
Their medicinable gum. Set you down this;
And say besides, that in Aleppo once,
Where a malignant and a turban'd Turk
Beat a Venetian and traduc'd the state,
I took by th' throat the circumcised dog,
And smote him—thus.

OTHELLO, *Othello*, V.II.338

CHARACTER—PAROLLES

Believe it, my lord, in mine own direct knowledge, without
any malice, but to speak of him
as my kinsman, he's a most notable coward, an infinite and
endless liar, an hourly promise-
breaker, the owner of no one good quality

SECOND LORD, *All's Well That Ends Well*, III.VI.7

CHARACTER—PETRUCHIO

Though he be blunt, I know him passing wise;
Though he be merry, yet withal he's honest.

TRANIO, *The Taming of the Shrew*, III.II.24

CHARACTER—PINCH

They brought one Pinch, a hungry lean-fac'd villain,
A mere anatomy, a mountebank,
A threadbare juggler and a fortune-teller,
A needy, hollow-ey'ed, sharp-looking wretch,
A living dead man.

ANTIPHOLUS OF EPHESUS, *The Comedy of Errors*, V.I.238

CHARACTER—PUCK

Are not you he
That frightens the maidens of the villagery,
Skim milk, and sometimes labor in the quern,
And bootless make the breathless huswife churn,
And sometime make the drink to bear no barm,
Mislead night-wanderers, laughing at their harm?
Those that Hobgoblin call you, and sweet Puck,
You do their work, and they shall have good luck.

FAIRY, *A Midsummer Night's Dream*, II.1.34

CHARACTER—KING RICHARD II

I have been studying how I may compare
This prison where I live unto the world;
And for because the world is populous,
And here is not a creature but myself,
I cannot do it; yet I'll hammer it out.

My brain I'll prove the female to my soul,
My soul the father, and these two beget
A generation of still-breeding thoughts;
And these same thoughts people this little world,
In humors like the people of this world:
For no thought is contented. The better sort,
As thoughts of things divine, are intermix'd
With scruples and do set the word itself
Against the word,
As thus: "Come, little ones," and then again,
"It is as hard to come as for a camel
To thread the postern of a small needle's eye."
Thoughts tending to ambition, they do plot
Unlikely wonders: how these vain weak nails
May tear a passage through the flinty ribs
Of this hard world, my ragged prison walls;
And for thy cannot, die in their own pride.
Thoughts tending to content flatter themselves
That they are not the first of fortune's slaves,
Nor shall not be the last—like seely beggars
Who sitting in the stocks refuge their shame,
That many have and others must sit there;
And in this thought they find a kind of ease,
Bearing their own misfortunes on the back
Of such as have before endur'd the like,
Thus play I in one person many people,
And none contented. Sometimes am I king;
Then treasons make me wish myself a beggar,
And so I am. Then crushing penury
Persuades me I was better when a king;
Then am I king'd again, and by and by
Think that I am unking'd by Bullingbrook,
And straight am nothing. But what e'er I be,
Nor I, nor any man that but man is,
With nothing shall be pleas'd, till he be eas'd
With being nothing.

KING RICHARD, *Richard II*, V.v.1

CHARACTER—RICHARD III

Now is the winter of our discontent
Made glorious summer by this sun of York;
And all the clouds that low'r'd upon our house
In the deep bosom of the ocean buried.
Now are our brows bound with victorious wreaths,
Our bruised arms hung up for monuments,
Our stern alarums chang'd to merry meetings,
Our dreadful marches to delightful measures.

Grim-visag'd War hath smooth's his wrinkled front;
And now, instead of mounting barbèd steeds
To fright the souls of fearful adversaries,
He capers nimbly in a lady's chamber
To the lascivious pleasing of a lute.
But, I that am not shap'd for sportive tricks,
Nor made to court an amorous looking glass;
I, that am rudely stamp'd, and want love's majesty
To strut before a wanton ambling nymph;
I, that am curtail'd of this fair proportion,
Cheated of feature by dissembling nature,
Deform'd, unfinish'd, set before my time
Into this breathing world, scarce half made up,
And that so lamely and unfashionable
That dogs bark at me as I halt by them—
Why, I, in this weak piping time of peace,
Have no delight to pass away the time,
Unless to see my shadow in the sun
And descant on mine own deformity.
And therefore, since I cannot prove a lover
To entertain these fair well-spoken days,
I am determinèd to prove a villain
And hate the idle pleasures of these days.
Plots have I laid, inductions dangerous,
By drunken prophecies, libels, and dreams,
To set my brother Clarence and the King
In deadly hate the one against the other;
And if King Edward be as true and just
As I am subtle, false, and treacherous,
This day should Clarence closely be mew'd up
About a prophecy, which says that *G*
Of Edward's heirs the murderer shall be.
Dive, thoughts, down to my soul, here Clarence comes!
RICHARD, DUKE OF GLOUCESTER, Richard III, I.I.I

CHARACTER—TROILUS

True swains in love shall in the world to come
Approve their truth by Troilus. When their rhymes,
Wants similes, truth tir'd with iteration,
"As true as steel, as plantage to the moon,
As sun to day, as turtle to her mate,
As iron to adamant, as earth to th' center,"
Yet after all comparisons of truth
(As truth authentic author to be cited)
"As true as Troilus" shall crown up the verse,
And sanctify the numbers.
TROILUS, Troilus and Cressida, III.II.173

CHARITY
see also GENEROSITY; HELP

> Who can sever love from charity?
>
> > BEROWNE, *Love's Labor's Lost*, IV.III.362

> Your honor has through Ephesus pour'd forth
> Your charity, and hundreds call themselves
> Your creatures, who by you have been restored.
>
> > GENTLEMAN, *Pericles*, III.II.43

> He hath a tear for pity, and a hand
> Open as day for melting charity.
>
> > KING HENRY IV, *2 Henry IV*, IV.IV.31

> But I perceive
> Men must learn now with pity to dispense,
> For policy sits above conscience.
>
> > FIRST STRANGER, *Timon of Athens*, III.II.85

> 'Tis not enough to help the feeble up,
> But to support him after.
>
> > TIMON, *Timon of Athens*, IV.III.1

> I gave it freely ever, and there's none
> Can truly say he gives if he receives.
>
> > TIMON, *Timon of Athens*, I.II.10

CHASTITY
see also ABSTINENCE; SELF-RESTRAINT; VIRGINITY

> Happ'ly that name of "chaste" unhappp'ly set
> this bateless edge on his keen appetite.
>
> > *The Rape of Lucrece*, 8

> It is the very emblem of a maid;
> For when the west wind courts her gently,
> How modestly she blows, and paints the sun
> With her chaste blushes! When the north comes near her,
> Rude and impatient, then, like chastity,
> She locks her beauties in her bud again,
> And leaves him to base briers.
>
> > EMILIA, *The Two Noble Kinsmen*, II.II.137

> Chaste, and immaculate in very thought,
> Whose maiden blood, thus rigorously effus'd,
> Will cry for vengeance at the gates of heaven.
>
> > JOAN DE PUCELLE, *1 Henry VI*, V.IV.51

> When I am dead, good wench,
> Let me be us'd with honor; strew me over
> With maiden flowers, that all the world may know
> I was a chaste wife to my grave.
>
> > KATHERINE, *Henry VIII*, IV.II.167

I will find you twenty lascivious turtles ere one chaste
man.

MISTRESS PAGE, *The Merry Wives of Windsor*, II.I.80

She'll not be hit
With Cupid's arrow, she hath Dian's wit;
And in strong proof of chastity well arm'd,
From Love's weak childish bow she lives uncharm'd.
She will not stay the siege of loving terms,
Nor bide th' encounter of assailing eyes,
Nor ope her lap to saint-seducing gold.
O, she is rich in beauty, only poor
That, when she dies, with beauty dies her store.

ROMEO, *Romeo and Juliet*, I.I.208

The moon methinks looks with wat'ry eye;
And when she weeps, weeps every little flower,
Lamenting some enforced chastity.

TITANIA, *A Midsummer Night's Dream*, III.I.198

Honesty coupled to beauty is to have honey a sauce to sugar.

TOUCHSTONE, *As You Like It*, III.III.30

CHILDREN
see also BABIES; CHILDREN OF UNMARRIED PARENTS; DAUGHTERS; GROWING UP;
SONS; YOUTH

Whilst her neglected child holds her in chase,
Cries to catch her whose busy care is bent
To follow that which flies before her face,
Not prizing her poor infant's discontent;
So run'st thou after that which flies from thee,
Whilst I, thy babe, chase thee afar behind.

SONNET 143, 5–10

Triumphs for nothing, and lamenting toys,
Is jollity for apes, and grief for boys.

GUIDERIUS, *Cymbeline*, IV.II.193

Your children were vexation to your youth.

KING RICHARD, *Richard III*, IV.IV.305

I think I shall never have the blessing of God till I have
issue o' my body; for they say barnes are blessings.

LAVATCH, *All's Well That Ends Well*, I.III.24

'Tis not good that children should know any wickedness.

MISTRESS QUICKLY, *The Merry Wives of Windsor*, II.II.128

How sweet a plant have you untimely cropp'd!
You have no children, butchers; if you had,

The thought of them would have stirr'd up remorse,
But if you ever chance to have a child,
Look in his youth to have him so cut off
As, deathsmen, you have rid this sweet young prince!

QUEEN MARGARET, *3 Henry VI*, V.v.62

CHILDREN OF UNMARRIED PARENTS
see also CHILDREN

I grow, I prosper:
Now, gods, stand up for bastards!

EDMUND, *King Lear*, I.II.21

Wherefore should I
Stand in the plague of custom, and permit
The curiosity of nations to deprive me,
For that I am some twelve or fourteen moonshines
Lag of a brother? Why bastard? Wherefore base?
When my dimensions are as well compact,
My mind as generous, and my shape as true,
As honest madam's issue? Why brand they us
With base? with baseness? bastardy? base, base?

EDMUND, *King Lear*, I.II.2

But, mother, I am not Sir Robert's son,
I have disclaim's Sir Robert and my land,
Legitimation, name, and all is gone;
Then, good my mother, let me know my father,
Some proper man, I hope. Who was it, mother?

PHILIP THE BASTARD, *King John*, I.I.246

He slander'd me with bastardy.
But whe'er I be as true begot or no,
That still I lay upon my mother's head,
But that I am as well begot, my liege
(Fair fall the bones that took the pains for me!)
Compare our faces, and be judge yourself.
If Old Sir Robert did beget us both,
And were our father and this son like him,
Old Sir Robert, father, on my knee
I give heaven thanks I was not like to thee!

PHILIP THE BASTARD, *King John*, I.I.74

We are all bastards,
And that most venerable man which I
Did call my father, was I know not where
When I was stamp'd.

POSTHUMUS, *Cymbeline*, II.v.2

CIVIL DISOBEDIENCE
see also CIVIL RIGHTS; REBELLION

> Faith, I have been a truant in the law,
> And never yet could frame my will to it,
> And therefore frame the law unto my will.
>
> EARL OF SUFFOLK, *1 Henry VI*, II.iv.7

> Civil dissension is a viperous worm
> That gnaws the bowels of the commonwealth.
>
> KING HENRY, *1 Henry VI*, III.i.72

> If they perceive dissension in our looks,
> And that within ourselves we disagree,
> How will their grudging stomachs be provok'd
> To willful disobedience, and rebel!
>
> KING HENRY, *1 Henry VI*, IV.i.139

CIVIL RIGHTS
see also CIVIL DISOBEDIENCE; DEMOCRACY; EQUALITY; FREEDOM

> Help, master, help! here's a fish hangs in
> the net, like poor man's right in the law; 'twill hardly
> come out.
>
> FISHERMAN, *Pericles*, II.i.116

> Did you perceive
> He did solicit you in free contempt
> When he did need your loves; and do you think
> That his contempt shall not be bruising to you
> When he hath power to crush? Why, had your bodies
> No heart among you? Or had you tongues to cry
> Against the rectorship of judgment?
>
> JUNIUS BRUTUS, *Coriolanus*, II.iii.199

CLERGY
see also PRAYER; SPIRITUALITY AND RELIGION

> And see, a book of prayer in his hand—
> True ornaments to know a holy man.
>
> BUCKINGHAM, *Richard III*, III.vii.98

> When holy and devout religious men
> Are at their beads, 'tis much to draw them thence,
> So sweet is zealous contemplation.
>
> BUCKINGHAM, *Richard III*, III.vii.92

> O holy sir,
> My reverend father, let it not be so!
> Out of your grace device, ordain, impose
> Some gentle order, and then we shall be blest
> To do your pleasure and continue friends.
>
> KING PHILIP, *King John*, III.i.248

But all his mind is bent to holiness,
To number Ave-Maries on his beads;
His champions are the prophets and apostles,
His weapons holy saws of sacred writ,
His study is his tilt-yard, and his loves
Are brazen images of canonized saints.
I would the college of the Cardinals
Would choose him Pope and carry him to Rome,
And set the triple crown upon his head—
That were a state fit for his holiness.

QUEEN MARGARET, 2 Henry VI, I.III.55

CLOTHING

see also FADS AND FASHION; JEWELRY

And look how well my garments sit upon me,
Much feater than before.

ANTONIO, The Tempest, II.I.273

Ne'er ask me what raiment I'll wear, for I have no more
doublets than backs, no more stockings than legs, no more
shoes than feet—nay, sometime more feet than shoes, or
such shoes as my toes look through the overleather.

CHRISTOPHER SLY, The Taming of the Shrew, IND.II.8

Youth no less becomes
The light and careless livery that it wears
Than settled age his sables and his weeds,
Importing health and graveness.

CLAUDIUS, Hamlet, IV.VII.78

Mur. What trade art thou? Answer me directly.
Cob. A trade, sir, that I hope I may use with a safe
conscience, which is indeed, sir, a mender of bad soles. . .
Truly, sir, all that I live by is with the awl:
I meddle with no tradesman's matters, nor women's
matters; but withal I am indeed, sir, a surgeon to old
shoes; when they are in great danger, I recover them.
As proper men as ever trod upon neat's-leather have
gone upon my handiwork.

COBBLER, MURELLUS, Julius Caesar, I.I.12

Put your bonnet to his right use, 'tis for the head.

HAMLET, Hamlet, V.II.92

The soul of this man is his clothes. Trust him not in
matter of heavy consequence.

LAFEW, All's Well That Ends Well, II.V.43

The scarfs and the bannerets about thee did manifoldly
dissuade me from believing thee a vessel of too great a
burden.

> LAFEW, *All's Well That Ends Well*, II.III.203

Sir, I would advise you to shift a shirt; the violence of
action hath made you reek as a sacrifice. Where air comes
out, air comes in; there's none abroad so wholesome as that
you vent.

> LORD, *Cymbeline*, I.II.1

Their cloths are after such a pagan cut to't,
That sure th' have worn out Christendom.

> LORD CHAMBERLAIN, *Henry VIII*, I.III.14

Our purses shall be proud, our garments poor,
For 'tis the mind that makes the body rich;
And as the sun breaks through the darkest clouds,
So honor peereth in the meanest habit.
What, is the jay more precious than the lark,
Because his feathers are more beautiful?
Or is the adder better than the eel,
Because his painted skin contents the eye?

> PETRUCHIO, *The Taming of the Shrew*, IV.III.171

Costly thy habit as thy purse can buy,
But not express'd in fancy, rich, not gaudy,
For the apparel oft proclaims the man.

> POLONIUS, *Hamlet*, I.III.70

Ah, cut my lace asunder,
That my pent heart may have some scope to beat,
Or else I swoon with this dead-killing news!

> QUEEN ELIZABETH, *Richard III*, IV.I.33

These clothes are good enough to drink in, and so be these
boots too; and they be not, let them hang themselves in
their own straps.

> SIR TOBY, *Twelfth Night*, I.III.11

CLOUDS

Sometime we see a cloud that's dragonish,
A vapor sometime like a bear or lion,
A tower'd citadel, a pendant rock,
A forked mountain, or blue promontory
With trees upon't that nod unto the world,
And mock our eyes with air. Thou hast seen these signs,
They are black vesper's pageants.

> ANTONY, *Antony and Cleopatra*, IV.XI.3

When clouds are seen, wise men put on their cloaks.

> CITIZEN, *Richard III*, II.III.32

Ham. Do you see yonder cloud that's almost in shape
of a camel?
Pol. By th' mass and 'tis, like a camel indeed.
Ham. Methinks it is like a weasel.
Pol. It is back'd like a weasel.
Ham. Or like a whale.
Pol. Very like a whale.

HAMLET, POLONIUS, *Hamlet*, III.II.376

COMFORT
see also COMPASSION; HOSPITALITY

You cloudy princes and heart-sorrowing peers
That bear this heavy mutual load of moan,
Now cheer each other in each other's love.

BUCKINGHAM, *Richard III*, II.II.112

Comfort's in heaven, and we are on the earth,
Where nothing lives but crosses, cares, and grief.

DUKE OF YORK, *Richard II*, II.II.78

Give me thy hand,
That I may dew it with my mournful tears;
Nor let the rain of heaven wet this place
To wash away my woeful monuments.

EARL OF SUFFOLK, *2 Henry VI*, III.II.339

He receives comfort like cold porridge.

SEBASTIAN, *The Tempest*, II.I.10

COMPANY
see also HOSPITALITY

Of much less value is my company
Than your good words.

BULLINGBROOK, *Richard II*, II.III.19

And I have heard it said, unbidden guests
Are often welcomest when they are gone.

DUKE OF BEDFORD, *1 Henry VI*, II.II.55

He would have all as merry
As, first, good company, good wine, good welcome,
Can make good people.

SIR HENRY GUILFORD, *Henry VIII*, I.IV.5

COMPASSION
see also COMFORT; EMPATHY; PITY

Melt at my tears and be compassionate!
Soft pity enters at an iron gate.

The Rape of Lucrece, 594

A wretched soul, bruis'd with adversity,
We bid be quiet when we hear it cry;
But were we burd'ned with like weight of pain,
As much, or more, we should ourselves complain.

ADRIANA, The Comedy of Errors, II.I.33

For why, the senseless brands will sympathize
The heavy accent of thy moving tongue,
And in compassion weep the fire out,
And some will mourn in ashes, some coal-black,
For the deposing of a rightful king.

KING RICHARD, Richard II, V.I.46

COMPETITION
see also BATTLE

The very dice obey him,
And in our sports my better cunning faints
Under his chance. If we draw lots, he speeds;
His cocks do win the battle still of mine,
When it is all to nought; and his quails ever
Beat mine, inhoop'd, at odds.

ANTONY, Antony and Cleopatra, II.III.34

We are not bred to talk, man. When we are arm'd
And both upon our guards, then let our fury,
Like meeting of two tides, fly strongly from us,
And then to whom the birthright of this beauty
Truly pertains (without obbraidings, scorns,
Despising of our persons, and such poutings,
Fitter for girls and schoolboys) will be seen,
And quickly, yours or mine.

ARCITE, The Two Noble Kinsmen, III.VI.28

Blood hath bought blood, and blows have answer'd blows;
Strength match'd with strength, and power confronted power:
Both are alike, and both alike we like
One must prove greatest. While they weigh so even
We hold our town for neither; yet for both.

HUBERT, King John, II.I.328

COMPLEXITY

I am not a day of season,
For thou mayest see a sunshine and a hail
In me at once.

KING OF FRANCE, All's Well That Ends Well, V.III.32

COMRADERY
see also FRIENDSHIP

> And here being thus together,
> We are an endless mine to one another;
> We are one another's wife, ever begetting
> New births of love; we are father, friends, acquaintance;
> We are, in one another, families:
> I am your heir, and you are mine; this place
> Is our inheritance.
>
> ARCITE, *The Two Noble Kinsmen*, II.II.78

> 'Tis a main goddess, cousin, that our fortunes
> Were twin'd together. 'Tis most true, two souls
> Put in two noble bodies, let 'em suffer
> The gall of hazard, so they grow together,
> Will never sink; they must not, say they could;
> A willing man dies sleeping, and all's done.
>
> PALAMON, *The Two Noble Kinsmen*, II.II.63

CONCLUSIONS

> We have no friend
> But resolution and the briefest end.
>
> CLEOPATRA, *Antony and Cleopatra*, IV.XV.90

> If it were done, when 'tis done, then 'twere well
> It were done quickly. If th' assassination
> Could trammel up the consequence, and catch
> With his surcease, success; that but this blow
> Might be the be-all and the end-all.
>
> MACBETH, *Macbeth*, I.VII.1

CONFESSION
see also GUILT

> Confess thy treasons ere thou fly the realm;
> Since thou hast far to go, bear not along
> The clogging burden of a guilty soul.
>
> BULLINGBROOK, *Richard II*, I.III.198

> I see a strange confession in thine eye.
> Thou shak'st thy head, and hold'st it fear or sin
> To speak a truth.
>
> EARL OF NORTHUMBERLAND, *2 Henry VI*, III.I.74

CONFIDENCE
see also ARROGANCE; PRIDE

> As confident as is the falcon's flight
> Against a bird, do I with Mowbray fight.
>
> BULLINGBROOK, *Richard II*, I.III.61

Ah, what's more dangerous than this fond affiance!

QUEEN MARGARET, *2 Henry VI*, III.i.74

CONFLICT

So doth my heart misgive me, in these conflicts
What may befall him, to his harm and ours.

DUKE OF SOMERSET, *3 Henry VI*, IV.vi.94

'Tis dangerous when the baser nature comes
Between the pass and fell incensed points
Of mighty opposites.

HAMLET, *Hamlet*, V.ii.60

Ay, marry, uncle, for I always thought
It was both impious and unnatural
That such immanity and bloody strife
Should reign among professors of one faith.

KING HENRY, *1 Henry VI*, V.i.11

For it is you
Have blown this coal betwixt my lord and me—
Which God's dew quench!

QUEEN KATHERINE, *Henry VIII*, II.iv.78

CONFUSION
see also BEWILDERMENT

Am I in earth, in heaven, or in hell?
Sleeping or waking, mad or well-advis'd?

ANTIPHOLUS OF SYRACUSE, *The Comedy of Errors*, II.ii.212

Cas. Did Cicero say anything?
Casca. Ay, he spoke Greek.
Cas. To what effect?
Casca. Nay, and I tell you that, I'll ne'er look you i' th'
face again. But those that understood him smiled at one
another, and shook their heads; but, for mine own part, it
was Greek to me.

CASSIUS, CASCA, *Julius Caesar*, I.ii.278

My thoughts are whirled like a potter's wheel,
I know not where I am, nor what I do.

LORD TALBOT, *1 Henry VI*, I.v.19

Confusion now hath made his masterpiece!

MACDUFF, *Macbeth*, II.iii.66

What most he should dislike seems pleasant to him;
What like, offensive.

OSWALD, *King Lear*, IV.ii.10

Methought I was enarmor'd of an ass.

TITANIA, *A Midsummer Night's Dream*, IV.i.77

CONSCIENCE

see also GUILT; THOUGHT

> Love is too young to know what conscience is,
> Yet who knows not conscience is born of love?
>
> SONNET 151, 1–2

> Leave her to heaven,
> And to those thorns that in her bosom lodge
> To prick and sting her.
>
> GHOST, *Hamlet*, I.v.86

> Thus conscience does make cowards of us all.
>
> HAMLET, *Hamlet*, III.i.82

> Stars, hide you fires,
> Let not light see my black and deep desires;
> The eye wink at the hand; yet let that be
> Which the eye fears, when it is done, to see.
>
> MACBETH, *Macbeth*, I.IV.50

> 'Tis a blushing sham-fac'd spirit that mutinies in a man's
> bosom. It fills a man full of obstacles. It made me once
> restore a purse of gold that (by chance) I found.
> It beggars any man that keeps it. It is turn'd out of
> towns and cities for a dangerous thing, and every man
> that means to live well endeavors to trust to himself
> and live without it.
>
> SECOND MURDERER, *Richard III*, I.IV.137

> Every man's conscience is a thousand men,
> To fight against this guilty homicide.
>
> OXFORD, *Richard III*, V.II.17

> The worm of conscience still begnaw thy soul!
>
> QUEEN MARGARET, *Richard III*, I.III.220

CONSERVATISM

see also MODERATION; TEMPERANCE

> Old fashions please me best; I am not so nice
> To change true rules for odd inventions.
>
> BIANCA, *The Taming of the Shrew*, III.i.80

> But since all is well, keep it so, wake not a sleeping wolf.
>
> LORD CHIEF JUSTICE, *2 Henry IV*, I.II.153

CONSPIRACY

see also REBELLION; TREASON

> O Conspiracy,
> Sham'st thou to show thy dang'rous brow by night,
> When evils are most free? O then, by day

Where wilt thou find a cavern dark enough
To mask thy monstrous visage? Seek none, Conspiracy!
Hide it in smiles and affability;
For if thou path, thy native semblance on,
Not Erebus itself were dim enough
To hide thee from prevention.

BRUTUS, Julius Caesar, II.I.77

CONSTANCY

I am constant as the northern star,
Of whose true-fix'd and resting quality
There is no fellow in the firmament.
The skies are painted with unnumb'red sparks,
They are all fire, and every one doth shine;
But there's but one in all doth hold his place.
So in the world: 'tis furnish'd well with men,
And men are flesh and blood, and apprehensive;
Yet in the number I do know but one
That unassailable holds on his rank,
Unshak'd of motion; and that I am he,
Let me a little show it.

CAESAR, Julius Caesar, III.I.60

CONTEMPT
see also HATRED

When thou shalt be dispos'd to set me light,
And place my merit in the eye of scorn,
Upon thy side against myself I'll fight,
And prove thee virtuous, though thou art forsworn.

SONNET 88, 1–4

Poor queen of love, in thine own law forlorn,
To love a cheek that smiles at thee in scorn!

Venus and Adonis, 251

The time seems long, their blood thinks scorn
Till it fly out and show them princes born.

BELARIUS, Cymbeline, IV.IV.53

Jaq. God buy you, let's meet as little as we can.
Orl. I do desire we may be better strangers.

JAQUES, ORLANDO, As You Like It, III.II.257

You nimble lightnings, dart your blinding flames
Into her scornful eyes!

LEAR, King Lear, II.IV.164

I have too long borne
Your blunt unbraidings and your bitter scoffs.

By heaven, I will acquaint his Majesty
Of those gross taunts that oft I have endur'd.
I had rather be a country servant maid
Than a great queen with this condition,
To be so baited, scorn'd and stormèd at.
QUEEN ELIZABETH, Richard III, I.III.102

Teach not thy lip such scorn; for it was made
For kissing, lady, not for such contempt.
RICHARD, DUKE OF GLOUCESTER, Richard III, I.II.171

Were I like thee I'd throw myself away.
TIMON, Timon of Athens, IV.III.219

CONVERSATION
see also SPEAKING AND SPEECH; VERBOSITY

Are my discourses dull? Barren my wit?
If voluble and sharp discourse be marred,
Unkindness blunts it more than marble hard.
ADRIANA, The Comedy of Errors, II.I.91

These high wild hills and rough uneven ways
Draws out our miles and makes them wearisome,
And yet your fair discourse hath been as sugar,
Making the hard way sweet and delectable.
EARL OF NORTHUMBERLAND, Richard II, II.III.4

More of your conversation would infect my brain.
MENENIUS AGRIPPA, Coriolanus, II.I.94

His eye begets occasions for his wit,
For every object that the one doth catch
The other turns to a mirth-moving jest,
Which his fair tongue, conceit's expositor,
Delivers in such apt and gracious words
That aged ears play truant at his tales,
And younger hearings are quite ravished,
So sweet and voluble is his discourse.
ROSALINE, Love's Labor's Lost, II.I.69

CORRUPTION
see also BRIBERY; CRIME; DECEIT; INJUSTICE; THEFT

I like not fair terms and a villain's mind.
BASSANIO, The Merchant of Venice, I.III.179

By heaven, I had rather coin my heart
And drop my blood for drachmas than to wring
From the hard hands of peasants their vile trash
By any indirection.
BRUTUS, Julius Caesar, IV.III.72

In the corrupted currents of this world
Offense's gilded hand may shove by justice,
And oft 'tis seen the wicked prize itself
Buys out the law, but 'tis not so above.

CLAUDIUS, *Hamlet*, III.III.57

Virtue is chok'd with foul ambition,
And charity chas'd hence by rancor's hand.

DUKE OF GLOUCESTER, *2 Henry VI*, III.I.143

These kind of knaves I know, which in this plainness
Harbor more craft and more corrupter ends
Than twenty silly-ducking observants
That stretch their duties nicely.

DUKE OF CORNWALL, *King Lear*, II.II.101

Thy sumptuous buildings and thy wife's attire
Have cost a mass of public treasury.

DUKE OF SOMERSET, *2 Henry VI*, I.III.129

We did train him on,
And his corruption being ta'en from us,
We as the spring of all shall pay for all.

EARL OF WORCESTER, *1 Henry IV*, V.II.19

Rank corruption, mining all within,
Infects unseen.

HAMLET, *Hamlet*, III.IV.148

So, oft it chances in particular men,
That for some vicious mole of nature in them,
As in their birth, wherin they are not guilty
(Since nature cannot choose his origin),
By their o'ergrowth of some complexion
Oft breaking down the pales and forts of reason,
Or by some habit, that too much o'er-leavens
The form of plausive manners—that these men,
Carrying, I say, the stamp of one defect,
Being nature's livery, or fortune's star,
His virtues else, be they as pure as grace,
As infinite as man may undergo,
Shall in the general censure take corruption
From that particular fault: the dram of evil
Doth all the noble substance of a doubt
To his own scandal.

HAMLET, *Hamlet*, I.IV.23

How weary, stale, flat, and unprofitable
Seem to me all the uses of this world!

Fie on't, ah fie! 'tis an unweeded garden
That grows to seed, things rank and gross in nature
Possess it merely.

HAMLET, Hamlet, I.II.133

Then we are like to have biting
statutes, unless his teeth be pull'd out.

JOHN HOLLAND, 2 Henry VI, IV.VII.16

Know'st thou not any whom corrupting gold
Will tempt unto a close exploit of death?

KING RICHARD, Richard III, IV.II.34

The mounting Bullingbrook ascends my throne,
The time shall not be many hours of age
More than it is, ere foul sin gathering head
Shall break into corruption.

KING RICHARD, Richard II, V.I.56

A good and virtuous nature may recoil
In an imperial charge.

MALCOLM, Macbeth, IV.II.19

Something is rotten in the state of Denmark.

MARCELLUS, Hamlet, I.IV.89

I have seen corruption boil and bubble,
Till it o'errun the stew.

VINCENTIO, DUKE OF VIENNA, Measure for Measure, V.I.316

COSMETICS
see also BEAUTY; PLASTIC SURGERY

Look on beauty,
An you shall see 'tis purchas'd by the weight,
Which therein works a miracle in nature,
Making them lightest that wear most of it.

BASSANIO, The Merchant of Venice, III.II.88

Your mistresses dare never come in rain,
For fear their colors should be wash'd away.

BEROWNE, Love's Labor's Lost, IV.III.266

COUNTRY
see also PATRIOTISM

If any think brave death outweighs bad life,
And that his country's dearer than himself;
Let him alone, or so many minded,
Wave thus to express his disposition,
And follow Martius.

CAIUS MARTIUS, Coriolanus, I.VI.71

Be just, and fear not;
Let all he ends thou aim'st at be thy country's,
Thy God's, and truth's.

CARDINAL WOLSEY, *Henry VIII*, III.II.446

I do love
My country's good with a respect more tender,
More holy and profound, than mine own life.

COMINIUS, *Coriolanus*, III.III.111

O, for honor of our land,
Let us not hang like roping icicles
Upon our houses' thatch, whiles a more frosty people
Sweat drops of gallant youth in our rich fields!
Poor we call them in their native lords!

CONSTABLE OF FRANCE, *Henry V*, III.V.22

Alas, poor country,
Almost afraid to know itself! It cannot
Be call'd our mother, but our grave; where nothing,
But who knows nothing, is once seen to smile;
Where sighs, and groans, and shrieks that rent the air
Are made, not mark'd; where violent sorrow seems
A modern ecstasy. The dead man's knell
Is there scarce ask'd for who, and good men's lives
Expire before the flowers in their caps,
Dying or ere they sicken.

ROSSE, *Macbeth*, IV.III.164

COURAGE
see also BRAVADO; FEARLESSNESS; STRENGTH

All's brave that youth mounts and folly guides.

CELIA, *As You Like It*, III.V.45

Winning will put any man into courage.

CLOTEN, *Cymbeline*, II.III.7

I saw him beat the surges under him,
And ride upon their backs. He trod the water,
Whose enmity he flung aside, and breasted
The surge most swoll'n that met him. His bold head
'Bove the contentious waves he kept, and oared
Himself with his good arms in lusty stroke
To th' shore, that o'er his wave-worn basis bowed,
As stooping to relieve him.

FRANCISCO, *The Tempest*, II.I.115

'Tis true that we are in great danger,
The greater therefore should our courage be.

KING HENRY, *Henry V*, IV.I.1

If we be English deer, be then in blood,
Not rascal-like, to fall down with a pinch,
But rather, moody-mad; and, desperate stags,
Turn on the bloody hounds with heads of steel,
And make the cowards stand aloof at bay.

LORD TALBOT, *1 Henry VI*, V.ii.48

For courage mounteth with occasion.
Let them be welcome then, we are prepar'd.

LYMOGES, DUKE OF AUSTRIA, *King John*, II.i.82

Think you a little din can daunt mine ears?
Have I not in my time heard lions roar?
Have I not heard the sea, puff'd up with winds,
Rage like an angry boar chafed with sweat?
Have I not heard great ordnance in the field,
And heaven's artillery thunder in the skies?
Have I not in a pitched battle heard
Loud 'larums, neighing steeds, and trumpets' clang?

PETRUCHIO, *The Taming of the Shrew*, I.ii.199

With what his valor did enrich his wit,
His wit set down to make his valure live.

PRINCE EDWARD, *Richard III*, III.i.85

Why, courage then! what cannot be avoided,
'Twere childish weakness to lament or fear.

QUEEN MARGARET, *3 Henry VI*, V.iv.37

He's truly valiant that can wisely suffer
The worst that man can breathe, and make his wrongs
His outsides, to wear them like his raiment, carelessly,
And ne'er prefer his injuries to his heart,
To bring it into danger.

SENATOR, *Timon of Athens*, III.v.31

COURTING
see also ATTRACTION

She is a woman, therefore may be woo'd,
She is a woman, therefore may be won,
She is Lavinia, therefore must be lov'd.

DEMETRIUS, *Titus Andronicus*, II.i.82

Albeit I will confess thy father's wealth
Was the first motive that I woo'd thee, Anne;
Yet wooing thee, I found thee of more value
Than stamps in gold, or sums in sealed bags;
And 'tis the very riches of thyself
That now I aim at.

FENTON, *The Merry Wives of Windsor*, III.iv.13

Your wrongs do set a scandal on my sex.
We cannot fight for love, as men may do.
We should be woo'd, and were not made to woo.

HELENA, *A Midsummer Night's Dream*, II.i.240

And little of this great world can I speak
More than pertains to feats of broils and battle,
And therefore little shall I grace my cause
In speaking for myself. Yet (by your gracious patience)
I will a round unvarnish'd tale deliver
Of my whole course of love—what drugs, what charms,
What conjuration, and what mighty magic
(For such proceeding I am charg'd withal)
I won his daughter.

OTHELLO, *Othello*, I.iii.86

Say that she rail, why then I'll tell her plain
She sings as sweetly as a nightingale;
Say that she frown, I'll say she looks as clear
As morning roses newly wash'd with dew;
Say she be mute, and will not speak a word,
Then I'll commend her volubility,
And say she uttereth piercing eloquence
If she do bid me pack, I'll give her thanks,
As though she bid me stay be her a week;
If she deny to wed, I'll crave the day
When I shall ask the banes, and when be married.

PETRUCHIO, *The Taming of the Shrew*, II.i.170

There is no love-broker in the world can more prevail in
man's commendation with woman than report of valor.

SIR TOBY, *Twelfth Night*, III.ii.36

That man hath a tongue, I say is no man,
If with his tongue he cannot win a woman.

VALENTINE, *The Two Gentlemen of Verona*, III.i.93

COWARDICE
see also INACTION; WEAKNESS

Manhood is melted into cur'sies, valor into compliment, and
men are only turn'd into tongue,
and trim ones too. He is now as valiant as Hercules
that only tells a lie, and swears
it.

BEATRICE, *Much Ado About Nothing*, IV.i.319

Hollow men, like horses hot at hand,
Make gallant show and promise of their mettle;
But when they should endure the bloody spur,

They fall their crests, and like deceitful jades
Sink in the trial.

BRUTUS, Julius Caesar, IV.II.23

Cowards die many times before their deaths,
The valiant never taste of death but once.

CAESAR, Julius Caesar, II.II.32

You souls of geese,
That bear the shapes of men, how you have run
From slaves that apes would beat!

CAIUS MARTIUS, Coriolanus, I.IV.34

You scarcely have the hearts to tell me so,
And therefore cannot have the hearts to do it.

CLARENCE, Richard III, I.IV.175

Turn head, and stop pursuit; for coward dogs
Most spend their mouths when what they seem to threaten
Runs far before them.

DOLPHIN, Henry V, II.IV.69

That which in mean men we entitle patience
Is pale cold cowardice in noble breasts.

DUCHESS OF GLOUCESTER, Richard II, I.II.33

Show me one scar character'd on thy skin:
Men's f lesh perserv'd so whole do seldom win.

DUKE OF YORK, 2 Henry VI, III.I.300

And all my followers to the eager foe
Turn back and f ly, like ships before the wind,
Or lambs pursu'd by hunger-starved wolves.

DUKE OF YORK, 3 Henry VI, I.IV.3

Am I a coward?
Who calls me villain, breaks my pate across,
Plucks off my beard and blows it in my face,
Tweaks me by the nose, gives me the lie i' th' throat
As deep as to the lungs? Who does me this?
Hah, 'swounds, I should take it; for it cannot be
But I am pigeon-liver'd, and lack gall
To make oppression bitter, or ere this
I should 'a' fatted all the region kites
With this slave's offal.

HAMLET, Hamlet, II.II.571

Thou kill'd him sleeping. O brave touch!
Could not a worm, an adder, do so much?

HERMIA, A Midsummer Night's Dream, III.II.70

You fled for vantage, every one will swear;
But if I bow, they'll say it was for fear.
There is no hope that ever I will stay,
If the first hour I shrink and run away.

JOHN TALBOT, 1 Henry VI, IV.v.28

There let him sink, and be the seas on him!
White-liver'd runagate, what doth he there?

KING RICHARD, Richard III, IV.iv.463

Hark, countrymen, either renew the fight,
Or tear the lions out of England's coat;
Renounce your soil, give sheep in lion's stead:
Sheep run not half so treacherous from the wolf,
Or horse or oxen from the leopard,
As you fly from your oft-subdued slaves.

LORD TALBOT, 1 Henry VI, I.v.27

Thou coward, art thou bragging to the stars,
Telling the bushes that thou look'st for wars,
And wilt not come?

PUCK, A Midsummer Night's Dream, III.ii.407

Manhood and honor
Should have hare hearts, would they but fat their thoughts
With this cramm'd reason; reason and respect
Make livers pale and lustihood deject.

TROILUS, Troilus and Cressida, II.ii.47

CRIME
see also BRIBERY; CORRUPTION; PUNISHMENT; THEFT

This dying virtue, this surviving shame,
Whose crime will bear an ever-enduring blame.

The Rape of Lucrece, 223

If by this crime he owes the law his life,
Why, let the war receive't in valiant gore,
For law is strict, and war is nothing more.

ALCIBIADES, Timon of Athens, III.v.82

This shows you are above,
You justicers, that these our nether crimes
So speedily can venge!

DUKE OF ALBANY, King Lear, IV.ii.78

Foul deeds will rise,
Though all the earth o'erwhelm them, to men's eyes.

HAMLET, Hamlet, I.ii.256

That one may smile, and smile, and be a villain!

HAMLET, Hamlet, I.v.108

One sin, I know, another doth provoke:
Murder's as near to lust as flame to smoke.

PERICLES, *Pericles*, I.I.137

Crimes, like lands,
Are not inherited.

SENATOR, *Timon of Athens*, V.IV.37

The evil that thou causest to be done,
That is thy means to live. Do thou but think
What 'tis to cram a maw or clothe a back
From such a filthy vice; say to thyself,
From their abominable and beastly touches
I drink, eat, array myself, and live.
Canst thou believe thy living is a life,
So stinkingly depending?

VINCENTIO, DUKE OF VIENNA, *Measure for Measure*, III.II.20

CRITICISM
see also EDITING; OPINION

When thou reviewest this, thou dost review
The very part was consecrate to thee.

SONNET 74, 5–6

I will chide no breather in the world but myself, against
whom I know most faults.

ORLANDO, *As You Like It*, III.II.280

Many wearing rapiers are afraid of goose-quills.

ROSENCRANTZ, *Hamlet*, II.II.343

CRUELTY

When we in our viciousness grow hard
(O misery on't!), the wise gods seel our eyes,
In our own filth drop our clear judgments, make us
Adore our errors, laugh at 's while we strut
To our confusion.

ANTONY, *Antony and Cleopatra*, III.XIII.111

Beauford's red sparkling eyes blab his heart's malice.

DUKE OF GLOUCESTER, *2 Henry VI*, III.I.154

I would not see thy cruel nails
Pluck out his poor old eyes, nor thy fierce sister
In his anointed flesh rash boarish fangs.

EARL OF GLOUCESTER, *King Lear*, III.VII.56

So looks the pent-up lion o'er the wretch
That trembles under his devouring paws.

EARL OF RUTLAND, *3 Henry VI*, I.III.12

I must be cruel only to be kind.

> HAMLET, *Hamlet*, III.IV.178

And as the butcher takes away the calf,
And binds the wretch, and beats it when it strays,
Bearing it to the bloody slaughter-house,
Even so remorseless have they borne him hence.

> KING HENRY, *2 Henry VI*, III.I.210

Thou hid'st a thousand daggers in thy thoughts,
Whom thou hast whetted on they stony heart
To stab at half an hour of my life.

> KING HENRY IV, *2 Henry IV*, IV.V.106

Come, you spirits
That tend on mortal thoughts, unsex me here,
And fill me from the crown to the toe topful
Of direst cruelty! Make thick my blood,
Stop up th' access and passage to remorse,
That no compunctious visitings of nature
Shake my fell purpose, nor keep peace between
Th' effect and it! Come to my woman's breasts,
And take my milk for gall, you murth'ring ministers,
Wherever in your sightless substances
You wait on nature's mischief! Come, thick night,
And pall thee in the dunest smoke of hell,
That my keen knife see not the wound it makes,
Nor heaven peep through the blanket of the dark
To cry, "Hold, hold!"

> LADY MACBETH, *Macbeth*, I.V.40

She hath abated me of half my train;
Look'd black upon me, strook me with her tongue,
Most serpent-like, upon the very heart.

> LEAR, *King Lear*, II.IV.159

Why, what a monstrous fellow art thou, thus
to rail on one that is neither known of thee nor knows
thee?

> OSWALD, *King Lear*, II.II.25

O you gods!
Why do you make us love your goodly gifts
And snatch them straight away?

> PERICLES, *Pericles*, III.I.22

In cruelty will I seek out my fame.

> YOUNG CLIFFORD, *2 Henry VI*, V.II.60

CRYING AND TEARS
see also GRIEF; MOURNING; SADNESS; SORROW

Dost thou drink tears, that thou provok'st such weeping?

Venus and Adonis, 949

Ah, but those tears are pearls which thy love sheeds,
And thy are rich, and ransom all ill deeds.

SONNET 34, 13–14

O how her eyes and tears did lend and borrow!
Her eye seen in the tears, tears in her eye,
Both crystals, where thy view'd each other's sorrow,
Sorrow that friendly sighs sought still to dry.

Venus and Adonis, 961

O father, what a hell of witchcraft lies
In the small orb of one particular tear!

A Lover's Complaint, 289

The April's in her eyes, it is love's spring,
And these showers to bring it on.

ANTONY, *Antony and Cleopatra*, III.II.43

His tears runs down his beard like winter's drops
From eaves of reeds.

ARIEL, *The Tempest*, V.I.16

The pretty and sweet manner of it forc'd
Those waters from me which I would have stopp'd,
But I had not so much of man in me,
And all my mother came into mine eyes
And gave me up to tears.

DUKE OF EXETER, *Henry V*, IV.VI.28

My plenteous joys,
Wanton in fullness, seek to hide themselves
In drops of sorrow.

DUNCAN, *Macbeth*, I.IV.33

Look, they weep,
And I, an ass, am onion-ey'd.

ENOBARBUS, *Antony and Cleopatra*, IV.II.34

How came her eyes so bright? Not with salt tears;
If so, my eyes are oft'ner wash'd than hers.

HELENA, *A Midsummer Night's Dream*, II.II.92

Back, foolish tears, back to your native spring,
Your tributary drops belong to woe,
Which you, mistaking, offer up to joy.

JULIET, *Romeo and Juliet*, III.II.102

Weep, wretched man; I'll aid thee tear for tear,
And let our hearts and eyes, like civil war,
Be blind with tears, and break o'ercharg'd with grief.

KING HENRY, 3 Henry VI, II.v.76

We'll make foul weather with despisèd tears;
Our signs and they shall lodge the summer corn,
And make a dearth in this revolting land.
Or shall we play the wantons with our woes
And make some pretty match with shedding tears?
As thus to drop them still upon one place,
Till they have fretted us a pair of graves
Within the earth, and, therein laid—there lies
Two kinsmen digg'd their graves with weeping eyes.
Would not this ill do well?

KING RICHARD, Richard II, III.III.161

Uncle, give me your hands; nay, dry your eyes—
Tears show their love, but want their remedies.

KING RICHARD, Richard II, III.III.202

If the river were dry, I am able to fill it with my tears.

LAUNCE, The Two Gentlemen of Verona, II.III.51

This would make a man a man of salt
To use his eyes for garden water-pots.

LEAR, King Lear, IV.VI.195

Venus smiles not in a house of tears.

PARIS, Romeo and Juliet, IV.I.8

All springs reduce their currents to mine eyes,
That I being govern'd by the watery moon,
May send forth plenteous tears to drown the world!

QUEEN ELIZABETH, Richard III, II.II.68

I am about to weep; but thinking that
We are a queen (or long have dream'd so), certain
The daughter of a king, my drops of tears
I'll turn to sparks of fire.

QUEEN KATHERINE, Henry VIII, II.IV.70

I cannot weep; for all my body's moisture
Scarce serves to quench my furnace-burning heart;
Nor can my tongue unload my heart's great burden.

RICHARD, DUKE OF GLOUCESTER, 3 Henry VI, II.I.79

Your eyes drop millstones, when fools' eyes fall tears.

RICHARD, DUKE OF GLOUCESTER, Richard III, I.III.352

Weep not, sweet queen, for trickling tears are vain.

SIR JOHN FALSTAFF, 1 Henry IV, II.IV.391

CURSES
see also INSULTS; THREATS

> The curses he shall have, the tortures he shall feel,
> will break the back of man, the heart of monster.
>
> AUTOLYCUS, *The Winter's Tale*, IV.IV.769

> She speaks poniards, and every word stabs.
>
> BENEDICK, *Much Ado About Nothing*, II.I.247

> All the infections that the sun sucks up
> From bogs, fens, flats, on Prosper fall, and make him
> By inch-meal a disease! His spirits hear me,
> And yet I needs must curse.
>
> CALIBAN, *The Tempest*, II.II.1

> You taught me language, and my profit on't
> Is, I know how to curse. The red-plague rid you
> For learning me your language!
>
> CALIBAN, *The Tempest*, I.II.363

> Curses never pass
> The lips of those that breathe them in the air.
>
> DUKE OF BUCKINGHAM, *Richard III*, I.III.284

> Would curses kill, as doth the mandrake's groan,
> I would invent as bitter searching terms,
> As curst, as harsh, and horrible to hear,
> Deliver'd strongly through my fixed teeth,
> With full as many signs of deadly hate,
> As lean-fac'd Envy in her loathsome cave.
> My tongue should stumble in mine earnest words,
> Mine eyes should sparkle like the beaten flint,
> Mine hair be fix'd an end, as one distract;
> Ay, every joint should seem to curse and ban;
> And even now my burden'd heart would break,
> Should I not curse them.
>
> EARL OF SUFFOLK, *2 Henry VI*, III.II.310

> A curse upon him, die he like a thief,
> That robs thee of thy goodness!
>
> LYSIMACHUS, *Pericles*, IV.VI.114

> A plague a' both houses!
>
> MERCUTIO, *Romeo and Juliet*, III.I.91

> Can curses pierce the clouds and enter heaven?
> Why then give way, dull clouds, to my quick curses!
>
> QUEEN MARGARET, *Richard III*, I.III.194

> Forbear to sleep the nights, and fast the days;
> Compare dead happiness with living woe;

Think that thy babes were sweeter than they were,
And he that slew them fouler than he is.
Bett'ring thy loss makes the bad causer worse;
Revolving this will teach thee how to curse.

QUEEN MARGARET, Richard III, IV.IV.118

The common curse of mankind, folly and ignorance, be
thine in great revenue!

THERSITES, Troilus and Cressida, II.III.27

Double, double, toil and trouble;
Fire burn, and cauldron bubble.

WITCHES (ALL), Macbeth, IV.I.10

DANCING
see also ART

Let's have a dance ere we are married, that we may lighten
our own hearts and our wives' heels.

BENEDICK, Much Ado About Nothing, V.IV.117

Ah, my mistresses, which of you all
Will now deny to dance? She that makes dainty,
She I'll swear hath corns.

CAPULET, Romeo and Juliet, I.V.18

When you do dance, I wish you
A wave o' th' sea, that you might ever do
Nothing but that; move still, still so,
And own no other function.

FLORIZEL, The Winter's Tale, IV.IV.140

I think you have
As little skill to fear as I have purpose
To put you to't. But come, our dance, I pray.
Your hand, my Perdita. So turtles pair
That never mean to part.

FLORIZEL, The Winter's Tale, IV.IV.152

My legs can keep no measure in delight,
When my poor heart no measure keeps in grief;
Therefore no dancing, girl, some other sport.

QUEEN, Richard II, III.IV.7

You have dancing shoes
With nimble soles, I have a soul of lead
So stakes me to the ground I cannot move.

ROMEO, Romeo and Juliet, I.IV.14

Swim with your bodies,
And carry it sweetly and deliverly,
And now and then a favor and a frisk.

SCHOOLMASTER, The Two Noble Kinsmen, III.V.28

DANGER
see also RISK; THREATS

Here pale with fear he doth premeditate
The dangers of his loathsome enterprise.

The Rape of Lucrece, 183

Into what dangers would you lead me, Cassius,
That you would have me seek into myself
For that which is not in me?

BRUTUS, *Julius Caesar,* I.II.63

It is the bright day that brings forth the adder,
And that craves wary walking.

BRUTUS, *Julius Caesar,* II.I.14

By a divine instinct men's minds mistrust
Ensuing danger; as by proof we see
The water swell before a boist'rous storm.

CITIZEN, *Richard III,* II.III.42

If he not answer'd, I should call a wolf,
And do him but that service. I have heard
Strange howls this livelong night; why may't not be
They have made prey of him? He has no weapons
He cannot run, the jingling of his gyves
Might call fell things to listen, who have in them
A sense to know a man unarm'd, and can
Smell where resistance is. I'll set it down
He's torn to pieces. They howl'd many together,
And then they fed on him.

DAUGHTER, *The Two Noble Kinsmen,* III.II.10

Where we are,
There's daggers in men's smiles; the near in blood,
The nearer bloody.

DONALBAIN, *Macbeth,* II.III.139

And that engenders thunder in his breast,
And makes him roar these accusations forth.

DUKE OF GLOUCESTER, *1 Henry VI,* III.I.39

But I must go and meet with danger there,
Or it will seek me in another place.

EARL OF NORTHUMBERLAND, *2 Henry IV,* II.III.48

Though I am not splenitive and rash.
Yet have I in me something dangerous,
Which let thy wisdom fear.

HAMLET, *Hamlet,* V.I.261

Out of this nettle,
danger, we pluck this flower, safety.

HOTSPUR, 1 Henry IV, II.III.9

But in the midst of this bright-shining day,
I spy a black, suspicious, threat'ning cloud,
That will encounter with our glorious sun,
Ere he attain his easeful western bed.

KING EDWARD, 3 Henry VI, V.III.2

We have scorch'd the snake, not kill'd it;
She'll close and be herself, whilest our poor malice
Remains in danger of her former tooth.

MACBETH, Macbeth, III.II.13

Men may sleep, and they may have their throats about
them at that time, and some say knives have edges.

NYM, Henry V, II.I.21

In thy danger
(If ever danger do environ thee)
Commend thy grievance to my holy prayers,
For I will be thy beadsman, Valentine.

PROTEUS, The Two Gentlemen of Verona, I.I.15

Such safety finds
The trembling lamb environed with wolves.

QUEEN MARGARET, 3 Henry VI, I.I.241

Now 'tis the spring, and weeds are shallow-rooted;
Suffer them now, and they'll o'ergrown the garden,
And choke the herbs for want of husbandry.

QUEEN MARGARET, 2 Henry VI, III.I.31

DAUGHTERS
see also BABIES; CHILDREN; CHILDREN OF UNMARRIED PARENTS; FATHERHOOD;
MOTHERHOOD

Fathers, from hence trust not your daughters' minds
By what you see them act. Is there not charms
By which the property of youth and maidhood
May be abus'd?

BRABANTIO, Othello, I.I.170

And that most deeply to consider is
The beauty of his daughter. He himself
Calls her a nonpareil.

CALIBAN, The Tempest, III.II.98

You have begot me, bred me, lov'd me: I
Return those duties back as are right fit,
Obey you, love you, and most honor you.

Why have my sister husbands, if they say
They love you all? Happily, when I shall wed,
That lord whose hand must take my plight shall carry
Half my love with him, half my care and duty.
Sure I shall never marry like my sisters,
To love my father all.

CORDELIA, *King Lear*, I.i.96

My noble father,
I do perceive here a divided duty:
To you I am bound for life and education;
My life and education both do learn me
How to respect you; you are the lord of duty;
I am hitherto your daughter. But here's my husband;
And so much duty as my mother show'd
To you, preferring you before her father,
So much I challenge that I may profess
Due to the Moor, my lord.
Is dearly bought as mine, and I will have it.

DESDEMONA, *Othello*, I.iii.181

Sir, I love you more than words can wield the matter,
Dearer than eyesight, space, and liberty,
Beyond what can be valued, rich or rare,
No less than life, with grace, health, beauty, honor;
As much as child e'er lov'd, or father found;
A love that makes breath poor, and speech unable:
Beyond all manner of so much I love you.

GONERIL, *King Lear*, I.i.54

What heinous sin is it in me
To be ashamed to be my father's child!
But though I am a daughter to his blood,
I am not to his manners.

JESSICA, *The Merchant of Venice*, II.iii.16

I embrace you.
Give me my robes. I am wild in my beholding.
O heavens bless my girl!

PERICLES, *Pericles*, V.i.222

DAY
see also LIGHT; SUNRISE; SUNSET

O Night, thou furnace of foul reeking smoke!
Let not the jealous Day behold that face,
Which underneath thy black all-hiding cloak
Immodestly lies martyr'd with disgrace.

The Rape of Lucrece, 799

Revealing day through every cranny spies.

The Rape of Lucrece, 1086

In the posteriors of this day, which the rude multitude call
the afternoon.

ARMADO, *Love's Labor's Lost*, V.I.89

The wolves have preyed, and look, the gentle day,
Before the wheels of Phoebus, round about
Dapples the drowsy east with spots of grey.

DON PEDRO, *Much Ado About Nothing*, V.III.25

But soft, what light through yonder window breaks?
It is the east, and Juliet is the sun.
Arise, fair sun, and kill the envious moon,
Who is already sick and pale with grief
That thou, her maid, art far more fair than she.

ROMEO, *Romeo and Juliet*, II.II.2

Night's candles are burnt out, and jocund day
Stands tiptoe on the misty mountain tops.

ROMEO, *Romeo and Juliet*, III.v.9

The busy day,
Wak'd by the lark, hath rous'd the ribald crows,
And dreaming night will hide our joys no longer.

TROILUS, *Troilus and Cressida*, IV.II.8

DAYDREAMING
see also DREAMS; SLEEP

Good lady,
Make yourself mirth with your particular fancy,
And leave me out on't.

ANNE BULLEN, *Henry VIII*, II.III.100

I' th' name of something holy, sir, why stand you
In this strange stare?

GONZALO, *The Tempest*, III.III.94

This is a strange repose, to be asleep
With eyes wide open—standing, speaking, moving—
And yet so fast asleep.

SEBASTIAN, *The Tempest*, II.I.213

DEATH
see also AFTERLIFE; DYING WORDS; EPITAPH; EULOGY; EUTHANASIA; FUNERALS;
GRIEF; HUMAN CONDITION; LOSS; MOURNING; SORROW; SUICIDE

"Hard-favor'd tyrant, ugly, meager, lean,
Hateful divorce of love"—thus chides she Death—

"Grim-grinning ghost, earth's worm, what dost thou mean
To stifle beauty, and to steal his breath?"

Venus and Adonis, 931

O mighty Caesar! dost thou lie so low?
Are all thy conquests, glories, triumphs, spoils,
Shrunk to this little measure?

ANTONY, *Julius Caesar*, III.i.148

Of all the wonders that I yet have heard,
It seems to me most strange that men should fear,
Seeing that death, a necessary end,
Will come when it will come.

CAESAR, *Julius Caesar*, II.ii.34

The breath no sooner left his father's body,
But that his wildness, mortified in him,
Seem'd to die too; yea, at that very moment,
Consideration like an angel came
And whipped th'offending Adam out of him,
Leaving his body as a paradise
T'envelop and contain celestial spirits.

CANTERBURY, *Henry V*, I.i.25

O son, the night before thy wedding-day
Hath death lain with thy wife. There she lies,
Flower as she was, deflowered by him.
Death is my son-in-law, Death is my heir,
My daughter he hath wedded. I will die,
And leave him all; life, living, all is Death's.

CAPULET, *Romeo and Juliet*, IV.v.35

Life and these lips have long been separated.
Death lies on her like an untimely frost
Upon the sweetest flower of all the field.

CAPULET, *Romeo and Juliet*, IV.v.27

Casca. He that cuts off twenty years of life
Cuts off so many years of fearing death.
Bru. Grant that, and then is death a benefit;
So are we Caesar's friends, that have abridg'd
His time of fearing death.

CASCA, BRUTUS, *Julius Caesar*, III.i.101

'Tis a vile thing to die, my gracious lord,
When men are unprepar'd and look not for it.

CATESBY, *Richard III*, III.ii.62

To die, and go we know not where;
To lie in cold obstruction, and to rot;

This sensible warm motion to become
A kneaded clod; and the delighted spirit
To bathe in fiery floods, or to reside
In thrilling region of thick-ribbèd ice;
To be imprison'd in the viewless winds
And blown wit restless violence round about
The pendant world; or to be worse than worst
Of those that lawless and incertain thought
Imagine howling—'tis too horrible!
The weariest and most loathèd worldly life
That age, ache, penury, and imprisonment
Can lay on nature is a paradise
To what we fear of death.

CLAUDIO, Measure for Measure, III.I.117

If I must die,
I will encounter darkness as a bride,
And hug it in mine arms.

CLAUDIO, Measure for Measure, III.I.82

Death, death. O amiable lovely death!
Thou odoriferous stench! sound rottenness!
Arise forth from the couch of lasting night,
Thou hate and terror to prosperity,
And I will kiss thy detestable bones,
And put my eyeballs in thy vaulty brows,
And ring these fingers with thy household worms,
And stop this gap of breath with fulsome dust,
And be a carrion monster like thyself.

CONSTANCE, King John, III.IV.25

To die by thee were but to die in jest,
From thee to die were torture more than death.

EARL OF SUFFOLK, 2 Henry VI, III.II.400

Men must endure
Their going hence even as their coming hither,
Ripeness is all.

EDGAR, King Lear, V.II.9

My joy is death;
Death, at whose name I oft have been afeared,
Because I wish'd this world's eternity.

ELEANOR, 2 Henry VI, II.IV.88

By my troth I care not; a man can die but
once, we owe God a death.

FEEBLE, 2 Henry IV, III.II.234

Come away, come away, death,
And in sad cypress let me be laid.
Fly away, fly away, breath,

I am slain by a fair cruel maid.
My shroud of white, stuck all with yew,
O, prepare it!
My part of death, no one so true
Did share it.
Not a flower, not a flower sweet
On my black coffin let there be strown.
Not a friend, not a friend greet
My poor corpse, where my bones
shall be thrown.
A thousand thousand sighs to save,
Lay me, O, where
Sad true lover never find my grave,
To weep there.

FESTE, *Twelfth Night*, II.IV.51

Do not forever with thy vailèd lids
Seek for thy noble father in the dust.
Thou know'st 'tis common, all that lives must die,
Passing through nature to eternity.

GERTRUDE, *Hamlet*, I.II.70

This fell sergeant, Death,
Is strict in his arrest.

HAMLET, *Hamlet*, V.II.336

Your worm is your only emperor for diet: we fat all
creatures else to fat us, and we fat ourselves for maggots;
your fat king and your lean beggar is but variable service,
two dishes, but to one table—that's the end.

HAMLET, *Hamlet*, IV.III.21

My oil-dried lamp and time-bewasted light
Shall be extinct with age and endless night;
My inch of taper will be burnt and done,
And blindfold Death not let me see my son.

JOHN OF GAUNT, *Richard II*, I.III.221

This sight of death is as a bell
That warns my old age to a sepulcher.

LADY CAPULET, *Romeo and Juliet*, V.III.206

A man that apprehends death no more dreadfully but as a
drunken sleep, careless, reckless, and fearless of what's
past, present, or to come; insensible of mortality, and
desperately mortal.

PROVOST, *Measure for Measure*, IV.II.142

This world's a city full of straying streets,
And death's the market-place, where each one meets.

QUEEN, *The Two Noble Kinsmen*, I.V.14

Ah, dear Juliet,
Why art thou yet so fair? Shall I believe
That unsubstantial Death is amorous,
And that the lean abhorrèd monster keeps
Thee here in dark to be his paramour?

> ROMEO, *Romeo and Juliet*, V.III.101

Thou detestable maw, thou womb of death,
Gorg'd with the dearest morsel of the earth,
Thus I enforce thy rotten jaws to open,
And in despite I'll cram thee with more food.

> ROMEO, *Romeo and Juliet*, V.III.45

Death's a great disguiser.

> VINCENTIO, DUKE OF VIENNA, *Measure for Measure*, IV.II.174

Death unloads thee.

> VINCENTIO, DUKE OF VIENNA, *Measure for Measure*, III.I.28

DEBTS
see also RESTITUTION

In common worldly things 'tis call'd ungrateful
With dull unwillingness to repay a debt,
Which with a bounteous hand was kindly lent.

> DORSET, *Richard III*, II.II.89

His days and times are past,
And my reliances on his fracted dates
Have smit my credit. I love and honor him,
But must not break my back to heal his finger.
Immediate are my needs, and my relief
Must not be toss'd and turn'd to me in words,
But find supply immediate.

> SENATOR, *Timon of Athens*, II.I.21

He that dies pays all debts.

> STEPHANO, *The Tempest*, III.II.131

DECEIT
see also APPEARANCE; CORRUPTION; DISGUISE; LIES

O' what authority and show of truth
Can cunning sin cover itself withal!

> CLAUDIO, *Much Ado About Nothing*, IV.I.35

Who makes the fairest show means most deceit.

> CLEON, *Pericles*, I.IV.75

Ah! that deceit should steal such gentle shape,
And with a virtuous visor hide deep vice!

> DUCHESS OF YORK, *Richard III*, II.II.27

Smooth runs the water where the brook is deep,
And in his simple show he harbors treason.
The fox barks not when he would steal the lamb.
EARL OF SUFFOLK, 2 Henry VI, III.I.53

Be it by gins, by snares, by subtlety,
Sleeping, or waking, 'tis no matter how,
So he be dead; for that is good deceit
Which mates him first that first intends deceit.
EARL OF SUFFOLK, 2 Henry VI, III.I.262

Dangerous conceits are in their natures poisons,
Which at the first are scarce found to distaste,
But with a little act upon the blood
Burn like the mines of sulphur.
IAGO, Othello, III.III.326

To beguile the time,
Look like the time; bear welcome in your eye,
Your hand, your tongue; look like th' innocent flower,
But be the serpent under't.
LADY MACBETH, Macbeth, I.v.63

DECISION

There is a tide in the affairs of men,
Which taken at the flood, leads on to fortune;
Omitted, all the voyage of their life
Is bound in shallows and in miseries.
BRUTUS, Julius Caesar, IV.III.218

Now, York, or never, steel thy fearful thoughts,
And change misdoubt to resolution.
DUKE OF YORK, 2 Henry VI, III.I.331

I had rather see a wren hawk at a fly
Than this decision.
EMILIA, The Two Noble Kinsmen, V.III.3

DEMOCRACY
see also EQUALITY; GOVERNMENT; POLITICS AND POWER; PUBLIC OPINION

Sir, the people
Must have their voices; neither will they bate
One jot of ceremony.
SICINIUS VELUTUS, Coriolanus, II.II.139

I do demand
If you submit you to the people's voices,
Allow their officers, and are content

To suffer lawful censure for such faults
As shall be prov'd upon you.
SICINIUS VELUTUS, Coriolanus, III.III.44

DEPENDENCE
see also NEED AND NECESSITY

I'll be a park, and thou shalt be my deer:
Feed where thou wilt, on mountain or in dale.
Venus and Adonis, 231

These strong Egyptian fetters I must break,
Or lose myself in dotage.
ANTONY, Antony and Cleopatra, I.II.116

DEPRESSION
see also MADNESS AND MENTAL ILLNESS; SADNESS; SORROW

O Melancholy,
Who ever yet could sound thy bottom? find
Mightst easil'est harbor in? Thou blessèd thing,
Jove knows what man thou mightst have made; but I,
Thou diedst, a most rare boy, of melancholy.
BELARIUS, Cymbeline, IV.II.204

I have of late—but wherefore I know not—lost all my mirth,
forgone all custom of exercises; and indeed it goes so
heavily with my disposition, that this goodly frame, the
earth, seems to me a sterile promontory; this most excellent
canopy, the air, look you, this brave o'erhanging firmament,
this majestical roof fretted with golden fire, why, it
appeareth nothing to me but a foul and pestilent
congregation of vapors.
HAMLET, Hamlet, II.II.295

She is continually in a harmless distemper,
sleeps little, altogether without appetite, save often
drinking, dreaming of another world and a better.
JAILER, The Two Noble Kinsmen, IV.III.3

I have neither the scholar's melancholy, which is emulation;
nor the musician's, which is fantastical; nor the
courtier's, which is proud; nor the soldier's, which is
ambitious; nor the lawyer's, which is politic; not the
lady's, which is nice; nor the lover's, which is all these:
but it is a melancholy of mine own, compounded of many
simples, extracted from many objects, and indeed the sundry
contemplation of my travels, in which my often rumination
wraps me in a most humorous sadness.
JAQUES, As You Like It, IV.I.10

He straight declin'd, droop'd, took it deeply,
Fasten'd and fix'd the shame on't in himself,
Threw off his spirit, his appetite, his sleep,
And downright languish'd.

LEONTES, *The Winter's Tale*, II.III.14

Melancholy is the nurse of frenzy.

MESSENGER, *The Taming of the Shrew*, IND.II.133

Why should this change of thoughts,
The sad companion, dull-ey'd melancholy,
Be my so us'd a guest as not an hour
In the day's glorious walk or peaceful night,
The tomb where grief should sleep, can breed me quiet?

PERICLES, *Pericles*, I.II.1

My lord leans wondrously to dis-
content. His comfortable distemper has forsook him,
he's much out of health, and keeps his chamber.

SERVILIUS, *Timon of Athens*, III.IV.70

DESIRE
see also ATTRACTION; LONGING; LUST; NEED AND NECESSITY; WILL

But nothing can affection's course control,
Or stop the headlong fury of his speed.

The Rape of Lucrece, 500

My woeful self that did in freedom stand,
And was my own fee-simple (not in part),
What with his art in youth and youth in art,
Threw my affections in his charmed power,
Reserv'd the stalk and gave him all my flower.

A Lover's Complaint, 143

The flesh being proud, Desire doth fight with Grace.

The Rape of Lucrece, 712

The sea hath bounds, but deep desire hath none.

Venus and Adonis, 389

Now quick desire hath caught the yielding prey,
And glutton-like she feeds, yet never filleth;
Her lips are conquerors, his lips obey.

Venus and Adonis, 547

Drunken Desire must vomit his receipt
Ere he can see his own abomination.

The Rape of Lucrece, 703

The little Love-god, lying once asleep,
Laid by his side his heart-inflaming brand,
Whilst many nymphs that vow'd chaste life to keep
Came tripping by, but in her maiden hand

The fairest votary took up that fire,
Which many legions of true hearts have warm'd.

SONNET 154, 1–6

All impediments in fancy's course
Are motives of more fancy.

BERTRAM, *All's Well That Ends Well*, V.III.214

Expectation fainted,
Longing for what it had not.

CAESAR (OCTAVIUS), *Antony and Cleopatra*, III.VI.47

Now old desire doth in his death-bed lie,
And young affection gapes to be his heir.

CHORUS, *Romeo and Juliet*, II.PRO.1

Thy desires
Are wolvish, bloody, starv'd, and ravenous.

GRATIANO, *The Merchant of Venice*, IV.I.137

Keep you in the rear of your affection,
Out of the shot and danger of desire.

LAERTES, *Hamlet*, I.III.34

Fire that's closest kept burns most of all.

LUCETTA, *The Two Gentlemen of Verona*, I.II.30

O, when mine eyes did see Olivia first,
Methought she purg'd the air of pestilence!
That instant was I turn'd into a hart,
And my desires, like fell and cruel hounds,
E'er since pursue me.

ORSINO, DUKE OF ILLYRIA, *Twelfth Night*, I.I.18

O cousin,
That we should things desire which do cost us
The loss of our desire! that nought could buy
Dear love but loss of dear love!

PALAMON, *The Two Noble Kinsmen*, V.IV.109

Is it not strange that desire should so many
years outlive performance?

POINS, *2 Henry IV*, II.IV.260

Wherefore waste I time to counsel thee
That art a votary to fond desire?

VALENTINE, *The Two Gentlemen of Verona*, I.I.51

Happy thou art not,
For what thou hast not, still thou striv'st to get,
And what thou hast, forget'st.

VINCENTIO, DUKE OF VIENNA, *Measure for Measure*, III.I.21

DESPAIR

see also DESPERATION; MISERY; SUFFERING

O, whither hast thou led me, Egypt?

ANTONY, *Antony and Cleopatra*, III.XI.51

This is all our world:
We shall know nothing here but one another,
Hear nothing but the clock that tells our woes;
The vine shall grow, but we shall never see it;
Summer shall come, and with her all delights,
But dead-cold winter must inhabit here still.

ARCITE, *The Two Noble Kinsmen*, II.II.40

O madam, my old heart is crack'd, it's crack'd!

EARL OF GLOUCESTER, *King Lear*, II.IV.147

O that this too too sallied flesh would melt,
Thaw, and resolve itself into a dew!
Or that the Everlasting had nor fix'd
His canon 'gainst self-slaughter! O God, God,
How weary, stale, flat, and unprofitable
Seem to me all the uses of this world!
Fie on't, ah fie! 'tis an unweeded garden
That grows to seed, things rank and gross in nature
Possess it merely.

HAMLET, *Hamlet*, I.II.129

Pol. My lord, I will take my leave of you.
Ham. You cannot take from me anything that I
will not more willingly part withal—except my life,
except my life, except my life.

HAMLET, POLONIUS, *Hamlet*, II.II.213

O, beat away the busy meddling fiend
That lays strong siege unto this wretch's soul,
And from his bosom purge this black despair!

KING HENRY, *2 Henry VI*, III.III.21

Why should nature build so foul a den,
Unless the gods delight in tragedies?

MARCUS, *Titus Andronicus*, IV.I.59

I will despair, and be at enmity
With cozening hope.

QUEEN, *Richard II*, II.II.68

I'll join with black despair against my soul,
And to myself become an enemy.

QUEEN ELIZABETH, *Richard III*, II.II.36

I am sick of this false world, and will love nought
But even the mere necessities upon't.

TIMON, Timon of Athens, IV.III.375

When I do tell thee there my hopes lie drown'd,
Reply not in how many fadoms deep
They lie indrench'd.

TROILUS, Troilus and Cressida, I.I.49

DESPERATION
see also DESPAIR

Let's leave this town, for they are harebrain'd slaves,
And hunger will enforce them to be more eager.
Of old I know them; rather with their teeth
The walls they'll tear down than forsake the siege.

CHARLES, 1 Henry VI, I.II.37

Desperation
Is all the policy, strength, and defense
That Rome can make against them.

COMINIUS, Coriolanus, IV.VI.126

O, bid me leap, rather than marry Paris,
From off the battlements of any tower,
Or walk in thievish ways, or bid me lurk
Where serpents are; chain me with roaring bears,
Or hide me nightly in a charnel-house,
O'ercover'd quite with dead men's rattling bones,
With reeky shanks and yellow chapless skulls;
Or bid me go into a new-made grave,
And hid me with a dead man in his shroud—
Things that, to hear them told, have made me tremble—
And I will do it without fear or doubt,
To live an unstain'd wife to my sweet love.

JULIET, Romeo and Juliet, IV.I.77

So cowards fight when they can fly no further,
So doves do peck the falcon's piercing talons,
So desperate thieves, all hopeless of their lives,
Breathe out invectives 'gainst the officers.

LORD CLIFFORD, 3 Henry VI, I.IV.39

The time and my intents are savage-wild,
More fierce and more inexorable far
Than empty tigers or the roaring sea.

ROMEO, Romeo and Juliet, V.III.37

O mischief, thou art swift
To enter in the thoughts of desperate men!

ROMEO, Romeo and Juliet, V.I.35

DESTINY
see also FATE

> Stand fast, good Fate
> to his hanging, make the rope of his destiny our cable,
> for our own doth little advantage. If he be not born to
> be hang'd, our case is miserable.
>
> GONZALO, *The Tempest*, I.I.30

> Be quiet then, as men should be,
> Till he hath pass'd necessity.
>
> GOWER, *Pericles*, II.CHO.5

> All unavoided is the doom of destiny.
>
> KING RICHARD, *Richard III*, IV.IV.218

DETERMINATION
see also DEVOTION; STRENGTH

> I will set this foot of mine as far
> As who goes farthest.
>
> CASCA, *Julius Caesar*, I.III.119

> Therein, ye gods, you make the weak most strong;
> Therein, ye gods, you tyrants do defeat;
> Nor stony tower, nor walls of beaten brass,
> Nor airless dungeon, nor strong links of iron,
> Can be retentive to the strength of spirit.
>
> CASSIUS, *Julius Caesar*, I.III.91

> Now from head to foot
> I am marble-constant; now the fleeting moon
> No planet is of mine.
>
> CLEOPATRA, *Antony and Cleopatra*, V.II.238

> Let not conscience,
> Which is but bold in f laming, thy lone bosom
> Inf lame too nicely, nor let pity, which
> Even woman have cast off, melt thee, but be
> A soldier to thy purpose.
>
> DIONYZA, *Pericles*, IV.I.4

> For being not propp'd by ancestry, whose grace
> Chalks successors their way, nor call'd upon
> For high feats done to th' crown, neither allied
> To eminent assistants, but spider-like
> Out of his self-drawing web, 'a give us note
> The force of his own merit makes his way.
>
> DUKE OF NORFOLK, *Henry VIII*, I.I.59

> The sun will set before I shall discharge
> What I must strive to do.
>
> FERDINAND, *The Tempest*, III.I.22

How high a pitch his resolution soars!

KING RICHARD, *Richard II*, I.I.109

Screw your courage to the sticking place,
And we'll not fail.

LADY MACBETH, *Macbeth*, I.VII.60

I have, Antiochus, and with a soul
Embold'ned with the glory of her praise,
Think death no hazard in this enterprise.

PERICLES, *Pericles*, I.I.3

Fearless minds climb soonest unto crowns.

RICHARD, DUKE OF GLOUCESTER, *3 Henry VI*, IV.VII.62

I am no pilot, yet, wert thou as far
As that vast shore wash'd with the farthest sea,
I should adventure for such merchandise.

ROMEO, *Romeo and Juliet*, II.II.82

DEVOTION
see also DETERMINATION; LOVE; PASSION

You look pale to-day.
In sooth, I would you were a little sick,
That I might sit all night and watch with you.
I warrant I love you more than you do me.

ARTHUR, *King John*, IV.I.29

Thus Indian-like,
Religious in mine error, I adore
The sun, that looks upon his worshipper,
But knows of him no more.

HELENA, *All's Well That Ends Well*, I.III.204

The sun was not so true unto the day
As he to me.

HERMIA, *A Midsummer Night's Dream*, III.II.50

A true-devoted pilgrim is not weary
To measure kingdoms with his feeble steps.

JULIA, *The Two Gentlemen of Verona*, II.VII.9

Doubt thou the stars are on fire,
Doubt that the sun doth move,
Doubt truth to be a liar,
But never doubt I love.

POLONIUS (READING FROM LETTER), *Hamlet*, II.II.116

DIGNITY
see also HONOR; VIRTUE

Stay but a little, for my cloud of dignity

Is held from falling with so weak a wind
That it will quickly drop; my day is dim.

KING HENRY IV, *2 Henry IV*, IV.v.98

She now begs
That little thought, when she set footing here,
She should have bought her dignities so dear.

QUEEN KATHERINE, *Henry VIII*, III.i.182

DIPLOMACY
see also PEACE; PERSUASION

Words before blows.

BRUTUS, *Julius Caesar*, V.i.27

Your gentleness shall force,
More than your force move us to gentleness.

DUKE SENIOR, *As You Like It*, II.vii.102

And now instead of bullets wrapp'd in fire
To make a shaking fever in your walls,
They shoot but calm words folded up in smoke,
To make a faithless error in your ears.

KING JOHN, *King John*, II.i.227

Touch you the sourest points with sweetest terms,
Nor curstness grow to th' matter.

LEPIDUS, *Antony and Cleopatra*, II.ii.24

To be generous, guiltless, and of free disposition, is to
take those things for bird-bolts that you deem your
cannon-bullets.

OLIVIA, *Twelfth Night*, I.v.91

DISABILITY
see also BLINDNESS

I have no way, and therefore want no eyes;
I stumbled when I saw. Full oft 'tis seen,
Our means secure us, and our mere defects
Prove our commodities.

EARL OF GLOUCESTER, *King Lear*, IV.i.18

DISCIPLINE
see also NEATNESS; ORDER

'Tis government that makes then seem divine,
The want thereof makes thee abominable.

DUKE OF YORK, *3 Henry VI*, I.iv.132

For those that tame wild horses
Pace 'em not in their hands to make 'em gentle,

But stop their mouths with stubborn bits and spur 'em
Till they obey the manage.

GARDINER, *Henry VIII*, V.II.56

Now, as fond fathers,
Having bound up the threat'ning twigs of birch
Only to stick it in their children's sight
For terror, not to use, in time the rod
Becomes more mock'd than fear'd; so our decrees,
Dead to infliction, to themselves are dead,
And liberty plucks justice by the nose;
The baby beats the nurse, and quite athwart
Goes all decorum.

VINCENTIO, DUKE OF VIENNA, *Measure for Measure*, I.III.23

DISCRETION
see also TASTE

Distinction, with a broad and powerful fan,
Puffing at all, winnows the light away,
And what hath mass or matter, by itself
Lies rich in virtue and unmingled.

AGAMEMNON, *Troilus and Cressida*, I.III.22

Of all the men alive
I never yet beheld that special face
Which I could fancy more than any other.

BIANCA, *The Taming of the Shrew*, II.I.10

No, I warrant you, I will not adventure my
discretion so weakly. Will you laugh me asleep, for I
am very heavy?

GONZALO, *The Tempest*, II.I.187

Let your own discretion be your tutor.

HAMLET, *Hamlet*, III.II.16

Look you to the guard to-night.
Let's teach ourselves that honorable stop,
Not to outsport discretion.

OTHELLO, *Othello*, II.III.1

It is as proper to our age
To cast beyond ourselves in our opinions,
As it is commonly for the younger sort
To lack discretion.

POLONIUS, *Hamlet*, II.I.111

A golden mind stoops not to shows of dross.

PRINCE OF MOROCCO, *The Merchant of Venice*, II.VII.20

The better
part of valor is discretion, in the which better part
I have sav'd my life.

SIR JOHN FALSTAFF, 1 Henry IV, V.IV.119

DISGUISE

see also APPEARANCE; DECEIT; FACE

Those crisped snaky golden locks,
Which make such wanton gambols with the wind
Upon supposed fairness, often known
To be the dowry of a second head,
The skull that bred them in the sepulcher.
Thus ornament is but the guilèd shore
To a most dangerous sea; the beauteous scarf
Veiling an Indian beauty; in a word,
The seeming truth which cunning times put on
To entrap the wisest.

BASSANIO, The Merchant of Venice, III.II.73

My face I'll grime with filth,
Blanket my loins, elf all my hairs in knots,
And with presented nakedness outface
The winds and persecutions of the sky.

EDGAR, King Lear, II.III.9

The devil hath power
T'assume a pleasing shape.

HAMLET, Hamlet, II.II.599

O serpent heart, hid with a flow'ring face!
Did ever dragon keep so fair a cave?
Beautiful tyrant! fiend angelical!
Dove-feather'd raven! wolvish ravening lamb!
Despised substance of divinest show!
Just opposite to what thou justly seem'st.
A damned saint, an honorable villain!

JULIET, Romeo and Juliet, III.II.73

I prithee speak, we will not trust our eyes
Without our ears: thou are not what thou seem'st.

PRINCE HENRY, 1 Henry IV, V.IV.136

Seems he a dove? his feathers are but borrow'd,
For he's disposed as the hateful raven.
Is he a lamb? his skin is surely lent him,
For he's inclin'd as is the ravenous wolves.
Who cannot steal a shape that means deceit?

QUEEN MARGARET, 2 Henry VI, III.I.75

Trust not those cunning waters of his eyes,
For villainy is not without such rheum,
And he, long traded in it, makes it seem
Like rivers of remorse and innocency.

SALISBURY, *King John*, IV.III.107

O, what may man within him hide,
Though angel on the outward side!

VINCENTIO, DUKE OF VIENNA, *Measure for Measure*, III.II.271

Disguise, I see thou art a wickedness
Wherein the pregnant enemy does much.

VIOLA, *Twelfth Night*, II.II.27

DISHONESTY
see also DECEIT; LIES

Would you were half so honest!
Men's prayers then would seek you, not their fears.

CROMWELL, *Henry VIII*, V.II.117

I think't no sin
To cozen him that would unjustly win.

DIANA, *All's Well That Ends Well*, IV.II.75

Such smiling rogues as these,
Like rats, oft bite the holy cords a-twain
Which are t' intrinse t' unloose; smooth every passion
That in the natures of their lords rebel,
Being oil to fire, snow to the colder moods;
Renege, affirm, and turn their halcyon beaks
With every gale and vary of their masters.

EARL OF KENT, *King Lear*, II.II.73

For things are often spoke and seldom meant;
But that my heart accordeth with my tongue,
Seeing the deed is meritorious,
And to preserve my sovereign from his foe,
Say but the word, and I will be his priest.

EARL OF SUFFOLK, *2 Henry VI*, III.I.268

If thou inclin'st that way, thou art a coward,
Which hoxes honesty behind, restraining
From course requir'd.

LEONTES, *The Winter's Tale*, I.II.244

DISILLUSIONMENT

Strange it is
That nature must compel us to lament
Our most persisted deeds.

AGRIPPA, *Antony and Cleopatra*, V.I.28

The words of Mercury are harsh after the songs of Apollo.
>   ARMADO, *Love's Labor's Lost*, V.II.930

Strange it is that our bloods,
Of color, weight, and heat, pour'd all together,
Would quite confound distinction, yet stands off
In differences so mighty.
>   KING OF FRANCE, *All's Well That Ends Well*, II.III.118

DISORDER
see also ANARCHY AND CHAOS

Her vine, the merry cheerer of the heart,
Unprunèd dies; her hedges even-pleach'd,
Like prisoners wildly overgrown with hair,
Put forth disorder'd twigs; her fallow leas
The darnel, hemlock, and rank femetary
Doth root upon, while that the coulter rusts
That should deracinate such savagery;
The even mead, that erst brought sweetly forth
The freckled cowslip, burnt, and green clover,
Wanting the scythe withal, uncorrected, rank,
Conceives by idleness, and nothing teems
But hateful docks, rough thistles, kecksies, burs,
Losing both beauty and utility;
And all our vineyards, fallows, meads, and hedges
Defective in their natures, grow to wildness.
>   DUKE OF BURGUNDY, *Henry V*, V.II.41

How irksome is this music to my heart!
When such strings jar, what hope of harmony?
>   KING HENRY, *2 Henry VI*, II.I.54

Fear frames disorder, and disorder wounds
where it should guard.
>   YOUNG CLIFFORD, *2 Henry VI*, V.II.32

DISTRUST
see also DOUBT; FAITHLESSNESS

Away he steals with open list'ning ear,
Full of foul hope, and full of fond mistrust;
Both which, as servitors to the unjust.
>   *The Rape of Lucrece*, 283

I wonder men dare trust themselves with men. Methinks they
should invite them without knives: Good for their meat, and
safer for their lives. There's much example for't: the
fellow that sits next him, now parts bread with him, pledges
the breath of him in a divided draught, is the readiest man
to kill him; 't 'as been prov'd.
>   APEMANTUS, *Timon of Athens*, I.II.43

I hold it cowardice
To rest mistrustful where a noble heart
Hath pawn'd an open hand in sign of love.

 EARL OF WARWICK, *3 Henry VI*, IV.II.7

He's mad that trusts in the tameness of a
wolf, a horse's health, a boy's love, or a whore's oath.

FOOL, *King Lear*, III.VI.17

I must no more believe thee in this point
(Though in't I know thou dost believe thyself)
Than I will trust a sickly appetite,
That loathes even as it longs.

HIPPOLYTA, *The Two Noble Kinsmen*, I.III.87

The bird that hath been limed in a bush,
With trembling wings misdoubteth every bush.

KING HENRY, *3 Henry VI*, V.VI.13

DIVORCE
see also MARRIAGE

And out of all these to restore the King,
He counsels a divorce, a loss of her
That, like a jewel, has hung twenty years
About his neck, yet never lost her luster.

DUKE OF NORFOLK, *Henry VIII*, II.II.29

No; God forbid that I should wish them sever'd
Whom God hath join'd together; ay, and 'twere pity
To sunder them that yoke so well together.

RICHARD, DUKE OF GLOUCESTER, *3 Henry VI*, IV.I.21

DOGS

O, 'tis a foul thing, when a cur cannot keep himself in all
companies!

LAUNCE, *The Two Gentlemen of Verona*, IV.IV.9

I think Crab my dog be the sourest-natur'd dog that lives:
my mother weeping, my father wailing, my sister crying, our
maid howling, our cat wringing her hands, and all our house
in a great perplexity, yet did not this cruel-hearted cur
shed one tear. He is a stone, a very pebble stone, and has
no more pity in him than a dog.

LAUNCE, *The Two Gentlemen of Verona*, II.III.5

I have dogs, my lord,
Will rouse the proudest panther in the chase,
And climb the highest promontory top.

MARCUS, *Titus Andronicus*, II.II.20

O Buckingham, take heed of yonder dog!
Look when he fawns he bites; and when he bites,
His venom tooth will rankle to the death.

QUEEN MARGARET, *Richard III*, I.III.288

My hounds are bred out of the Spartan kind;
So flew'd, so sanded; and their heads are hung
With ears that sweep away the morning dew;
Crook-knee'd, and dewlapp'd like Thessalian bulls;
Slow in pursuit; but match'd in mouth like bells,
Each under each. A cry more tuneable
Was never hollo'd to, nor cheer'd with horn,
In Crete, in Sparta, nor Thessaly.

THESEUS, *A Midsummer Night's Dream*, IV.I.119

DOUBT
see also DISTRUST; FAITHLESSNESS

Some sudden qualm hath struck me at the heart,
And dimm'd mine eyes, that I can read no further.

DUKE OF GLOUCESTER, *2 Henry VI*, I.I.54

This is, sir, a doubt
In such a time nothing becoming you,
Nor satisfying us.

GUIDERIUS, *Cymbeline*, IV.IV.14

Nought's had, all's spent,
Where our desire is got without content;
'Tis safer to be that which we destroy
Than by destruction dwell in doubtful joy.

LADY MACBETH, *Macbeth*, III.II.4

Our doubts are traitors,
And makes us lose the good we oft might win,
By fearing to attempt.

LUCIO, *Measure for Measure*, I.IV.77

DOWNFALL
see also BANKRUPTCY; POVERTY; RESIGNATION

'Tis certain, greatness, once fall'n out with fortune,
Must fall out with men too. What the declin'd is,
He shall as soon read in the eyes of others
As feel in his own fall; for men, like butterflies,
Show not their mealy wings but to the summer,
And not a man, for being simply man,
Hath any honor, but honor for those honors
That are without him, as place, riches, and favor—
Prizes of accident as oft as merit,

Which when they fall, as beign slippery standers,
The love that lean'd on them as slippery too,
Doth one pluck down another, and together
Die in the fall.

ACHILLES, *Troilus and Cressida*, III.III.75

I should fear those that dance before me now
Would one day stamp upon me. 'T 'as been done;
Men shut their doors against a setting sun.

APEMANTUS, *Timon of Athens*, I.II.143

Nay then, farewell!
I have touch'd the highest point of all my greatness,
And from that full meridian of my glory,
I haste now to my setting. I shall fall
Like a bright exhalation in the evening,
And no man see me more.

CARDINAL WOLSEY, *Henry VIII*, III.II.223

These mouths who, but of late, earth, sea, and air
Were all too little to content and please,
Although they gave their creatures in abundance,
As houses are defiled for want of use,
They are now starv'd for want of exercise;
Those palates who, not yet two summers younger,
Must have inventions to delight the taste,
Would now be glad of bread and beg for it.

CLEON, *Pericles*, I.IV.34

Ah, Richard! with the eyes of heavy mind
I see thy glory like a shooting star
Fall to the base earth from the firmament.

EARL OF SALISBURY, *Richard II*, II.IV.18

The younger rises when the old doth fall.

EDMUND, *King Lear*, III.III.25

Our hap is loss, our hope but sad despair,
Our ranks are broke, and ruin follows us.

GEORGE, *3 Henry VI*, II.III.9

Bad begins and worse remains behind.

HAMLET, *Hamlet*, III.IV.179

Now, France, thy glory droopeth to the dust.

JOAN DE PUCELLE, *1 Henry VI*, V.III.29

Press not a falling man too far! 'tis virtue.
His faults lie open to the laws, let them,
Not you correct him. My heart weeps to see him
So little of his great self.

LORD CHAMBERLAIN, *Henry VIII*, III.II.333

Be cheerful; wipe thine eyes:
Some falls are means the happier to arise.

LUCIUS, *Cymbeline*, IV.II.402

So now prosperity begins to mellow
And drop into the rotten mouth of death.

QUEEN MARGARET, *Richard III*, IV.IV.I

DREAMS
see also DAYDREAMING; IMAGINATION; SLEEP

Dreams are toys,
Yet for this once, yea, superstitiously,
I will be squar'd by this.

ANTIGONUS, *The Winter's Tale*, III.III.39

The eye of man hath not heard, the ear of man hath not seen,
man's hand is not able to taste, his tongue to conceive, nor
his heart to report, what my dream was.

BOTTOM, *A Midsummer Night's Dream*, IV.I.211

To die, to sleep—
To sleep, perchance to dream—ay, there's the rub,
For in that sleep of death what dreams may come,
When we have shuffled off this mortal coil,
Must give us pause.

HAMLET, *Hamlet*, III.I.65

Ham. O God, I could be bounded in a nutshell, and
count myself a king of infinite space—were it not that I
have bad dreams.
Guil. Which dreams indeed are ambition, for the very
substance of the ambitious is merely the shadow of a dream.
Ham. A dream itself is but a shadow.
Ros. Truly, and I hold ambition of so airy and light
a quality that it is but a shadow's shadow.

HAMLET, GUILDENSTERN, ROSENCRANTZ, *Hamlet*, II.II.254

Learn, good soul,
To think our former state a happy dream,
From which awak'd, the truth of what we are
Shows us but this. .

KING RICHARD, *Richard II*, V.I.17

And for his dreams, I wonder he's so simple
To trust the mock'ry of unquiet slumbers.

LORD HASTINGS, *Richard III*, III.II.26

True, I talk of dreams,
Which are the children of an idle brain,
Begot of nothing but vain fantasy,

Which is as thin of substance as the air,
And more inconstant than the wind, who woos
Even now the frozen bosom of the north,
And, being anger'd, puffs away from thence,
Turning his side to the dew-dropping south.

MERCUTIO, *Romeo and Juliet*, I.IV.96

Rom. I dreamt a dream tonight.
Mer. And so did I.
Rom. Well, what was yours?
Mer. That dreamers often lie.
Rom. In bed asleep, while they do dream things true.
Mer. O then I see Queen Mab hath been with you.
She is the fairies' midwife, and she comes
In shape no bigger than an agot-stone
On the forefinger of an alderman,
Drawn with a team of little atomi
Over men's noses as they lie asleep.
Her chariot is an empty hazel-nut,
Made by the joiner squirrel or old grub,
Time out a' mind the fairies' coachmakers.
Her wagon-spokes made of long spinners' legs,
The cover of the wings of grasshoppers,
Her traces of the smallest spider web,
Her collars of the moonshine's wat'ry beams,
Her whip of cricket's bone, the last of film,
Her wagoner a small grey-coated gnat,
Not half so big as round little worm
Prick'd from the lazy finger of a maid.
And in this state she gallops by night
Through lovers' brains, and then they dream of love;
O'er courtiers' knees, that dream on cur'sies straight;
O'er lawyers' fingers, who straight dream on fees;
O'er ladies' lips, who straight on kisses dream,
Which oft the angry Mab with blisters plagues,
Because their breath with sweetmeats tainted are.
Sometimes she gallops o'er a courtier's nose,
And then dreams he of smelling out a suit;
And sometime comes she with a tithe-pig's tail
Tickling a parson's nose as 'a lies asleep,
Then he dreams of another benefice.
Sometime she driveth o'er a soldier's neck,
And then dreams he of cutting foreign throats,
Of breaches, ambuscadoes, Spanish blades,
Of healths five fadom deep; and then anon
Drums in his ear, at which he starts and wakes,

And being frighted, swears a prayer or two,
And sleeps again.

MERCUTIO, ROMEO, *Romeo and Juliet*, I.IV.50

This dream of mine
Being now awake, I'll queen it no inch farther,
But milk my ewes, and weep.

PERDITA, *The Winter's Tale*, IV.IV.448

These our actors
(As I foretold you) were all spirits, and
Are melted into air, into thin air,
And like the baseless fabric of this vision,
The cloud-capp'd tow'rs, the gorgeous palaces,
The solemn temples, the great globe itself,
Yea, all which it inherit, shall dissolve,
And like this insubstantial pageant faded
Leave not a rack behind. We are such stuff
As dreams are made on; and our little life
(His glassy essence), like an angry ape
Plays such fantastic tricks before high heaven
As makes the angels weep; who, with our spleens,
Would all themselves laugh mortal.

PROSPERO, *The Tempest*, IV.I.148

Why then I do but dream on sovereignty,
Like one that stands upon a promontory
And spies a far-off shore where he would tread,
Wishing his foot were equal with his eye,
And chides the sea that sunders him from thence,
Saying, he'll lade it dry to have his way.

RICHARD, DUKE OF GLOUCESTER, *3 Henry VI*, III.II.134

O blessèd, blessèd night! I am afeard,
Being in night, all this is but a dream,
Too flattering-sweet to be substantial.

ROMEO, *Romeo and Juliet*, II.II.139

DROWNING
see also SWIMMING

O Lord, methought what pain it was to drown!
What dreadful noise of waters in my ears!
What sights of ugly death within my eyes!
Methoughts I saw a thousand fearful wracks;
A thousand men that fishes gnaw'd upon;
Wedges of gold, great anchors, heaps of pearl,
Inestimable stones, unvalued jewels,
All scatt'red in the bottom of the sea:

Some lay in dead men's skulls, and in the holes
Where eyes did once inhabit, there were crept
(As 'twere in scorn of eye) reflecting gems,
That woo'd the slimy bottom of the deep,
And mock'd the dead bones that lay scatt'red by.

CLARENCE, Richard III, I.IV.21

Down her weedy trophies and herself
Fell in the weeping brook. Her clothes spread wide,
And mermaid-like awhile they bore her up,
Which time she she chanted snatches of old lauds,
As one incapable of her own distress,
Or like a creature native and indued
Unto that element. But long it could not be.
Till that her garments, heavy with their drink,
Pull'd the poor wretch from her melodious lay
To muddy death.

GERTRUDE, Hamlet, IV.VII.174

If thou wilt needs damn thyself, do it a more delicate
way than drowning.

IAGO, Othello, I.III.353

I had been drown'd, but that the shore was shelvy and
shallow—a death that I abhor; for the water swells a man.

SIR JOHN FALSTAFF, The Merry Wives of Windsor, III.V.12

I have had a kind of alacrity in sinking; and the bottom
were as deep as hell, I should down

SIR JOHN FALSTAFF, The Merry Wives of Windsor, III.V.12

DRUGS AND MEDICATION

see also HEALING; NATURAL MEDICINE; PHYSICIAN; RECOVERY; SICKNESS

I do know her spirit,
And will not trust one of her malice with
A drug of such damn'd nature. Those she has
Will stupefy and dull the sense awhile,
Which first (perchance) she'll prove on cats and dogs,
Then afterward up higher.

CORNELIUS, Cymbeline, I.V.34

Doct. The patient must minister to himself.
Macb. Throw physic to the dogs, I'll none of it.

DOCTOR, MACBETH, Macbeth, V.III.47

The drug he gave me, which he said was precious
And cordial to me, have I not found it
Murd'rous to th' senses?

IMOGEN, Cymbeline, IV.II.326

I have seen a medicine
That's able to breathe life into a stone,
Quicken a rock, and make you dance canary
With spritely fire and motion, whose simple touch
Is powerful to araise King Pippen, nay,
To give great Charlemain a pen in's hand
And write to her a love-line.

LAFEW, *All's Well That Ends Well*, II.I.72

DRUNKENNESS

see also ALCOHOL; ALCOHOLISM

Her more than haste is mated with delays,
Like the proceedings of a drunken brain.

Venus and Adonis, 909

They were red-hot with drinking,
So full of valor that they smote the air
For breathing in their faces; beat the ground
For kissing of their feet; yet always bending
Towards their project. Then I beat my tabor,
At which like unback'd colts they prick'd their ears,
Advanc'd their eyelids, lifted up their noses
As they smelt music.

ARIEL, *The Tempest*, IV.I.171

It's monstrous labor when I wash my brain
And it grow fouler.

CAESAR (OCTAVIUS), *Antony and Cleopatra*, II.VII.99

Oli. What's a drunken man like, fool?
Clo. Like a drown'd man, a fool, and a madman.
One draught above heat makes him a fool, the second
mads him, and a third drowns him.

FESTE, OLIVIA, *Twelfth Night*, I.v.130

You come
in faint for want of meat, depart reeling with too much
drink; sorry that you have paid too much, and sorry
that you are paid too much; purse and brain both
empty; the brain the heavier for being too light, the
purse too light, being drawn of heaviness. O, of
this contradiction you shall now be quit.

JAILER, *Cymbeline*, V.IV.160

DUTY

see also FAITHFULNESS; HONOR; LOYALTY; RESPONSIBILITY; SERVICE

For fleet-wing'd duty with thought's feathers flies.

The Rape of Lucrece, 1216

Lord of my love, to whom in vassalage
Thy merit hath my duty strongly knit,
To thee I send this written ambassage
To witness duty, not to show my wit;
Duty so great, which wit so poor as mine
May make seem bare, in wanting words to show it,
But that I hope some good conceit of thine
In thy soul's thought (all naked) will bestow it.

SONNET 26, 1–8

I do profess
That for your Highness' good I ever labor'd
More than mine own; that am, have, and will be
(Though all the world should crack their duty to you
And throw it from their soul, though perils did
Abound, as thick as thought could make 'em, and
Appear in forms more horrid), yet my duty,
As doth a rock against the chiding flood,
Should the approach of this wild river break,
And stand unshaken yours.

CARDINAL WOLSEY, *Henry VIII*, III.II.190

If neglection
Should therein make me vile, the common body,
By you reliv'd, would force me to my duty.

CLEON, *Pericles*, III.III.20

I do perceive here a divided duty.

DESDEMONA, *Othello*, I.III.181

Were you well serv'd, you would be taught your duty.

EARL RIVERS, *Richard III*, I.III.249

Think'st thou that duty shall have dread to speak
When power to flattery bows?

EARL OF KENT, *King Lear*, I.I.147

Weigh'd between loathness and obedience, at
Which end o' th' beam should bow.

SEBASTIAN, *The Tempest*, II.I.131

DYING WORDS
see also DEATH; EPITAPH; EULOGY

The miserable change now at my end
Lament nor sorrow at; but please your thoughts
In feeding them with those my former fortunes
Where in I liv'd, the greatest prince of th' world,
The noblest; and do now not basely die,
Not cowardly put off my helmet to

My countryman—a Roman by a Roman
Valiantly vanquish'd. Now my spirit is going.
I can no more.

ANTONY, *Antony and Cleopatra*, IV.xv.51

Come, tears, confound,
Out, sword, and wound
The pap of Pyramus;
Ay, that left pap,
Where heart doth hop.
Thus die I, thus, thus, thus.
Now am I dead,
Now am I fled;
My soul is the sky.
Tongue, lose thy light,
Moon, take thy flight,
Now die, die, die, die, die.

BOTTOM AS PYRAMUS, *A Midsummer Night's Dream*, V.i.295

Et tu, Brute?—Then fall Caesar!

CAESAR, *Julius Caesar*, III.i.77

Caesar, thou art reveng'd,
Even with the sword that kill'd thee.

CASSIUS, *Julius Caesar*, V.iii.45

Peace, peace!
Dost thou not see my baby at my breast,
That sucks the nurse asleep?
As sweet as balm, as soft as air, as gentle—
O Antony!—Nay, I will take thee too:
[Applying another asp to her arm.]
What should I stay—

CLEOPATRA, *Antony and Cleopatra*, V.ii.308

Direct mine arms I may embrace his neck,
And in his bosom spend my latter gasp.
O, tell me when my lips do touch his cheeks,
That I may kindly give one fainting kiss.

EDMUND MORTIMER, *1 Henry VI*, II.v.37

No, no, the drink, the drink—O my dear Hamlet—
The drink, the drink! I am pois'ned.

GERTRUDE, *Hamlet*, V.ii.309

O God, Horatio, what a wounded name,
Things standing thus unknown, shall I leave behind me!
If thou didst ever hold me in thy heart,
Absent thee from felicity a while,
And in this harsh world draw thy breath in pain

To tell my story. . . O, I die, Horatio,
The potent poison quite o'er-crows my spirit.
I cannot live to hear the news from England,
But I do prophesy th' election lights
On Fortinbras, he has my dying voice.
So tell him, with the' occurrents more and less
Which have solicited—the rest is silence.

HAMLET, Hamlet, V.II.344

O but they say the tongues of dying men
Enforce attention like deep harmony.

JOHN OF GAUNT, Richard II, II.I.5

What's here? A cup clos'd in my true love's hand?
Poison, I see, hath been his timeless end.
O churl, drunk all, and left no friendly drop
To help me after? I will kiss thy lips,
Haply some poison yet doth hang on them,
To make me die with a restorative.
Thy lips are warm
Yea, noise? Then I'll be brief. O happy dagger,
This is thy sheath [stabs herself]; there rust, and let me
die.

JULIET, Romeo and Juliet, V.III.161

To bed, to bed, there's knocking at the gate. Come, come,
come, come, give me your hand. What's done cannot be
undone. To bed, to bed, to bed, to bed.

LADY MACBETH, Macbeth, V.II.66

Help me into some house, Benvolio,
Or I shall faint. A plague a' both your houses!
They have made worms' meat of me. I have it,
And soundly too. Your houses!

MERCUTIO, Romeo and Juliet, III.I.105

Eyes, look your last!
Arms, take your last embrace! and, lips, O you
The doors of breath, seal with a righteous kiss
A dateless bargain to engrossing death!
Come, bitter conduct, come, unsavory guide!
Thou desperate pilot, now at once run on
The dashing rocks thy sea-sick weary bark!
Here's to my love! [Drinks.] O true apothecary!
Thy drugs are quick. Thus with a kiss I die.

ROMEO, Romeo and Juliet, V.III.112

EARTHQUAKE

Casca. Who ever knew the heavens menace so?
Cas. Those that have known the earth so full of faults.

CASSIUS, CASCA, *Julius Caesar*, I.III.44

Diseased nature oftentimes breaks forth
In strange eruptions; oft the teeming earth
Is with a kind of colic pinch'd and vex'd
By the imprisoning of unruly wind
Within her womb, which for enlargement striving,
Shakes the old beldame earth, and topples down
Steeples and moss-grown towers.

HOTSPUR, *1 Henry IV*, III.I.26

EDITING

see also CRITICISM; WRITING

Pol. This is too long.
Ham. It shall to the barber's with your beard.

HAMLET, POLONIUS, *Hamlet*, II.II.498

EDUCATION

see also TEACHERS

All delights are vain, but that most vain
Which, with pain purchas'd, doth inherit pain:
As, painfully to pore upon a book
To seek the light of truth, while truth the while
Doth falsely blind the eyesight of his look.
Light, seeking light, doth light of light beguile;
So ere you find where light in darkness lies,
Your light grows dark by losing of your eyes.
Study me how to please the eye indeed
By fixing it upon a fairer eye,
Who dazzling so, that eye shall be his heed,
And give him light that it was blinded by.
Study is like the heaven's glorious sun,
That will not be deep searched with saucy looks;
Small have continual plodders ever won,
Save base authority from others' books.
These earthly godfathers of heaven's lights,
That give a name to every fixèd star,
Have no more profit of their shining nights
Than those that walk and wot not what they are.
Too much to know is to know nought but fame;
And every godfather can give a name.

BEROWNE, *Love's Labor's Lost*, I.I.72

Learning is but an adjunct to ourself,
And where we are, our learning likewise is.
                              BEROWNE, *Love's Labor's Lost*, IV (?)

My love is thine to teach; teach it but how,
And thou shalt see how apt it is to learn
Any hard lesson that may do thee good.
                              DON PEDRO, *Much Ado About Nothing*, I.I.291

Now to Marina bend your mind,
Whom our fast-growing scene must find
At Tharsus, and by Cleon train'd
In music's letters, who hath gain'd
Of education all the grace,
Which makes her both th' heart and place
Of general wonder.
                              GOWER, *Pericles*, IV.CHO.5

O this learning, what a thing it is!
                              GREMIO, *The Taming of the Shrew*, I.II.159

From his cradle
He was a scholar, and a ripe and good one;
Exceeding wise, fair-spoken, and persuading;
Lofty and sour to them that lov'd him not,
But to those men that sought him, sweet as summer.
                              GRIFFITH, *Henry VIII*, IV.II.50

The gentleman is learn'd, and a most rare speaker,
To nature none more bound; his training such
That he may furnish and instruct great teachers
And never seek for aid out of himself.
                              KING HENRY, *Henry VIII*, I.II.111

I am, in all affected as yourself,
Glad that you thus continue your resolve
To such the sweets of sweet philosophy.
Only, good master, while we do admire
This virtue and this moral discipline,
Let's be no stoics nor no stocks, I pray.
Or so devote to Aristotle's checks
As Ovid be an outcast quite abjur'd.
Balk logic with acquaintance that you have,
And practice rhetoric in your common talk.
Music and poesy use to quicken you,
The mathematics and the metaphysics,
Fall to them as you find your stomach serves you.
No profit grows where is no pleasure ta'en.
In brief, sir, study what you most affect.
                              TRANIO, *The Taming of the Shrew*, I.I.26

ELEMENTS
see also AIR; STORMS

> The elements,
> Of whom your swords are temper'd may as well
> Wound the loud winds, or with bemock'd-at stabs
> Kill the still-closing waters, as diminish
> One dowle that's in my plume.
>
> ARIEL, The Tempest, III.III.61

> Methinks King Richard and myself should meet
> With no less terror than the elements
> Of fire and water, when their thund'ring shock
> At meeting tears the cloudy cheeks of heaven.
> Be he the fire, I'll be the yielding water;
> The rage be his, whilst on the earth I rain
> My waters—on the earth, and not on him.
>
> BULLINGBROOK, Richard II, III.III.54

> I tax not you, you elements, with unkindness;
> I never gave you kingdom, call'd you children;
> You owe me no subscription. Then let fall
> Your horrible pleasure. Here I stand your slave,
> A poor, infirm, weak, and despis'd old man;
> But yet I call you servile ministers.
>
> LEAR, King Lear, III.II.16

> Thou hast as chiding a nativity
> As fire, air, water, earth, and heaven can make
> To herald thee from the womb.
>
> PERICLES, Pericles, III.I.32

> Th' unfriendly elements
> Forgot thee utterly, nor have I time
> To give thee hallow'd to thy grave.
>
> PERICLES, Pericles, III.I.57

EMOTION

> And that deep torture may be call'd a hell,
> When more a felt than one hath power to tell.
>
> The Rape of Lucrece, 1287

> Deep sounds make lesser noise than shallow fords,
> And sorrow ebbs, being blown with wind of words.
>
> The Rape of Lucrece, 1329

> Let the superfluous and lust-dieted man,
> That slaves your ordinance, that will not see
> Because he does not feel, feel your pow'r quickly.
>
> EARL OF GLOUCESTER, King Lear, IV.I.67

EMPATHY
see also COMPASSION; GRIEF; MOURNING; PITY; SADNESS; SORROW; SUFFERING

> Yet, cousin,
> Even from the bottom of these miseries,
> From all that fortune can inflict upon us,
> I see two comforts rising, two mere blessings,
> If the gods please—to hold here a brave patience,
> And the enjoying of our griefs together.
>> ARCITE, *The Two Noble Kinsmen*, II.II.55

> A friend should bear his friend's infirmities.
>> CASSIUS, *Julius Caesar*, IV.III.86

> My Dionyza, shall we rest here,
> And by relating tales of others' griefs,
> See if 'twill teach us to forget our own?
>> CLEON, *Pericles*, I.IV.1

> Had he been slaughter-man to all my kin,
> I should not for my life but weep with him,
> To see how only sorrow gripes his soul.
>> EARL OF NORTHUMBERLAND, *3 Henry VI*, I.IV.169

> I bleed inwardly for my lord.
>> FLAVIUS, *Timon of Athens*, I.II.204

> It is foul weather in us all, good sir,
> When you are cloudy.
>> GONZALO, *The Tempest*, II.I.142

> O! I have suffered
> With those that I saw suffer.
>> MIRANDA, *The Tempest*, I.II.5

> O, the cry did knock
> Against my very heart.
>> MIRANDA, *The Tempest*, I.II.8

> Hearts of most hard temper
> Melt and lament for her.
>> OLD LADY, *Henry VIII*, II.II.12

> O, could this kiss be printed in thy hand,
> That thou mightst think upon these by the seal,
> Through whom a thousand signs are breath'd for thee!
>> QUEEN MARGARET, *2 Henry VI*, III.II.343

ENEMY
see also BATTLE; BETRAYAL; TREASON; WAR

> That I did love thee, Caesar, O, 'tis true;
> If then thy spirit look up us now,
> Shall it not grieve thee dearer than thy death,

To see thy Antony making his peace,
Shaking the bloody fingers of thy foes,
Most noble! in the presence of thy corse?
Had I as many eyes as thou hast wounds,
Weeping as fast as they stream forth thy blood,
It would become me better than to close
In terms of friendship with thine enemies.

ANTONY, *Julius Caesar*, III.i.194

His foes are so enrooted with his friends
That, plucking to unfix an enemy,
He doth unfasten so and shake a friend,
So that this land, like an offensive wife
That hath enrag'd him on to offer strokes,
As he is striking, holds him infant up
And hangs resolv'd correction in the arm
That was uprear'd to execution.

ARCHBISHOP, *2 Henry IV*, IV.i.205

Be able for thine enemy
Rather in power than use.

COUNTESS OF ROSSILLION, *All's Well That Ends Well*, I.i.65

Name not religion, for thou lov'st the flesh,
And ne'er throughout the year to church thou go'st
Except it be to pray against thy foes.

DUKE OF GLOUCESTER, *1 Henry VI*, I.i.41

By my troth, this is the old fashion, you two
never meet but you fall to some discord. You are both,
i' good truth, as rheumatic as two dry toasts, you cannot one bear with another's confirmities.

HOSTESS QUICKLY, *2 Henry IV*, II.iv.55

Yield stinging nettles to mine enemies;
And when they from thy bosom pluck a flower,
Guard it, I pray thee, with a lurking adder,
Whose double tongue may with a mortal touch
Throw death upon thy sovereign's enemies.

KING RICHARD, *Richard II*, III.ii.18

Who not needs shall never lack a friend,
And who in want a hollow friend doth try,
Directly seasons him his enemy.

PLAYER KING, *Hamlet*, III.ii.207

ENTERTAINMENT
see also PLEASURE

Sweet recreation barr'd, what doth ensue
But moody and dull melancholy,

Kinsman to grim and comfortless despair,
And at her heels a huge infectious troop
Of pale distemperatures and foes to life?
                    ABBESS, *The Comedy of Errors*, V.I.78

Do not dull thy palm with entertainment.
                    POLONIUS, *Hamlet*, I.III.64

What sport shall we devise here in this garden
To drive away the heavy thought of care?
                    QUEEN, *Richard II*, III.IV.I

Say, what abridgement have you for this evening?
What masque? What music? How shall we beguile
The lazy time, if not with some delight?
                    THESEUS, *A Midsummer Night's Dream*, V.I.39

ENVIRONMENTALISM
see also ELEMENTS; FLOWERS; GARDENING; NATURE

Nature's bequest gives nothing, but doth lend,
And being frank she lends to those are free.
                    SONNET 4, 3–4

I have begun to plant thee, and will labor
To make thee full of growing.
                    DUNCAN, *Macbeth*, I.IV.28

The earth that's nature's mother is her tomb;
What is her burying grave, that is her womb;
And from her womb children of divers kind
We sucking on her natural bosom find:
Many for many virtues excellent,
None but for some, and yet all different.
O, mickle is the powerful grace that lies
In plants, herbs, stones, and their true qualities;
For nought so vile that on the earth doth live
But to the earth some special good doth give;
Nor aught so good but, strain'd from that fair use,
Revolts from true birth, stumbling on abuse.
                    FRIAR LAWRENCE, *Romeo and Juliet*, II.III.9

Thorough this distemperature, we see
The seasons alter: hoary-headed frosts
Fall in the fresh lap of the crimson rose,
And on old Hiems' thin and icy crown
An odorous chaplet of sweet summer buds
is, as in mockery, set; the spring, the summer,
The childing autumn, angry winter, change
Their wonted liveries; and the mazed world,
By their increase, now knows not which is which.

And this same progeny of evils comes
From our debate, from our dissension;
We are their parents and original.

TITANIA, A Midsummer Night's Dream, II.i.106

ENVY
see also JEALOUSY

When in disgrace with Fortune and men's eyes
I all alone beweep my outcast state,
And trouble deaf heaven with my bootless cries,
And look upon myself and curse my fate,
Wishing me like to one more rich in hope,
Featur'd like him, like him with friends possess'd,
Desiring this man's art, and that man's scope,
With what I most enjoy contented least.

SONNET 29, 1–8

Virtue cannot live out of the teeth of emulation.

ARTEMIDORUS, Julius Caesar, II.III.13

One flourishing branch of his most royal root,
Is crack'd, and all the precious liquor split,
Is hack'd down, and his summer leaves all faded,
By envy's hand and murder's bloody axe.

DUCHESS OF GLOUCESTER, Richard II, I.II.18

No black envy
Shall make my grave.

DUKE OF BUCKINGHAM, Henry VIII, II.i.85

But alack,
That monster Envy, oft the wrack
Of earned praise, Marina's life
Seeks to take off by treason's knife.

GOWER, Pericles, IV.CHO.11

No metal can,
No nor the hangman's axe, bear half the keenness
Of thy sharp envy.

GRATIANO, The Merchant of Venice, IV.i.123

How bitter a thing it is to look at happiness through
another man's eyes!

ORLANDO, As You Like It, V.II.43

A man can no more separate age and covetousness than 'a
can part young limbs and lechery; but the gout galls the
one, and the pox pinches the other, and so both the
degrees prevent my curses.

SIR JOHN FALSTAFF, 2 Henry IV, I.II.228

'Tis much, when scepters are in children's hands;
But more, when envy breeds unkind division:
There comes the ruin, there begins confusion.
                              DUKE OF EXETER, *1 Henry VI*, IV.I.192

EPITAPH
see also DEATH; DYING WORDS; EULOGY; FUNERALS

Or I shall live your epitaph to make,
Or you survive when I in earth am rotten.
                              SONNET 81, 1–2

Her monument
Is almost finished, and her epitaphs
In glitt'ring golden characters express
A general praise to her, and care in us
At whose expense 'tis done.
                              DIONYZA, *Pericles*, IV.III.42

"The fairest, sweetest, and best lies here,
Who withered in her spring of year.
She was of Tyrus the King's daughter,
On whom four death hath made this slaughter.
Marina was she call'd, and at her birth,
Thetis, being proud, swallowed some part a' th' earth.
Therefore the earth, fearing to be o'erflowed,
Hath Thetis' birth-child on the heavens bestowed;
Wherefore she does, and swears she'll never stint,
Make raging battery upon shores of flint."
                              GOWER, *Pericles*, IV.IV.34

Fear no more the hear o' th' sun,
Nor the furious winter's rages,
Thou thy worldly task hast done,
Home are gone, and ta'en thy wages.
Golden lads and girls all must,
As chimney-sweepers, come to dust.
                              GUIDERIUS, *Cymbeline*, IV.II.258

Adieu, and take thy praise with thee to heaven!
Thy ignominy sleep with thee in the grave,
But not rememb'red in thy epitaph!
                              PRINCE HENRY, *1 Henry IV*, V.IV.99

EQUALITY
see also CIVIL RIGHTS; DEMOCRACY; FEMINISM; FREEDOM

I was born as free as Caesar, so were you;
We both have fed as well, and we can both
Endure the winter's cold as well as he.
                              CASSIUS, *Julius Caesar*, I.II.97

We came into the world like brother and brother;
And now let's go hand in hand, not one before another.
Dromio of Ephesus, The Comedy of Errors, V.I.425

Ham. Your worm is your only emperor for diet: we fat all
creatures else to fat us, and we fat ourselves for maggots;
your fat king and your lean beggar is but variable service,
two dishes, but to one table—that's the end.
King. Alas, alas!
Ham. A man may fish with the worm that hath eat of a king,
and eat of the fish that hath fed of that worm.
King. What dost thou mean by this?
Ham. Nothing but to show you how a king may go a progress
through the guts of a beggar.
Hamlet, Claudius, Hamlet, IV.III.21

Why, sir, I pray, are not the streets as free
For me as for you?
Tranio, The Taming of the Shrew, I.II.231

EULOGY
see also DEATH; DYING WORDS; EPITAPH; FUNERALS; PARTING

Friends, Romans, countrymen, lend me your ears!
I come to bury Caesar, not to praise him.
The evil that men do lives after them,
The good is oft interred with their bones;
So let it be with Caesar. The noble Brutus
Hath told you Caesar was ambitious;
If it were so, it were a grievous fault,
And grievously hath Caesar answer'd it.
Here, under leave of Brutus and the rest
(For Brutus is an honorable man,
So are they all, all honorable men),
Come I to speak in Caesar's funeral.
He was my friend, faithful and just to me;
But Brutus says he was ambitious,
And Brutus is an honorable man.
He hath brought many captives home to Rome,
Whose ransoms did the general coffers fill;
Did this in Caesar seem ambitious?
When that the poor hath cried, Caesar hath wept;
Ambition should be made of sterner stuff.
Yet Brutus says he was ambitious,
And Brutus is an honorable man.
You all did see that on the Lupercal
I thrice presented him a kingly crown,
Which he did thrice refuse. Was this ambition?
Yet Brutus says he was ambitious,

And sure he is an honorable man.
I speak not disprove what Brutus spoke,
But here I am to speak what I do know.
You all did love him once, not without cause;
What cause withholds you then to mourn for him?
O judgment! thou art fled to brutish beats,
And men have lost their reason. Bear with me,
My heart is in the coffin there with Caesar,
And I must pause till it come back to me.

ANTONY, *Julius Caesar*, III.II.73

When the sun sets, the earth doth drizzle dew,
But for the sunset of my brother's son
It rains downright.

CAPULET, *Romeo and Juliet*, III.V.126

Sweets to the sweet, farewell!

GERTRUDE, *Hamlet*, V.I.243

He lives in fame, that died in virtue's cause.

LUCIUS, *Titus Andronicus*, I.I.390

Angels are bright still, though the brightest fell.

MALCOLM, *Macbeth*, IV.III.22

Nothing in his life
Became him like the leaving of it. He died
As one that had been studied in his death,
To throw away the dearest thing he own'd,
As 'twere a careless trifle.

MALCOLM, *Macbeth*, I.IV.7

His part is play'd, and though it were too short,
He did it well; your day is length'ned and
The blissful dew of heaven does arrouse you.

PALAMON, *The Two Noble Kinsmen*, V.IV.102

If there be
A place prepar'd for those that sleep in honor,
I wish his weary soul that falls may win it.

PALAMON, *The Two Noble Kinsmen*, III.VI.98

EUTHANASIA
see also DEATH; SUICIDE

Now put it, God, in the physician's mind
To help him to his grave immediately!

KING RICHARD, *Richard II*, I.IV.59

It is silliness to live, when to live is torment;
and then have we a prescription to die, when death is
our physician.

RODERIGO, *Othello*, I.III.308

And why not death, rather than living torment?

VALENTINE, *The Two Gentlemen of Verona*, III.i.169

EVIL

see also HELL; SIN; SUPERNATURAL; VICE

For unstain'd thoughts do seldom dream on evil.

The Rape of Lucrece, 87

The devil can cite Scripture for his purpose.
An evil soul producing holy witness
is like a villain with a smiling cheek,
A goodly apple rotten at the heart.,
O, what a goodly outside falsehood hath!

ANTONIO, *The Merchant of Venice*, I.III.98

The prince of darkness is a gentleman.

EDGAR, *King Lear*, III.IV.144

Men's evil manners live in brass, their virtues
We write in water.

GRIFFITH, *Henry VIII*, IV.II.45

The devil hath power
T'assume a pleasing shape.

HAMLET, *Hamlet*, II.II.599

Ah, what a sign it is of evil life,
Where death's approach is seen so terrible!

KING HENRY, *2 Henry VI*, III.III.5

The love of wicked men converts to fear,
That fear to hate, and hate turns one or both
To worthy danger and deserved death.

KING RICHARD, *Richard II*, V.I.66

What do you tremble? are you all afraid?
Alas, I blame you not, for you are mortal,
And mortal eyes cannot endure the devil.

LADY ANNE, *Richard III*, I.II.43

A devil, a born devil, on whose nature
Nurture can never stick; on whom my pains,
Humanely taken, all, all lost, quite lost;
And as with age his body uglier grows,
So his mind cankers.

PROSPERO, *The Tempest*, IV.I.188

Ay, thou wast born to be a plague to men.

QUEEN MARGARET, *3 Henry VI*, V.v.28

I cannot tell, the world is grown so bad
That wrens make prey where eagles dare not perch.

RICHARD, DUKE OF GLOUCESTER, *Richard III*, I.III.69

For now the devil that told me I did well
Say that this deed is chronicled in hell.

SIR PIERCE OF EXTON, *Richard II*, V.v.115

EXCESS
see also GREED; WEALTH

With eager feeding food doth choke the feeder.

JOHN OF GAUNT, *Richard II*, II.i.37

A surfeit of the sweetest things
The deepest loathing to the stomach brings.

LYSANDER, *A Midsummer Night's Dream*, II.ii.137

Can one desire too much of a good thing?

ROSALIND, *As You Like It*, IV.i.123

Therefore, to be possess'd with double pomp,
To guard a title that was rich before,
To gild refined gold, to paint the lily,
To throw a perfume on the violet,
To smooth the ice, or add another hue
Unto the rainbow, or with taper-light
To seek the beauteous eye of heaven to garnish,
Is wasteful and ridiculous excess.

SALISBURY, *King John*, IV.ii.9

EXCUSES

When workmen strive to do better than well,
They do confound their skill in covetousness,
And oftentimes excusing of a fault
Doth make the fault the worse by th' excuse:
As patches set upon a little breach
Discredit more in hiding of the fault
Than did the fault before it was so patch'd.

PEMBROKE, *King John*, IV.ii.28

I will not excuse you, you shall not be
excus'd, excuses shall not be admitted, there is no
excuse shall serve, you shall not be excus'd.

SHALLOW, *2 Henry IV*, V.i.4

EXILE
see also PARTING

Banishment!
It comes not ill; I hate not to be banish'd,
It is a cause worthy my spleen and fury.

ALCIBIADES, *Timon of Athens*, III.v.110

This must my comfort be,
That sun that warms you here shall shine on me,

And those his golden beams to you here lent
Shall point on me and gild my banishment.
BULLINGBROOK, *Richard II*, I.III.144

One of our souls had wand'red in the air,
Banish'd this frail sepulcher of our flesh,
As now our flesh is banish'd from this land.
BULLINGBROOK, *Richard II*, I.III.195

You common cry of curs, whose breath I hate
As reek a' th' rotten fens, whose loves I prize
As the dead carcasses of unburied men
That do corrupt my air—I banish you!
CORIOLANUS, *Coriolanus*, III.III.120

Some word there was, worser than Tybalt's death,
That murd'red me: I would forget it fain,
But O, it presses to my memory,
Like damned guilty deeds to sinners' minds:
"Tybalt is dead, and Romeo banished."
That "banished," that one word "banished,"
Hath slain ten thousand Tybalts.
JULIET, *Romeo and Juliet*, III.II.108

The sly, slow hours shall not determinate
The dateless limit of thy dear exile;
The hopeless word of "never of return"
Breathe I against thee, upon pain of life.
KING RICHARD, *Richard II*, I.III.150

They hurried us abroad a bark,
Bore us some leagues to sea, where they prepared
A rotten carcass of a butt, not rigg'd,
Nor tackle, sail, nor mast, the very rats
Instinctively have quit it. There they hoist us,
To cry to th' sea, that roar'd to us; to sigh
To th' winds, whose pity, sighing back again,
Did us but loving wrong.
PROSPERO, *The Tempest*, I.II.144

I do find more pain in banishment
Than death can yield me here by my abode.
QUEEN MARGARET, *Richard III*, I.III.167

"Banished" is banish'd from the world,
And world's exile is death; then "banished"
Is death misterm'd. Calling death "banished,"
Thou cut'st my head off with a golden axe,
And smilest upon the stroke that murders me.
ROMEO, *Romeo and Juliet*, III.III.13

EXPERIENCE
see also KNOWLEDGE; WISDOM

> Experience is by industry achiev'd
> And perfected by the swift course of time.
>> ANTONIO, *The Two Gentlemen of Verona*, I.III.22

> Experience, O, thou disprov'st report!
>> IMOGEN, *Cymbeline*, IV.II.34

> Make bold her bashful years with your experience.
>> KING RICHARD, *Richard III*, IV.IV.326

> A thousand more mischances than this one
> Have learn'd me how to brook this patiently.
>> SILVIA, *The Two Gentlemen of Verona*, V.III.3

EXPLOITATION
see also POLITICS AND POWER; PROSTITUTION

> The leanness that afflicts us, the object of our
> misery, is as an inventory to particularize their abundance;
> our sufferance is a gain to them.
>> CITIZEN, *Coriolanus*, I.I.20

> The great ones eat
> up the little ones. I can compare our rich misers to
> nothing so fitly as to a whale: 'a plays and tumbles,
> driving the poor fry before him, and at last devour
> them all at a mouthful.
>> FISHERMAN, *Pericles*, II.I.28

> That to's power he would
> Have made them mules, silenc'd their pleaders, and
> Dispropertied their freedoms, holding them,
> In human action and capacity,
> Of no more soul nor fitness for the world
> Than camels in their war, who have their provand
> Only for bearing burdens, and sore blows
> For sinking under them.
>> JUNIUS BRUTUS, *Coriolanus*, II.I.246

> You have, as it appears to me, practic'd upon the
> easy-yielding spirit of this woman, and made her serve
> your uses both in purse and in person.
>> LORD CHIEF JUSTICE, *2 Henry IV*, II.I.114

EYES AND SIGHT
see also BLINDNESS; SENSUALITY

> Since I left you, mine eye is in my mind,
> And that which governs me to go about
> Doth part his function, and is partly blind,
> Seems seeing, but effectually is out.
>> SONNET 113, 1–4

Mine eye and heart are at a mortal war,
How to divide the conquest of thy sight:
Mine eye my heart thy picture's sight would bar,
My heart mine eye the freedom of that right.

SONNET 46, 1–4

If eyes, corrupt by over-partial looks,
Be anchor'd in the bay where all men ride,
Why of eyes' falsehood hast thou forgèd hooks,
Whereto the judgment of my heart is tied?

SONNET 137, 5–8

O what a war of looks was then between them!
Her eyes petitioners to his eyes suing,
His eyes saw her eyes as they had not seen them,
Her eyes wooed still, his eyes disdain'd the wooing.

Venus and Adonis, 355

Sometime diverted their poor balls are tied
To th' orbed earth; sometimes they do extend
Their view right on.

A Lover's Complaint, 24

When most I wink, then do mine eyes best see,
For all the day they view things unrespected.

SONNET 43, 1–2

The eye sees not itself
But by reflection, by some other things.

BRUTUS, *Julius Caesar*, I.ii.52

She is alive; behold
Her eyelids, cases to those heavenly jewels
Which Pericles hath lost, begin to part
Their fringes of bright gold. The diamonds
Of a most praised water doth appear,
To make the world twice rich.

CERIMON, *Pericles*, III.ii.97

To what, my love, shall I compare thine eyne?
Crystal is muddy.

DEMETRIUS, *A Midsummer Night's Dream*, III.ii.138

See better, Lear, and let me still remain
The true blank of thine eye.

EARL OF KENT, *King Lear*, I.i.157

These eyes, that now are dimm'd with death's black veil,
Have been as piercing as the midday sun
To search the secret treasons of the world.

EARL OF WARWICK, *3 Henry VI*, V.ii.16

These eyes, like lamps whose wasting oil is spent,
Wax dim, as drawing to their exigent.

EDMUND MORTIMER, 1 Henry VI, II.v.8

Lo, in these windows that let forth thy life
I pour the helpless balm of my poor eyes.

LADY ANNE, Richard III, I.II.12

No eyes in
your head, nor no money in your purse? Your eyes are
in a heavy case, your purse in a light, yet you see how
this world goes.

LEAR, King Lear, IV.VI.145

What stars do spangle heaven with such beauty,
As those two eyes become that heavenly face?

PETRUCHIO, The Taming of the Shrew, IV.V.31

Thou tell'st me there is murder in mine eye:
'Tis pretty, sure, and very probable,
That eyes, that are the frail'st and softest things.
Who shut their coward gates on atomies,
Should be called tyrants, butchers, murderers!
Now I do frown on thee with all my heart,
And if mine eyes can wound, now let them kill thee.

PHEBE, As You Like It, III.V.10

Two of the fairest stars in all the heaven,
Having some business, do entreat her eyes
To twinkle in their spheres till they return.
What if her eyes were there, they in her head?
The brightness of her cheek would shame those stars,
As daylight doth a lamp; her eyes in heaven
Would through the airy region stream so bright
That birds would sing and think it were not night.

ROMEO, Romeo and Juliet, II.II.15

We wordly men
Have miserable, mad, mistaking eyes.

TITUS, Titus Andronicus, V.II.65

If these be true spies which I wear in my
head, here's a goodly sight.

TRINCULO, The Tempest, V.I.259

FACE
see also APPEARANCE; DISGUISE

Yet in good faith some say that thee behold,
Thy face hath not the power to make love groan.

SONNET 131, 5–6

And as the bright sun glorifies the sky,
So is her face illumin'd with her eye.

Venus and Adonis, 485

His face was as the heav'ns, and therein stuck
A sun and moon, which kept their course, and lighted
The little O, th' earth.

CLEOPATRA, *Antony and Cleopatra*, V.II.79

There's no art
To find the mind's construction in the face.

DUNCAN, *Macbeth*, I.IV.11

Thou tremblest, and the whiteness in thy cheek
Is apter than thy tongue to tell thy errand.

EARL OF NORTHUMBERLAND, 2 *Henry IV*, I.I.68

Yes, this man's brow, like to a title-leaf,
Foretells the nature of a tragic volume.
So looks the strond whereon the imperious flood
Hath left a witness'd usurpation.

EARL OF NORTHUMBERLAND, 2 *Henry IV*, I.I.60

What see you in those papers that you lose
So much complexion?—Look ye how they change!
Their cheeks are paper.

KING HENRY, *Henry V*, II.II.72

O flatt'ring glass,
Like to my followers in prosperity,
Thou dost beguile me! Was this face the face
That every day under his household roof
Did keep ten thousand men? Was this the face
That like the sun, did make beholders wink?
Is this the face which fac'd so many follies,
That was at least out-fac'd by Bullingbrook?
A brittle glory shineth in this face,
As brittle as the glory is the face.

KING RICHARD, *Richard II*, IV.I.279

Your face, my Thane, is as a book, where men
May read strange matters.

LADY MACBETH, *Macbeth*, I.V.62

For by his face straight shall you know his heart.

LORD HASTINGS, *Richard III*, III.IV.53

All men's faces are true, whatsome'er their hands are.

MENAS, *Antony and Cleopatra*, II.VI.97

The tartness of his face sours ripe grapes.

MENENIUS AGRIPPA, *Coriolanus*, V.IV.17

Her face the book of praises, where is read
Nothing but curious pleasures, as from thence
Sorrow were ever raz'd, and testy wrath
Could never be her mild companion.
PERICLES, Pericles, I.I.15

Ye have angels' faces, but heaven knows your hearts.
QUEEN KATHERINE, Henry VIII, III.I.145

FADS AND FASHION
see also CLOTHING

Seest thou not, I say, what a deformed thief this fashion
is, how giddily 'a turns about all the hot-bloods between
fourteen and five-and-thirty, sometimes fashioning them like
Pharaoh's soldiers in the reechy painting, sometime like
god Bel's priests in the old church-window, sometime like
the shaven Hercules in the smirch'd worm-eaten tapestry,
where his codpiece seems as massy as his club.
BORACHIO, Much Ado About Nothing, III.III.130

Report of fashions in proud Italy,
Whose manners still our tardy, apish nation
Limps after in base imitation.
DUKE OF YORK, Richard II, II.I.21

New customs,
Though they be never so ridiculous
(Nay, let 'em be unmanly), yet are follow'd.
LORD SANDS, Henry VIII, I.III.3

The pox of such antic, lisping, affecting phantasimes, these
new tuners of accent! "By Jesu, a very good blade! a very
tall man! a very good whore!" Why, is not this a lamentable
thing, grandsire, that we should be thus afflicted with
these strange flies, these fashion-mongers, these
pardon-me's, who stand so much on the new form, that they
cannot sit at ease on the old bench? O, their bones, their
bones!
MERCUTIO, Romeo and Juliet, II.IV.28

What's this? a sleeve? 'tis like a demi-cannon.
What, up and down carv'd like an apple-tart?
Here's snip and nip and cut and slish and slash,
Like to a censer in a barber shop.
Why, what a' devil's name, tailor, call'st thou this?
PETRUCHIO, The Taming of the Shrew, IV.III.88

How oddly he is suited! I think he bought his doublet in
Italy, his round hose in France, his bonnet in France, and
his behavior everywhere.
PORTIA, The Merchant of Venice, I.II.73

FAILURE

> Finish, good lady, the bright day is done,
> And we are for the dark.
>
> IRAS, *Antony and Cleopatra*, V.II.193

> Losers will have leave
> To ease their stomachs with their bitter tongues.
>
> TITUS, *Titus Andronicus*, III.I.232

FAIRIES

see also SUPERNATURAL

> This is the fairy land. O spite of spites!
> We talk with goblins, owls, and sprites;
> If we obey them not, this will ensue:
> They'll suck our breath, or pinch us black and blue.
>
> DROMIO OF SYRACUSE, *The Comedy of Errors*, II.II.189

> Over hill, over dale,
> Thorough bush, thorough brier,
> Over park, over pale,
> Thorough flood, thorough fire,
> I do wander every where,
> Swifter than the moon's sphere;
> And I serve the Fairy Queen,
> To dew her orbs upon the green.
> The cowslips tall her pensioners be,
> In their gold coats spots you see:
> Those be rubies, fairy favors,
> In those freckles live their savors.
>
> FAIRY, *A Midsummer Night's Dream*, II.I.2

> With female fairies will his tomb be haunted,
> And worms will not come to thee.
>
> GUIDERIUS, *Cymbeline*, IV.II.217

> Now it is the time of night
> That the graves, all gaping wide
> Every one lets forth his sprite,
> In the church-way paths to glide.
> And we fairies, that do run
> By the triple Hecat's team
> From the presence of the sun,
> Following darkness like a dream,
> Now are frolic.
>
> PUCK, *A Midsummer Night's Dream*, V.I.379

> Come, now a roundel and a fairy song;
> Then, for the third part of a minute, hence,
> Some to kill cankers in the musk-rose buds,

Some war with rere-mice for their leathern wings
To make my small elves coats, and some keep back
The clamorous owl, that nightly hoots and wonders
At our quaint spirits.

TITANIA, A Midsummer Night's Dream, II.II.1

FAITH
see also DEVOTION; HIGHER POWER; HOPE; SPIRITUALITY AND RELIGION

There are no tricks in plain and simple faith.

BRUTUS, Julius Caesar, IV.II.22

O, if thou grant my need,
Which only lives but by the death of faith,
That need must needs infer this principle,
That faith would live again by death of need.
O then tread down my need, and faith mounts up;
Keep my need up, and faith is trodden down!

CONSTANCE, King John, III.I.212

My desires
Run not before mine honor, nor my lusts
Burn hotter than my faith.

FLORIZEL, The Winter's Tale, IV.IV.33

O Fortune, Fortune, all men call thee fickle;
If thou art fickle, what dost thou with him
That is reknowned for faith? Be fickle, Fortune:
For then I hope thou wilt not keep him long,
But send him back.

JULIET, Romeo and Juliet, III.v.60

Now God be prais'd, that to believing souls
Gives light in darkness, comfort in despair!

KING HENRY, 2 Henry VI, II.I.64

Thou hast no faith left now, unless thou'dst two,
And that's far worse than none: better have none
Than plural faith, which is too much by one.

SILVIA, The Two Gentlemen of Verona, V.IV.50

There's no more faith in thee than in a stew'd prune.

SIR JOHN FALSTAFF, 1 Henry IV, III.III.111

FAITHFULNESS
see also DUTY; LOYALTY

For know my heart stands armed in mine ear,
And will not let a false sound enter there.

Venus and Adonis, 779

Your rule direct to any; if to me,
Day serves not light more faithful than I'll be.

HELICANUS, Pericles, I.II.109

Harp on it still shall I till heart-strings break.

QUEEN ELIZABETH, Richard III, IV.IV.365

FAITHLESSNESS
see also DISTRUST; DOUBT

So shall I live, supposing thou art true,
Like a deceived husband, so love's face
May still seem love to me, though alter'd new:
Thy looks with me, thy hear in other place.

SONNET 93, 1–4

It cannot fail, but by
The violation of my faith, and then
Let nature crush the sides o' th' earth together,
And mar the seeds within!

FLORIZEL, The Winter's Tale, IV.IV.477

FAME
see also GLORY; HONOR; IMMORTALITY; SELF-PROMOTION

But yesterday the word of Caesar might
Have stood against the world; now lies he there,
And none so poor to do him reverence.

ANTONY, Julius Caesar, III.II.118

By my troth, I think fame but stammers
'em, they stand a grise above the reach of report.

DAUGHTER, The Two Noble Kinsmen, II.I.27

Let fame, that all hunt after in their lives,
Live regist'red upon our brazen tombs,
And then grace us in the disgrace of death;
When spite of cormorant devouring Time,
Th' endeavor of this present breath may buy
That honor which shall bate his scythe's keen edge,
And make us heirs of all eternity.

FERDINAND, KING OF NAVARRE, Love's Labor's Lost, I.I.1

The heavens,
Through you, increase our wonder, and sets up
Your fame for ever.

GENTLEMEN, Pericles, III.II.95

Fame, at the which he aims,
In whom already he's well grac'd, cannot

Better be held nor more attain'd than by
A place below the first.

JUNIUS BRUTUS, *Coriolanus*, I.I.263

I live with bread like you, feel want,
Taste grief, need friends: subjected thus,
How can you say to me I am a king?

KING RICHARD, *Richard II*, III.II.175

Death makes no conquest of this conqueror,
For now he lives in fame though not in life.

PRINCE EDWARD, *Richard III*, III.I.87

Glory grows guilty of detested crimes,
When for fame's sake, for praise, an outward part,
We bend to that the working of the heart.

PRINCESS OF FRANCE, *Love's Labor's Lost*, IV.I.31

Remember that your fame
Knolls in the ear o' th' world; what you do quickly
Is not done rashly; your first thought is more
Than others' labored meditance; your premeditating
More than their actions.

QUEEN, *The Two Noble Kinsmen*, I.I.132

His fame lives in the world, his shame in you.

SIR WILLIAM LUCY, *1 Henry VI*, IV.IV.46

FATE

see also CHANCE; DESTINY; FORTUNE

Come what can come,
The worst is death.

ARCITE, *The Two Noble Kinsmen*, II.III.17

What can be avoided
Whose end is purpos'd by the mighty gods?

CAESAR, *Julius Caesar*, II.II.26

Men at some times are masters of their fates;
The fault, dear Brutus, is not in our stars,
But in ourselves, that we are underlings.

CASSIUS, *Julius Caesar*, I.II.139

But heaven hath a hand in these events,
To whose high will we bound our calm contents.

DUKE OF YORK, *Richard II*, V.II.37

What must be shall be.

JULIET, *Romeo and Juliet*, IV.I.21

What fates impose, that men must needs abide;
It boots not to resist both wind and tide.

KING EDWARD, 3 Henry VI, IV.III.58

If chance will have me king, why, chance may crown me
Without my stir.

MACBETH, Macbeth, I.III.143

Though wayward fortune did malign my state,
My derivation was from ancestors
Who stood equivalent with mighty kings,
But time hath rooted out my parentage,
And to the world and awkward casualties
Bound me in servitude.

MARINA, Pericles, V.I.89

Fate, show thy force: ourselves we do not owe;
What is decreed must be; and this be so.

OLIVIA, Twelfth Night, I.V.310

We cannot but obey
The powers above us. Could I rage and roar
As doth the sea she lies in, yet the end
Must be as 'tis.

PERICLES, Pericles, III.III.9

Our will and fates do so contrary run
That our devices still are overthrown,
Our thoughts are ours, their ends none of our own.

PLAYER KING, Hamlet, III.II.211

My mind misgives
Some consequence yet hanging in the stars
Shall bitterly begin his fearful date
With this night's revels, and expire the term
Of a despised life clos'd in my breast
By some vile forfeit of untimely death.
But He that hath the steerage of my course
Direct my sail!

ROMEO, Romeo and Juliet, I.IV.106

FATHERHOOD
see also BABIES; CHILDREN; CHILDREN OF UNMARRIED PARENTS; DAUGHTERS;
GRANDPARENTS; HEREDITY; MEN; SONS

As a decrepit father takes delight
To see his active child do deeds of youth,
So I, made lame by Fortune's dearest spite,
Take all my comfort of thy worth and truth.

SONNET 37, 1–4

With cunning hast thou filch'd my daughter's heart,
Turn'd her obedience (which is due to me)
To stubborn harshness.

EGEUS, A Midsummers Night's Dream, I.1.36

The pleasure that some fathers feed upon
Is my strict fast—I mean, my children's looks;
And therein fasting, hast thou made me gaunt.

JOHN OF GAUNT, Richard II, II.1.79

You urg'd me as a judge, but I had rather
You would have bid me argue like a father.
O, had't been a stranger, not my child,
To smooth his fault I should have been more mild.

JOHN OF GAUNT, Richard II, I.III.237

For this the foolish over-careful fathers
Have broke their sleep with thoughts, their brains with
care,
Their bones with industry;
For this they have engrossèd and pil'd up
The cank'red heaps of strange-achievèd gold;
For this they have been thoughtful to invest
Their sons with arts and martial exercises;
When like the bee tolling from every flower
The virtuous sweets,
Our thighs pack'd with wax, our mouths with honey,
We bring it to the hive, and like the bees,
Are murd'red for our pains. This bitter taste
Yields his engrossments to the ending father.

KING HENRY IV, 2 Henry IV, IV.v.64

Bring me a father that so lov'd his child,
Whose joy of her is overwhelm'd like mine,
And bid him speak of patience;
Measure his owe the length and breadth of mine,
And let it answer every strain for strain,
As thus for thus, and such a grief for such,
In every lineament, branch, shape, and form;
If such a one will smile and stroke his beard,
And sorrow wag, cry "hem!" when he should groan,
Patch grief with proverbs, make misfortune drunk
With candle-wasters, bring him yet to me,
And I of him will gather patience.

LEONATO, Much Ado About Nothing, V.I.8

Looking on the lines
Of my boy's face, methoughts I did recoil
Twenty-three years, and saw myself unbreech'd

In my green velvet coat, my dagger muzzled,
Lest it should bit its master, and so prove
(As ornament oft does) too dangerous.

LEONTES, *The Winter's Tale*, I.II.152

Thou, being a king, blest with a goodly son,
Didst yield consent to disinherit him,
Which argued thee a most unloving father.
Unreasonable creatures feed their young,
And though man's face be fearful to their eyes,
Yet in protection of their tender ones,
Who hath not seen them, even with those wings
Which sometime they have us'd with fearful flight,
Make war with him that climb'd unto their nest,
Offering their own lives in their young's defense?
For shame, my liege, make they your president!
Were it not pity that this goodly boy
Should lose his birthright by his father's fault.

LORD CLIFFORD, *3 Henry VI*, II.II.23

He makes a July's day short as December,
And with his varying childness cures in me
Thoughts that would thick my blood.

POLIXENES, *The Winter's Tale*, I.II.169

O, a cherubin
Thou wast that did preserve me. Thou didst smile,
Infusèd with a fortitude from heaven,
When I have deck'd the sea with drops full salt,
Under my burden groan'd, which rais'd in me
An undergoing stomach, to bear up
Against what should ensue.

PROSPERO, *The Tempest*, I.II.153

And that I love the tree from whence thou sprang'st,
Witness the loving kiss I give the fruit.

RICHARD, DUKE OF GLOUCESTER, *3 Henry VI*, V.VII.31

God knows thou art a collop of my flesh,
And for thy sake have I shed many a tear.

SHEPHERD, *1 Henry VI*, V.IV.18

FATIGUE

Let it be to-night
For now they are oppress'd with travail, they
Will not, nor cannot, use such vigilance
As when they are fresh.

ANTONIO, *The Tempest*, III.III.14

For strokes receiv'd and many blows repaid
Have robb'd my strong-knit sinews of their strength,
And spite of spite needs must I rest awhile.

EARL OF WARWICK, *3 Henry VI*, II.III.3

My little body is a-weary of this great world.

PORTIA, *The Merchant of Venice*, I.II.1

With signs of war about his aged neck.
O, full of careful business are his looks!

QUEEN, *Richard II*, II.II.74

FAULTS
see also MISTAKES; VICE

Men's faults do seldom to themselves appear,
Their own transgressions partially they smother.

The Rape of Lucrece, 632

You gods will give us
Some faults to make us men.

AGRIPPA, *Antony and Cleopatra*, V.I.32

I am very proud, revengeful, ambitious, with more offenses
at my beck than I have thoughts to put them in, imagination
to give them shape, or time to act them in.

HAMLET, *Hamlet*, III.I.123

I must not think there are
Evils enow to darken all his goodness:
His faults, in him, seem as the spots of heaven
More fiery by night's blackness; hereditary,
Rather than purchas'd; what he cannot change,
Than what he chooses.

LEPIDUS, *Antony and Cleopatra*, I.IV.10

They say best men are molded out of faults,
And for the most, become much more the better
For being a little bad.

MARIANA, *Measure for Measure*, V.I.439

FEAR
see also CARE AND CONCERN; WORRY

Not mine own fears, nor the prophetic soul
Of the wide world, dreaming on things to come,
Can yet the lease of my true love control,
Suppos'd as forfeit to a confin'd doom.

SONNET 107, 1–4

Wrapp'd and confounded in a thousand fears,
Like to a new-kill'd bird she trembling lies.

The Rape of Lucrece, 456

So at his bloody view her eyes are fled
Into the deep-dark cabins of her head.

Venus and Adonis, 1037

I rather tell thee what is to be fear'd
Than what I fear.

CAESAR, *Julius Caesar*, I.II.211

Truly, the hearts of men are full of fear.
You cannot reason (almost) with a man
That looks not heavily and full of dread.

CITIZEN, *Richard III*, II.III.38

Thou shalt be punish'd for thus frighting me,
For I am sick and capable of fears,
Oppress'd with wrongs, and therefore full of fears,
A widow, husbandless, subject to fears,
A woman, naturally born to fears.

CONSTANCE, *King John*, III.I.11

To fear the worst oft cures the worse.

CRESSIDA, *Troilus and Cressida*, III.II.73

Let pale-fac'd fear keep with the mean-born man,
And find no harbor in a royal heart.

DUKE OF YORK, *2 Henry VI*, III.I.335

What should be the fear?
I do not set my life at a pin's fee,
And for my soul, what can it do to that,
Being a thing immortal as itself?

HAMLET, *Hamlet*, I.IV.64

Of all base passions, fear is most accurs'd.

JOAN DE PUCELLE, *1 Henry VI*, V.II.18

I have a faint cold fear thrills through my veins,
That almost freezes up the heat of life.

JULIET, *Romeo and Juliet*, IV.III.15

When our actions do not,
Our fears do make us traitors.

LADY MACDUFF, *Macbeth*, IV.II.3

Best safety lies in fear.

LAERTES, *Hamlet*, I.III.43

Where love is great, the littlest doubts are fear;
Where little fears grow great, great love grows there.

PLAYER QUEEN, *Hamlet*, III.II.171

Cruel are the times when we are traitors,
And do not know ourselves; when we hold rumor
From what we fear, yet know not what we fear,

But float upon a wild and violent sea
Each way, and none.

ROSSE, Macbeth, IV.II.18

I cannot speak, nor think,
Nor dare to know that which I know.

SHEPHERD, The Winter's Tale, IV.IV.451

FEARLESSNESS
see also BRAVADO; COURAGE

Let him approach.
But that we fear the gods in him, he brings not
A jot of terror to us.

ARCITE, The Two Noble Kinsmen, I.II.94

But fear not thou, until thy foot be snar'd,
Nor never seek prevention of thy foes.

ELEANOR, 2 Henry VI, II.IV.56

Teeth hadst thou in thy head when thou wast born,
To signify thou cam'st to bite the world.

KING HENRY, 3 Henry VI, V.VI.53

FEMINISM
see also EQUALITY; WOMEN

For me, I am the mistress of my fate.

The Rape of Lucrece, 1069

Methinks a woman of this valiant spirit
Should, if a coward heard her speak these words,
Infuse his breast with magnanimity,
And make him, naked, foil a man at arms.

PRINCE EDWARD, 3 Henry VI, V.IV.39

And, being a woman, I will not be slack
To play my part in Fortune's pageant.

ELEANOR, 2 Henry VI, I.II.66

'Tis not a year or two shows us a man:
They are all but stomachs, and we all but food;
They eat us hungerly, and when they are full
They belch us.

EMILIA, Othello, III.IV.103

Let husbands know
Their wives have sense like them; they see, and smell,
And have their palates both for sweet and sour,
As husbands have.

EMILIA, Othello, IV.III.93

And have not we affections,
Desires for sport, and frailty, as men have?
Then let them use us well; else let them know,
The ills we do, their ills instruct us so.

EMILIA, Othello, IV.III.100

There is no honesty in such
dealing, unless a woman should be made an ass and a
beast, to bear every knave's wrong.

HOSTESS QUICKLY, 2 Henry IV, II.I.36

My daughter weeps, she'll not part with you,
She'll be a soldier too, she'll to the wars.

OWEN GLENDOWER, 1 Henry IV, III.I.193

Would all other women
Could speak this with as free a soul as I do!

QUEEN KATHERINE, Henry VIII, III.I.31

Make the doors upon a woman's wit, and it will out at the
casement; shut that, and 'twill out at the key-hole; stop
that, 'twill fly with the smoke out at the chimney.

ROSALIND, As You Like It, IV.I.161

She is pistol-proof, sir; you shall not hardly
offend her.

SIR JOHN FALSTAFF, 2 Henry IV, II.IV.116

FISHING

3. Fish. Master, I marvel how the fishes live in the sea.
1. Fish. Why, as men do a-land; the great ones eat up the
little ones.

FISHERMEN, Pericles, II.I.26

The imperious seas breed monsters, for the dish,
Poor tributary rivers as sweet fish.

IMOGEN, Cymbeline, IV.II.35

How from the finny subject of the sea
These fishers tell the infirmities of men,
And from their wat'ry empire recollect
All that may men approve or men detect!—
Peace be at your labor, honest fishermen.

PERICLES, Pericles, II.I.48

The pleasant'st angling is to see the fish
Cut with her golden oars the silver stream,
And greedily devour the treacherous bait.

URSULA, Much Ado About Nothing, III.I.26

FLATTERY
see also PRAISE

He that loves to be flatter'd is worthy
o' th' flatterer.

APEMANTUS, *Timon of Athens*, I.i.226

O that men's ears should be
To counsel deaf, but not to flattery!

APEMANTUS, *Timon of Athens*, I.ii.249

These couchings and these lowly courtesies
Might fire the blood of ordinary men,
And turn preordinance and first decree
Into the law of children. Be not fond
To think that Caesar bears such rebel blood
That will be thaw'd from the true quality
With that which melteth fools—I mean sweet words,
Low-crooked curtsies, and base spaniel fawning.

CAESAR, *Julius Caesar*, III.i.36

When I tell him he hates flatterers
He says he does, being then most flattered.

DECIUS, *Julius Caesar*, II.i.207

Why should the poor be flatter'd?
No, let the candied tongue lick absurd pomp,
And crook the pregnant hinges of the knee
Where thrift may follow fawning.

HAMLET, *Hamlet*, III.ii.59

They do abuse the King that flatter him,
For flattery is the bellows blows up sin,
The thing the which is flattered, but a spark
To which that blast gives heat and stronger glowing.

HELICANUS, *Pericles*, I.ii.38

A thousand flatterers sit within thy crown,
Whose compass is no bigger than thy head.

JOHN OF GAUNT, *Richard II*, II.i.100

He does me double wrong
That wounds me with the flatteries of his tongue.

KING RICHARD, *Richard II*, III.ii.215

'Twas never merry world
Since lowly feigning was call'd compliment.

OLIVIA, *Twelfth Night*, III.i.98

Nay, never paint me now;
Where fair is not, praise cannot mend the brow.

PRINCESS OF FRANCE, *Love's Labor's Lost*, IV.i.16

I had rather have a fool to make me merry than experience
to make me sad.

> ROSALIND, *As You Like It*, IV.i.27

FLOWERS
see also ENVIRONMENTALISM; GARDENING; NATURE

Fair flowers that are not gather'd in their prime
Rot and consume themselves in little time.

> *Venus and Adonis*, 131

Flowers distill'd, though they with winter meet.
Leese but their show; their substance still lives sweet.

> SONNET 5, 13–14

Keep these flowers,
We'll see how near art can come near their colors.

> EMILIA, *The Two Noble Kinsmen*, II.ii.148

Beauty's a flower.

> FESTE, *Twelfth Night*, I.v.52

Within the infant rind of this weak flower
Poison hath residence and medicine power;
For this, being smelt, with that part cheers each part,
Being tasted, stays all sense with the heart.
Two such opposed kings encamp them still
In man as well as herbs, grace and rude will;
And here the worser is predominant,
Full soon the canker death eats up that plant.

> FRIAR LAWRENCE, *Romeo and Juliet*, II.ii.23

Bid her steal into the pleached bower,
Where honeysuckles, ripened by the sun,
Forbid the sun to enter, like favorites
Made proud by princes, that advance their pride
Against the power that bred it.

> HERO, *Much Ado About Nothing*, III.i.8

These flow'rs are like the pleasures of the world.

> IMOGEN, *Cymbeline*, IV.ii.296

I know a bank where the wild thyme blows,
Where oxlips and the nodding violet grows,
Quite over-canopied with lusty woodbine,
With sweet musk-roses and with eglantine.

> OBERON, *A Midsummer Night's Dream*, II.i.249

FOOD
see also BARS AND RESTAURANTS; VEGETARIANISM

Unquiet meals make ill digestions.

> ABBESS, *The Comedy of Errors*, V.i.73

Their tables were stor'd full, to glad the sight,
And not so much to feed on as delight.

CLEON, *Pericles*, I.IV.28

Friend, you must eat no white bread; if you do,
Your teeth will bleed extremely.

DAUGHTER, *The Two Noble Kinsmen*, III.V.80

Sea-water shalt thou drink; thy food shall be
The fresh-brook mussels, wither'd roots, and husks
Wherein the acorn cradled.

PROSPERO, *The Tempest*, I.II.462

Buy food, and get thyself in flesh.

ROMEO, *Romeo and Juliet*, V.I.84

Though the chameleon Love can feed on the air, I am one
that am nourish'd by my victuals, and would fain have meat.

SPEED, *Two Gentlemen of Verona*, II.I.172

Each man to his stool, with that spur as he
would to the lip of his mistress; your diet shall be in all
places alike. Make not a city feast of it, to let the meat
cool ere we can agree upon the first place; sit, sit.
The gods require our thanks.

TIMON, *Timon of Athens*, III.VI.65

FOOLISHNESS

That noble lady
Or gentleman that is not freely merry
Is not my friend.

CARDINAL WOLSEY, *Henry VIII*, I.IV.35

And you shall find his vanities forespent
Were but the outside of the Roman Brutus,
Covering discretion with a coat of folly,
As gardeners do with ordure hide those roots
That shall first spring and be most delicate.

CONSTABLE OF FRANCE, *Henry V*, II.IV.36

If you love an addle egg as much as you love an idle head,
you would eat chickens i' th' shell.

CRESSIDA, *Troilus and Cressida*, I.II.133

God give them wisdom that have it; and those that are fools,
let them use their talents.

FESTE, *Twelfth Night*, I.V.14

This is the silliest stuff that I ever heard.

HIPPOLYTA, *A Midsummer Night's Dream*, III.II.115

Folly in fools bears not so strong a note
As fool'ry in the wise, when wit doth dote,
Since all the power thereof it doth apply
To prove, by wit, worth in simplicity.

> MARIA, *Love's Labor's Lost*, V.II.75

Well, thus we play the fools with the time, and the spirits
of the wise sit in the clouds and mock us.

> PRINCE HENRY, *2 Henry IV*, II.II.141

None are so surely caught, when they are catch'd,
As wit turn'd fool; folly, in wisdom hatch'd,
Hath wisdom's warrant and the help of school,
And wit's own grace to grace a learned fool.

> PRINCESS OF FRANCE, *Love's Labor's Lost*, V.II.69

I am too childish-foolish for this world.

> RICHARD, DUKE OF GLOUCESTER, *Richard III*, I.III.141

O you heavenly charmers,
What things you make of us! For what we lack
We laugh, for what we have are sorry, still
Are children in some kind.

> THESEUS, *The Two Noble Kinsmen*, V.IV.131

I hold him but a fool that will endanger
His body for a girl that loves him not.

> THURIO, *The Two Gentlemen of Verona*, V.IV.133

Pro. So, by your circumstance, you call me fool.
Val. So, by your circumstance, I fear you'll prove.
Pro. 'Tis love you cavil at, I am not Love.
Val. Love is your master, for he masters you;
And he that is yoked by a fool,
Methinks should not be chronicled for wise.

> VALENTINE, PROTEUS, *The Two Gentlemen of Verona*, I.I.36

This fellow is wise enough to play the fool,
And to do that well craves a kind of wit.
He must observe their mood on whom he jests,
The quality of persons, and the time;
And like the haggard, check at every feather
That comes before his eye. This is a practice
As full of labor as a wise man's art;
For folly that he wisely shows is fit,
But wise men, folly-fall'n, quite taint their wit.

> VIOLA, *Twelfth Night*, III.I.60

FOREIGN LANGUAGE

My language? heavens!
I am the best of them that speak this speech,
Were I but where 'tis spoken.

FERDINAND, *The Tempest*, I.II.429

Your Majestee ave fausse French enough to
deceive de most sage demoiselle dat is en France.

KATHERINE, *Henry V*, V.II.218

Come, your answer is broken music;
for thy voice is music and thy English broken; therefore,
Queen of all, Katherine, break thy mind to me in
broken English.

KING HENRY, *Henry V*, V.II.243

I' faith, Kate, my wooing is fit for thy understanding.
I am glad thou canst speak no better English, for if
thou couldst, thou wouldst find me such a plain king
that thou wouldst think I had sold my farm to buy
my crown. I know no ways to mince it in love, but
directly to say "I love you."

KING HENRY, *Henry V*, V.II.122

It is as easy for me, Kate, to
conquer the kingdom as to speak so much more
French. I shall never move thee in French, unless it be
to laugh at me.

KING HENRY, *Henry V*, V.II.184

O fair Katherine, if you will love me
soundly with your French heart, I will be glad to
hear you confess it brokenly with your English tongue.

KING HENRY, *Henry V*, V.II.104

I understand thy kisses, and thou mine,
And that a feeling disputation,
But I will never be a truant, love,
Till I have learn'd thy language, for thy tongue
Makes Welsh as sweet as ditties highly penn'd,
Sung by a fair queen in a summer's bow'r,
With ravishing division, to her lute.

LORD MORTIMER, *1 Henry IV*, III.I.202

This is the deadly spite that angers me:
My wife can speak no English, I no Welsh.

LORD MORTIMER, *1 Henry IV*, III.I.190

They have been at a great feast of languages, and stol'n
the scraps.

MOTH, *Love's Labor's Lost*, V.I.36

The language I have learnt these forty years,
My native English, now I must forgo,
And now my tongue's use is to me no more
Than an unstringed viol or a harp,
Or like a cunning instrument cas'd up,
Or being open, put into his hands
That knows no touch to tune the harmony.
Within my mouth you have enjail'd my tongue,
Doubly portcullis'd with my teeth and lips,
And dull unfeeling barren ignorance
Is made my jailer to attend on me.
I am too old to fawn upon a nurse,
Too far in years to be a pupil now.
What is thy sentence then but speechless death,
Which robs my tongue from breathing native breath?

MOWBRAY, Richard II, I.III.159

FORGIVENESS
see also GRACE; MERCY; REPENTANCE

Thine eye begins to speak, set thy tongue there;
Or in thy piteous heart plant thou thine ear,
That hearing how our plaints and prayers do pierce,
Pity may move thee "pardon" to rehearse.

DUCHESS OF YORK, Richard II, V.III.125

Mercy is not itself that oft looks so;
Pardon is still the nurse of second woe.

ESCALUS, Measure for Measure, II.I.283

Use every man after his desert, and who shall scape
whipping? Use them after your own honor and dignity—the
less they deserve, the more merit is in your bounty.

HAMLET, Hamlet, II.II.529

When thou dost ask me blessing, I'll kneel down
And ask of thee forgiveness. So we'll live,
And pray, and sing, and tell old tales, and laugh
At gilded butterflies, and hear poor rogues
Talk of court news.

LEAR, King Lear, V.III.10

But I shall live, my lord, to give them thanks
That were the cause of my imprisonment.

LORD HASTINGS, Richard III, I.I.127

These words have turn'd my hate to love,
And I forgive and quite forget old faults.

QUEEN MARGARET, 3 Henry VI, III.III.199

If thy revengeful heart cannot forgive,
Lo here I lend thee this sharp-pointed sword,
Which if thou please to hide in this true breast,
And let the soul forth that adoreth thee,
I lay it naked to the deadly stroke,
And humbly beg the death upon my knee.

RICHARD, DUKE OF GLOUCESTER, Richard III, I.II.173

Ay, even such heaps and sums of love and wealth
As shall to thee blot out what wrongs were theirs,
And write in thee the figures of their love,
Ever to read them thine.

SENATOR, Timon of Athens, V.I.152

I do beseech your Grace, for charity,
If ever any malice in your heart
Were hid against me, now to forgive me frankly.

SIR THOMAS LOVELL, Henry VIII, II.I.79

I'll bring a bevy,
A hundred black-ey'd maids that love as I do,
With chaplets on their heads of daffadillies,
With cherry lips and cheeks of damask roses,
And all we'll dance an antic 'fore the Duke,
And beg his pardon.

WOOER, The Two Noble Kinsmen, IV.I.71

FORMALITY
see also MANNERS; NAMES AND TITLES

When love begins to sicken and decay
It useth an enforced ceremony.

BRUTUS, Julius Caesar, IV.II.20

His ceremonies
laid by, in his nakedness he appears but a man.

KING HENRY, Henry V, IV.I.104

Ceremony was but devis'd at first
To set a gloss on faint deeds, hollow welcomes,
Recanting goodness, sorry ere 'tis shown;
But where there is true friendship, there needs none.

TIMON, Timon of Athens, I.II.15

FORTUNE
see also CHANCE; FATE; GAMBLING; LUCK

Fortune knows
We scorn her most when most she offers blows.

ANTONY, Antony and Cleopatra, III.XI.73

Fortune is merry,
And in this mood will give us any thing.

ANTONY, *Julius Caesar*, III.II.266

Fortune, good night; smile once more, turn thy wheel.

EARL OF KENT, *King Lear*, II.II.173

Blest are those
Whose blood and judgment are so well co-meddled,
That they are not a pipe for Fortune's finger
To sound what stop she please.

HAMLET, *Hamlet*, III.II.68

Therefore that I may conquer fortune's spite
By living low, where fortune cannot hurt me,
And that the people of this blessed land
May not be punish'd with my thwarting stars.

KING HENRY, *3 Henry VI*, IV.VI.19

Will Fortune never come with both hands full,
But write her fair words still in foulest terms?
She either gives a stomach and no food—
Such are the poor, in health; or else a feast
And takes away the stomach—such are the rich,
That have abundance and enjoy it not.

KING HENRY IV, *2 Henry IV*, IV.IV.103

Never fortune
Did play a subtler game.

PALAMON, *The Two Noble Kinsmen*, V.IV.113

I have ere now, sir, been better known to you, when I have
held familiarity with fresher clothes; but I am now, sir,
muddied in Fortune's mood, and smell somewhat strong of her
strong displeasure.

PAROLLES, *All's Well That Ends Well*, V.II.2

All other doubts, by time let them be clear'd,
Fortune brings in some boats that are not steer'd.

PISANIO, *Cymbeline*, IV.III.45

I know not
What counts harsh Fortune casts upon my face,
But in my bosom shall never come,
To make my heart her vassal.

POMPEY, *Antony and Cleopatra*, II.VI.53

Every man shift for all the rest, and let no man
take care for himself; for all is but fortune.

STEPHANO, *The Tempest*, V.I.257

FREEDOM
see also CIVIL RIGHTS; EQUALITY

>   Every bondman in his own hand bears
>   The power to cancel his captivity.
>
>   CASCA, *Julius Caesar*, I.III.101

>   Thou shalt be as free
>   As mountain winds.
>
>   PROSPERO, *The Tempest*, I.II.499

>   Then to the elements
>   Be free, and fare thou well!
>
>   PROSPERO, *The Tempest*, V.I.318

FRIENDSHIP
see also COMRADERY

>   Am not I liable to those affections,
>   Those joys, griefs, angers, fears, my friend shall suffer?
>
>   ARCITE, *The Two Noble Kinsmen*, II.II.188

>   I count myself in nothing else so happy
>   As in a soul rememb'ring my good friends,
>   And as my fortune ripens with thy love,
>   It shall be still thy true love's recompense.
>   My heart this covenant makes, my hand thus seals it.
>
>   BULLINGBROOK, *Richard II*, II.III.46

>   Thy friendship makes us fresh.
>
>   CHARLES, *1 Henry VI*, III.III.86

>   Assure thee,
>   If I do vow a friendship, I'll perform it
>   To the last article.
>
>   DESDEMONA, *Othello*, III.III.20

>   To wail friends lost
>   Is not by much so wholesome-profitable
>   As to rejoice at friends but newly found.
>
>   FERDINAND, KING OF NAVARRE, *Love's Labor's Lost*, V.II.749

>   We, Hermia, like two artificial gods,
>   Have with our needles created both one flower,
>   Both on one sampler, sitting on one cushion,
>   Both warbling of one song, both in one key,
>   As if our hands, our sides, voices, and minds
>   Had been incorporate. So we grew together,
>   Like to a double cherry, seeming parted,
>   But yet an union in partition,
>   Two lovely berries molded on one stem;

So with two seeming bodies, but one heart,
Two of the first, like coats in heraldry,
Due but to one, and crowned with one crest.

> HELENA, *A Midsummer Night's Dream*, III.II.203

I will upon all hazards well believe
Thou art my friend that know'st my tongue so well.

> HUBERT, *King John*, V.VI.8

And, will they take the offer of our grace,
Both he and they and you, yea, every man
Shall be my friend again, and I'll be his.

> KING HENRY, *1 Henry IV*, V.I.106

'Twixt such friends as we
Few words suffice.

> PETRUCHIO, *The Taming of the Shrew*, I.II.65

Those friends thou hast, and their adoption tried,
Grapple them unto thy soul with hoops of steel.

> POLONIUS, *Hamlet*, I.III.62

In companions
That do converse and waste the time together,
Whose souls do bear an egall yoke of love,
There must be needs a like proportion
Of lineaments, of manners, and of spirit.

> PORTIA, *The Merchant of Venice*, III.IV.11

You do surely bar the door upon your own liberty if you deny
your griefs to your friend.

> ROSENCRANTZ, *Hamlet*, III.II.338

Nature teaches beasts to know their friends.

> SICINIUS VELUTUS, *Coriolanus*, II.I.6

I am not of that feather to shake off
My friend when he must need me.

> TIMON, *Timon of Athens*, I.I.100

O you gods, think I, what need we have any
friends, if we should ne'er have need of 'em? They
were the most needless creatures living, should we
ne'er have use for 'em; and would most resemble sweet
instruments hung up in cases, that keep their sounds to
themselves.

> TIMON, *Timon of Athens*, I.II.95

The amity that wisdom knits not, folly may easily untie.

> ULYSSES, *Troilus and Cressida*, II.III.101

FUNERALS
see also DEATH; DYING WORDS; EPITAPH; EULOGY; GRIEF; LOSS; MOURNING; SORROW

Lo in this hollow cradle take thy rest,
My throbbing heart shall rock thee day and night.

Venus and Adonis, 1185

May he continue
Long in his Highness' favor, and do justice
For truth's sake and his conscience, that his bones,
When he has run his course and sleeps in blessings,
May have a tomb of orphans' tears wept on him!

CARDINAL WOLSEY, *Henry VIII*, III.II.395

With twenty thousand kisses, and to drain
Upon his face an ocean of salt tears,
To tell my love unto his dumb deaf trunk,
And with my fingers feel his hand unfeeling.
But all in vain are these mean obsequies.

KING HENRY, *2 Henry VI*, III.II.142

Set down, set down your honorable load,
If honor may be shrouded in a hearse.

LADY ANNE, *Richard III*, I.II.1

Inter their bodies as become their births.

RICHMOND, *Richard III*, V.V.15

FUTILITY
see also HOPELESSNESS; IMPOSSIBILITY

Thus are my blossoms blasted in the bud,
And caterpillars eat my leaves away.

DUKE OF YORK, *2 Henry VI*, III.I.89

To say nothing, to do nothing, to know nothing, and to have
nothing, is to be a great part of your title, which is
within a very little of nothing.

LAVATCH, *All's Well That Ends Well*, II.IV.24

Had I but died an hour before this chance,
I had liv'd a blessèd time; for from this instant
There's nothing serious in mortality:
All is but toys: renown and grace is dead,
The wine of life is drawn, and the mere lees
Is left this vault to brag of.

MACBETH, *Macbeth*, II.III.91

FUTURE
see also PROPHECY; TIME

The woe's to come; the children yet unborn
Shall feel this day as sharp to them as thorn.

BISHOP OF CARLISLE, *Richard II*, IV.I.322

O that a man might know
The end of this day's business ere it come!
But it sufficeth that the day will end,
And then the end is known.

BRUTUS, Julius Caesar, V.I.122

The fringèd curtains of thine eye advance,
And say what thou seest yond.

PROSPERO, The Tempest, I.II.409

GAMBLING
see also CHANCE; FORTUNE; LUCK

As false as dicers' oaths.

HAMLET, Hamlet, III.IV.45

Your life, good master,
Must shuffle for itself.

IMOGEN, Cymbeline, V.V.104

If Hercules and Lichas play at dice
Which is the better man, the greater throw
May turn by fortune from the weaker hand.

PRINCE OF MOROCCO, The Merchant of Venice, II.I.32

GARDENING
see also AGRICULTURE; ENVIRONMENTALISM; FLOWERS; NATURE

This garden has a world of pleasures in't.

ARCITE, The Two Noble Kinsmen, II.II.118

We at time of year
Do wound the bark, the skin of our fruit-trees,
Lest being over-proud in sap and blood,
With too much riches it confound itself.

GARDENER, Richard II, III.IV.57

Go bind thou up young dangling apricocks,
Which like unruly children make their sire
Stoop with oppression of their prodigal weight;
Give some supportance to the bending twigs.
Go thou, and like an executioner
Cut off the heads of too fast growing sprays,
That look too lofty in our commonwealth.

GARDENER, Richard II, III.IV.29

Superfluous branches
We lop away, that bearing boughs may live.

GARDENER, Richard II, III.IV.63

Blessed garden,
And fruit and flowers more blessed, that still blossom
As her bright eyes shine on ye, would I were,

For all the fortune of my life hereafter,
Yon little tree, yon blooming apricock!

PALAMON, *The Two Noble Kinsmen*, II.II.232

GENDER
see also FEMINISM; MEN; MISOGYNY; SEX; WOMEN

Thou art no man, though of a man's complexion
For men will kiss even by their own direction.

Venus and Adonis, 215

Be that you are,
That is a woman; if you be more, you're none;
If you be one (as you are well-express'd
By all external warrants), show it now,
By putting on the destin'd livery.

ANGELO, *Measure for Measure*, II.IV.134

Art thou a man? Thy form cries out thou art;
Thy tears are womanish, thy wild acts denote
The unreasonable fury of a beast.
Unseemly woman in a seeming man,
And ill-seeming beast in seeming both,
Thou hast amaz'd me!

FRIAR LAWRENCE, *Romeo and Juliet*, III.III

Thy beauty hath made me effeminate,
And in my temper soft'ned valor's steel!

ROMEO, *Romeo and Juliet*, III.I.113

If I were a woman I would kiss as many of you as had beards
that pleas'd me, complexions that lik'd me, and breaths that
I defied not.

ROSALIND, *As You Like It*, EPILOGUE.18

GENEROSITY
see also CHARITY; GIFTS; KINDNESS

I seek not to wax great by others' waning,
Or gather wealth, I care not with what envy.
Sufficeth that I have maintains my state
And sends the poor well pleased from my gate.

ALEXANDER IDEN, *2 Henry VI*, IV.X.20

And even as willingly at thy feet I leave it
As others would ambitiously receive it.

DUKE OF GLOUCESTER, *2 Henry VI*, II.III.35

O Antony,
Thou mine of bounty, how wouldst thou have paid
My better service, when my turpitude

Thou dost so crown with gold!
> ENOBARBUS, *Antony and Cleopatra*, IV.VI.30

For what doth cherish weeds but gentle air?
And what makes robbers bold but too much lenity?
> LORD CLIFFORD, *3 Henry VI*, II.VI.21

That churchman bears a bounteous mind indeed,
A hand as fruitful as the land that feeds us;
His dews fall every where.
> SIR THOMAS LOVELL, *Henry VIII*, I.III.55

I take all and your several visitations
So kind to heart, 'tis not enough to give;
Methinks, I could deal kingdoms to my friends,
And ne'er be weary.
> TIMON, *Timon of Athens*, I.II.218

He is gone happy, and has left me rich.
Then, as in grateful virtue I am bound
To your free heart, I do return those talents,
Doubled with thanks and service, from whose help
I deriv'd liberty.
> VENTIDIUS, *Timon of Athens*, I.II.4

GENTLENESS
see also KINDNESS

Since men prove beasts, let beasts bear gentle minds.
> *The Rape of Lucrece*, 1148

They are as gentle
As zephyrs blowing below the violet,
Not wagging his sweet head.
> BELARIUS, *Cymbeline*, IV.II.171

This milky gentleness and course of yours
Though I condemn not, yet, under pardon,
You are much more attax'd for want of wisdom
Than prais'd for harmful mildness.
> GONERIL, *King Lear*, I.IV.341

Your bear a gentle mind, and heav'nly blessings
Follow such creatures.
> LORD CHAMBERLAIN, *Henry VIII*, II.III.57

As I can remember, by my troth
I never did her hurt in all my life.
I never spake bad word, nor did ill turn
To any living creature. Believe me law,
I never kill'd a mouse, nor hurt a fly;

I trod upon a worm against my will,
But I wept for't.

MARINA, Pericles, IV.I.73

He is not the flower of courtesy, but I'll warrant him, as
gentle as a lamb.

NURSE, Romeo and Juliet, II.v.43

GHOSTS
see also SUPERNATURAL

Come, poor babe.
I have heard (but not believ'd) the spirits o' th' dead
May walk again. If such thing be, thy mother
Appear'd to me last night; for ne'er was dream
So like a waking. To me comes a creature,
Sometimes her head on one side, some another—
I never say a vessel of like sorrow,
So fill'd, and so becoming; in pure white robes,
Like very sanctity, she did approach
My cabin where I lay; thrice bow'd before me,
And (gasping to begin some speech) her eyes
Became two spouts.

ANTIGONUS, The Winter's Tale, III.III.15

Vex not his ghost. O, let him pass, he hates him
That would upon the rack of this tough world
Stretch him out longer.

EARL OF KENT, King Lear, V.III.314

Oft have I seen a timely-parted ghost,
Of ashy semblance, meager, pale, and bloodless,
Being all descended to the laboring heart,
Who, in the conflict that it holds with death,
Attracts the same for aidance 'gainst the enemy,
Which with the heart there cools an ne'er returneth
To blush and beautify the cheek again.
But see, his face is black and full of blood.

EARL OF WARWICK, 2 Henry VI, III.II.161

No more, you petty spirits of region low,
Offend our hearing; hush! How dare you ghosts
Accuse the Thunderer, whose bolt, you know,
Sky-planted, batters all rebelling coasts?

JUPITER, Cymbeline, V.IV.93

By the apostle Paul, shadows to-night
Have strook more terror to the soul of Richard
Than can the substance of ten thousand soldiers
Armèd in proof and led by shallow Richmond.

KING RICHARD, Richard III, V.III.216

Were I the ghost that walk'd, I'd bid you mark
Her eye, and tell me for what dull part in't
You chose her; then I'd shriek, that even your ears
Should rift to hear me, and the words that follow'd
Should be "Remember mine."

PAULINA, The Winter's Tale, V.I.63

Sometime he talks as if Duke Humphrey's ghost
Were by his side; sometime he calls the King,
And whispers to his pillow as to him
The secrets of his overcharged soul.

VAUX, 2 Henry VI, III.II.373

GIFTS
see also CHARITY; GENEROSITY

Thy gift, thy tables, are within my brain
Full character'd with lasting memory,
Which shall above that idle rank remain
Beyond all date, even to eternity.

SONNET 122, 1–4

What need the bridge much broader than the flood?
The fairest grant is the necessity.

DON PEDRO, Much Ado About Nothing, I.I.316

The gifts she looks from me are pack'd and lock'd
Up in my heart, which I have given already,
But not deliver'd.

FLORIZEL, The Winter's Tale, IV.IV.358

Pray'rs and tears have mov'd me, gifts could never.

LORD SAY, 2 Henry VI, IV.VII.68

Rich gifts wax poor when givers prove unkind.

OPHELIA, Hamlet, III.I.100

My recompense is thanks, that's all,
Yet my good will is great, though the gift small.

THAISA, Pericles, III.IV.17

GLORY
see also FAME; GREATNESS; HONOR

Princes have but their titles for their glories,
An outward honor for an inward toil,
And for unfelt imaginations
They often feel a world of restless cares;
So that between their titles and low name
There's nothing differs but the outward fame.

BRAKENBURY, Richard III, I.IV.78

Glory is like a circle in the water,
Which never ceaseth to enlarge itself,
Till by broad spreading it disperse to nought.
With Henry's death the English circle ends.

JOAN DE PUCELLE, *1 Henry VI*, I.II.133

Outside or inside, I will not return
Till my attempt so much be glorified
As to my ample hope was promised
Before I drew this gallant head of war,
And cull'd these fiery spirits from the world,
To outlook conquest and to win renown
Even in the jaws of danger and of death.

LEWIS, *King John*, V.II.110

Ha, majesty! how high thy glory tow'rs
When the rich blood of kings is set on fire!

PHILIP THE BASTARD, *King John*, II.I.350

GOOD
see also INNOCENCE; PURITY; VIRTUE

And when old Time shall lead him to his end,
Goodness and he fill up one monument!

DUKE OF BUCKINGHAM, *Henry VIII*, II.I.93

Some good I mean to do,
Despite mine own nature.

EDMUND, *King Lear*, V.III.244

Poor honest lord, brought low by his own heart,
Undone by goodness! Strange, unusual blood,
When man's worst sin is, he does too much good!
Who then dares to be half so kind again?

FLAVIUS, *Timon of Athens*, IV.II.36

There is some soul of goodness in things evil,
Would men observing distill it out.

KING HENRY, *Henry V*, IV.I.4

As I intend more good to you and yours
Than ever you or yours by me were harm'd!

KING RICHARD, *Richard III*, IV.IV.237

Good alone
Is good, without a name; vileness is so:
The property by what it is should go,
Not by the title.

KING OF FRANCE, *All's Well That Ends Well*, II.III.128

There's nothing ill can dwell in such a temple
If the ill spirit have so fair a house,

Good things will strive to dwell with't.
MIRANDA, The Tempest, I.II.458

Your honor and your goodness teach me to't
Without your vows.
PERICLES, Pericles, III.III.26

GOSSIP
see also RUMORS; SCANDAL

Shall she live to betray this guilt of ours,
A long-tongu'd babbling gossip.
AARON, Titus Andronicus, IV.II.150

Truths would be tales,
Where now half tales be truths.
AGRIPPA, Antony and Cleopatra, II.II.133

What great ones do, the less will prattle of.
CAPTAIN, Twelfth Night, I.II.33

You have heard of the news abroad,
I mean the whisper'd ones, for they are yet but
ear-bussing arguments?
CURAN, King Lear, II.I.6

Thou find'st to be too busy is some danger.
HAMLET, Hamlet, III.IV.33

His forward voice now is to speak well
of his friend; his backward voice is to utter foul
speeches and to detract.
STEPHANO, The Tempest, II.II.90

GOVERNMENT
see also AUTHORITY; DEMOCRACY; LEADERSHIP; POLITICS AND POWER; PUBLIC OPIN-
ION; TYRANNY

Mine's not an idle cause; The Duke himself,
Or any of my brothers of the state,
Cannot but feel this wrong as 'twere their own;
For if such actions may have passage free,
Bond-slaves and pagans shall our statesmen be.
BRABANTIO, Othello, I.II.95

He shall well know
The noble tribunes are the people's mouth,
And we their hands.
CITIZEN, Coriolanus, III.I.269

In him there is a hope of government,
Which is his nonage, council under him,

And in his full and ripened years, himself,
No doubt shall then, and till then, govern well.

CITIZEN, Richard III, II.III.12

For government, tough high, and low, and lower,
Put into parts, doth keep in one consent,
Congreeing in a full and natural close,
Like music.

DUKE OF EXETER, Henry V, I.II.180

There's not, I think, a subject
That sits in heart-grief and uneasiness
Under the sweet shade of your government.

EARL OF CAMBRIDGE, Henry V, II.II.26

They say there's but five upon this isle: we are three
of them; if th' other two be brain'd like us, the state
totters.

TRINCULO, The Tempest, III.II.5

GRACE
see also MERCY; SPIRITUALITY AND RELIGION

Alack, when one our grace we have forgot,
Nothing goes right—we would, and we would not.

ANGELO, Measure for Measure, IV.IV.33

Be now as prodigal of all dear grace
As nature was in making graces dear,
When she did starve the general world beside
And prodigally gave them all to you.

BOYET, Love's Labor's Lost, II.I.9

Every wink of any eye some new grace
will be born.

GENTLEMEN, The Winter's Tale, V.II.110

O momentary grace of mortal men,
Which we more hunt for than the grace of God!

LORD HASTINGS, Richard III, III.IV.96

Though all things foul would wear the brow of grace,
Yet grace must still look so.

MALCOLM, Macbeth, IV.III.22

The hand that hath made you fair hath made you good; the
goodness that is cheap in beauty makes beauty brief in
goodness; but grace, soul of your complexion, shall keep the
body of it ever fair.

VINCENTIO, DUKE OF VIENNA, Measure for Measure, III.I.180

If I cannot persuade thee
Rather to show a noble grace to both parts
Than seek the end of one, thou shalt no sooner
March to assault thy country than to tread
(Trust to't, thou shalt not) on thy mother's womb
That brought thee to this world.

VOLUMNIA, *Coriolanus*, V.III.120

GRANDPARENTS
see also DAUGHTERS; FATHERHOOD; HEREDITY; MOTHERHOOD; SONS

Thy famous grandfather
Doth live again in thee. Long mayst thou live
To bear his image and renew his glories!

EARL OF OXFORD, *3 Henry VI*, V.IV.52

A grandam's name is little less in love
Than is the doting title of a mother.

KING RICHARD, *Richard III*, IV.IV.299

I should sin
To think but nobly of my grandmother.
Good wombs have borne bad sons.

MIRANDA, *The Tempest*, I.II.117

GRATITUDE
see also BLESSING

Thanks to men
Of noble minds is honorable meed.

BASSIANUS, *Titus Andronicus*, I.I.215

For your great graces
Heap'd upon me, poor undeserver, I
Can nothing render but allegiant thanks.

CARDINAL WOLSEY, *Henry VIII*, II.II.174

Ingratitude is monstrous,
and for the multitude to be ungrateful were to
make a monster of the multitude; of the which we
being members, should bring ourselves to be monstrous
members.

CITIZEN, *Coriolanus*, II.III.9

The sin of my ingratitude even now
Was heavy on me. Thou art so far before,
That swiftest wing of recompense is slow
To overtake thee. Would thou hadst less deserv'd,
That the proportion both of thanks and payment
Might have been mine! Only I have left to say,
More is thy due than more than all can pay.

DUNCAN, *Macbeth*, I.IV.15

The thanks I give
Is telling you that I am poor of thanks,
And scarce can spare them.

IMOGEN, *Cymbeline*, II.III.87

My life itself, and the best heart of it,
Thanks you for this great care.

KING HENRY, *Henry VIII*, I.II.I

Thou better know'st
The offices of nature, bond of childhood,
Effects of courtesy, dues of gratitude.

LEAR, *King Lear*, II.IV.177

The poorest service is repaid with thanks.

PETRUCHIO, *The Taming of the Shrew*, IV.III.45

Time as long again
Would be fill'd up, my brother, with our thanks.

POLIXENES, *The Winter's Tale*, I.II.3

To be more thankful to thee
shall be my study, and my profit therein the heaping
friendships.

POLIXENES, *The Winter's Tale*, IV.II.18

GREATNESS
see also FAME; GLORY; HERO; HONOR; NOBILITY; ROYALTY

Why, man, he doth bestride the narrow world
Like a Colussus, and we petty men
Walk under his huge legs, and peep about
To find ourselves dishonorable graves.
Men at some time are masters of their fates;
The fault, dear Brutus, is not in our stars,
But in ourselves, that we are underlings.
Brutus and Caesar: what should be in that "Caesar"?
Why should that name be sounded more than yours?
Write them together, yours is as fair a name;
Sound them, it doth become the mouth as well;
Weigh them, it is as heavy; conjure with 'em,
"Brutus" will start a spirit as soon as "Caesar."
Now in the names of all the gods at once,
Upon what meat doth this our Caesar feed
That he is grown so great?

CASSIUS, *Julius Caesar*, I.II.135

The soul and body rive not more in parting
Than greatness going off.

CHARMIAN, *Antony and Cleopatra*, IV.XIII.5

Be it known that we, the greatest, are misthought
For things that others do; and when we fall,
We answer others' merits in our name,
Are therefore to be pitied.

CLEOPATRA, *Antony and Cleopatra*, V.II.176

But in short space
It rain'd down fortune show'ring on your head,
And such a flood of greatness fell on you,
What with our help, what with the absent King,
What with the injuries of a wanton time.

EARL OF WORCESTER, *1 Henry IV*, V.I.46

Rightly to be great
Is not to stir without great argument,
But greatly to find quarrel in a straw
When honor's at the stake.

HAMLET, *Hamlet*, IV.IV.53

And yet but justice; for though
This king were great, his greatness was no guard
To bar heaven's shaft, but sin had his reward.

HELICANUS, *Pericles*, II.IV.13

Some are born great, some achieve greatness, and some have
greatness thrust upon 'em.

MALVOLIO (READING), *Twelfth Night*, II.V.145

So doth the greater glory dim the less:
A substitute shines brightly as a king
Until a king be by, and then his state
Empties itself, as doth an inland brook
Into the main of waters.

PORTIA, *The Merchant of Venice*, V.I.93

If I do grow great, I'll
grow less, for I'll purge and leave sack, and live
cleanly as a nobleman should do.

SIR JOHN FALSTAFF, *1 Henry IV*, V.IV.163

Base men by his endowments are made great.

WILLOUGHBY, *Richard II*, II.III.139

GREED
see also MONEY; WEALTH

Let me tell you, Cassius, you yourself
Are much condemn'd to have an itching palm,
To sell and mart your offices for gold
To undeservers.

BRUTUS, *Julius Caesar*, IV.III.9

See, sons, what things you are!
How quickly nature falls into revolt
When gold becomes her object!
KING HENRY IV, 2 Henry IV, IV.v.64

There grows
In my most ill-compos'd affection such
A stanchless avarice that, were I king,
I should cut off the nobles for their lands,
Desire his jewels, and this other's house,
And my more-having would be as a sauce
To make me hunger more, that I should forge
Quarrels unjust against the good and loyal,
Destroying them for wealth.
MALCOLM, Macbeth, IV.III.76

For their love
Lies in their purses, and whoso empties them
By so much fills their hearts with deadly hate.
SIR JOHN BAGOT, Richard II, II.II.129

O thou sweet king-killer, and dear divorce
'Twixt natural son and sire! thou bright defiler
Of Hymen's purest bed! thou valiant Mars!
Thou ever young, fresh, lov'd, and delicate wooer,
Whose blush doth thaw the consecrated snow
That lies on Dian's lap! thou visible god,
That sold'rest close impossibilities,
And mak'st them kiss? that speak'st with every tongue
To every purpose! O thou touch of hearts,
Think thy slave man rebels, and by thy virtue
Set them into confounding odds, that beasts
May have the world in empire!
TIMON, Timon of Athens, IV.III.381

GRIEF
see also CRYING AND TEARS; LOSS; MOURNING; SADNESS; SORROW

Grief hath two tongues, and never woman yet
Could rule them both without ten women's wit.
Venus and Adonis, 1007

Every one can master a grief but he that has it.
BENEDICK, Much Ado About Nothing, III.II.28

Honest plain words best pierce the ear of grief.
BEROWNE, Love's Labor's Lost, V.II.753

My particular grief
Is of so flood-gate and o'erbearing nature

That it engluts and swallows other sorrows,
And it is still itself.
BRABANTIO, *Othello*, I.III.55

I will instruct my sorrows to be proud,
For grief is proud and makes his owner stoop.
To me and to the state of my great grief
Let kings assemble; for my grief's so great
That no supporter but the huge firm earth
Can hold it up.
CONSTANCE, *King John*, III.i.68

Grief boundeth where it falls,
Not with the empty hollowness, but weight.
DUCHESS OF GLOUCESTER, *Richard II*, I.ii.58

No joyful tongue gave him his welcome home,
But dust was thrown upon his sacred head,
Which with such gentle sorrow he shook off,
His face still combating tears and smiles,
The badges of his grief and patience.
DUKE OF YORK, *Richard II*, V.ii.29

Better I were distract,
So should my thoughts be sever'd from my griefs,
And woes by wrong imaginations lose
The knowledge of themselves.
EARL OF GLOUCESTER, *King Lear*, IV.vi.281

Alas, poor Yorick! I knew him, Horatio, a fellow of
infinite jest, of most excellent fancy. He hath bore me on
his back a thousand times, and now how abhorr'd in my
imagination it is! My gorge rises at it. Here hung those
lips that I have kiss'd know not how oft. Where be your
gibes now, your gambols, your songs, your flashes of
merriment, that were wont to set the table on a roar? Not
one now to mock your own grinning?—Quite chap-fall'n.
HAMLET, *Hamlet*, V.i.184

'Tis not alone my inky cloak, good mother
Nor customary suits of solemn black,
Nor windy suspiration of forc'd breath,
No, nor the fruitful river in the eye,
Nor the dejected havior on the visage,
Together with all forms, moods, shapes of grief,
That can denote me truly. These indeed seem,
For they are actions that a man might play,
But I have that within which passes show,
These but the trappings and the suits of woe.
HAMLET, *Hamlet*, I.ii.77

Good my lords,
I am not prone to weeping, as our sex
Commonly are, the want of which vain dew
Perchance shall dry your pities; but I have
That honorable grief lodg'd here which burns
Worse than tears drown.

HERMIONE, *The Winter's Tale*, II.I.107

Thy grief is but thy absence for a time.

JOHN OF GAUNT, *Richard II*, I.III.258

'Tis very true, my grief lies all within,
And these external manners of laments
Are merely shadows to the unseen grief
That swells with silence in the tortur'd soul.

KING RICHARD, *Richard II*, IV.I.295

Some grief shows much of love,
But much of grief shows still some want of wit.

LADY CAPULET, *Romeo and Juliet*, III.V.72

The grief that does not speak
Whispers the o'er-fraught heart, and bids it break.

MALCOLM, *Macbeth*, IV.III.209

A heavy heart bears not a humble tongue.

PRINCESS OF FRANCE, *Love's Labor's Lost*, V.II.737

He's something stain'd
With grief (that's beauty's canker).

PROSPERO, *The Tempest*, I.II.414

Oft have I heard that grief soften the mind,
And makes it fearful and degenerate.

QUEEN MARGARET, *2 Henry VI*, IV.IV.I

To weep is to make less the depth of grief.

RICHARD, DUKE OF GLOUCESTER, *3 Henry VI*, II.I.85

GROWING UP
see also AGING; CHILDREN; YOUTH

I had rather
Have skipp'd from sixteen years of age to sixty,
To have turn'd my leaping time into a crutch,
Than have seen this.

ARVIRAGUS, *Cymbeline*, IV.II.198

"Ay," quoth my uncle Gloucester,
"Small herbs have grace, great weeds do grow apace."

And since, methinks I would not grow so fast,
Because sweet flow'rs are slow and weeds make haste.
DUKE OF YORK, Richard III, II.IV.12

Marry (they say) my uncle grew so fast
That he could gnaw at two hours old.
DUKE OF YORK, Richard III, II.IV.27

O Harry, thou hast robb'd me of my youth!
I better brook the loss of brittle life
Than those proud titles thou has won of me.
HOTSPUR, 1 Henry IV, V.IV.77

We were, fair queen,
Two lads that thought there was no more behind
But such a day to-morrow as to-day,
And to be boy eternal.
POLIXENES, The Winter's Tale, I.II.63

I would there were no age between ten and
three-and-twenty, or that youth would sleep out
the rest; for these is nothing in the between but getting
wenches with child, wronging the ancientry, stealing,
fighting.
SHEPHERD, The Winter's Tale, III.III.59

GUILT
see also ACCUSATION; CONFESSION; CONSCIENCE; SHAME

The guilt being great, the fear doth still exceed.
The Rape of Lucrece, 229

Red cheeks and fiery eyes blaze forth her wrong.
Venus and Adonis, 219

Pray can I not,
Though inclination be as sharp as will.
My stronger guilt defeats my strong intent,
And, like a man to double business bound,
I stand in pause where I shall first begin,
And both neglect.
CLAUDIUS, Hamlet, III.III.38

So full of artless jealousy is guilt,
It spills itself in fearing to be spilt.
GERTRUDE, Hamlet, IV.V.19

All three of them are desperate; their great guilt
(Like poison given to work a great time after)
Now 'gins to bite the spirits.
GONZALO, The Tempest, III.III.104

I could accuse me of such things that it were better my
mother had not borne me.

HAMLET, Hamlet, III.I.22

The guilt of conscience take thou for thy labor,
But neither my good word nor princely favor.
With Cain go wander through shades of night,
And never show thy head by day nor light.

BULLINGBROOK, Richard II, V.VI.41

Lady M. Out, damn'd spot! out I say! One—two—why then
'tis time to do't. Hell is murky. Fie, my lord, fie, a
soldier, and afeared? What need we fear who knows it, when
none can call our pow'r to accompt? Yet who would have
thought the old man to have had so much blood in him?
Doct. Do you mark that?
Lady M. The Thane of Fife had a wife; where is she now?
What, will these hands ne'er be clean?

LADY MACBETH, DOCTOR, Macbeth, V.I.35

Close pent-up guilts,
Rive your concealing continents, and cry
These dreadful summoners grace. I am a man
More sinn'd against than sinning.

LEAR, King Lear, III.II.57

What hands are here? Hah! they pluck out mine eyes.
Will all great Neptune's ocean wash this blood
Clean from my hand? No; this my hand will rather
The multitudinous seas incarnadine,
Making the green one red.

MACBETH, Macbeth, II.II.56

HABIT

Custom calls me to't.
What custom wills, in all things should we do't,
The dust on antique time would lie unswept,
And mountainous error be too highly heap'd
For truth to o'erpeer.

CORIOLANUS, Coriolanus, II.III.117

That monster custom, who all sense doth eat,
Of habits devil, is angel yet in this,
That to the use of actions fair and good
He likewise gives a frock or livery
That aptly is put on.

HAMLET, Hamlet, III.IV.161

How use doth breed a habit in a man!

VALENTINE, The Two Gentlemen of Verona, V.IV.1

HAPPINESS
see also JOY; PLEASURE; SATISFACTION

> O happiness enjoy'd but of a few,
> And if posssess'd, as soon decay'd and done
> As is the morning's silver melting dew
> Against the golden splendor of the sun!
>
> *The Rape of Lucrece*, 22

> A merry heart goes all the day.
>
> AUTOLYCUS, *The Winter's Tale*, IV.III.125

> Many years of happy days befall
> My gracious sovereign, my most loving liege!
>
> BULLINGBROOK, *Richard II*, I.I.20

> How bitter a thing it is to look into happiness through
> another man's eyes.
>
> ORLANDO, *As You Like It*, V.II.43

> I fear our happiness is at the height.
>
> QUEEN ELIZABETH, *Richard III*, I.III.41

HASTE
see also RASHNESS; SPEED

> Those that with haste will make a mighty fire
> Begin it with weak straws.
>
> CASSIUS, *Julius Caesar*, I.III.107

> Although I joy in thee
> I have no joy of this contract to-night.
> It is too rash, too unadvis'd, too sudden,
> Too like the lightning, which doth cease to be
> Ere one can say it lightens.
>
> JULIET, *Romeo and Juliet*, II.II.116

> If it were done, when 'tis done, then 'twere well
> It were done quickly.
>
> MACBETH, *Macbeth*, I.VII.1

> Rom. O, let us hence, I stand on sudden haste.
> Fri. L. Wisely and slowly, they stumble that run fast.
>
> ROMEO, FRIAR LAWRENCE, *Romeo and Juliet*, II.III.93

HATRED
see also BIGOTRY AND INTOLERANCE; CONTEMPT; MISANTHROPY; MISOGYNY

> But that thou none lov'st is most evident;
> For thou are so possess'd with murd'ous hate,
> That 'gainst thyself thou stick'st not to conspire,
> Seeking that beauteous roof to ruinate
> Which to repair should be thy chief desire.
>
> SONNET 10, 4–8

There is no hate in loving.

The Rape of Lucrece, 240

Speak, Winchester, for boiling choler chokes
The hollow passage of my poison'd voice,
By sight of these our baleful enemies.

DUKE OF YORK, *1 Henry VI*, V.IV.120

See what a scourge is laid upon your hate,
That heaven finds means to kill your joys with love.

ESCALUS, PRINCE OF VERONA, *Romeo and Juliet*, V.III.292

Deep malice makes too deep incision.

KING RICHARD, *Richard II*, I.I.155

And, by my soul, this pale and angry rose,
As cognizance of my blood-drinking hate,
Will I for ever and my faction wear,
Until it wither with me to my grave,
Or flourish to the height of my degree.

RICHARD PLANTAGENET, *1 Henry VI*, II.IV.107

Bass. Do all men kill the things they do not love?
Shy. Hates any man the thing he would not kill?
Bass. Every offense is not a hate at first.
Shy. What, wouldst thou have a serpent sting thee twice?

SHYLOCK, BASSANIO, *The Merchant of Venice*, IV.I.66

HEALING

see also DRUGS AND MEDICATION; NATURAL MEDICINE; PHYSICIANS; RECOVERY

Diseases desperate grown
By desperate appliance are reliev'd,
Or not at all.

CLAUDIUS, *Hamlet*, IV.III.9

Please her appetite,
And do it home; it cures her ipso facto
The melancholy humor that infects her.

DOCTOR, *The Two Noble Kinsmen*, V.II.37

Give me leave
To speak my mind, and I will through and through
Cleanse the foul body of th' infected world,
If they will patiently receive my medicine.

JAQUES, *As You Like It*, II.VII.58

We have done deeds of charity,
Made peace of enmity, fair love of hate,
Between these swelling wrong-incensèd peers.

KING EDWARD, *Richard III*, II.I.50

Canst thou not minister to a mind diseas'd,
Pluck from the memory a rooted sorrow,
Raze out the written troubles of the brain,
And with some sweet oblivious antidote
Cleanse the stuff'd bosom of that perilous stuff
Which weighs upon the heart?

MACBETH, Macbeth, V.III.40

Before the curing of a strong disease,
Even in the instant of repair and health,
The fit is strongest, evils that take leave,
On their departure most of all show evil.

PANDULPH, King John, III.IV.112

HEART
see also DESIRE; LOVE

For lovers say, the heart hath treble wrong
When it is barr'd the aidance of the tongue.

Venus and Adonis, 329

But his hot heart, which fond desire doth scorch,
Puffs forth another wind that fires the torch.

The Rape of Lucrece, 314

Heart, once be stronger than thy continent,
Crack thy frail case!

ANTONY, Antony and Cleopatra, IV.XIV.40

But his flaw'd heart
(Alack, too weak the conflict to support!)
'Twist two extremes of passion, joy and grief,
Burst smilingly.

EDGAR, King Lear, V.III.197

A light heart lives long.

KATHERINE, Love's Labor's Lost, V.I.18

But a good heart, Kate, is the sun and the
moon, or rather the sun and not the moon; for it shines
bright and never changes, but keeps his course truly.

KING HENRY, Henry V, V.II.162

Yes, my good lord, a pure unspotted heart,
Never yet taint with love, I send the King.

MARGARET, 1 Henry VI, V.III.182

No, no, my heart will burst and if I speak,
And I will speak, that so my heart may burst.

QUEEN MARGARET, 3 Henry VI, V.V.59

By innocence I swear, and by my youth,
I have one heart, one bosom, and one truth,
And that no woman has, nor never none
Shall mistress be of it, save I alone.

VIOLA, Twelfth Night, III.I.157

HEAVEN
see also AFTERLIFE; ANGELS; HIGHER POWER; SPIRITUALITY AND RELIGION

The sun that shines from heaven shines but warm,
And lo I lie between that sun and thee.

Venus and Adonis, 193

My robe,
And my integrity to heaven, is all
I dare now call mine own.

CARDINAL WOLSEY, Henry VIII, III.II.452

Heaven has an end in all.

DUKE OF BUCKINGHAM, Henry VIII, II.I.124

Look how the floor of heaven
Is thick inlaid with patens of bright gold.
There's not the smallest orb which thou behold'st
But in his motion like an angel sings,
Still quiring to young-ey'd cherubins;
Such harmony is in immortal souls,
But whilst this muddy vesture of decay
Doth grossly close it in, we cannot hear it.

LORENZO, The Merchant of Venice, V.I.58

Heaven is above all yet; there sits judge
That no king can corrupt.

QUEEN KATHERINE, Henry VIII, III.I.100

Simple plain Clarence, I do love thee so
That I will shortly send thy soul to heaven,
If heaven will take the present at our hands.

RICHARD, DUKE OF GLOUCESTER, Richard III, I.I.118

HELL
see also AFTERLIFE; EVIL; SPIRITUALITY AND RELIGION

And after all this fearful homage done,
Give thee thy hire and send thy soul to hell,
Pernicious blood-sucker of sleeping men!

EARL OF WARWICK, 2 Henry VI, III.II.224

He, my lady,
Hath into monstrous habits put the graces
That once were his, and is become as black
As if besmear'd in hell.

KING HENRY, Henry VIII, I.II.121

Then since the heavens have shap'd my body so,
Let hell make crook'd my mind to answer it.
RICHARD, DUKE OF GLOUCESTER, *3 Henry VI*; V.VI.78

HELP
see also CHARITY

O, help me, help me! Pluck but off these
rags; and then, death, death!
AUTOLYCUS, *The Winter's Tale*, V.III.52

True it is that we have seen better days,
And have with holy bell been knoll'd to church,
And sat at good men's feasts, and wip'd our eyes
Of drops that sacred pity hath engend'red;
And therefore sit you down in gentleness,
And take upon command what help we have
That to your wanting may be minist'red.
DUKE SENIOR, *As You Like It*, II.VII.120

Alas, poor souls, it griev'd my heart to
hear what pitiful cries they made to us to help them,
when, well a day, we could scarce help ourselves.
FISHERMAN, *Pericles*, II.I.20

What I have been I have forgot to know,
But what I am, want teaches me to think on:
A man throng'd up with cold, my veins are chill,
And have no more of life than may suffice
To give my tongue that heat to ask your help;
Which if you shall refuse, when I am dead,
For that I am a man, pray you see me buried.
PERICLES, *Pericles*, II.I.71

HEREDITY
see also BIRTH; CHILDREN; CHILDREN OF UNMARRIED PARENTS; DAUGHTERS;
FATHERHOOD; GRANDPARENTS; MOTHERHOOD; SONS

But that thy face is vizard-like, unchanging,
Made impudent with use of evil deeds,
I would assay, proud queen, to make thee blush.
To tell thee whence thou cam'st, of whom deriv'd,
Were shame enough to shame thee, wert thou not shameless.
DUKE OF YORK, *3 Henry VI*, I.IV.116

This is a stem
Of that victorious stock; and let us fear
The native mightiness and fate of him.
FRENCH KING, *Henry V*, II.IV.62

But his body
And fiery mind illustrate a brave father.

HIPPOLYTA, *The Two Noble Kinsmen*, II.V.22

God pardon thee! yet let me wonder, Harry,
At thy affections, which do hold a wing
Quite from the flight of all thy ancestors.

KING HENRY, *1 Henry IV*, III.II.29

Behold, my lords,
Although the print be little, the whole matter
And copy of the father—eye, nose, lip,
The trick of 's frown, his forehead, nay, the valley,
The pretty dimples of his chin and cheek, his smiles,
The very mold and frame of hand, nail, finger.
And thou, good goddess Nature, which hast made it
So like him that got it, if thou hast
The ordering of the mind too, 'mongst all colors
No yellow in't, lest she suspect, as he does,
Her children not her husband's!

PAULINA, *The Winter's Tale*, II.III.98

Do you not read some tokens of my son
In the large composition of this man?

QUEEN ELINOR, *King John*, I.I.87

If then the tree may be known by
the fruit, as the fruit by the tree, then peremptorily I
speak it, there is virtue in that Falstaff.

SIR JOHN FALSTAFF, *1 Henry IV*, II.IV.428

HERESY
see also REBELLION; SPIRITUALITY AND RELIGION

Then, by the lawful power that I have,
Thou shalt stand curs'd and excommunicate,
And blessed shall he be that doth revolt
From his allegiance to an heretic,
And meritorious shall that hand be call'd,
That takes away by any secret course
Thy hateful life.

PANDULPH, *King John*, III.I.172

It is an heretic that makes the fire,
Not she which burns in't.

PAULINA, *The Winter's Tale*, II.III.115

HERO
see also COURAGE; GREATNESS

He stopp'd the fliers,

And by his rare example made the coward
Turn terror into sport; as weeds before
A vessel under sail, so men obey'd
And fell below his stem. His sword, death's stamp,
Where it did mark, it took; from face to foot
He was a thing of blood, whose every motion
Was tim'd with dying cries.

COMINIUS, Coriolanus, II.II.103

Lo, there thou stand'st, a breathing valiant man,
Of an invincible unconquer'd spirit!

GENERAL, 1 Henry VI, IV.II.31

For those that could speak low and tardily
Would turn their own perfection to abuse,
To seem like him; so that in speech, in gait,
In diet, in affections of delight,
In military rules, humors of blood,
He was the mark and glass, copy and book,
That fashion'd others.

LADY PERCY, 2 Henry IV, II.III.26

Close by the battle, ditch'd and wall'd with turf,
Which gave advantage to an ancient soldier
(An honest one, I warrant), who deserv'd
So long a breeding as his white beard came to,
In doing this for 's country.

POSTHUMUS, Cymbeline, V.III.14

HIGHER POWER
see also FAITH; SPIRITUALITY AND RELIGION

An idiot holds his bauble for a god,
And keeps the oath which by that god he swears.

AARON, Titus Andronicus, V.I.79

There's a divinity that shapes our ends,
Rough-hew them how we will.

HAMLET, Hamlet, V.II.10

It is not so with Him that all things knows
As 'tis with us that square our guess by shows;
But most it is presumption in us when
The help of heaven we count the act of men.

HELENA, All's Well That Ends Well, II.I.149

If my suspect be false, forgive me, God,
For judgment only doth belong to thee.

KING HENRY, 2 Henry VI, III.II.139

God shall be my hope,
My stay, my guide, and lanthorn to my feet.
                    KING HENRY, *2 Henry VI*, II.III.24

You should be rul'd and led
By some discretion that discerns your state
Better than you yourself.
                    REGAN, *King Lear*, II.IV.148

God have mercy upon one of our souls! He may have mercy
upon mine, but my hope is better, so look to thyself.
                    SIR TOBY (READING), *Twelfth Night*, III.IV.166

HISTORY
see also KNOWLEDGE; MEMORY; PAST; STORYTELLING

And therefore will he wipe his tables clean
And keep no tell-tale to his memory
That may repeat and history his loss
To new remembrance.
                    ARCHBISHOP, *2 Henry IV*, IV.I.199

There is a history in all men's lives,
Figuring the natures of the times deceas'd,
The which observ'd, a man may prophesy,
With a near aim, of the main chance of things
As yet not come to life, who in their seeds
And weak beginning lie intreasurèd.
                    EARL OF WARWICK, *2 Henry IV*, III.I.80

There are many events in the
womb of time which will be deliver'd.
                    IAGO, *Othello*, I.III.369

Either our history shall with full mouth
Speak freely of our acts, or else our grave,
Like Turkish mute, shall have a tongueless mouth,
Not worshipp'd with a waxen epitaph.
                    KING HENRY, *Henry V*, I.II.230

Sir, he made a chimney in my father's house,
and the bricks are alive at this day to testify it; therefore deny it not.
                    SMITH THE WEAVER, *2 Henry VI*, IV.II.148

HOME

You had much ado to make his anchor hold,
When you cast out, it still came home.
                    CAMILLO, *The Winter's Tale*, I.II.213

And all th' unsettled humors of the land,
Rash, inconsiderate, fiery voluntaries,
With ladies' faces and fierce dragons' spleens,
Have sold their fortunes at their native homes,
Bearing their birthrights proudly on their backs,
To make a hazard of new fortunes here.

CHATILLION, King John, II.I.66

For where thou art, there is the world itself,
With every several pleasure in the world.

EARL OF SUFFOLK, 2 Henry VI, III.II.362

By my troth, I will speak my conscience
of the King: I think he would not wish himself any
where but where he is.

KING HENRY, Henry V, IV.I.118

Home-keeping youth have ever homely wits.

VALENTINE, The Two Gentlemen of Verona, I.I.2

HOMELESSNESS
see also HUNGER; POVERTY

Hail, thou fair heaven!
We house i' th' rock, yet use thee not so hardly
As prouder livers do.

BELARIUS, Cymbeline, III.III.7

Then was I as a tree
Whose boughs did bend with fruit; but in one night,
A storm or robbery (call it what you will)
Shook down my mellow hangings, nay, my leaves,
And left me bare to weather.

BELARIUS, Cymbeline, III.III.60

O then, my father,
Will you permit that I shall stand condemn'd
A wandering vagabond, my rights and royalties
Plucked from my arms perforce—and given away
To upstart unthrifts? Wherefore was I born?

BULLINGBROOK, Richard II, II.III.118

You houseless poverty—
Nay, get thee in; I'll pray, and then I'll sleep.
Poor naked wretches, wheresoe'er you are,
That bide the pelting of this pitiless storm,
How shall your houseless heads and unfed sides,
Your loop'd and window'd raggedness, defend you
From seasons such as these?

LEAR, King Lear, III.IV.26

And of thy boundless goodness take some note
That for our crowned heads we have no roof.
QUEEN, The Two Noble Kinsmen, I.I.51

And I—like one lost in a thorny wood,
That rents the thorns, and is rent with the thorns,
Seeking a way, and straying from the way,
Not knowing how to find the open air,
But toiling desperately to find it out—
Torment myself to catch the English crown;
And from that torment I will free myself.
RICHARD, DUKE OF GLOUCESTER, 3 Henry VI, III.II.174

Who cannot keep his wealth must keep his house.
THIRD SERVANT, Timon of Athens, III.III.41

Here's neither bush nor shrub to bear off any
weather at all.
TRINCULO, The Tempest, II.II.18

No matter what, he's poor, and
that's revenge enough. Who can speak broader than
he that has no house to put his head in? Such may rail
against great buildings.
VARRO'S SECOND SERVANT, Timon of Athens, III.IV.62

HONESTY
see also HONOR; TRUTH

Honor and honesty
I cherish and depend on, howsoev'r
You skip them in me, and with the, fair coz,
I'll maintain my proceedings. Pray be pleas'd
To show in generous terms your griefs, since that
Your question's with your equal, who professes
To clear his own way with the mind and sword
Of a true gentleman.
ARCITE, The Two Noble Kinsmen, III.I.50

Mistake me not, I speak but as I find.
BAPTISTA, The Taming of the Shrew, II.I.66

An honest man, sir, is able to speak for himself, when a
a knave is not.
DAVY, 2 Henry IV, V.I.45

I cannot hide what I am: I must be sad when I have cause,
and smile at no man's jests; eat when I have stomach, and
wait for no man's leisure; sleep when I am drowsy, and tend
on no man's business; laugh when I am merry, and claw no
man in his humor.
DON JOHN, Much Ado About Nothing, I.III.13

A heart unspotted is not easily daunted.

> DUKE OF GLOUCESTER, *2 Henry VI*, III.i.100

I do profess to be no less than I seem, to
serve him truly that will put me in trust, to love him
that is honest, to converse with him that is wise
and says little, to fear judgment, to fight when I cannot
choose, and to eat no fish.

> EARL OF KENT, *King Lear*, I.iv.13

The weight of this sad time we must obey,
Speak what we feel, not what we ought to say.

> EDGAR, *King Lear*, V.iii.324

To be honest, as this world goes, is to be one man pick'd
out of ten thousand.

> HAMLET, *Hamlet*, II.ii.178

When truth kills truth, O devilish holy fray!

> HELENA, *A Midsummer Night's Dream*, III.ii.129

Because I cannot flatter and look fair,
Smile in men's faces, smooth, deceive, and cog,
Duck with French nods and apish courtesy,
I must be held a rancorous enemy.

> RICHARD, DUKE OF GLOUCESTER, *Richard III*, I.iii.47

Never any thing can be amiss,
When simpleness and duty tender it.

> THESEUS, *A Midsummer Night's Dream*, V.i.82

HONOR
see also DUTY; FAME; GLORY; GREATNESS; NOBILITY; REPUTATION

His word is more than the miraculous harp.

> ANTONIO, *The Tempest*, II.i.87

If I lose mine honor,
I lose myself.

> ANTONY, *Antony and Cleopatra*, III.iv.22

There is no terror, Cassius, in your threat;
For I am arm'd so strong in honesty
That they pass by me as the idle wind.

> BRUTUS, *Julius Caesar*, IV.iii.66

Set honor in one eye and death i' th' other,
And I will look on both indifferently;
For let the gods so speed me as I love
The name of honor more than I fear death.

> BRUTUS, *Julius Caesar*, I.ii.86

Life every man holds dear, but the dear man
Holds honor far more precious-dear than life.

HECTOR, *Troilus and Cressida*, V.III.27

My friends were poor, but honest.

HELENA, *All's Well That Ends Well*, I.III.195

Send danger from the east unto the west,
Do honor cross it from the north to south.

HOTSPUR, *1 Henry IV*, I.III.195

By Jove, I am not covetous for gold,
Nor care I who doth feed upon my cost'
It yearns me not if men my garments wear;
Such outward things dwell not in my desires.
But if it be a sin to covet honor,
I am the most offending soul alive.

KING HENRY, *Henry V*, IV.III.24

See that you come
Not to woo honor, but to wed it, when
The bravest questant shrinks. Find what you seek,
That fame may cry you loud.

KING OF FRANCE, *All's Well That Ends Well*, II.I.14

Honors thrive,
When rather from our acts we them derive
Than our foregoers. The mere word's a slave
Debosh'd on every tomb, on every grave
A lying trophy, and as oft is dumb
Where dust and damn'd oblivion is the tomb
Of honor'd bones indeed.

KING OF FRANCE, *All's Well That Ends Well*, II.III.135

Mine honor is my life, both grow in one,
Take honor from me, and my life is done.
Then, dear my liege, mine honor let me try;
In that I live, and for that will I die.

MOWBRAY, *Richard II*, I.I.182

Honor's train
Is longer than his foreskirt.

OLD LADY, *Henry VIII*, II.III.97

'Tis not my profit that does lead mine honor;
Mine honor, it.

POMPEY, *Antony and Cleopatra*, II.VII.76

O that estates, degrees, and offices
Were not deriv'd corruptly, and that clear honor
Were purchas'd by the merit of the wearer!

How many then should cover that stand bare?
How many be commanded that command?
How much low peasantry would then be gleaned
From the true seed of honor? and how much honor
Pick'd from the chaff and ruin of the times
To be new varnish'd?

PRINCE OF ARRAGON, The Merchant of Venice, II.IX.41

You stand upon your honor! Why, thou unconfinable baseness,
it is as much as I can do to keep the terms of honor
precise. I, I, I myself sometimes, leaving the fear of God
on the left hand and hiding mine honor in my necessity, am
fain to shuffle, to hedge, and to lurch; and yet you, rogue,
will ensconce your rages, your cat-a-mountain looks, you
red-lattice phrases, and your bold-beating oaths, under the
shelter of your honor!

SIR JOHN FALSTAFF, The Merry Wives of Windsor, II.II.20

Well, 'tis no matter, honor pricks
me on. Yea, but how if honor prick me off when
I come on? how then? Can honor set to a leg? No.
Or an arm? No. Or take away the grief of a wound?
No. Honor hath no skill in surgery then? No. What
is honor? A word. What is in that word honor?
What is that honor? Air. A trim reckoning!
Who hath it? He that died a' Wednesday. Doth he
feel it? No. Doth he hear it? No. 'Tis insensible
then? Yea, to the dead. But will't not live with the
Took it in rage, though calm'd have given't again.
I thank thee for't. My shipwrack now's no ill,
Since I have here my father gave in his will.

SIR JOHN FALSTAFF, 1 Henry IV, V.I.129

HOPE
see also FAITH; OPTIMISM; WISHES

O, out of that no hope
What great hope have you! No hope, that way, is
Another way so high a hope that even
Ambition cannot pierce a wink beyond,
But doubt discovery there.

ANTONIO, The Tempest, II.I.239

Earth hath swallowed all my hopes but she;
She's the hopeful lady of my earth.

CAPULET, Romeo and Juliet, I.II.14

The miserable have no other medicine
But only hope.

CLAUDIO, Measure for Measure, III.I.2

Look what thy soul holds dear, imagine it
To lie that way thou goest, not whence thou com'st.
Suppose the singing birds musicians,
The grass whereon thou tread'st the presence strow'd,
The flowers fair ladies, and thy steps no more
Than a delightful measure or a dance,
For gnarling sorrow hath less power to bite
The man that mocks as it and sets it light.

JOHN OF GAUNT, *Richard II*, I.III.286

And all the ruins of distressful times
Repair'd with double riches of content.
What? we have many goodly days to see:
The liquid drops of tears that you have shed
Shall come again, transform'd to orient pearl,
Advantaging their love with interest
Of ten times double gain of happiness.

KING RICHARD, *Richard III*, IV.IV.318

Was the hope drunk
Wherein you dress'd yourself? Hath is slept since?
And wakes it now to look so green and pale
At what it did so freely?

LADY MACBETH, *Macbeth*, I.VII.35

It was, my lord, who lin'd himself with hope,
Eating the air, and promise of supply,
Flatt'ring himself in project of a power
Much smaller than the smallest of thoughts,
And so with great imagination,
Proper to madmen, led his powers to death,
And winking, leapt into destruction.

LORD BARDOLPH, *2 Henry IV*, I.III.27

Hope is a curtal dog in some affairs.

PISTOL, *The Merry Wives of Windsor*, II.I.110

Hope is a lover's staff; walk hence with that
And manage it against despairing thoughts.

PROTEUS, *The Two Gentlemen of Verona*, III.I.248

Dowagers, take hands,
Let us be widows to our woes; delay
Commends us to a famishing hope.

QUEEN, *The Two Noble Kinsmen*, I.I.165

Till then fair hope must hinder live's decay.

QUEEN ELIZABETH, *3 Henry VI*, IV.IV.16

True hope is swift and flies with swallow's wings.

RICHMOND, *Richard III*, V.II.23

I am giddy; expectation whirls me round;
Th' imaginary relish is so sweet
That it enchants my sense.

TROILUS, Troilus and Cressida, III.II.18

HOPELESSNESS
see also FAITHLESSNESS; FUTILITY; IMPOSSIBILITY

Those hopes are prisoners with us.

ARCITE, The Two Noble Kinsmen, II.II.26

The hope and expectation of thy time
Is ruin'd, and the soul of every man
Prophetically do forethink thy fall.

KING HENRY, 1 Henry IV, III.II.36

Thus do the hopes we have in him touch ground
And dash themselves to pieces.

LORD MOWBRAY, 2 Henry IV, IV.I.17

HORROR

O, full of scorpions is my mind.

MACBETH, Macbeth, III.II.36

O horror, horror, horror! Tongue nor heart
Cannot conceive nor name thee!

MACDUFF, Macbeth, II.III.63

On horror's head horrors accumulate.

OTHELLO, Othello, III.III.370

HORSES AND HORSEBACK RIDING

His ears up-pric'd, his braided hanging mane
Upon his compass'd crest now stand on end,
His nostrils drink the air, and forth again
As from a furnace, vapors doth he send.

Venus and Adonis, 271

Sometime he trots, as if he told the steps,
With gentle majesty and modest pride;
Anon he rears upright, curvets, and leaps.

Venus and Adonis, 277

Imperiously he leaps, he neighs, he bounds,
And now his woven girth he breaks asunder;
The bearing earth with his hard hoof he wounds,
Whose hollow womb resounds like heaven's thunder.

Venus and Adonis, 265

Look what a horse should have he did not lack,
Save a proud rider on so proud a back.

Venus and Adonis, 299

Well could he ride, and often men would say,
'That horse his mettle from his rider rakes;
Proud of subjection, noble by the sway,
What rounds, what bounds, what course, what stop he makes!'

A Lover's Complaint, 106

It is the prince of palfreys: his neigh is like
the bidding of a monarch, and his countenance enforces
homage.

DOLPHIN, *Henry V*, III.VII.27

I will not change
my horse with any that treads but on four pasterns.
Ca, ha! he bounds from the earth, as if his entrails were
hairs; le cheval volant, the Pegasus, chez les narines de
feu! When I bestride him, I soar, I am a hawk; he
trots the air; the earth sings when he touches it; the
basest horn of his hoof is more musical than the pipe of
Hermes.

DOLPHIN, *Henry V*, III.VII.11

Be warn'd by me than: thy that ride so, and
ride not warily, fall into foul bogs. I had rather have
my horse to my mistress.

DOLPHIN, *Henry V*, III.VII.56

It is a beast for
Perseus. He is pure air and fire; and the dull elements
of earth and water never appear in him, but only in
patient stillness while his rider mounts him.

DOLPHIN, *Henry V*, III.VII.20

A horse, a horse! my kingdom for a horse!

KING RICHARD, *Richard III*, V.IV.7

As he thus went counting
The flinty pavement, dancing as 'tween to th' music
His own hoofs made (for as they say from iron
Came music's origin), what envious flint,
Cold as old Saturn, and like him possess'd
With fire malevolent, darted a spark,
Or what fierce sulphur else, to this end made,
I comment not—the hot horse, hot as fire,
Took toy at this, and fell to what disorder
His power could give his will, bounds, comes on end,
Forgets school-doing, being therein train'd,
And of kind manage.

PIRITHOUS, *The Two Noble Kinsmen*, V.IV.58

With that he gave his able horse the head,
And ending forward strook his armèd heels
Against the panting sides of his poor jade
Up to the rowel-head, and starting so
He seem'd in running to devour the way,
Staying no longer question.

TRAVERS, *2 Henry IV*, I.I.43

HOSPITALITY
see also COMFORT; COMPANY

Such comfort as do lusty young men feel
When well-apparel'd April on the heel
Of limping winter treads, even such delight
Among fresh fennel buds shall you this night
Inherit at my house.

CAPULET, *Romeo and Juliet*, I.II.26

I am your host,
With robber's hands my hospitable favors
You should not ruffle thus.

EARL OF GLOUCESTER, *King Lear*, III.VII.39

Come, thou
shalt go home, and we'll have flesh for holidays, fish
for fasting-days, and moreo'er, puddings and flap-
jacks, and thou shalt be welcome.

FISHERMAN, *Pericles*, II.I.80

See, your guests approach,
Address yourself to entertain them sprightly,
And let's be red with mirth.

FLORIZEL, *The Winter's Tale*, IV.IV.53

Th' appurtenance of welcome is fashion and ceremony.

HAMLET, *Hamlet*, II.II.371

You are as welcome, worthy sir, as I
Have words to bid you, and shall find it so
In all that I can do.

IMOGEN, *Cymbeline*, I.VI.29

Embrace him, love him, give him welcome hither.

KING PHILIP, *King John*, II.I.11

To feed were best at home;
From thence, the sauce to meat is ceremony,
Meeting were bare without it.

LADY MACBETH, *Macbeth*, III.V.34

What cannot be eshew'd must be embrac'd.

PAGE, *The Merry Wives of Windsor*, V.V.237

Sir, you are very welcome to our house.
It must appear in other ways than words,
Therefore I scant this breathing courtesy.

PORTIA, *The Merchant of Venice*, V.I.139

HUMAN CONDITION
see also BIRTH; DEATH; LIFE

That we shall die, we know, 'tis but the time,
And drawing days out, that men stand upon.

BRUTUS, *Julius Caesar*, III.I.99

We were born to die.

CAPULET, *Romeo and Juliet*, III.IV.4

This is the state of man: to-day he puts forth
The tender leaves of hopes, to-morrow blossoms,
And bears his blushing honors thick upon him;
The third day comes a frost, a killing frost,
And when he thinks, good easy man, full surely
His greatness is a-ripening, nips his root,
And then he falls as I do.

CARDINAL WOLSEY, *Henry VIII*, III.II.352

Humanity must perforce prey on itself,
Like monsters of the deep.

DUKE OF ALBANY, *King Lear*, IV.II.48

What a piece of work is man, how noble in reason, how
infinite in faculties, in form and moving, how express and
admirable in action, how like an angel in apprehension, how
like a god! the beauty of the world; the paragon of animals;
and yet to me what is this quintessence of dust? Man
delights not me.

HAMLET, *Hamlet*, II.II.303

We all are men,
In our own natures frail, and capable
Of our flesh; few are angels.

LORD CHANCELLOR, *Henry VIII*, V.II.45

How beauteous mankind is! O brave new world
That has such people in't!

MIRANDA, *The Tempest*, V.I.183

In the reproof of chance
Lies the true proof of men.

NESTOR, *Troilus and Cressida*, I.III.33

Lord, what fools these mortals be!

PUCK, *A Midsummer Night's Dream*, III.II.115

Merely, thou art death's fool,
For him thou labor'st by thy flight to shun,
And yet run'st toward him still.

VINCENTIO, DUKE OF VIENNA, Measure for Measure, II.I.11

HUMILITY
see also MODESTY

Verily,
I swear, 'tis better to be lowly born,
And range with humble livers in content.

ANNE BULLEN, Henry VIII, II.III.18

Wherefore did you so much tempt the heavens?
It is the part of men to fear and tremble
When the most mighty gods by tokens send
Such dreadful heralds to astonish us.

CASCA, Julius Caesar, I.III.53

And then I stole all courtesy from heaven,
And dress'd myself in sick humility
That I did pluck allegiance from men's hearts,
Loud shouts and saluations from their mouths,
Even in the presence of the crowned King.

KING HENRY, 1 Henry IV, III.II.50

But if it did infect my blood with joy,
Or swell my thoughts to any strain of pride,
If any rebel or vain sport of mine
Did with the least affection of a welcome
Give entertainment to the might of it,
Let God for ever keep it from my head,
And make me as the poorest vassal is
That doth with awe and terror kneel to it!

PRINCE HENRY, 2 Henry IV, IV.V.169

I have sounded the
very base-string of humility.

PRINCE HENRY, 1 Henry IV, II.IV.5

HUMOR
see also SMILE

Oh, I am stabb'd with laughter.

BOYET, Love's Labor's Lost, V.II.79

The world may laugh again.

DUKE OF GLOUCESTER, 2 Henry VI, II.IV.82

I do well believe your Highness, and did it to
minister occasion to these gentlemen, who are of such

sensible and nimble lungs that they always use to
laugh at nothing.

GONZALO, The Tempest, II.I.173

Jesters do oft prove prophets.

REGAN, King Lear, V.III.71

I will laugh like a hyen, and that when thou art inclined
to sleep.

ROSALIND, As You Like It, IV.I.155

A jest's prosperity lies in the ear
Of him that hears it, never in the tongue
Of him that makes it.

ROSALINE, Love's Labor's Lost, V.II.861

HUNGER
see also FOOD; HOMELESSNESS; POVERTY; SUFFERING

At thy heel
Did famine follow, whom thou fought'st against
(Though daintily brought up) with patience more
Than savages could suffer. Thou didst drink
The stale of horses and the gilded puddle
Which beasts would cough at; thy palate then did deign
The roughest berry on the rudest hedge;
Yea, like the stag, when snow the pasture sheets,
The barks of trees thou brows'd. On the Alps
It is reported thou didst eat strange flesh,
Which some did die to look on; and all this
(It wounds thine honor that I speak it now)
Was borne so like a soldier, that thy cheek
So much as lank'd not.

CAESAR (OCTAVIUS), Antony and Cleopatra, I.IV.58

That hunger broke stone walls, that dogs must eat,
That meat was made for mouths, that the gods sent not
Corn for the rich men only.

CAIUS MARTIUS, Coriolanus, I.I.206

Who wanteth food and will not say he wants it,
Or can conceal his hunger till he famish?

CLEON, Pericles, I.IV.II

So sharp are hunger's teeth, that man and wife
Draw lots who first shall die to lengthen life.
Here stands a lord, and there a lady weeping;
Here many sink, yet those which see them fall
Have scarce strength left to give them burial.
Is not this true?

CLEON, Pericles, I.IV.45

Nay then thou wilt starve sure; for here's
nothing to be got now-a-days unless thou canst fish
for't.

> FISHERMAN, *Pericles*, II.I.68

My hunger's gone; but even before I was
At point to sink for food.

> IMOGEN, *Cymbeline*, III.VI.16

For I, that never
fear'd any, am vanquish'd by famine, not by valor.

> JACK CADE, *2 Henry VI*, IV.x.74

But now am I so
hungry that, if I might have a lease of my life for a
thousand years, I could stay no longer.

> JACK CADE, *2 Henry VI*, IV.x.4

HUNTING

And sometime sorteth with a heard of deer:
Danger deviseth shifts, wit waits on fear.

> *Venus and Adonis*, 689

But up to th' mountains!
This is not hunters' language. He that strikes
The venison first shall be the lord o' th' feast,
To him the other two shall minister,
And we will fear no poison, which attends
In place of greater state.

> BELARIUS, *Cymbeline*, III.III.73

Well, 'tis done.
We'll hunt no more to-day, nor seek for danger
Where there's no profit.

> BELARIUS, *Cymbeline*, IV.II.162

Am I your bird? I mean to shift my bush,
And then pursue me as you draw your bow.

> BIANCA, *The Taming of the Shrew*, V.II.46

Come, shall we go and kill us venison?
And yet it irks me the poor dappled fools,
Being native burghers of this desert city,
Should in their own confines with forked heads
Have their round haunches gor'd.

> DUKE SENIOR, *As You Like It*, II.I.21

And like a jolly troop of huntsmen come
Our lusty English, all with purpled hands,
Dy'd in the dying slaughter of their foes.

> ENGLISH HERALD, *King John*, III.I.321

All things that are,
Are with more spirit chased than enjoy'd.

GRATIANO, *The Merchant of Venice*, II.VI.8

HUSBANDS
see also MARRIAGE; MEN; WIDOWHOOD; WIVES

O husband, hear me! ay, alack, how new
Is "husband" in my mouth! even for that name
Which till this time my tongue did ne'er pronounce.

BLANCH OF SPAIN, *King John*, III.I.305

Thy husband is thy lord, thy life, thy keeper,
Thy head, thy sovereign; one that cares for thee,
And for thy maintenance, commits his body
To painful labor both by sea and land;
To watch the night in storms, the day in cold,
Whilst thou li'st warm at home, secure and safe.

KATE, *The Taming of the Shrew*, V.II.146

A young man married is a man that's marr'd.

PAROLLES, *All's Well That Ends Well*, II.III.298

To me she's married, not unto my clothes.

PETRUCHIO, *The Taming of the Shrew*, III.II.117

My queen, my mistress!
O lady, weep no more, lest I give cause
To be suspected of more tenderness
Than doth become a man. I will remain
The loyal'st husband that did e'er plight troth.

POSTHUMUS, *Cymbeline*, I.I.93

As a wall'd town is more worthier than a village, so is the
forehead of a married man more honorable than the bare brow
of a bachelor.

TOUCHSTONE, *As You Like It*, III.III.59

HYPOCRISY
see also DECEIT; DISGUISE

And since the wisdom of their choice is rather to have
my hat than my heart, I will practice the insinuating nod
and be off to them most counterfeitly; that is,
sir, I will counterfeit the bewitchment of some popular
man, and give it bountiful to the desirers.

CORIOLANUS, *Coriolanus*, II.III.98

Please he in earnest? Look upon his face:
His eyes do drop no tears, his prayers are in jest,
His words come from his mouth, ours from our breast;

He prays but faintly, and would be denied,
We pray with heart and soul, and all beside;
His weary joints would gladly rise, I know,
Our knees still kneel till to the ground they grow;
His prayers are full of false hypocrisy,
Ours of true zeal and deep integrity;
Our prayers do outpray his, then let them have
That mercy which true prayer ought to have.

DUCHESS OF YORK, *Richard II*, V.III.100

Most mischievous foul sin, in chiding sin:
For thou thyself hast been a libertine,
As sensual as the brutish sting itself.

DUKE SENIOR, *As You Like It*, II.VII.64

King. But now, my cousin Hamlet, and my son—
Ham. [Aside.] A little more than kin, and a little less
kind.

HAMLET, CLAUDIUS, *Hamlet*, I.II.64

Lucio. Thou conclud'st like the sanctimonious
pirate, that went to sea with the Ten Commandments,
but scrap'd one out of the table.
2. Gent. "Thou shalt not steal"?
Lucio. Ay, that he raz'd.

LUCIO, SECOND GENTLEMAN, *Measure for Measure*, I.II.7

Do not, as some ungracious pastors do,
Show me the steep and thorny way to heaven,
Whiles, like a puff'd and reckless libertine,
Himself the primrose path of dalliance treads,
And recks not his own rede.

OPHELIA, *Hamlet*, I.III.47

'Tis too much prov'd—that with devotion's visage
And pious action we do sugar o'er
The devil himself.

POLONIUS, *Hamlet*, III.I.46

He who the sword of heaven will bear
Should be as holy as severe;
Pattern in himself to know,
Grace to stand, and virtue go;
More nor less to others paying
Than by self-offenses weighing.
Shame to him whose cruel striking
Kills for faults of his own liking!

VINCENTIO, DUKE OF VIENNA, *Measure for Measure*, III.II.261

IDENTITY
see also NAMES AND TITLES; SELF-KNOWLEDGE

> O villain, thou hast stol'n both mine office and my name:
> The one ne'er got me credit, the other mickle blame.
>
> DROMIO OF EPHESUS, *The Comedy of Errors*, III.I.43

> Thou wast a pretty fellow when thou hadst
> no need to care for her frowning, now thou are an O
> without a figure. I am better than thou art now, I am
> a Fool, thou art nothing.
>
> FOOL, *King Lear*, I.IV.191

> Does any here know me? This is not Lear.
> Does Lear walk thus? speak thus? Where are his eyes?
> Either his notion weakens, his discernings
> Are lethargied—ha! waking? 'Tis not so,
> Who is it that can tell me who I am?
>
> LEAR, *King Lear*, I.IV.226

> Who dares not stir by day must walk by night,
> And have is have, however men do catch.
> Near or far off, well won is still well shot,
> And I am I, howe'er I was begot.
>
> PHILIP THE BASTARD, *King John*, I.I.172

> By a name
> I know not how to tell thee who I am.
> My name, dear saint, is hateful to myself,
> Because it is an enemy to thee;
> Had I written, I would tear the word.
>
> ROMEO, *Romeo and Juliet*, II.II.53

IGNORANCE
see also BIGOTRY AND INTOLERANCE; STUPIDITY

> There is no darkness but ignorance, in which thou art more
> puzzled than the Egyptians in their fog.
>
> FESTE, *Twelfth Night*, IV.II.42

> He has no more directions
> in the true disciplines of the wars, look you, of the
> Roman disciplines, than is a puppy-dog.
>
> FLUELLEN, *Henry V*, III.II.71

> Ang. Either you are ignorant,
> Or seem so craftily; and that's not good.
> Isab. Let me be ignorant, and in nothing good,
> But graciously to know I am no better.
>
> ISABELLA, ANGELO, *Measure for Measure*, II.IV.74

He hath never fed of the dainties that are bred in a book;
he hath not eat paper, as it were; he hath not drunk ink;
his intellect is not replenished; he is only an animal, only
sensible in the duller parts.

NATHANIEL, *Love's Labor's Lost*, IV.II.24

ILLUSION
see also IMAGINATION; MADNESS AND MENTAL ILLNESS; PARANOIA

Nothing that is so is so.

FESTE, *Twelfth Night*, IV.I.8

Nothing is
But what is not.

MACBETH, *Macbeth*, I.III.141

Is this a dagger I see before me,
The handle toward my hand? Come, let me clutch thee:
I have thee not, and yet I see thee still.
Art thou not, fatal vision, sensible
To feeling as to sight? or art thou but
A dagger of the mind, a false creation,
Proceeding from the heat-oppressed brain?
I see thee yet, in form as palpable
As this which now I draw.
Thou marshal'st me the way that I was going,
And such an instrument I was to use.
Mine eyes are made the fools o' th' other senses,
Or else worth all the rest. I see thee still;
And on thy blade and dudgeon gouts of blood,
Which was not so before. There's no such thing:
It is the bloody business which informs
Thus to mine eyes.

MACBETH, *Macbeth*, II.I.33

IMAGINATION
see also DREAMS; ILLUSION; STORYTELLING

O, who can hold a fire in his hand
By thinking on the frosty Caucasus?
Or cloy the hungry edge of appetite
By bare imagination of a feast?
Or wallow naked in December snow
By thinking on fantastic summer's heat?

BULLINGBROOK, *Richard II*, I.III.294

Imagination of some great exploit
Drives him beyond the bounds of patience.

EARL OF NORTHUMBERLAND, *1 Henry IV*, I.III.199

Conceit in weakest bodies strongest works.

GHOST, *Hamlet*, III.IV.114

There are more things in heaven and earth, Horatio,
Than are dreamt of in your philosophy.
HAMLET, Hamlet, I.v.166

The current that with gentle murmur glides,
Thou know'st, being stopp'd, impatiently doth rage;
But when his fair course is not hindered,
He makes sweet music with th' enamell'd stones,
Giving a gentle kiss to every sedge
He overtaketh in his pilgrimage;
And so by many winding nooks he strays
With willing sport to the wild ocean.
JULIA, The Two Gentlemen of Verona, II.VII.25

Give me an ounce of civet; good apothecary,
Sweeten my imagination.
LEAR, King Lear, IV.VI.130

Present fears
Are less than horrible imaginings.
MACBETH, Macbeth, I.III.137

Lovers and madmen have such seething brains,
Such shaping fantasies, that apprehend
More than cool reason ever comprehends.
The lunatic, the lover, and the poet
Are of imagination all compact.
One sees more devils than vast hell can hold;
That is the madman. The lover, all as frantic,
Sees Helen's beauty in a brow of Egypt.
The poet's eye, in a fine frenzy rolling,
Doth glance from heaven to earth, from earth to heaven;
And as imagination bodies forth
The forms of things unknown, the poet's pen
Turns them to shapes, and gives to airy nothing
A local habitation and a name.
Such tricks hath strong imagination,
That if it would but apprehend some joy,
It comprehends some bringer of that joy;
Or in the night, imagining some fear,
How easy is a bush suppos'd a bear!
THESEUS, A Midsummer Night's Dream, V.1.4

IMMORTALITY
see also FAME; POSTERITY

I hold it ever
Virtue and cunning were endowments greater
Than nobleness and riches. Careless heirs

May the two latter darken and expend,
But immortality attends the former,
Making a man a god.

CERIMON, *Pericles*, III.II.27

I have immortal longings in me.

CLEOPATRA, *Antony and Cleopatra*, V.II.280

Erect his statue and worship it,
And make my image but a alehouse sign.

QUEEN MARGARET, *2 Henry VI*, III.II.80

IMPATIENCE

Here all enrag'd, such passion her assails
That patience is quite beaten from her breast.

The Rape of Lucrece, 1562

I stand on fire:
Come to the matter.

CYMBELINE, *Cymbeline*, V.v.169

All the pow'r of his wits have given way to
his patience.

EARL OF KENT, *King Lear*, III.VI.4

So tedious is this day
As is the night before some festival
To an impatient child that hath new robes
And may not wear them.

JULIET, *Romeo and Juliet*, III.II.28

Sir, sir, impatience hath his privilege.

PEMBROKE, *King John*, IV.III.32

O, but impatience waiteth on true sorrow.
And see where comes the breeder of my sorrow!

QUEEN MARGARET, *3 Henry VI*, III.III.42

IMPOSSIBILITY
see also FUTILITY

'Tis as impossible that he's undrown'd,
As he that sleeps here swims.

ANTONIO, *The Tempest*, II.I.237

Then let the pebbles on the hungry beach
Fillop the stars; then let the mutinous winds
Strike the proud cedars 'gainst the fiery sun,
Murd'ring impossibility, to make
What cannot be, slight work.

CORIOLANUS, *Coriolanus*, V.III.58

Therefore, thou happy father,
Think that the clearest gods, who make them honors
Of men's impossibilities, have preserved thee.

EDGAR, *King Lear*, IV.VI.72

Alas, poor duke, the task he undertakes
Is numb'ring sands and drinking oceans dry.

SIR HENRY GREEN, *Richard II*, II.II.145

IMPRISONMENT

Let's think this prison holy sanctuary
To keep us from corruption of worse men.

ARCITE, *The Two Noble Kinsmen*, II.II.71

Our cage
We make a choir, as doth the prison'd bird,
And sing our bondage freely.

ARVIRAGUS, *Cymbeline*, III.III.42

The prison itself is proud of 'em;
and they have all the world in their chamber.

DAUGHTER, *The Two Noble Kinsmen*, II.I.24

All corners else o' th' earth
Let liberty make use of; space enough
Have I in such a prison.

FERDINAND, *The Tempest*, I.II.492

You shall not now be stol'n, you have locks upon you;
So graze, as you find pasture.

JAILER, *Cymbeline*, V.IV.1

Ay, such a pleasure as incagèd birds
Conceive, when, after many moody thoughts,
At last by notes of household harmony
They quite forget their loss of liberty.

KING HENRY, *3 Henry VI*, IV.VI.12

Most welcome, bondage! for thou art a way,
I think, to liberty; yet am I better
Than one that's sick o' th' gout, since he had rather
Groan so in perpetuity than be cur'd
By th' sure physician, death, who is the key
T' unbar these locks.

POSTHUMUS, *Cymbeline*, V.IV.3

What, are my doors oppos'd against my passage?
Have I been ever free, and must my house
Be my retentive enemy? my jail?
The place which I have feasted, does it now
(Like all mankind) show me an iron heart?

TIMON, *Timon of Athens*, III.IV.79

INACTION
see also BOREDOM; COWARDICE; PROCRASTINATION

Come, I have learn'd that fearful commenting
Is leaden servitor to dull delay;
Delay leads impotent and snail-pac'd beggary.

BUCKINGHAM, *Richard III*, IV.III.51

If we shall stand still,
In fear our motion will be mock'd or carp'd at,
We should take root here where we sit, or sit
State-statues only.

CARDINAL WOLSEY, *Henry VIII*, I.II.85

What is a man,
If his chief good and market of his time
Be but to sleep and feed? a beast, no more.
Sure He that made us with such large discourse,
Looking before and after, gave us not
That capability and godlike reason
To fust in us unus'd. Now whether it be
Bestial oblivion, or some craven scruple
Or thinking too precisely on th' event—
A thought which quarter'd hath but one part wisdom
And ever three parts coward—I do not know
Why yet I live to say, "This thing's to do,"
Sith I have cause, and will, and strength, and means
To do't.

HAMLET, *Hamlet*, IV.IV.33

Thus conscience does make cowards of us all,
And thus the native hue of resolution
Is sicklied o'er with the pale cast of thought,
And enterprises of great pitch and moment
With this regard their currents turn awry,
And lose the name of action.

HAMLET, *Hamlet*, III.I.82

Art thou afeard
To be the same in thine own act and valor
As thou art in desire?

LADY MACBETH, *Macbeth*, I.VII.39

Who mak'st a show but dar'st not strike, thy conscience
Is so possess'd with guilt.

PROSPERO, *The Tempest*, I.II.471

INCEST

This king unto him took a peer,
Who died and left a female heir,

So buxom, blithe, and full of face
As heaven had lent her all his grace;
With whom the father liking took,
And he to incest did provoke—
Bad child, worse father, to entice his own
To evil should be done by none.

GOWER, Pericles, I.CHO.21

Antiochus from incest lived not free;
For which, the most high gods not minding longer
To withhold the vengeance that they had in store,
Due to this heinous capital offense,
Even in the height and pride of all his glory,
When he was seated in a chariot
Of an inestimable value, and his daughter with him,
A fire from heaven came and shrivell'd up
Those bodies, even to loathing, for they so stunk,
That all those eyes ador'd them ere their fall
Scorn now their hand should give them burial.

HELICANUS, Pericles, II.IV.2

INCONSTANCY
see also FADS AND FASHION; TRANSIENCE

He wears his faith but as the fashion of his hat; it ever
changes with the next block.

BEATRICE, Much Ado About Nothing, I.I.75

Young men's love then lies
Not truly in their hearts, but in their eyes.
Jesu Maria, what a deal of brine
Hath wash'd thy sallow cheeks for Rosaline!
How much salt water thrown away in waste,
To season love, that of it doth not taste!
The sun not yet thy sighs from heaven clears,
Thy old groans yet ringing in mine ancient ears;
Lo here upon thy cheek the stain doth sit
Of an old tear that is not wash'd off yet.
If e'er thou wast thyself and these woes thine,
Thou and these woes were all for Rosaline.
And art thou chang'd? Pronounce this sentence then:
Women may fall, when there's no strength in men.

FRIAR LAWRENCE, Romeo and Juliet, II.III.67

One day he gives us diamonds, next day stones.

LORD, Timon of Athens, III.VI.120

Were man
But constant, he were perfect; that one error

Fills him with faults; makes him run through all th' sins:
Inconstancy falls off ere it begins.

PROTEUS, The Two Gentlemen of Verona, V.IV.110

Even as one heat another heat expels,
Or as one nail by strength drives out another,
So the remembrance of my former love
Is by a newer object quite forgotten.

PROTEUS, The Two Gentlemen of Verona, II.IV.192

Thou art not certain,
For thy complexion shifts to strange effects,
After the moon.

VINCENTIO, DUKE OF VIENNA, Measure for Measure, III.I.23

INDEPENDENCE

You do me double wrong
To strive for that which resteth in my choice.
I am no breeching scholar in the schools,
I'll not be tied to hours, nor 'pointed times,
But learn my lessons as I please myself.

BIANCA, The Taming of the Shrew, III.I.16

I will not choose what many men desire,
Because I will not jump with common spirits,
And rank me with the barbarous multitudes.

PRINCE OF ARRAGON, The Merchant of Venice, II.IX.31

INFATUATION
see also ATTRACTION; LOVE—GENERAL

They seem'd almost,
with staring on one another, to tear the cases of their
eyes. There was speech in their dumbness, language in
their very gesture; they look'd as they had heard of a
world ranson'd, or one destroy'd. A notable
passion of wonder appear'd in them; but the wisest
beholder, that knew no more but seeing, could not say
if th' importance were joy or sorrow; but in the
extremity of the one, it must needs be.

AUTOLYCUS, The Winter's Tale, V.II.11

For several virtues
Have I lik'd several women, never any
With so full soul but some defect in her
Did quarrel with the noblest grace she ow'd,
And put it to the foil. But you, O you,
So perfect and so peerless, are created
Of every creature's best!

FERDINAND, The Tempest, III.I.42

Hear my soul speak:
The very instant that I saw you, did
My heart fly to your service, there resides,
To make me slave to it, and for your sake
Am I this patient log-man.

FERDINAND, The Tempest, III.i.63

I do, my lord, and in her eye I find
A wonder, or a wondrous miracle,
The shadow of my self form'd in her eye,
Which being but the shadow of your son,
Becomes a sun and makes your son a shadow.
I do protest I never lov'd myself
Till now infixèd I beheld myself
Drawn in the flattering table of her eye.

LEWIS, King John, II.i.496

INFIDELITY
see also ADULTERY; BETRAYAL

Hath not else his eye
Stray'd his affection in unlawful love—
A sin prevailing much in youthful men,
Who give their eyes the liberty of gazing?

ABBESS, The Comedy of Errors, V.i.50

How dearly would it touch thee to the quick,
Shouldst thou but hear I were licentious,
And that this body, consecrate to thee,
By ruffian lust should be contaminate?

ADRIANA, The Comedy of Errors, II.ii.130

Since mine own doors refuse to entertain me,
I'll knock elsewhere, to see if they'll disdain me.

ANTIPHOLUS OF EPHESUS, The Comedy of Errors, III.i.120

I had rather be a toad
And live upon the vapor of a dungeon
Than keep a corner in the thing I love
For others' uses.

OTHELLO, Othello, III.iii.270

But when to my good lord I prove untrue,
I'll choke myself. There's all I'll do for you.

PISANIO, Cymbeline, I.v.86

Know thou first,
I lov'd the maid I married; never man
Sigh'd truer breath; but that I see thee here,
Thou noble thing, more dances my rapt heart

Than when I first my wedded mistress saw
Bestride my threshold.

TULLUS AUFIDIUS, Coriolanus, IV.V.113

INFLATION
see also MONEY

Poor fellow never joy'd since the price of
oats rose, it was the death of him.

CARRIER, 1 Henry IV, II.I.11

INFLUENCE
see also PERSUASION; POLITICS AND POWER

That hard heart of thine,
Hath taught them scornful tricks, and such disdain
That they have murd'red this poor heart of mine.

Venus and Adonis, 500

You did know
How much you were my conqueror, and that
My sword, made weak by my affection, would
Obey it on all cause.

ANTONY, Antony and Cleopatra, III.XI.65

I have made you mad;
And even with such-like valor men hang and drown
Their proper selves.

ARIEL, The Tempest, III.III.58

Sir, in good faith, in sincere verity,
Under th' allowance of your great aspect,
Whose influence, like the wreath of radiant fire
On flick'ring Phoebus' front.

EARL OF KENT, King Lear, II.II.105

It is a wonderful thing to
see the semblable coherence of his men's spirits
and his. They, by observing him, do bear themselves like
foolish justices; he, by conversing with them, is
turn'd into a justice-like servingman. Their spirits are
so marred in conjunction with the participation of
society that they flock together in consent, like so
many wild geese.

SIR JOHN FALSTAFF, 2 Henry IV, V.I.64

INGRATITUDE
see also RUDENESS; UNKINDNESS

Brutus, as you know, was Caesar's angel.
Judge, O you gods, how dearly Caesar lov'd him!

This was the most unkindest cut of all;
For when the noble Caesar saw him stab,
Ingratitude, more strong than traitor's arms,
Quite vanquish'd him.

ANTONY, *Julius Caesar*, III.II.181

I know my lord hath spent Timon's wealth,
And now ingratitude makes it worse than stealth.

HORTENSIUS, *Timon of Athens*, III.IV.26

Ingratitude! thou marble-hearted fiend,
More hideous when thou show'st thee in a child
Than the sea-monster.

LEAR, *King Lear*, I.IV.259

O you hard hearts, you cruel men of Rome,
Knew you not Pompey? Many a time and oft
Have you climb'd up to walls and battlements,
To tow'rs and windows, yea, to chimney-tops,
Your infants in your arms, and there have sate
The livelong day, with patient expectation,
To see great Pompey pass the streets of Rome;
And when you saw his chariot but appear,
Have you not made an universal shout,
That Tiber trembled underneath her banks
To hear the replication of your sounds
Made in her concave shores?
And do you now put on your best attire?
And do you now cull out a holiday?
And do you now strew flowers in his way,
That comes in triumph over Pompey's blood?
Be gone!
Run to your houses, fall upon your knees,
Pray to the gods to intermit the plague
That needs must light on this ingratitude.

MURELLUS, *Julius Caesar*, I.I.36

I am rapt and cannot cover
The monstrous bulk of this ingratitude
With any size of words.

POET, *Timon of Athens*, V.I.64

These old fellows
Have their ingratitude in them hereditary:
Their blood is cak'd, 'tis cold, it seldom flows;
'Tis lack of kindly warmth they are not kind.

TIMON, *Timon of Athens*, II.II.214

I hate ingratitude more in a man
Than lying, vainness, babbling, drunkenness,

Or any taint of vice whose strong corruption
Inhabits our frail blood.

VIOLA, Twelfth Night, III.IV.335

INHERITANCE

The old bees die, the young possess their hive.

The Rape of Lucrece, 1769

This small inheritance my father left me
Contenteth me, and worth a monarchy.

ALEXANDER IDEN, 2 Henry VI, IV.x.18

For in the book of Numbers is it writ,
When the man dies, let the inheritance
Descend unto the daughter.

CANTERBURY, Henry V, I.II.98

Since I had my office,
I have kept you next my heart, have not alone
Employ'd you where high profits might come home,
But par'd my present havings, to bestow
My bounties upon you.

KING HENRY, Henry VIII, III.II.156

Let's choose executors and talks of wills;
And yet not so, for what can we bequeath
Save our deposed bodies to the ground?

KING RICHARD, Richard II, III.II.148

Only we shall retain
The name, and all th' addition to a king;
The sway, revenue, execution of the rest,
Beloved sons, be yours, which to confirm,
This coronet part between you.

LEAR, King Lear, I.I.135

I am a man
That from my first have been inclin'd to thrift,
And my estate deserves an heir more rais'd
Than one which holds a trencher.

OLD ATHENIAN, Timon of Athens, I.I.117

Thou givest me somewhat to repair myself;
And though it was mine own, part of my heritage,
Which my dead father did bequeath to me,
With this strict charge, even as he left his life,
"Keep it, my Pericles, it hath been a shield
'Twist me and death"—and pointed to this brace—
"For that it sav'd me, keep it. In like necessity—
The which the gods protect thee from!—may defend thee."

It kept were I kept, I so dearly lov'd it,
Till the rough seas, that spares not any man,
Took it in rage, though calm'd have given't again.
I thank thee for't. My shipwrack now's no ill,
Since I have here my father gave in his will.

PERICLES, Pericles, II.I.121

INJURY
see also PAIN

Rom. Courage, man, the hurt cannot be much.
Mer. No, 'tis not so deep as a well, nor so wide as
a church-door, but 'tis enough, 'twill serve. Ask for
me to-morrow, and you shall find me a grave man. I
am pepper'd, I warrant, for this world. A plague a'
both your houses! 'Zounds, a dog, a rat, a mouse,
a cat, to scratch a man to death! a braggart, a rogue, a
villain, that fights by the book of arithmetic!

MERCUTIO, ROMEO, Romeo and Juliet, III.I.95

I had a wound here that was like a <i>T</i>,
But now 'tis made an <i>H</i>.

SCARUS, Antony and Cleopatra, IV.VII.7

INJUSTICE
see also CORRUPTION; LAW; TYRANNY

Some innocents 'scape not the thunderbolt.

CLEOPATRA, Antony and Cleopatra, II.V.77

Was there ever any man thus beaten out of season,
When in the why and the wherefore is neither rhyme
nor reason?

DROMIO OF SYRACUSE, The Comedy of Errors, II.II.47

Therefore proceed.
But yet hear this—mistake me not; no life
(I prize it not a straw), but for mine honor,
Which I would free—if I shall be condemned
Upon surmises (all proofs sleeping else
But what your jealousies awake), I tell you
'Tis rigor and not law.

HERMIONE, The Winter's Tale, III.II.108

Apollo's angry, and the heavens themselves
Do strike at my injustice.

LEONTES, The Winter's Tale, III.II.147

I think the echoes of his shames have deaf'd
The ears of heav'nly justice.

PALAMON, The Two Noble Kinsmen, I.II.80

My comfort is, that heaven will take our souls,
And plague injustice with the pains of hell.

SIR HENRY GREEN, *Richard II*, III.I.33

INNOCENCE
see also GOOD; PURITY

Though my gross blood be stain'd with this abuse,
Immaculate and spotless is my mind.

The Rape of Lucrece, 1655

For thou hast kill'd the sweetest innocent
That e'er did lift up eye.

EMILIA, *Othello*, V.II.199

This hand of mine
Is yet a maiden and an innocent hand,
Not painted with the crimson spots of blood.
Within this bosom never ent'red yet
The dreadful motion of a murderous thought,
And you have slander'd nature in my form,
Which howsoever rude exteriorly,
Is yet the cover of a fairer mind
Than to be butcher of an innocent child.

HUBERT, *King John*, IV.II.251

The trust I have is in mine innocence,
And therefore am I bold and resolute.

LORD SAY, *2 Henry VI*, IV.IV.59

How green you are and fresh in this old world!

PANDULPH, *King John*, III.IV.145

Sweet Prince, the untainted virtue of your years
Hath not yet div'd into the world's deceit.

RICHARD, DUKE OF GLOUCESTER, *Richard III*, III.I.7

INSOMNIA
see also SLEEP

Is it thy will image should keep open
My heavy eyelids to the weary night?
Dost thou desire my slumbers should be broken
While shadows like to thee to mock my sight?

SONNET 61, 1–4

A heavy summons lies like lead upon me,
And yet I would not sleep. Merciful powers,
Restrain in me the cursed thoughts that nature
Gives way to in repose!

BANQUO, *Macbeth*, II.I.6

Not poppy, nor mandragora,
Nor all the drowsy syrups of the world
Shall ever medicine thee to that sweet sleep
Which thou ow'dst yesterday.

IAGO, Othello, III.III.330

You lack the season of all natures, sleep.

LADY MACBETH, Macbeth, III.IV.140

Thy spirit within thee hath been so at war,
And thus hath so bestirr'd thee in they sleep,
That beads of sweat have stood upon thy brow,
Like bubbles in a late-disturbed stream,
And in thy face strange motions have appear'd
Such as we see when men restrain their breath
On some great sudden hest.

LADY PERCY, 1 Henry IV, II.III.56

O polish'd peturbation! golden care!
That keep'st the ports of slumber open wide
To many a watchful night, sleep with it now!

PRINCE HENRY, 2 Henry IV, IV.V.23

INSTINCT
see also INTUITION

'Tis wonder
That an invisible instinct should frame them
To royalty unlearn'd, honor untaught,
Civility not seen from other, valor
That wildly grows in them but yields a crop
As if it had been sow'd.

BELARIUS, Cymbeline, IV.II.176

I'll never
Be such a gosling to obey instinct, but stand
As if a man were author of himself,
And knew no other kin.

CORIOLANUS, Coriolanus, V.III.34

Instinct is a great matter.

SIR JOHN FALSTAFF, 1 Henry IV, II.IV.272

INSULTS
see also CURSES

Boys, apes, braggarts, Jacks, milksops!

ANTHONY, Much Ado About Nothing, V.I.91

You are not worth the dust which the rude wind
Blows in your face.

DUKE OF ALBANY, King Lear, IV.II.30

'Tis beauty that doth oft make women proud,
But God he knows thy share thereof is small.
DUKE OF YORK, 3 Henry VI, I.IV.128

These words of yours draw life-blood from my heart.
JOHN TALBOT, 1 Henry VI, IV.VI.32

Get you gone, you dwarf;
You minimus, of hind'ring knot-grass made;
You bead, you acorn.
LYSANDER, A Midsummer Night's Dream, III.II.328

Asses, fools, dolts! chaff and bran, chaff and bran!
porridge after meat!
PANDARUS, Troilus and Cressida, I.II.241

Thou flea, thou nit, thou winter-cricket thou!
PETRUCHIO, The Taming of the Shrew, IV.III.109

Live loath'd, and long,
Most smiling, smooth, detested parasites,
Courteous destroyers, affable wolves, meek bears,
You fools of fortune, trencher-friends, time's flies,
Cap-and-knee slaves, vapors, and minute-jacks!
TIMON, Timon of Athens, III.VI.93

INTENTIONS
see also PURPOSE; WILL

When good will is show'd, though't come too short,
The actor may plead pardon.
CLEOPATRA, Antony and Cleopatra, II.V.8

If but as well I other accents borrow,
That can my speech defuse, my good intent
May carry through itself to that full issue.
EARL OF KENT, King Lear, I.IV.1

INTUITION
see also INSTINCT

If your mind dislike any thing, obey it.
HORATIO, Hamlet, V.II.217

Cease, no more.
You smell this business with a sense as cold
As is a dead man's nose; but I do see't, and feel't,
As you feel doing thus—and see withal
The instruments that feel.
LEONTES, The Winter's Tale, II.I.150

There is a thing within my bosom tells me
That no conditions of our peace can stand.
LORD MOWBRAY, 2 Henry IV, IV.I.181

IRRATIONALITY

see also MADNESS AND MENTAL ILLNESS

I love him beyond love and beyond reason,
Or wit, or safety. I have made him know it.
I care not, I am desperate.

DAUGHTER, *The Two Noble Kinsmen*, II.VI.11

O, who can find the bent of a woman's fancy?
I am a fool, my reason is lost in me;
I have no choice, and I have lied so lewdly
That women ought to beat me.

EMILIA, *The Two Noble Kinsmen*, IV.II.33

My reason
Sits in the wind against me.

ENOBARBUS, *Antony and Cleopatra*, III.X.35

I am a feather for each wind that blows.

LEONTES, *The Winter's Tale*, II.III.154

JEALOUSY

see also ENVY

For where Love reigns, disturbing Jealousy
Doth call himself Affection's sentinel,
Gives false alarms, suggesteth mutiny
And in a peaceful hour doth cry, 'Kill, kill!'

Venus and Adonis, 649

To both these sisters have I sworn my love;
Each jealous of the other, as the stung
Are of the adder.

EDMUND, *King Lear*, V.I.55

But jealous souls will not be answer'd so;
They are not ever jealous for the cause,
But jealous for they're jealous. It is a monster
Begot upon itself, born on itself.

EMILIA, *Othello*, III.IV.159

Or failing so, yet that I put the Moor
At least into a jealousy so strong
That judgment cannot cure.

IAGO, *Othello*, II.I.300

O, beware, my lord, of jealousy!
It is the green-ey'd monster which doth mock
The meat it feeds on.

IAGO, *Othello*, III.III.165

How many fond fools serve mad jealousy?
> LUCIANA, *The Comedy of Errors*, II.I.116

Why? why is this?
Think'st thou I'd make a life of jealousy?
To follow still the changes of the moon
With fresh suspicions? No! to be once in doubt
Is once to be resolv'd. Exchange me for a goat,
When I shall turn the business of my soul
To such exsufflicate and blown surmises,
Matching thy inference.
> OTHELLO, *Othello*, III.III.176

This jealousy
Is for a precious creature: as she's rare,
Must it be great; and as his person's mighty,
Must it be violent; and as he does conceive
He is dishonor'd by a man which ever
Profess'd to him, why, his revenges must
In that be made more bitter.
> POLIXENES, *The Winter's Tale*, I.II.451

I will be more jealous of thee than a Barbary cock-pigeon
over his hen.
> ROSALIND, *As You Like It*, IV.I.149

JEWELRY

Torches are made to light, jewels to wear,
Dainties to taste, fresh beauty for the use.
> *Venus and Adonis*, 163

Believe't, dear lord,
You mend the jewel by wearing it.
> JEWELLER, *Timon of Athens*, I.I.171

In argument and proof of which contract,
Bear her this jewel, pledge of my affection.
> KING HENRY, *1 Henry VI*, V.I.46

Sparkles this stone as it was wont, or is't not
Too dull for your good wearing?
> POSTHUMUS, *Cymbeline*, II.IV.40

And when the dusty sky began to rob
My earnest-gaping sight of thy land's view,
I took a costly jewel from my neck,
A heart it was, bound in with diamonds,
And threw it towards thy land. The sea receiv'd it,
And so I wish'd thy body might my heart.
> QUEEN MARGARET, *2 Henry VI*, III.II.104

Jewels lose their glory if neglected.

SIMONIDES, *Pericles*, II.II.12

JOY
see also HAPPINESS; PLEASURE

Give me your hands.
Let grief and sorrow still embrace his heart
That doth not wish you joy!

ALONSO, *The Tempest*, V.I.213

Joy had the like conception in our eyes,
And at that instant like a babe sprung up.

APEMANTUS, *Timon of Athens*, I.II.110

To men in joy, but grief makes one hour ten.

BULLINGBROOK, *Richard II*, I.III.261

Sound drums and trumpets! Farewell sour annoy!
For here I hope begins our lasting joy.

KING EDWARD, *3 Henry VI*, V.VII.45

How much better it is to weep at joy that to joy at weeping!

LEONATO, *Much Ado About Nothing*, I.I.27

Give me a gash, put me to present pain,
Lest this great sea of joys rushing upon me
O'erbear the shores of my mortality,
And drown me with their sweetness.

PERICLES, *Pericles*, V.I.191

Come what sorrow can,
It cannot countervail the exchange of joy
That one short minute gives me in her sight.

ROMEO, *Romeo and Juliet*, II.VI.3

JUDGMENT
see also JUSTICE; LAW; OPINION

O appetite, from judgment stand aloof!

A Lover's Complaint, 166

'Tis better to be vile than vile esteemed,
When not to be receives reproach of being,
And the just pleasure lost, which is so deemed
Not by our feeling, but by others's seeing.
For why should others' false adulterate eyes
Give salutation to my sportive blood?

SONNET 121, 1–6

Eleanor, the law, thou seest, hath judgèd thee;
I cannot justify whom the law condemns.

DUKE OF GLOUCESTER, *2 Henry VI*, II.III.14

I see men's judgments are
A parcel of their fortunes, and things outward
Do draw the inward quality after them,
To suffer all alike.

ENOBARBUS, *Antony and Cleopatra*, III.XII.31

My judgment is we should not step too far
Till we had his assistance by the hand.
For in a theme so bloody-fac'd as this,
Conjecture, expectation, and surmise
Of aids incertain should not be admitted.

LORD BARDOLPH, *2 Henry IV*, I.III.20

Take each man's censure, but reserve thy judgment.

POLONIUS, *Hamlet*, I.III.69

'Twas you inces'd the rabble;
Cats, that can judge as fitly of his worth
As I can of those mysteries which heaven
Will not have earth to know.

VOLUMNIA, *Coriolanus*, IV.II.33

JUSTICE
see also JUDGMENT; LAW; PUNISHMENT

Isab. Yet show some pity.
Ang. I show it most of all when I show justice;
For then I pity those I do not know,
Which a dismiss'd offense would after gall.

ANGELO, ISABELLA, *Measure for Measure*, II.II.99

Had you rather Caesar were living, and die all slaves, than
that Caesar were dead, to live
all freemen?

BRUTUS, *Julius Caesar*, III.II.22

Remember March, the ides of March remember:
Did not great Julius bleed for justice' sake?
What villain touch'd his body, that did stab
And not for justice? What? shall one of us,
That struck the foremost man of all this world
But for supporting robbers, shall we now
Contaminate our fingers with base bribes?
And sell the mighty space of our large honors
For so much trash as may be grasped thus?
I had rather be a dog, and bay the moon,
Moon, take thy flight,
Now die, die, die, die, die.

BRUTUS, *Julius Caesar*, IV.III.18

Let Hercules himself do what he may,
The cat will mew, and dog will have his day.

HAMLET, *Hamlet*, V.I.291

O worthy Prince, dishonor not your eye
By throwing it on any other object,
Till you have heard me in my true complaint,
And given me justice, justice, justice, justice!

ISABELLA, *Measure for Measure*, V.I.22

But since correction lieth in those hands
Which made the fault that we cannot correct,
Put we our quarrel to the will of heaven.

JOHN OF GAUNT, *Richard II*, I.II.4

Well, for this night we will repose us here;
To-morrow toward London back again,
To look into this business thoroughly,
And call these foul offenders to their answers,
And poise the cause in justice' equal scales,
Whose beam stands sure, whose rightful cause prevails.

KING HENRY, *2 Henry VI*, II.I.196

If little faults, proceeding on distemper,
Shall not be wink'd at, how shall we stretch our eye
When capital crimes, chew'd, swallow'd, and digested,
Appear before us?

KING HENRY, *Henry V*, II.II.54

Thus may we gather honey from the weed,
And make a moral of the devil himself.

KING HENRY, *Henry V*, IV.I.11

Such neighbor nearness to our sacred blood
Should nothing privilege him nor partialize
The unstooping firmness of my upright soul.

KING RICHARD, *Richard II*, I.I.119

And even there, methinks an angel spake.
Look where the holy legate comes apace,
To give us warrant from the hand of heaven,
And on our actions set the name of right
With holy breath.

LEWIS, *King John*, V.II.65

We still have judgment here, that we but teach
Bloody instructions, which, being taught, return
To plague th' inventor. This even-handed justice
Commends th' ingredients of our poison'd chalice
To our own lips.

MACBETH, *Macbeth*, I.VII.8

If the great gods be just, they shall assist
The deeds of justest men.

POMPEY, Antony and Cleopatra, II.I.1

For though usurpers sway the rule a while,
Yet heav'ns are just, and time suppresseth wrongs.

QUEEN MARGARET, 3 Henry VI, III.II.76

I'll have my bond, speak not against my bond,
I have sworn an oath that I will have my bond.

SHYLOCK, The Merchant of Venice, III.III.4

We may not think the justness of each act
Such and no other than event doth form it.

TROILUS, Troilus and Cressida, II.II.119

KINDNESS
see also GENEROSITY; GENTLENESS

I fear thy nature,
It is too full o' th' milk of human kindness
To catch the nearest way.

LADY MACBETH, Macbeth, I.V.16

Your present kindness
Makes my past miseries sports.

PERICLES, Pericles, V.III.40

This is a way to kill a wife with kindness.

PETRUCHIO, The Taming of the Shrew, IV.I.208

Be brief, lest that the process of thy kindness
Last longer telling then thy kindness' date.

QUEEN ELIZABETH, Richard III, IV.IV.254

I know not how they sold themselves, but
thou like a kind fellow gavest thyself away gratis,
And I thank thee for thee.

SIR JOHN FALSTAFF, 2 Henry IV, IV.III.68

Commend me to them,
And tell them that, to ease them of their griefs,
Their fears of hostile strokes, their aches, losses,
Their pangs of love, with other incident throes
That nature's fragile vessel doth sustain
In life's uncertain voyage, I will some kindness do them.

TIMON, Timon of Athens, V.I.202

KISS
see also AFFECTION; LOVE—GENERAL; SEX

Even so she kiss'd his brow, his cheek, his chin,
And where she ends, she doth anew begin.

Venus and Adonis, 59

The warm effects which she in him finds missing
She seeks to kindle with continual kissing.

Venus and Adonis, 605

A thousand kisses buys my heart from me,
And pay them at thy leisure, one by one.
What is ten hundred touches unto thee?

Venus and Adonis, 517

Peace, I will stop your mouth.

BENEDICK, *Much Ado About Nothing*, V.IV.98

Once he kiss'd me—
I lov'd my lips the better ten days after.
Would he would do so ev'ry day!

DAUGHTER, *The Two Noble Kinsmen*, II.IV.25

This kiss, if it durst speak,
Would stretch thy spirits up into the air.

GONERIL, *King Lear*, IV.II.22

He took the bride about the neck,
And kiss'd her lips with such a clamorous smack
That at the parting all the church did echo.

GREMIO, *The Taming of the Shrew*, III.II.177

You kiss by th' book.

JULIET, *Romeo and Juliet*, I.V.110

I can express no kinder sign of love
Than this kind kiss.

KING HENRY, *2 Henry VI*, I.I.18

You have witchcraft in
your lips, Kate; there is more eloquence in a sugar
touch of them than in the tongues of the French council.

KING HENRY, *Henry V*, V.II.275

One kiss shall stop our mouths, and dumbly part;
Thus give I mine, and thus take I thy heart.

KING RICHARD, *Richard II*, V.I.95

Upon thy cheek lay I this zealous kiss
As seal to this indenture of my love

LYMOGES, DUKE OF AUSTRIA, *King John*, II.I.19

That kiss is comfortless
As frozen water to a starved snake.

MARCUS, *Titus Andronicus*, III.I.250

If I profane with my unworthiest hand
This holy shrine, the gentle sin is this,
My lips, two blushing pilgrims, ready stand

To smooth that rough touch with a tender kiss.

ROMEO, *Romeo and Juliet*, I.V.93

Their lips were four red roses on a stalk,
Which in their summer beauty kiss'd each other.

TYRREL, *Richard III*, IV.III.12

KNOWLEDGE
see also EXPERIENCE; WISDOM

I ever
Have studied physic; through which secret art
By turning o'er authorities, I have,
Together with my practice, made familiar
To me and to my aid the blest infusions
That dwells in vegetives, in metals, stones;
And can speak of the disturbances
That nature works, and of her cures; which doth give me
A more content in course of true delight
Than to be thirsty after tottering honor,
Or tie my pleasure up in silken bags,
To please the fool and death.

CERIMON, *Pericles*, III.II.31

I speak not this in estimation,
As what I think might be, but what I know
Is ruminated, plotted, and set down,
And only stays but to behold the face
Of that occasion that shall bring it on.

EARL OF WORCESTER, *1 Henry IV*, I.III.272

And seeing ignorance is the curse of God,
Knowledge the wing wherewith we fly to heaven.

LORD SAY, *2 Henry VI*, IV.VII.73

LAW
see also INJUSTICE; JUDGMENT; JUSTICE; LAWYERS; PUNISHMENT

We must not make a scarecrow of the law,
Setting it up to fear the birds of prey,
And let it keep one shape, till custom make it
Their perch and not their terror.

ANGELO, *Measure for Measure*, II.I.1

The law hath not been dead, though it hath slept.

ANGELO, *Measure for Measure*, II.II.90

Only this fears me,
The law will have the honor of our ends.
Have at thy life!

ARCITE, *The Two Noble Kinsmen*, III.VI.129

In law, what plea so tainted and corrupt
But, being season'd with a gracious voice,
Obscures the show of evil?

BASSANIO, *The Merchant of Venice*, III.II.75

Wrest once the law to your authority:
To do a great right, do a little wrong,
And curb this cruel devil of his will.

BASSANIO, *The Merchant of Venice*, IV.I.215

Here is a hand to hold a scepter up,
And with the same to act controlling laws.

DUKE OF YORK, *2 Henry VI*, V.I.102

But in these nice sharp quillets of the law,
Good faith, I am no wiser than a daw.

EARL OF WARWICK, *1 Henry VI*, II.IV.17

We are for law, he dies, urge it no more
On height of our displeasure. Friend, or brother,
He forfeits his own blood that spills another.

SENATOR, *Timon of Athens*, III.V.85

Nay, John, it will be stinking law,
for his breath stinks with eating toasted cheese.

SMITH THE WEAVER, *2 Henry VI*, IV.VII.11

LAWYERS
see also JUSTICE; LAW

The first thing we do, let's kill all the lawyers.

DICK THE BUTCHER, *2 Henry VI*, IV.II.76

There's another skull. Why may not that be the skull of a
lawyer? Where be his quiddities now, his quillities, his
cases, his tenures, and his tricks? Why does he suffer this
mad knave now to knock him about the sconce with a dirty
shovel, and will not tell him of his action of battery?

HAMLET, *Hamlet*, V.I.98

Good counselors lack no clients.

POMPEY, *Measure for Measure*, I.II.106

Windy attorneys to their client's woes,
Airy succeeders of intestate joys,
Poor breathing orators of miseries,
Let them have scope! though what they will impart
Help nothing else, yet do they ease the heart.

QUEEN ELIZABETH, *Richard III*, IV.IV.127

Do as adversaries do in law,
Strive mightily, but eat and drink as friends.

TRANIO, *The Taming of the Shrew*, I.II.276

LAZINESS
see also INACTION; PROCRASTINATION

What is a man,
If his chief good and market of his time
Be but to sleep and feed? a beast, no more.

HAMLET, *Hamlet*, IV.IV.33

Y' are lazy knaves,
And here ye lie baiting of bombards, when
Ye should do service.

LORD CHAMBERLAIN, *Henry VIII*, V.III.80

LEADERSHIP
see also AUTHORITY; GOVERNMENT; POLITICS AND POWER; ROYALTY

He is their god; he leads them like a thing
Made by some other deity than Nature,
That shapes man better; and they follow him
Against us brats with no less confidence
Than boys pursuing summer butterflies,
Or butchers killing flies.

COMINIUS, *Coriolanus*, IV.VI.90

Gentlemen, will you go muster men? If I
Know how or which way to order these affairs
Thus disorderly thrust into my hands,
Never believe me.

DUKE OF YORK, *Richard II*, II.II.108

You have that in your countenance
which I would fain call master.

EARL OF KENT, *King Lear*, I.IV.27

And knowing this kingdom is without a head—
Like goodly buildings left without a roof
Soon fall to ruin—your noble self,
That best know how to rule and how to reign,
We thus submit unto—our sovereign.

LORD, *Pericles*, II.IV.35

He is a happy king, since he gains from his
subjects the name of good by his government.

PERICLES, *Pericles*, II.I.104

Be great in act, as you have been in thought.
Let not the world see fear and sad distrust

Govern the motion of a kingly eye.
Be stirring as the time, be fire with fire,
Threaten the threat'ner, and outface the brow
Of bragging horror; so shall inferior eyes,
That borrow their behaviors from the great,
Grow great by your example and put on
The dauntless spirit of resolution.

PHILIP THE BASTARD, *King John*, V.I.45

When that the general is not like the hive
To whom the foragers shall all repair,
What honey is expected?

ULYSSES, *Troilus and Cressida*, I.III.81

LETTERS
see also WRITING

Get posts and letters, and make friends with speed—
Never so few, and never yet more need.

EARL OF NORTHUMBERLAND, *2 Henry IV*, I.I.214

If he should write
And I not have it, 'twere a paper lost
As offer'd mercy is.

IMOGEN, *Cymbeline*, I.III.2

Thither write, my queen,
And with mine eyes I'll drink the words you send,
Though ink be made of gall.

POSTHUMUS, *Cymbeline*, I.I.99

LIES
see also DECEIT; DISHONESTY; DISGUISE; SLANDER

If but one of his pockets could speak, would it not say he
lies?

ANTONIO, *The Tempest*, II.I.66

Oftentimes, to win us to our harm,
The instruments of darkness tell us truths,
Win us with honest trifles, to betray's
In deepest consequence.

BANQUO, *Macbeth*, I.III.123

If I be false, or swerve a hair from truth,
When time is old and hath forgot itself,
When water-drops have worn the stones of Troy,
And blind oblivion swallow'd cities up,
And mighty states characterless are grated
To dusty nothing, yet let memory,
From false to false among false maids in love,
Upbraid my false hood! When th' have said as false

As air, as water, wind, or sandy earth,
As fox to lamb, or wolf to heifer's calf,
Pard to the hind, or step-dame to her son,
Yea, let them say, to stick the heart of falsehood,
"As false as Cressid."

CRESSIDA, Troilus and Cressida, III.II.184

He commands us to provide, and give great gifts,
And all out of an empty coffer;
Nor will he know his purse, or yield me this,
To show him what a beggar his heart is,
Being of no power to make his wishes good.

FLAVIUS, Timon of Athens, I.II.192

Why, what a candy deal of courtesy
This fawning greyhound then did proffer me!

HOTSPUR, 1 Henry IV, I.III.251

To lapse in fullness
Is sorer than to lie for need; and falsehood
Is worse, in kings than beggars.

IMOGEN, Cymbeline, III.VI.12

I say thou liest, Camillo, and I hate thee,
Pronounce thee a gross lout, a mindless salve,
Or else a hovering temporizer, that
Canst with thine eyes at once see good and evil,
Inclining to them both.

LEONTES, The Winter's Tale, I.II.300

These lies are like their father that begets
them, gross as a mountain, open, palpable.

PRINCE HENRY, 1 Henry IV, II.IV.225

LIFE
see also BIRTH; HUMAN CONDITION

By law of nature thou art bound to breed,
That thine may live, when thou thyself art dead.

Venus and Adonis, 171

Death may usurp on nature many hours,
And yet the fire of life kindle again
The o'erpress'd spirits.

CERIMON, Pericles, III.II.82

I love long life better than figs.

CHARMIAN, Antony and Cleopatra, I.II.32

I can no more: live thou to joy thy life;
Myself no joy in nought but that thou liv'st.

EARL OF SUFFOLK, 2 Henry VI, III.II.365

Why, what is pomp, rule, reign, but earth and dust?
And live we how we can, yet die we must.

EARL OF WARWICK, *3 Henry VI*, V.II.27

O gentlemen, the time of life is short!
To spend that shortness basely were too long
If life did rule upon a dial's point,
Still ending at the arrival of an hour.

HOTSPUR, *1 Henry IV*, V.II.81

All the world's a stage,
And all the men and women merely players;
They have their exits and their entrances,
And one man in his time plays many parts,
His acts being seven ages. At first the infant,
Mewling and puking in the nurse's arms.
Then the whining schoolboy, with his satchel
And shining morning face, creeping like snail
Unwillingly to school. And then the lover,
Sighing like furnace, with a woeful ballad
Made to his mistress' eyebrow. Then a soldier,
Full of strange oaths, and bearded like the pard,
Jealous in honor, sudden and quick in quarrel,
Seeking the bubble reputation
Even in the cannon's mouth. And then the justice,
In fair round belly with good capon lin'd,
With eyes severe and beard of formal cut,
Full of wise saws and modern instances;
And so he plays his part. The sixth age shifts
Into the lean and slipper'd pantaloon,
With spectacles on nose, and pouch on side,
His youthful hose, well sav'd, a world too wide
For his shrunk shank, and his big manly voice,
Turning again toward childish treble, pipes
And whistles in his sound. Last scene of all,
That ends this strange eventful history,
Is second childishness, and mere oblivion,
Sans teeth, sans eyes, sans taste, sans every thing.

JAQUES, *As You Like It*, II.VII.139

Love they to live that love and honor have.

JOHN OF GAUNT, *Richard II*, II.I.138

For in the shade of death I shall find joy;
In life by double death.

KING HENRY, *2 Henry VI*, III.II.54

The web of our life is of a mingled yarn, good and ill
together; our virtues would be proud, if our faults whipped

them not, and our crimes would despair, if they were not
cherish'd by our virtues.

First Lord, *All's Well That Ends Well*, IV.III.71

To-morrow, and to-morrow, and to-morrow,
Creeps in this petty pace from day to day,
To the last syllable of recorded time;
And all our yesterdays have lighted fools
The way to dusty death. Out, out, brief candle!
Life's but a walking shadow, a poor player,
That struts and frets his hour upon the stage,
And then is heard no more. It is a tale
Told by an idiot, full of sound and fury,
Signifying nothing.

Macbeth, *Macbeth*, V.V.19

Why grow the branches when the root is gone?
Why wither not the leaves that want their sap?
If you will live, lament; if die, be brief.

Queen Elizabeth, *Richard III*, II.II.41

Sir To. Does not our lives consist of
the four elements?
Sir And. Faith, so they say, but I think it rather
consists of eating and drinking.

Sir Andrew and Sir Toby, *Twelfth Night*, II.III.9

I fear not Goliath with a weaver's beam, because
I know also life is a shuttle.

Sir John Falstaff, *The Merry Wives of Windsor*, V.I.22

Reason thus with life:
If I do lose thee, I do lose a thing
That none but fools would keep.

Vincentio, Duke of Vienna, *Measure for Measure*, III.I.6

LIGHT
see also DAY; NIGHT

Lo in the orient when the gracious light
Lifts up his burning head, each under eye
Doth homage to his new-appearing sight,
Serving with looks his sacred majesty.

Sonnet 7, 1–4

This said, he sets his foot upon the light,
For light and lust are deadly enemies;
Shame folded up in blind concealing night,
When most unseen, then most doth tyrannize.

The Rape of Lucrece, 673

The flame o' th' taper
Bows toward her, and would under-peep her lids,
To see the enclosèd lights, nor canopied
Under these windows, white and azure lac'd
With blue of heaven's own tinct.

JACHIMO, Cymbeline, II.II.19

Jul. O now be gone, more light and light it grows.
Rom. More light and light, more dark and dark our woes!

JULIET, ROMEO, Romeo and Juliet, III.v.35

LITERACY
see also READING; WRITING

Find them out whose names are written here! It is written
that the shoemaker should meddle with his yard and the
tailor with his last, the fisher with his pencil and the
painter with his nets; but I am sent to find those persons
whose names are here writ, and can never find what names the
writing person hath here writ. I must to the learned.

CLOWN, Romeo and Juliet, I.II.38

To be a well-favor'd man is the gift of fortune, but to
write and read comes by nature.

DOGBERRY, Much Ado About Nothing, III.III.14

Many wearing rapiers are afraid of goose-quills.

ROSENCRANTZ, Hamlet, II.II.343

LONGING
see also DESIRE; NEED AND NECESSITY

Sir, you have sav'd my longing, and I feed
Most hungerly on your sight.

ALCIBIADES, Timon of Athens, I.1.251

The flow'r that I would pluck
And put between my breast (O then but beginning
To swell about the blossom), she would long
Till she had such another, and commit it
To the like innocent cradle, where phoenix-like
They died in perfume.

EMILIA, The Two Noble Kinsmen, I.III.66

How his longing
Follows his friend: since his depart, his sports,
Though craving seriousness and skill, pass'd slightly
His careless execution, where not gain
Made him regard, or loss consider, but
Playing o'er business in his hand, another
Directing in his head, his mind nurse equal

To these so diff'ring twins.

EMILIA, The Two Noble Kinsmen, I.III.27

LOSS
see also GRIEF; MOURNING; SADNESS; SORROW

If I lose thee, my loss is my love's gain,
And losing her, my friend hath found that loss;
Both find each other, and I lose both twain,
And both for my sake lay on me this cross.

SONNET 42, 9–12

Irreparable is the loss, and patience
Says it is past her cure.

ALONSO, The Tempest, V.I.140

What our contempts doth often hurl from us,
We wish it ours again. The present pleasure,
By revolution low'ring, does become
The opposite of itself. She's good, being gone;
The hand could pluck her back that shov'd her on.

ANTONY, Antony and Cleopatra, I.II.123

What we have we prize not to the worth
Whiles we enjoy it, but being lack'd and lost,
Why then we rack the value; then we find
The virtue that possession would not show us
Whiles it was ours.

FRIAR FRANCIS, Much Ado About Nothing, IV.I.218

Your loss is great, so your regard should be;
My worth is unknown, no loss is known in me.

JOHN TALBOT, 1 Henry VI, IV.V.22

1. Lord. How mightily sometimes we make us
comforts of our losses!
2. Lord. And how mightily some other times we
drown our gain in tears!

FIRST LORD, SECOND LORD, All's Well That Ends Well, IV.III.65

He hath lost his fellows,
And strays about to find 'em.

PROSPERO, The Tempest, I.II.417

LOVE AND EXPRESSION

I am sure my love's
More ponderous than my tongue.

CORDELIA, King Lear, I.I.77

Ah, Juliet, if the measure of thy joy
Be heat'd like mine, and that thy skill be more

To blazon it, then sweeten with thy breath
This neighbor air, and let rich music's tongue
Unfold the imagin'd happiness that both
Receive in either by this dear encounter.

ROMEO, *Romeo and Juliet*, II.VI.24

LOVE AND FIRE

Love's fire heats water, water cools not love.

SONNET 154, 14

Love is a spirit all compact of fire,
Not gross to sink, but light, and will aspire.

Venus and Adonis, 149

Didst thou but know the inly touch of love,
Thou wouldst as soon go kindle fire with snow
As seek to quench the fire of love with words.

JULIA, *The Two Gentlemen of Verona*, II.VII.18

Love is a smoke made with the fume of sighs,
Being purg'd, a fire sparkling in lovers' eyes,
Being vex'd, a sea nourish'd with loving tears.
What is it else? a madness most discreet,
A choking gall, and a preserving sweet.

ROMEO, *Romeo and Juliet*, I.I.190

LOVE AND PURSUIT

Love's heralds should be thoughts,
Which ten times faster glides than the sun's beams,
Driving back shadows over low'ring hills.

JULIET, *Romeo and Juliet*, II.V.4

Nature is fine in love, and where 'tis fine,
It sends some precious instance of itself
After the thing it loves.

LAERTES, *Hamlet*, IV.V.162

Love sought is good, but given unsought is better.

OLIVIA, *Twelfth Night*, III.I.156

LOVE AND THE SENSES

Thou blind fool, Love, what dost thou to mine eyes,
That they behold and see not what they see?

SONNET 137, 1–2

O me! what eyes hath Love put in my head,
Which have no correspondence with true sight.

SONNET 148, 1–2

Fie, fie, fond love, thou art as full of fear

As one with treasure laden, hemm'd with thieves.

Venus and Adonis, 1021

Love, first learned in a lady's eyes,
Lives not alone immurèd in the brain,
But with the motion of all elements,
Courses as swift as thought in every power,
And gives to every power a double power,
Above their functions and offices.
It adds a precious seeing to the eye:
A lover's eyes will gaze an eagle blind.
A lover's ear will hear the lowest sound,
When the suspicious head of theft is stopp'd.
Love's feeling is more soft and sensible
Than are the tender horns of cockled snails.
Love's tongue proves dainty Bacchus gross in taste.
For valor, is not Love a Hercules,
Still climbing trees in the Hesperides?
Subtle as Sphinx, as sweet and musical
As bright Apollo's lute, strung with his hair.
And when Love speaks, the voice of all the gods
Make heaven drowsy with the harmony.

BEROWNE, *Love's Labor's Lost*, IV.III.324

Love looks not with the eyes but with the mind;
And therefore is wing'd Cupid painted blind.
Nor hath Love's mind of any judgment taste;
Wings, and no eyes, figure unheedy haste;
And therefore is Love said to be a child,
Because in choice he is so oft beguil'd.
As waggish boys in game themselves forswear,
So the boy Love is perjur'd everywhere.

HELENA, *A Midsummer Night's Dream*, I.I.234

LOVE—CUPID

This wimpled, whining, purblind, wayward boy,
This senior-junior, giant-dwarf, Dan Cupid,
Regent of love rhymes, lord of folded arms,
Th' anointed sovereign of sighs and groans,
Liege of all loiterers and malecontents.

BEROWNE, *Love's Labor's Lost*, III.I.179

LOVE—GENERAL
see also AFFECTION; ATTRACTION; COURTING; DESIRE; DEVOTION; HEART; INFATUA-
TION; KISS; MARRIAGE; PASSION

So are you to my thoughts as food to life,
Or as sweet-season'd showers are to the ground.

SONNET 75, 1–2

Thy love is better than high birth to me,
Richer than wealth, prouder than garments' cost,
Of more delight than hawks or horses be;
And having thee, of all men's pride I boast.

SONNET 116, 1–4

Let me not to the marriage of true minds
Admit impediments; love is not love
Which alters when it alteration finds,
Or bends with the remover to remove.

SONNET 116, 1–4

O hard-believing love, how strange it seems!
Not to believe, and yet too credulous.

Venus and Adonis, 985

Love's arms are peace, 'gainst rule, 'gainst sense,
'gainst shame,
And sweetens, in the suff'ring pangs it bears,
The aloes of all forces, shocks, and fears.

A Lover's Complaint, 271

There's beggary in the love that can be reckon'd.

ANTONY, *Antony and Cleopatra*, I.I.15

Love's reason's without reason.

ARVIRAGUS, *Cymbeline*, IV.II.22

Prosperity's the very bond of love,
Whose fresh complexion and whose heart together
Affliction alters.

CAMILLO, *The Winter's Tale*, IV.IV.573

By heaven, my soul is purg'd from grudging hate,
And with my hand I seal my true heart's love.

EARL RIVERS, *Richard III*, II.I.9

That this his love was an external plant,
Whereof the root was fix'd in virtue's ground,
The leaves and fruit maintain'd with beauty's sun,
Exempt from envy, but not from disdain,
Unless the Lady Bona quit his pain.

EARL OF WARWICK, *3 Henry VI*, III.III.124

He says he loves my daughter.
I think so too; for never gaz'd the moon
Upon the water as he'll stand and read
As 'twere my daughter's eyes; and to be plain,
I think there is not half a kiss to choose
Who loves another best.

SHEPHERD, *The Winter's Tale*, IV.IV.171

LOVE—SKEPTICAL

The poor world is almost six thousand years old, and in all
this time there was not any man died in his own person,
videlicet, in a love-cause. Troilus had his brains dash'd
out with a Grecian club, yet he did what he could to die
before, and he is one of the patterns of love. Leander, he
would have liv'd many a fair year though Hero had turn'd
nun, if it had not been for a hot midsummer night; for, good
youth, he went but forth to wash him in the Hellespont, and
being taken with the cramp was drown'd; and the foolish
chroniclers of that age found it was—Hero of Sestos. But
these are all lies: men have died from time to time, and
worms have eaten them, but not for love.

ROSALIND, *As You Like It*, IV.i.94

Love is merely a madness, and I tell you, deserves as well a
dark house and a whip as madmen do; and the reason why they
are not so punish'd and cur'd is, that the lunacy is so
ordinary that the whippers are in love too.

ROSALIND, *As You Like It*, III.ii.400

LOVE—THE LOOK OF

Such as I am, all true lovers are,
Unstaid and skittish in all motions else,
Save in the constant image of the creature
That is belov'd.

ORSINO, DUKE OF ILLYRIA, *Twelfth Night*, II.iv.17

The sight of lovers feedeth those in love.

ROSALIND, *As You Like It*, III.iv.57

Val. Why, how know you that I am in love?
Speed. Marry, by these special marks: first, you have
learn'd, like Sir Proteus, to wreathe your arms, like a
malcontent; to relish a love-song, like a robin-redbreast;
to walk alone, like one that had the pestilence; to sigh,
like a schoolboy that had lost his A B C; to weep, like a
young wench that had buried her grandam; to fast, like one
that takes diet; to watch, like one that fears robbing; to
speak puling, like a beggar at Hallowmas. You were wont,
when you laugh'd, to crow like a cock, when you walk'd,
to walk like one of the lions; when you fasted, it was
presently after dinner; when you look'd sadly, it was for
want of money; and now you are metamorphis'd with a
mistress, that when I look on you, I can hardly think you
my master.

VALENTINE, SPEED, *The Two Gentlemen of Verona*, II.i.17

LOVE—TRAGIC

A pair of star-cross'd lovers take their life;
Whose misadventur'd piteous overthrows
Doth with their death bury their parents strife.

CHORUS, *Romeo and Juliet*, PRO.6

Love that comes too late,
Like a remorseful pardon slowly carried,
To the great sender turns a sour offense,
Crying, "That's good that's gone."

KING OF FRANCE, *All's Well That Ends Well*, V.III.57

So dear I lov'd the man that I must weep.
I took him for the plainest harmless creature
That breath'd upon the earth a Christian;
Made him my book, wherein my soul recorded
The history of all her secret thoughts.

RICHARD, DUKE OF GLOUCESTER, *Richard III*, III.v.24

My only love sprung from my only hate!
Too early seen unknown, and known too late!
Prodigious birth of love it is to me
That I must love a loathèd enemy.

JULIET, *Romeo and Juliet*, I.v.138

LOYALTY
see also DUTY; FAITHFULNESS; FRIENDSHIP

Master, go on, and I will follow thee
To the last gasp, with truth and loyalty.

ADAM, *As You Like It*, II.III.69

It is no vicious blot, murther, or foulness,
No unchaste action, or dishonored step,
That hath depriv'd me of your grace and favor,
But even for want of that for which I am richer—
A still-soliciting eye, and such a tongue
That I am glad I have not, though not to have it
Hath lost me in your liking.

CORDELIA, *King Lear*, I.I.228

The loyalty well held to fools does make
Our faith mere folly; yet he that can endure
To follow with allegiance a fall'n lord
Does conquer him that did his master conquer,
And earns a place i' th' story.

ENOBARBUS, *Antony and Cleopatra*, III.XIII.42

Yea, on his part I'll empty all these veins,
And shed my dear blood drop by drop in the dust.

HOTSPUR, *1 Henry IV*, I.III.133

This speedy and quick appearance argues proof
Of your accustom'd diligence to me.
JOAN DE PUCELLE, *1 Henry VI*, V.III.8

O, where is faith? O, where is loyalty?
If it be banish'd from the frosty head,
Where shall if find a harbor in the earth?
KING HENRY, *2 Henry VI*, VI.I.166

You have no cause to hold my friendship doubtful.
I never was nor never will be false.
LORD STANLEY, *Richard III*, IV.IV.493

End life when I end loyalty!
LYSANDER, *A Midsummer Night's Dream*, II.II.63

My duty pricks me on to utter that
Which else no worldly good should draw from me.
PROTEUS, *The Two Gentlemen of Verona*, III.I.8

I was a pack-horse in his great affairs:
A weeder-out of his proud adversaries,
A liberal rewarder of his friends;
To royalize his blood I spent mine own.
RICHARD, DUKE OF GLOUCESTER, *Richard III*, I.III.121

LUCK
see also FORTUNE; GAMBLING
And from this swarm of fair advantages
You took occasion to be quickly wooed
To gripe the general sway into your hand.
EARL OF WORCESTER, *1 Henry IV*, V.I.55

'Tis a lucky day, boy, and we'll do good
deeds on't.
SHEPHERD, *The Winter's Tale*, III.III.137

LUST
see also ATTRACTION; DESIRE; SEX
Her face doth reek and smoke, her blood doth boil,
And careless lust stirs up a desperate courage.
Venus and Adonis, 555

Love's gentle spring doth always fresh remain,
Lust's winter comes ere summer half be done.
Venus and Adonis, 801

Love comforteth like sunshine after rain,
But Lust's effect is tempest after sun.
Venus and Adonis, 799

This momentary joy breeds months of pain
This hot desire converts to cold disdain.

The Rape of Lucrece, 690

But virtue, as it never will be moved,
Though lewdness court it in a shape of heaven,
So lust, though to a radiant angel link'd,
Will sate itself in a celestial bed
And prey on garbage.

GHOST, *Hamlet*, I.v.53

To live
In the rank sweat of an enseamèd bed,
Stew'd in corruption, honeying and making love
Over the nasty sty!

HAMLET, *Hamlet*, III.IV.91

There are a kind of men, so loose of soul,
That in their sleeps will mutter their affairs.

IAGO, *Othello*, III.III.416

The cloyèd will—
That satiate yet unsatisfied desire, that tub
Both fill'd and running—ravening first the lamb,
Longs after for the garbage.

JACHIMO, *Cymbeline*, I.VI.48

Tell me else,
Could such inordinate and low desires,
Such poor, such bare, such lewd, such mean attempts,
Such barren pleasures, rude society,
As thou art match'd withal and grafted to,
Accompany the greatness of thy blood,
And hold their level with thy princely heart?

KING HENRY, *1 Henry IV*, III.II.11

Thy bed, lust-stain'd, shall with lust's blood be spotted.

OTHELLO, *Othello*, V.I.36

And both like serpents are, who though they feed
On sweetest flowers, yet they poison breed.

PERICLES, *Pericles*, I.I.132

Urge his hateful luxury
And bestial appetite in change of lust,
Which stretch'd unto their servants, daughters, wives,
Even where his raging eye or savage heart,
Without control, lusted to make a prey.

RICHARD, DUKE OF GLOUCESTER, *Richard III*, III.v.80

MADNESS AND MENTAL ILLNESS
see also DEPRESSION; ILLUSION; IRRATIONALITY; SICKNESS

Were such things here as we do speak about?
Or have we eaten on the insane root
That takes the reason prisoner?

BANQUO, *Macbeth*, I.III.83

Madness in great ones must not unwatch'd go.

CLAUDIUS, *Hamlet*, III.I.188

O you kind gods!
Cure this great breach in his abused nature,
Th' untun'd and jarring senses, O, wind up
Of this child-changed father!

CORDELIA, *King Lear*, IV.VII.13

Some strange commotion
Is in his brain; he bites his lip, and starts,
Stops on a sudden, looks upon the ground,
Then lays his finger on his temple; straight
Springs out into fast gait, then stops again,
Strikes his breast hard, and anon he casts
His eye against the moon.

DUKE OF NORFOLK, *Henry VIII*, III.II.112

I am but mad north-north-west. When the wind is southerly
I know a hawk from a hand-saw.

HAMLET, *Hamlet*, II.II.378

My wit's diseas'd.

HAMLET, *Hamlet*, III.II.321

There is a mutiny in 's mind.

KING HENRY, *Henry VIII*, III.II.120

O, let me not be mad, not mad, sweet heaven!
Keep me in temper, I would not be mad!

LEAR, *King Lear*, I.V.46

We are not ourselves
When nature, being oppress'd, commands the mind
To suffer with the body.

LEAR, *King Lear*, II.IV.107

Bear with her weakness, which I think proceeds
From wayward sickness and no grounded malice.

LORD STANLEY, *Richard III*, I.III.28

Better be with the dead,
Whom we, to gain our peace, have sent to peace,

Than on the torture of the mind to lie
In restless ecstasy.

MACBETH, Macbeth, III.II.19

Any madness I ever yet beheld seem'd but tameness, civility,
and patience to this his distemper he is in now.

MISTRESS PAGE, The Merry Wives of Windsor, IV.II.26

Though this be madness, yet there is method in't.

POLONIUS, Hamlet, II.II.205

Your noble son is mad:
Mad call I it, for to define true madness,
What is't but to be nothing else but mad?

POLONIUS, Hamlet, II.II.92

Fri. L. I see that madmen have no ears.
Rom. How should they when that wise men have no eyes?

ROMEO, FRIAR LAWRENCE, Romeo and Juliet, III.III.61

MANNERS
see also FORMALITY

Those that are good manners at the court are as ridiculous
in the country as the behavior of the country is most
mockable at the court. You told me you salute not at the
court but you kiss your hands; that courtesy would be
uncleanly if courtiers were shepherds.

CORIN, As You Like It, III.II.45

And if I were thy nurse, thy tongue to teach,
"Pardon" should be the first word of thy speech.

DUCHESS OF YORK, Richard II, V.III.113

Frame your manners to the time.

LUCENTIO, The Taming of the Shrew, I.I.227

He has been yonder i' the sun practicing behavior to his own
shadow this half hour.

MARIA, Twelfth Night, II.v.16

The thorny point
Of bare distress hath ta'en from me the show
Of smooth civility; yet am I inland bred,
And know some nurture.

ORLANDO, As You Like It, II.VII.94

He is as disproportion'd in his manners
As in his shape.

PROSPERO, The Tempest, V.I.291

Where good manners shall lie all in one or two men's hands,
and they unwash'd too, 'tis a foul thing.

SECOND SERVINGMAN, Romeo and Juliet, I.v.3

It is certain that either wise bearing or
ignorant carriage is caught, as men take diseases, one of
another; therefore let me take heed of their company.

SIR JOHN FALSTAFF, 2 Henry IV, V.i.75

MARRIAGE

see also COURTING; DIVORCE; HUSBANDS; LOVE—GENERAL; UNITY; WIDOWHOOD;
WIVES

Wooing, wedding, and repenting, is as a Scotch jig, a
measure, and a cinquepace; the first suite is hot and hasty,
like a Scotch jig, and full as fantastical; the wedding,
mannerly-modest, as a measure, full of state and ancientry;
and then comes repentance, and with his bad legs falls into
the cinquepace faster and faster, till he sink into his
grave.

BEATRICE, Much Ado About Nothing, II.i.73

Prince, thou art sad, get thee a wife, get thee a wife.

BENEDICK, Much Ado About Nothing, V.iv.122

Come, madam wife, sit by my side, and let the world slip,
we shall ne'er be younger.

CHRISTOPHER SLY, The Taming of the Shrew, IND.ii.142

Henry is able to enrich his queen,
And not to seek a queen to make him rich:
So worthless peasants bargain for their wives,
As market men for oxen, sheep, or horse.
Marriage is a matter of more worth
Than to be dealt in by attorneyship.

EARL OF SUFFOLK, 1 Henry VI, V.v.51

Look down, you gods,
And on this couple drop a blessed crown!

GONZALO, The Tempest, V.i.201

I say we will have no more marriage. Those that are married
(all but one) shall live, the rest shall keep as they are.
To a nunn'ry, go.

HAMLET, Hamlet, III.i.147

Father and mother is man and wife; man and wife is one
flesh.

HAMLET, Hamlet, IV.iii.51

Their knot of love
Tied, weav'd, entangled, with so true, so long,
And with a finger of so deep a cunning,
May be outworn, never undone.

HIPPOLYTA, The Two Noble Kinsmen, I.iii.41

He is the half part of a blessed man,
Left to be finished by such as she,
And she a fair divided excellence,
Whose fullness of perfection lies in him.
O, two such silver currents when they join
Do glorify the banks that bound them in;
And two such shores to two such streams made one,
Two such controlling bounds shall you be, kings,
To these two princes, if you marry them.

HUBERT, *King John*, II.I.437

We will have rings and things, and fine array;
And kiss me, Kate, we will be married a' Sunday.

PETRUCHIO, *The Taming of the Shrew*, II.I.323

One half of me is yours, the other half yours—
Mine own, I would say; but if mine, then yours,
And so all yours.

PORTIA, *The Merchant of Venice*, III.II.16

Fair encounter
Of two most rare affections! Heavens rain grace
On that which breeds between 'em!

PROSPERO, *The Tempest*, III.I.75

Look how my ring encompasseth thy finger,
Even so thy breast encloseth my poor heart:
And if thy poor devoted servant may
But beg one favor at thy gracious hand,
Thou dost confirm his happiness for ever.

RICHARD, DUKE OF GLOUCESTER, *Richard III*, I.II.203

Men are April when they woo, December when they wed; maids
are May when they are maids, but the sky changes when they
are wives.

ROSALIND, *As You Like It*, IV.I.147

The gods by their divine arbitrament
Have given you this knight: he is a good one
As ever strook at head. Give me your hands.
Receive you her, you him, be plighted with
A love that grows as you decay.

THESEUS, *The Two Noble Kinsmen*, V.III.107

MARTYRDOM
see also SACRIFICE

Though I think
I never shall enjoy her, yet I'll preserve

The honor of affection, and die for her,
Make death a devil.

ARCITE, The Two Noble Kinsmen, III.VI.167

"Done to death by slanderous tongues
Was the Hero that here lies.
Death, in guerdon of her wrongs,
Gives her fame which never dies.
So the life that died with shame
Lives in death with glorious fame."

CLAUDIO (READING), Much Ado About Nothing, V.III.3

If the law
Find me, and then condemn me for't, some wenches,
Some honest-hearted maids, will sing my dirge,
And tell to memory my death was noble,
Dying almost a martyr.

DAUGHTER, The Two Noble Kinsmen, II.VI.13

To-day shalt thou behold a subject die
For truth, for duty, and for loyalty.

EARL RIVERS, Richard III, III.III.3

From whose obedience I forbid my soul,
Kneeling before this ruin of sweet life,
And breathing to his breathless excellence
The incense of a vow, a holy vow,
Never to taste the pleasures of the world,
Never to be infected with delight,
Nor conversant with ease and idleness,
Till I have set a glory to this hand,
By giving it the worship of revenge.

SALISBURY, King John, IV.III.64

MATURITY
see also AGING; GROWING UP; OLD AGE

Though age from folly could not give me freedom,
It does from childishness.

CLEOPATRA, Antony and Cleopatra, I.III.57

The crow doth sing as sweetly as the lark
When neither is attended; and I think
The nightingale, if she should sing by day
When every goose is cackling, would be thought
No better a musician that the wren.
How many things by season, season'd are
To their right praise and true perfection!

PORTIA, The Merchant of Venice, V.I.102

The truth is, I am only
old in judgment and understanding.

SIR JOHN FALSTAFF, 2 Henry IV, I.II.191

MEMORY
see also HISTORY; PAST

When to the sessions of sweet silent thought
I summon up remembrance of things past,
I sigh the lack of many a thing I sought,
And with old woes new wail my dear time's waste.

SONNET 30, 1–4

The wrinkles which thy glass will truly show,
Of mouthèd graves will give thee memory.

SONNET 77, 5–6

These arms of mine shall be thy winding sheet;
My heart, sweet boy, shall be thy sepulcher,
For from my heart thine image ne'er shall go.

FATHER, 3 Henry VI, II.v.114

Remember thee!
Ay, thou poor ghost, whiles memory holds a seat
In this distracted globe. Remember thee!
Yea, from the table of my memory
I'll wipe away all trivial fond records,
All saws of books, all forms, all pressures past
That youth and observation copied there,
And thy commandment all alone shall live
Within the book and volume of my brain,
Unmix'd with baser matter.

HAMLET, Hamlet, I.v.95

Praising what is lost
Makes the remembrance dear.

KING OF FRANCE, All's Well That Ends Well, V.III.19

But how is it
That this lives in thy mind? What seest thou else
In the dark backward and abysm of time?

PROSPERO, The Tempest, I.II.48

Let us not burden our rememberance with
A heaviness that's gone.

PROSPERO, The Tempest, V.I.198

MEN
see also FATHERHOOD; GENDER; HUSBANDS; SONS

Sigh no more, ladies, sigh no more,
Men were deceivers ever,

One foot in sea, and one on shore,
To one thing constant never.
BALTHASAR (SONG), *Much Ado About Nothing*, II.III.62

I had rather hear my dog bark at a crow than a man swear he
loves me.
BEATRICE, *Much Ado About Nothing*, I.I.131

He that hath a beard is more than a youth, and he that hath
no beard is less than a man.
BEATRICE, *Much Ado About Nothing*, II.I.36

Manhood is call'd foolery when it stands against a falling
fabric.
COMINIUS, *Coriolanus*, III.I.245

Men are not gods,
Nor of them look for such observancy
As fit the bridal.
DESDEMONA, *Othello*, III.IV.146

So you serve us
Till we serve you; but when you have our roses,
You barely leave our thorns to prick ourselves,
And mock us with our bareness.
DIANA, *All's Well That Ends Well*, IV.II.17

What should such fellows as I do crawling between earth and
heaven? We are arrant knaves, believe none of us.
HAMLET, *Hamlet*, III.I.126

There's nothing situate under heaven's eye
But hath his bound in earth, in sea, in sky.
The beasts, the fishes, and the wingèd fowls
Are their males' subjects and at their controls:
Man, more divine, the master of all these,
Lord of the wide world and wild wat'ry seas,
Indu'd with intellectual sense and souls,
Of more pre-eminence than fish and fowls,
Are masters to their females, and their lords:
Then let your will attend on their accords.
Is dearly bought as mine, and I will have it.
LUCIANA, *The Comedy of Errors*, II.I.16

A man is master of his liberty.
LUCIANA, *The Comedy of Errors*, II.I.7

There's no trust,
No faith, no honesty in men, all perjur'd,
All forsworn, all naught, all dissemblers.
NURSE, *Romeo and Juliet*, III.II.85

However we do praise ourselves,
Our men's fancies are more giddy and unfirm,
More longing, wavering, sooner lost and worn,
Than women's are.

ORSINO, DUKE OF ILLYRIA, *Twelfth Night*, II.iv.32

Do you know what a man is? Is not birth, beauty, good
shape, discourse, manhood, learning, gentleness, virtue,
youth, liberality, and such-like, the spice and salt that
season a man?

PANDARUS, *Troilus and Cressida*, I.ii.252

If manhood, good manhood, be
not forgot upon the face of the earth, then am I a
shotten herring.

SIR JOHN FALSTAFF, *1 Henry IV*, II.iv.128

So true, so just, and now so comfortable?
It almost turns my dangerous nature mild.
Let me behold thy face. Surely, this man
Was born of woman.

TIMON, *Timon of Athens*, IV.iii.490

MERCY
see also FORGIVENESS; GRACE; REPENTANCE

We seek not
Thy breath of mercy, Theseus. 'Tis to me
A thing as soon to die as thee to say it,
And no more mov'd.

ARCITE, *The Two Noble Kinsmen*, III.vi.159

What if this cursèd hand
Were thicker than itself with brother's blood,
Is there not rain enough in the sweet heavens
To wash it white as snow? Whereto serves mercy
But to confront the visage of offense?

CLAUDIUS, *Hamlet*, III.iii.43

How shalt thou hope for mercy, rend'ring none?

DUKE OF VENICE, *The Merchant of Venice*, IV.i.88

Why, all the souls that were were forfeit once,
And He that might the vantage best have took
Found out the remedy. How would you be
If He, which is the top of judgment, should
But judge you as you are? O, think on that,
And mercy then will breathe within your lips,
Like man new made.

ISABELLA, *Measure for Measure*, II.ii.73

No ceremony that to great ones 'longs,
Not the king's crown, nor the deputed sword,
The marshal's truncheon, nor the judge's robe,
Become them with one half so good a grace
As mercy does.

ISABELLA, Measure for Measure, II.II.59

As I suck blood, I will some mercy show.

PISTOL, Henry V, IV.IV.64

The quality of mercy is not strain'd,
It droppeth as the gentle rain from heaven
Upon the place beneath. It is twice blest:
It blesseth him that gives and him that takes.
'Tis mightiest in the mightiest, it becomes
The thronèd monarch better than his crown.
His scepter shows the force of temporal power,
The attribute to awe and majesty,
Where in doth sit the dread and fear of kings;
But mercy is above this sceptred sway,
It is enthronèd in the hearts of kings,
It is an attribute to God himself.

PORTIA, The Merchant of Venice, IV.I.184

This good deed
Shall raze you out o' th' book of trespasses
All you are set down there.

QUEEN, The Two Noble Kinsmen, I.I.32

O, I hope some god,
Some god hath put his mercy in your manhood,
Whereto he'll infuse pow'r, and press you forth
Our undertaker.

QUEEN, The Two Noble Kinsmen, I.I.71

Nothing emboldens sin so much as mercy.

SENATOR, Timon of Athens, III.V.2

You show great mercy if you give him life
After the taste of much correction.

SIR THOMAS GREY, Henry V, II.II.50

Brother, you have a vice of mercy in you,
Which is better fits a lion than a man.

TROILUS, Troilus and Cressida, V.III.37

MIND
see also REASON; THOUGHT

Incapable of more, replete with you,
My most true mind thus maketh mine untrue.

SONNET 113, 13–14

Perish the man whose mind is backward now!

> EARL OF WESTMERLAND, *Henry V*, IV.III.72

If she be furnish'd with a mind so rare,
She is alone th' Arabian bird.

> JACHIMO, *Cymbeline*, I.VI.16

All things are ready, if our minds be so.

> KING HENRY, *Henry V*, IV.III.71

When the mind's free,
The body's delicate.

> LEAR, *King Lear*, III.IV.11

It is too late, the life of all his blood
Is touch'd corruptibly; and his pure brain
(Which some suppose the soul's frail dwelling-house)
Doth by the idle comments that it makes
Foretell the ending of mortality.

> PRINCE HENRY, *King John*, V.VII.1

MIRACLES

But you have done more miracles than I:
You made in a day, my lord, whole towns to fly.

> DUKE OF GLOUCESTER, *2 Henry VI*, II.I.159

Nothing almost sees miracles
But misery.

> EARL OF KENT, *King Lear*, II.II.165

Great seas have dried
When miracles have by the great'st been denied.

> HELENA, *All's Well That Ends Well*, II.I.140

MISANTHROPY
see also ALIENATION; BIGOTRY AND INTOLERANCE; HATRED; MEN

I had rather be a canker in a hedge than a rose in his
grace, and it better fits my blood to be disdain'd of all
than to fashion a carriage to rob love from any. In this
(though I cannot be said to be a flattering honest man) it
must not be denied but I am a plain-dealing villain. I am
trusted with a muzzle, and enfranchis'd with a clog,
therefore I have decreed not to sing in my cage. If I had
my mouth, I would bite; if I had my liberty, I would do my
liking. In the mean time let me be that I am, and seek not
to alter me.

> DON JOHN, *Much Ado About Nothing*, I.III.27

I am Misanthropos, and hate mankind.
For thy part, I do wish thou wert a dog.

That I might love thee something.

> TIMON, *Timon of Athens*, IV.III.54

Hate all, curse all, show charity to none,
But let the famish'd flesh slide from the bone
Ere thou relieve the beggar. Give to dogs
What thou deniest to me. Let prisons swallow 'em
Debts wither 'em to nothing; be men like blasted woods,
And may diseases lick up their false bloods!
And so farewell and thrive.

> TIMON, *Timon of Athens*, IV.III.527

If thou wert the lion, the fox would
beguile thee; if thou wert the lamb, the fox would eat
thee; if thou were the fox, the lion would suspect
thee, when peradventure thou wert accus'd by the ass;
if thou wert the ass, thy dullness would torment thee,
and still thou liv'dst but as a breakfast to the wolf; if
thou wert the wolf, thy greediness would afflict thee,
and oft thou shouldst hazard thy life for thy dinner;
wert thou the unicorn, pride and wrath would confound
thee and make thine own self the conquest of thy fury;
wert thou a bear, thou wouldst be kill'd by the horse;
wert thou a horse, thou wouldst be seiz'd by the
leopard; wert thou a leopard, thou wert germane
to the lion, and the spots of thy kindred were jurors on
thy life.

> TIMON, *Timon of Athens*, IV.III.328

MISCHIEF

Mischief, thou art afoot,
Take thou what course thou wilt!

> ANTONY, *Julius Caesar*, III.II.259

See, to beguile the old folks, how the young folks lay their
heads together!

> GRUMIO, *The Taming of the Shrew*, I.II.138

MISERY
see also DESPAIR; DESPERATION; SUFFERING

Though woe be heavy, yet it seldom sleeps,
And they that watch see time how slow it creeps.

> *The Rape of Lucrece*, 1574

O ill-dispersing wind of misery!
O my accursèd womb, the bed of death!
A cockatrice hast thou hatch'd to the world,
Whose unavoided eye is murderous.

> DUCHESS OF YORK, *Richard III*, IV.I.52

Dark shall be my light, and night my day;
To think upon my pomp shall be my hell.

ELEANOR, *2 Henry VI*, II.IV.40

Misery make sport to mock itself.

JOHN OF GAUNT, *Richard II*, II.I.85

Ay, Margaret; my heart is drown'd with grief,
Whose flood begins to flow within mine eyes;
My body round engirt with misery—
For what's more miserable than discontent?

KING HENRY, *2 Henry VI*, III.I.198

But kings and mightiest potentates must die,
For that's the end of human misery.

LORD TALBOT, *1 Henry VI*, III.II.136

Misery acquaints a man with
strange bedfellows.

TRINCULO, *The Tempest*, II.II.39

MISOGYNY

see also BIGOTRY AND INTOLERANCE; HATRED; WOMEN

Under a compelling occasion, let women die. It were pity to
cast them away for nothing, though between them and a great
cause, they should be esteem'd nothing.

ENOBARBUS, *Antony and Cleopatra*, I.II.137

Frailty, thy name is woman!

HAMLET, *Hamlet*, I.II.146

Two women plac'd together makes cold weather.

LORD CHAMBERLAIN, *Henry VIII*, I.IV.22

Women are as roses, whose fair flow'r
Being once display'd, doth fall that very hour.

ORSINO, DUKE OF ILLYRIA, *Twelfth Night*, II.IV.38

This is a way to kill a wife with kindness.
And thus I'll curb her mad and headstrong humor.
He that knows better how to tame a shrew,
Now let him speak; 'tis charity to shew.

PETRUCHIO, *The Taming of the Shrew*, IV.I.208

Women, being the weaker vessels, are ever thrust to the
wall.

SAMPSON, *Romeo and Juliet*, I.I.15

Win her with gifts if she respect not words:
Dumb jewels often in their silent kind
More than quick words do move a woman's mind.

VALENTINE, *The Two Gentlemen of Verona*, III.I.89

MISTAKES
see also FAULTS

Book both my willfulness and errors down,
And on just proof surmise accumulate;
Bring me within the level of your frown,
But shoot not at me in your wakened hate.

SONNET 117, 9–12

What wretched errors hath my heart committed,
Whilst it hath thought itself so blessed never!

SONNET 119, 5–6

Say that thou didst forsake me for some fault,
And I will comment upon that offense;
Speak of my lameness, and I straight will halt.

SONNET 89, 1–3

No more be griev'd at that which thou hast done:
Roses have thorns, and silver foundations mud,
Clouds and eclipses stain both moon and sun,
And loathsome canker lives in sweetest bud.
All men make faults.

SONNET 35, 1–5

If you miscarry,
Your business of the world hath so an end,
And machination ceases.

EDGAR, *King Lear*, V.I.44

O hateful error, melancholy's child,
Why dost thou show to the apt thoughts of men
The things that are not? O error, soon conceiv'd
Thou never com'st unto a happy birth,
But kill'st the mother that engend'red thee!

MESSALA, *Julius Caesar*, V.III.67

MODERATION
see also CONSERVATISM

These violent delights have violent ends,
And in their triumph die, like fire and powder,
Which as they kiss consume. The sweetest honey
Is loathsome in his own deliciousness,
And in the taste confounds the appetite.
Therefore love moderately: long love doth so;
Too swift arrives as tardy as too slow.

FRIAR LAWRENCE, *Romeo and Juliet*, II.VI.9

Boundless intemperance
In nature is a tyranny; it hath been

Th' untimely emptying of the happy throne,
And fall of many kings.

MALCOLM, Macbeth, IV.III.66

They are as sick that surfeit with too much as they that
starve with nothing. It is no mean happiness therefore to
be seated in the mean; superfluity comes sooner by white
hairs, but competency lives longer.

NERISSA, The Merchant of Venice, I.II.5

MODESTY
see also HUMILITY

I cannot tell what you and other men
Think of this life; but, for my single self,
I had as lief not be as live to be
In awe of such a thing as I myself.

CASSIUS, Julius Caesar, I.II.93

'Twere a concealment
Worse than a theft, no less than a traducement,
To hide your doings, and to silence that
Which, to the spire and top of praises vouch'd,
Would seem but modest.

COMINIUS, Coriolanus, I.IX.21

I had rather have one scratch my head i' th' sun
When the alarum were stuck than idly sit
To hear my nothings monster'd.

CORIOLANUS, Coriolanus, II.II.75

Your honors' pardon;
I had rather have my wounds to heal again
Than hear say how I got them.

CORIOLANUS, Coriolanus, II.II.68

It is the witness still of excellency
To put a strange face on his own perfection.

DON PEDRO, Much Ado About Nothing, II.III.46

Falseness cannot come from thee, for thou lookest
Modest as Justice, and thou seemest a palace
For the crown'd Truth to dwell in.

PERICLES, Pericles, V.I.120

You do yourselves
Much wrong, you bate too much of your own merits.

TIMON, Timon of Athens, I.II.205

MONEY
see also GREED; INFLATION; WEALTH

There is remuneration, for the best ward of mine honor is

rewarding my dependents.

> ARMADO, *Love's Labor's Lost*, III.i.131

He that wants money, means, and content is without three good friends.

> CORIN, *As You Like It*, III.ii.24

Whose large style
Agrees not with the leanness of his purse.

> DUKE OF GLOUCESTER, *2 Henry VI*, I.i.111

If money were as certain as your waiting,
'Twere sure enough.

> FLAVIUS, *Timon of Athens*, III.iv.47

If money go before, all ways do lie open.

> FORD, *The Merry Wives of Windsor*, II.ii.168

There is thy gold, worse poison to men's souls,
Doing more murder in this loathsome world,
Than these poor compounds that thou mayest not sell.
I sell thee poison, thou hast sold me none.

> ROMEO, *Romeo and Juliet*, V.i.80

MOON
see also NIGHT; STARS

These late eclipses of the sun and moon
portend no good to us.

> EARL OF GLOUCESTER, *King Lear*, I.ii.103

Here stood he in the dark, his sharp sword out,
Mumbling of wicked charms, conjuring the moon
To stand 's auspicious mistress.

> EDMUND, *King Lear*, II.i.38

Rom. Lady, by yonder blessed moon I vow,
That tips with silver all these fruit-tree tops—
Jul. O, swear not by the moon, th' inconstant moon,
That monthly changes in her circles orb,
Lest that thy love prove likewise variable.

> JULIET, ROMEO, *Romeo and Juliet*, II.ii.107

Snout. Doth the moon shine that night we play
our play?
Bot. A calendar, a calendar! Look in the almanac.
Find out moonshine, find out moonshine.

> SNOUT, BOTTOM, *A Midsummer Night's Dream*, III.i.51

The moon (the governess of floods),
Pale in her anger, washes all the air,
That rheumatic diseases do abound.

> TITANIA, *A Midsummer Night's Dream*, II.i.103

MORNING
see also SUNRISE

Full many a glorious morning have I seen
Flatter the mountain tops with sovereign eye,
Kissing with golden face the meadows green,
Gilding pale streams with heavenly alcumy.

SONNET 33, 1–4

And truly not the morning sun of heaven
Better becomes the grey cheeks of th' east,
Nor that full star that ushers in the even
Doth half that glory to the sober west,
As those two mourning eyes becomes thy face.

SONNET 132, 5–9

And solemn night with slow sad gait descended
To ugly hell, when lo the blushing morrow
Lends light to all fair eyes that light will borrow.

The Rape of Lucrece, 1081

This morning, like the spirit of a youth
That means to be of note, begins betimes.

ANTONY, *Antony and Cleopatra*, IV.IV.26

The grey-ey'd morn smiles on the frowning night,
Check'ring the eastern clouds with streaks of light,
And flecklèd darkens like a drunkard reels
From forth day's path and Titan's fiery wheels.

FRIAR LAWRENCE, *Romeo and Juliet*, II.III.1

And as the morning steals upon the night,
Melting the darkness, so their rising senses
Begin to chase the ignorant fumes that mantle
Their clearer reason.

PROSPERO, *The Tempest*, V.I.65

MOTHERHOOD
see also BABIES; CHILDREN; CHILDREN OF UNMARRIED PARENTS; DAUGHTERS;
GRANDPARENTS; HEREDITY; SONS; WOMEN

Par. Younger than she are happy mothers made.
Cap. And too soon marr'd are those so early made.

CAPULET, PARIS, *Romeo and Juliet*, I.II.12

A fever with the absence of her son;
A madness, of which her life's in danger.

CYMBELINE, *Cymbeline*, IV.III.1

A grievous burden was thy birth to me,
Tetchy and wayward was the infancy;

Thy school-days frightful, desp'rate, wild, and furious.
DUCHESS OF YORK, Richard III, IV.iv.168

Alas! you three on me, threefold distress'd,
Pour all your tears. I am your sorrow's nurse,
And I will pamper it with lamentation.
DUCHESS OF YORK, Richard III, II.ii.85

As a long-parted mother with her child
Plays fondly with her tears and smiles in meeting,
So weeping, smiling, greet I thee, my earth,
And do thee favors with my royal hands.
KING RICHARD, Richard II, III.ii.8

If she must teem,
Create her child of spleen, that it may live
And be a thwart disnatur'd torment to her.
Let it stamp wrinkles in her brow of youth,
With cadent tears fret channels in her cheeks,
Turn all her mother's pains and benefits
To laughter and contempt, that she may feel
How sharper than a serpent's tooth it is
To have a thankless child!
LEAR, King Lear, I.iv.281

There's no man in the world
More bound to 's mother, yet here he lets me prate
Like on i' th' stocks. Thou hast never in thy life
Show'd thy dear mother any courtesy,
When she, poor hen, fond of no second brood,
Has cluck'd thee to the wars, and safely home
Loaden with honor.
VOLUMNIA, Coriolanus, V.iii.158

MOUNTAINEERING

Now for our mountain sport: up to yond hill,
Your legs are young; I'll tread these flats.
BELARIUS, Cymbeline, III.iii.10

Well could I curse away a winter's night,
Though standing naked on a mountain top,
Where biting cold would never let grass grow,
And think it but a minute spent in sport.
EARL OF SUFFOLK, 2 Henry VI, III.ii.335

When we were boys,
Who would believe that there were mountaineers,
Dew-lapp'd, like bulls, whose throats has hanging at 'em

Wallets of flesh? or that there were such men
Whose heads stood in their breasts?

GONZALO, *The Tempest*, III.III.43

MOURNING
see also DEATH; EULOGY; FUNERALS; GRIEF; LOSS; SORROW

No longer mourn for me when I am dead
Than you shall hear the surly sullen bell
Give warning to the world that I am fled
From this vile world with vilest worms to dwell.

SONNET 71, 1–4

You must know your father lost a father,
That father lost, lost his, and the survivor bound
In filial obligation for some term
To do obsequious sorrow. But to persever
In obstinate condolement is a course
Of impious stubbornness, 'tis unmanly grief,
It shows a will most incorrect to heaven
A heart unfortified, or mind impatient,
An understanding simple and unschool'd.

CLAUDIUS, *Hamlet*, I.II.89

Grief fills the room up of my absent child,
Lies in his bed, walks up and down with me,
Puts on his pretty looks, repeats his words,
Remembers me of all his gracious parts,
Stuffs out his vacant garments with his form;
Then, have I reason to be fond of grief?
Fare you well! Had you such a loss as I,
I could give better comfort than you do.

CONSTANCE, *King John*, III.IV.93

It were lost sorrow to wail one that's lost.

DUCHESS OF YORK, *Richard III*, II.II.11

I honor'd him, I lov'd him, and will weep
My date of life out for his sweet live's loss.

HUBERT, *King John*, IV.III.105

And as the dam runs lowing up and down,
Looking the way her harmless young one went,
And can do nought but wail her darling's loss,
Even so myself bewails good Gloucester's case
With sad unhelpful tears.

KING HENRY, *2 Henry VI*, III.I.214

Come mourn with me for what I do lament,
And put on sullen black incontinent.

BULLINGBROOK, *Richard II*, V.VI.47

Moderate lamentation is the right of the dead, excessive
grief the enemy to the living.
LAFEW, All's Well That Ends Well, I.I.55

He has no children. All my pretty ones?
Did you say all?—O hell-kite—All?
What, all my pretty chickens, and their dam,
At one fell swoop?
MACDUFF, Macbeth, IV.III.216

Death remembered should be like a mirror,
Who tells us life's but breath, to trust it error.
PERICLES, Pericles, I.I.45

And if thine eyes can water for his death,
I give thee this to dry thy cheeks withal.
QUEEN MARGARET, 3 Henry VI, I.IV.82

Like a cloistress she will veilèd walk,
And water once a day her chamber round
With eye-offending brine; all this to season
A brother's dead love, which she would keep fresh
And lasting in her sad remembrance.
VALENTINE, Twelfth Night, I.I.27

MULTICULTURALISM

We have been call'd so many, not that
our heads are some brown, some black, some abram,
some bald, but that our wits are so diversely
color'd; and truly I think if all our wits were to issue
out of one skull, they would fly east, west, north, south,
and their consent of one direct way should be at once to
all points a' th' compass.
CITIZEN, Coriolanus, II.III.18

'Tis often seen
Adoption strives with nature, and choice breeds
A native slip to us from foreign seeds.
COUNTESS OF ROSILLION, All's Well That Ends Well, I.III.144

Strange is it that our bloods,
Of color, weight, and heat, pour'd all together,
Would quite confound distinction, yet stands off
In differences so mighty.
KING, All's Well That Ends Well, II.III.118

MURDER AND EXECUTION
see also CRIME; PUNISHMENT

The silly lambs: pure thoughts are dead and still,
While lust and murder wakes to stain and kill.
The Rape of Lucrece, 167

Here wast thou bay'd, brave hart,
Here didst thou fall, and here thy hunters stand,
Sign'd in thy spoil, and crimson'd in thy lethe.
O world! thou wast the forest to this hart,
And this indeed, O world, the heart of thee.

ANTONY, *Julius Caesar*, III.i.204

Let heaven kiss earth! now let not Nature's hand
Keep the wild flood confin'd! let order die!
And let this world no longer be a stage
To feed contention in a ling'ring act;
But let one spirit of the first-born Cain
Reign in all bosoms, that each heart being set
On bloody courses, the rude scene may end,
And darkness be the burier of the dead!

EARL OF NORTHUMBERLAND, *2 Henry IV*, I.i.153

Mercy but murders, pardoning those that kill.

ESCALUS, PRINCE OF VERONA, *Romeo and Juliet*, III.i.197

Murder most foul, as in the best it is,
But this most foul, strange, and unnatural.

GHOST, *Hamlet*, I.v.27

Murder, though it have no tongue, will speak
With most miraculous organ.

HAMLET, *Hamlet*, II.ii.593

It cannot be but thou hast murd'red him;
So should a murderer look—so dead, so grim.

HERMIA, *A Midsummer Night's Dream*, III.ii.56

Truth will come to light; murder cannot be hid long.

LAUNCELOT, *The Merchant of Venice*, II.ii.79

Your hangman is a more penitent trade than your bawd: he
doth oft'ner ask forgiveness.

POMPEY, *Measure for Measure*, IV.ii.49

Thy head (all indirectly) gave direction.
No doubt the murd'rous knife was dull and blunt
Till it was whetted on thy stone-hard heart
To revel in the entrails of my lambs.

QUEEN ELIZABETH, *Richard III*, IV.iv.226

MUSIC
see also ART; SONGS AND SINGING

Music to hear, why hear'st thou music sadly?
Sweets with sweets war not, joy delights in joy.

SONNET 8, 1–2

Is it not a strange that sheep's guts should hale souls out
of men's bodies?

BENEDICK, *Much Ado About Nothing*, II.III.59

Be not afeard, the isle is full of noises,
Sounds, and sweet airs, they give delight and hurt not.
Sometimes a thousand twangling instruments
Will hum about mine ears; and sometimes voices,
That if I then had wak'd after long sleep,
Will make me sleep again, and then in dreaming,
The clouds methought would open, and show riches
Ready to drop upon me, that when I wak'd
I cried to dream again.

CALIBAN, *The Tempest*, III.II.135

Give me some music; music, moody food
Of us that trade in love.

CLEOPATRA, *Antony and Cleopatra*, II.V.1

Where should this music be? I' th' air, or th' earth?
It sounds no more; and sure it waits upon
Some god o' th' island. Sitting on a bank,
Weeping again the King my father's wrack,
The music crept by me upon the waters,
Allaying both their fury and my passion
With its sweet air; thence I have follow'd it,
Or it hath drawn me rather. But 'tis gone.
No, it begins again.

FERDINAND, *The Tempest*, I.II.388

For notes of sorrow out of tune are worse
Than priests and fanes that lie.

GUIDERIUS, *Cymbeline*, IV.II.241

Cause the musicians play me that sad note
I nam'd my knell, whilst I sit meditating
On that celestial harmony I go to.

KATHERINE, *Henry VIII*, IV.II.78

Music do I hear?
Ha, ha keep time! How sour sweet music is
When time is broke, and no proportion kept!
So is it in the music of men's lives.
And here have I the daintiness of ear
To check time broke in a disordered string.

KING RICHARD, *Richard II*, V.V.41

Wilt thou have music? Hark, Apollo plays,
And twenty caged nightingales do sing.

LORD, *The Taming of the Shrew*, IND.II.35

Do but note a wild and wanton herd
Or race of youthful and unhandled colts,
Fetching mad bounds, bellowing and neighing loud,
Which is the hot condition of their blood,
If they but hear perchance a trumpet sound,
Or any air of music touch their ears,
You shall perceive them make a mutual stand,
Their savage eyes turn'd to a modest gaze,
By the sweet power of music; therefore the poet
Did feign that Orpheus drew trees, stones, and floods;
Since nought so stockish, hard, and full of rage,
But music for the time doth change his nature.
The man that hath no music in himself,
Nor is not moved with concord of sweet sounds,
Is fit for treasons, stratagems, and spoils;
The motions of his spirit are dull as night,
And his affections dark as Erebus;
Let no such man be trusted.

LORENZO, *The Merchant of Venice*, V.i.71

How sweet the moonlight sleeps upon this bank!
Here we will set, and let the sounds of music
Creep in our ears. Soft stillness and the night
Become the touches of sweet harmony.

LORENZO, *The Merchant of Venice*, V.i.54

Preposterous ass, that never read so far
To know the cause why music was ordain'd!
Was it not to refresh the mind of man
After his studies or his usual pain?

LUCENTIO, *The Taming of the Shrew*, III.i.9

If music be the food of love, play on,
Give me excess of it, that surfeiting,
The appetite may sicken, and so die.
That strain again, it had a dying fall,
O, it came o'er my ear like the sweet sound
That breathes upon a bank of violets,
Stealing and giving odor.

ORSINO, DUKE OF ILLYRIA, *Twelfth Night*, I.i.1

I am beholding to you
For your sweet music this last night. I do
Protest my ears were never better fed
With such delightful pleasing harmony.

SIMONIDES, *Pericles*, II.v.25

NAMES AND TITLES
see also FORMALITY; IDENTITY

Brutus and Caesar: what should be in that "Caesar"?
Why should that name be sounded more than yours?
Write them together, yours is as fair a name;
Sound them, it doth become the mouth as well;
Weigh them, it as heavy; conjure with 'em,
"Brutus" will start a spirit as soon as "Caesar."

CASSIUS, *Julius Caesar*, I.II.142

He was a kind of nothing, titleless,
Till he had forg'd himself a name a' th' fire
Of burning Rome.

COMINIUS, *Coriolanus*, V.I.13

Know, my name is lost,
By treason's troth bare-gnawn and canker-bit,
Yet am I noble as the adversary
I come to cope.

EDGAR, *King Lear*, V.III.122

O Romeo, Romeo, wherefore art thou Romeo?
Deny thy father and refuse thy name;
Or, if thou wilt not, be but sworn my love,
And I'll no longer be a Capulet.
'Tis but thy name that is my enemy;
Thou art thyself, though not a Montague.
What's Montague? It is nor hand nor foot,
Nor arm, nor face, nor any other part!
Belonging to a man. O, be some other name!
What's in a name? That which we call a rose
By any other word would smell as sweet;
So Romeo would, were he not Romeo call'd,
Retain that dear perfection which he owes
Without that title. Romeo, doff thy name,
And for thy name, which is no part of thee,
Take all myself.

JULIET, *Romeo and Juliet*, II.II.33

I have no name, no title,
No, not that name was given me at the font,
But 'tis usurp'd. Alack the heavy day,
That I have worn so many winters out
And know not now what name to call myself!

KING RICHARD, *Richard II*, IV.I.255

From lowest place when virtuous things proceed,
The place is dignified by th' doer's deed.
Where great additions swell's, and virtue none,

It is a dropsied honor. Good alone
Is good, without a name; vileness is so.
The property by what it is should go,
Not by the title.

KING OF FRANCE, All's Well That Ends Well, II.III.125

I cannot tell what the dickens his name is.

MISTRESS PAGE, The Merry Wives of Windsor, III.II.19

You are called plain Kate,
And bonny Kate, and sometimes Kate the curst;
But Kate, the prettiest Kate in Christendom,
Kate of Kate Hall, my super-dainty Kate,
For dainties are all Kates.

PETRUCHIO, The Taming of the Shrew, II.I.185

In what vile part of this anatomy
Doth my name lodge? Tell me, that I may sack
The hateful mansion.

ROMEO, Romeo and Juliet, III.III.106

I have a whole school of tongues in this belly
of mine, and not a tongue of them all speaks any other
word but my name.

SIR JOHN FALSTAFF, 2 Henry IV, IV.III.17

NATURAL MEDICINE
see also DRUGS AND MEDICATION; HEALING; PHYSICIANS; RECOVERY; SICKNESS

With a wound I must be cur'd.

ANTONY, Antony and Cleopatra, IV.XIV.78

What is infirm from your sounder parts shall fly,
Health shall live free, and sickness freely die.

HELENA, All's Well That Ends Well, II.I.167

Our remedies oft in ourselves do lie,
Which we ascribe to heaven.

HELENA, All's Well That Ends Well, I.I.216

NATURE
see also AGRICULTURE; ENVIRONMENTALISM; FLOWERS; GARDENING

Call the creatures
Whose naked natures live in all the spite
Of wreakful heaven, whose bare unhoused trunks
To the conflicting elements expos'd,
Answer mere nature; bid them flatter thee.

APEMANTUS, Timon of Athens, IV.III.227

Is't not mad lodging
Here in the wild woods, cousin?

ARCITE, The Two Noble Kinsmen, III.III.22

Nature must obey necessity.

BRUTUS, *Julius Caesar*, IV.III.227

Who with thy saffron wings upon my flow'rs
Diffusest honey-drops, refreshing show'rs,
And with each end of thy blue bow dost crown
My bosky acres and my unshrubb'd down,
Rich scarf to my proud earth.

CERES, *The Tempest*, IV.I.78

Hath not old custom made this life more sweet
Than that of painted pomp? Are not these woods
More free from peril than the envious court?
Here feel we not the penalty of Adam,
The seasons' difference, as the icy fang
And churlish chiding of the winter's wind,
Which when it bites and blows upon my body
Even till I shrink with cold, I smile and say,
"This is no flattery: these are counselors
That feelingly persuade me what I am."
Sweet are the uses of adversity
Which like the toad, ugly and venomous,
Wears yet a precious jewel in his head;
And this our life, exempt from public haunt,
Finds tongues in trees, books in the running brooks,
Sermons in stones, and good in every thing.

DUKE SENIOR, *As You Like It*, II.I.2

For nature doth abhor to make his bed
With the defunct, or sleep upon the dead.

LUCIUS, *Cymbeline*, IV.II.357

I know a bank where the wild thyme blows,
Where oxlips and the nodding violet grows,
Quite over-canopied with luscious woodbine,
With sweet musk-roses and with eglantine.

OBERON, *A Midsummer Night's Dream*, II.I.249

Yet Nature is made better by no mean
But Nature makes that mean; so over that art
Which you say adds to Nature, is an art
That Nature makes.

POLIXENES, *The Winter's Tale*, IV.IV.89

Behold, the earth has roots;
Within this mile break forth a hundred springs;
The oaks bear mast, the briers scarlet heps;
The bounteous huswife Nature on each bush
Lays her full mess before you.

TIMON, *Timon of Athens*, IV.III.417

Nature never lends
The smallest scruple of her excellence,
But like a thrifty goddess, she determines
Herself the glory of a creditor,
Both thanks and use.

VINCENTIO, DUKE OF VIENNA, *Measure for Measure*, I.I.36

NEATNESS
see also DISCIPLINE; ORDER

I will never trust a man again for keeping his sword clean,
nor believe he can have every thing in him by wearing his
apparel neatly.

SECOND LORD, *All's Well That Ends Well*, IV.III.144

NEED AND NECESSITY
see also BEGGING; DEPENDENCE; DESIRE; LONGING

Plenty and peace breeds cowards; hardness ever
Of hardiness is mother.

IMOGEN, *Cymbeline*, III.VI.21

Teach thy necessity to reason thus:
There is no virtue like necessity.

JOHN OF GAUNT, *Richard II*, I.III.277

The art of our necessities is strange
And can make vile things precious.

LEAR, *King Lear*, III.II.70

His approach,
So out of circumstance and sudden, tells us
'Tis not a visitation fram'd, but forc'd
By need and accident.

LEONTES, *The Winter's Tale*, V.I.89

The need I have of thee,
thine own goodness hath made.

POLIXENES, *The Winter's Tale*, IV.II.11

I am sworn brother, sweet,
To grim Necessity, and he and I
Will keep a league till death.

QUEEN, *Richard II*, V.I.20

NEWS

Ill news, by'r lady—seldom comes the better.
I fear, I fear 'twill prove a giddy world.

CITIZEN, *Richard III*, II.III.4

Though it be honest, it is never good
To bring bad news. Give to a gracious message
An host of tongues, but let ill tidings tell
Themselves when they be felt.

CLEOPATRA, Antony and Cleopatra, II.v.85

Would I could find a fine frog! he would tell me
News from all parts o' th' world.

DAUGHTER, The Two Noble Kinsmen, III.iv.12

Yet the first bringer of unwelcome news
Hath by a losing office, and his tongue
Sound ever after as a sullen bell,
Rememb'red rolling a departing friend.

EARL OF NORTHUMBERLAND, 2 Henry IV, I.i.100

This news, which is call'd true, is so
like an old tale, that the verity of it is
in strong suspicion.

SECOND GENTLEMAN, The Winter's Tale, V.i.27

Ham. What news?
Ros. None, my lord, but the world's grown honest.
Ham. Then is doomsday near.

HAMLET, ROSENCRANTZ, Hamlet, II.ii.236

O Lord, why lookest thou so sad?
Though news be sad, yet tell them merrily;
If good, thou shamest the music of sweet news
By playing it to me with so sour a face.

JULIET, Romeo and Juliet, II.v.21

Despiteful tidings, O unpleasing news!

LADY ANNE, Richard III, IV.i.36

None good, my liege, to please you with the hearing,
Nor none so bad but well may be reported.

LORD STANLEY, Richard III, IV.iv.457

But if you be afeard to hear the worst,
Then let the worst unheard fall on your head.

PHILIP THE BASTARD, King John, IV.ii.135

But what art thou, whose heavy looks foretell
Some dreadful story hanging on thy tongue?

RICHARD, DUKE OF GLOUCESTER, 3 Henry VI, II.i.43

Thy father's beard
is turn'd white with the news.

SIR JOHN FALSTAFF, 1 Henry IV, II.iv.358

NIGHT
see also MOON; STARS; SUNSET

> When I do count the clock that tells the time,
> And see the brave day sunk in hideous night.
>
> SONNET 12, 1–2

> Now entertain conjecture of a time
> When creeping murmur and the poring dark
> Fills the wide vessel of the universe.
> From camp to camp, through the foul womb of night,
> The hum of either army stilly sounds.
>
> CHORUS, *Henry V*, IV.CHO.1

> But day doth daily draw my sorrows longer,
> And night doth nightly make grief's length seem stronger.
>
> SONNET 28, 13–14

> And coal-black clouds that shadow heaven's light
> Do summon us to part, and bid good night.
>
> *Venus and Adonis*, 533

> O comfort-killing Night, image of hell,
> Dim register and notary of shame,
> Black stage for tragedies and murders fell,
> Vast sin-concealing chaos, nurse of blame!
>
> *The Rape of Lucrece*, 764

> The dragon-wing of night o'erspreads the earth.
>
> ACHILLES, *Troilus and Cressida*, V.VIII.17

> O grim-look'd night! O night with hue so black!
> O night, which ever art when day is not!
> O night, O night! alack, alack, alack.
>
> BOTTOM AS PYRAMUS, *A Midsummer Night's Dream*, V.I.170

> A great cause of the night is lack of the sun.
>
> CORIN, *As You Like It*, III.II.28

> The tyranny of the open night's too rough
> For nature to endure.
>
> EARL OF KENT, *King Lear*, III.IV.2

> Here's a night pities
> neither wise men nor fools.
>
> FOOL, *King Lear*, III.II.12

> This cold night will turn us all to fools and
> madmen.
>
> FOOL, *King Lear*, III.IV.79

> A night is but small breath, and little pause,
> To answer matters of this consequence.
>
> FRENCH KING, *Henry V*, II.IV.145

Dark night, that from the eye his function takes,
The ear more quick of apprehension makes;
Wherein it doth impair the seeing sense,
It pays the hearing double recompense.

HERMIA, A Midsummer Night's Dream, III.II.177

Hell and night
Must bring this monstrous birth to the world's light.

IAGO, Othello, I.III.403

The bright day is done,
And we are for the dark.

IRAS, Antony and Cleopatra, V.II.193

Spread thy close curtain, love-performing night,
That th' runaway's eyes may wink, and Romeo
Leap to these arms untalk'd of and unseen!
Lovers can see to do their amorous rites
By their own beauties, or, if love be blind,
It best agrees with night.

JULIET, Romeo and Juliet, II.II.5

That when the searching eye of heaven is hid
Behind the globe, that lights the lower world,
Then thieves and robbers range abroad unseen
In murders and in outrage boldly here.

KING RICHARD, Richard II, III.II.37

The lights burn blue. It is now dead midnight,
Cold fearful drops stand on my trembling flesh.

KING RICHARD, Richard III, V.III.180

Come, thick night,
And pall thee in the dunnest smoke of hell,
That my keen knife see not the wound it makes,
Nor heaven peep through the blanket of the dark
To cry, "Hold, hold!"

LADY MACBETH, Macbeth, I.v.50

The gaudy, blabbing, and remorseful day
Is crept into the bosom of the sea;
And now loud-howling wolves arouse the jades
That drag the tragic melancholy night;
Who with their drowsy, slow, and flagging wings
Cleep dead men's graves, and from their misty jaws
Breathe foul contagious darkness in the air.

LIEUTENANT, 2 Henry VI, IV.I.1

Come, seeling night,
Scarf up the tender eye of pitiful day,
And with thy bloody and invisible hand

Cancel and tear to pieces that great bond
Which keeps me pale! Light thickens, and the crow
Makes wing to th' rooky wood;
Good things of day begin to droop and drowse,
Whiles night's black agents to their preys do rouse.

MACBETH, Macbeth, III.ii.46

All so soon as the all-cheering sun
Should in the farthest east begin to draw
The shady curtains from Aurora's bed,
Away from light steals home my heavy son,
And private in his chamber pens himself,
Shuts up his windows, locks fair daylight out,
And makes himself an artificial night.

MONTAGUE, Romeo and Juliet, I.i.134

This night methinks is but the daylight sick,
It looks a little paler.

PORTIA, The Merchant of Venice, V.i.124

NOBILITY
see also GREATNESS; HONOR

A little of all noble qualities:
I could have kept a hawk, and well have hollow'd
To a deep cry of dogs; I dare not praise
My feat in horsemanship, yet they that knew me
Would say it was my best piece; last, and greatest,
I would be thought a soldier.

ARCITE, The Two Noble Kinsmen, II.v.10

For mine own part,
I shall be glad to learn of noble men.

BRUTUS, Julius Caesar, IV.iii.53

Signs of nobleness, like stars, shall shine
On all deservers.

DUNCAN, Macbeth, I.iv.41

True nobility is exempt from fear:
More can I bear than you dare execute.

EARL OF SUFFOLK, 2 Henry VI, IV.i.130

Sweet mercy is nobility's true badge.

TAMORA, Titus Andronicus, I.i.119

NOISE

O, 'twas a din to fright a monster's ear,
To make an earthquake; sure it was the roar
Of a whole herd of lions.

ANTONIO, The Tempest, II.i.314

Your native town you enter'd like a post,
And had no welcomes home, but he returns
Splitting the air with noise.

CONSPIRATORS, *Coriolanus*, V.VI.49

Let there be no noise made, my gentle friends,
Unless some dull and favorable hand
Will whisper music to my weary spirit.

KING HENRY IV, *2 Henry IV*, IV.V.1

NUMEROLOGY

They say there is divinity in odd numbers, either in
nativity, chance, or death.

SIR JOHN FALSTAFF, *The Merry Wives of Windsor*, V.I.3

OATHS

see also PROMISES; VOWS

Cas. Let us swear our resolution.
Bru. No, not an oath! If not the face of men,
The sufferance of our souls, the time's abuse—
If these be motives weak, break off betimes,
And every man hence to his idle bed;
So let high-sighted tyranny range on,
Till each man drop by lottery. But if these
(As I am sure they do) bear fire enough
To kindle cowards, and to steel with valor
The melting spirits of women, then, countrymen,
What need we any spur but our own cause
To prick us to redress what other bond
Than secret Romans, that have spoke the word
And will not palter? and what other oath
Than honesty to honesty engag'd
That this shall be, or we will fall for it?
Swear priests and cowards, and men cautelous,
Old feeble carrions, and such suffering souls
That welcome wrongs; unto bad causes swear
Such creatures as men doubt; but do not stain
The even virtue of our enterprise,
Nor th' insuppressive mettle of our spirits,
To think that our cause or our performance
Did need an oath; when every drop of blood
That every Roman bears, and nobly bears,
Is guilty of a several bastardy,
If he do break the smallest particle
Of any promise that hath pass'd from him.

BRUTUS, CASSIUS, *Julius Caesar*, II.I.113

When a gentleman is dispos'd to swear, it is
not for any standers-by to curtal his oaths.

CLOTEN, *Cymbeline*, II.I.10

Not for Bohemia, nor the pomp that may
Be thereat gleaned, for all the sun sees, or
The close earth wombs, or the profound seas hides
In unknown fathoms, will I break my oath
To this my fair belov'd.

FLORIZEL, *The Winter's Tale*, IV.IV.488

I here entail
The crown to thee and to thine heirs for ever,
Conditionally that here thou take an oath
To cease this civil war, and whilst I live
To honor me as thy king and sovereign,
And neither by treason nor hostility
To seek to put me down and reign thyself.

KING HENRY, *3 Henry VI*, I.I.194

What fool is not so wise
To lose an oath to win a paradise?

LONGAVILLE, *Love's Labor's Lost*, IV.III.70

The strongest oaths are straw
To th' fire i' th' blood. Be more abstemious.
Or else good night your now!

PROSPERO, *The Tempest*, IV.I.52

An oath is of no moment, being not took
Before a true and lawful magistrate
That hath authority over him that swears.

RICHARD, DUKE OF GLOUCESTER, *3 Henry VI*, I.II.22

OBEDIENCE
see also SERVICE; SUBMISSION

I do not know
What kind of my obedience I should tender.
More than my all is nothing: nor my prayers
Are not words duly harrowed, nor my wishes
More worth than empty vanities; yet prayers and wishes
Are all I can return.

ANNE BULLEN, *Henry VIII*, II.III.65

When Caesar says, "Do this," it is perform'd.

ANTONY, *Julius Caesar*, I.II.10

I will be correspondent to command
And do my spiriting gently.

ARIEL, *The Tempest*, I.II.297

The hearts of princes kiss obedience,
So much they love it; but to stubborn spirits
They swell and grown, as terrible as storms.

CARDINAL WOLSEY, Henry VIII, III.I.162

O heavens!
If you love old men, if your sweet sway
Allow obedience, if you yourselves are old,
Make it our cause; send down, and take my part.

LEAR, King Lear, II.IV.189

If I affect it more
Than as your honor and as your renown,
Let me no more from this obedience rise,
Which my most inward true and duteous spirit
Teacheth this prostrate and exterior bending.

PRINCE HENRY, 2 Henry IV, IV.V.144

Thy humble servant vows obedience
And humble service till the point of death.

RICHARD PLANTAGENET, 1 Henry VI, III.I.166

OBESITY

He's fat, and scant of breath.

GERTRUDE, Hamlet, V.II.287

He hath eaten me out of house and home, he hath put all my substance into that fat belly of his.

HOSTESS QUICKLY, 2 Henry IV, II.I.74

Fal. My honest lads, I will tell you what I am
about.
Pist. Two yards, and more.

PISTOL, FALSTAFF, The Merry Wives of Windsor, I.III.38

Sher. A gross fat man.
Car. As fat as butter.

SHERIFF, CARRIER, 1 Henry IV, II.IV.510

OFFICE POLITICS
see also POLITICS AND POWER; WORK

The general's disdain'd
By him one step below, he by the next
That next by him beneath; so every step,
Exampled by the first pace that is sick
Of his superior, grows to an envious fever
Of pale and bloodless emulation.

ULYSSES, Troilus and Cressida, I.III.129

Better to leave undone, than by our deed
Acquire too high a fame when him we serve's away.
VENTIDIUS, Antony and Cleopatra, III.I.14

OLD AGE
see also AGING; MATURITY

The aim of all is but to nurse the life
With honor, wealth, and ease, in waning age.
The Rape of Lucrece, 141

Time had not scythèd all that youth begun,
Nor Youth all quit, but spite of heaven's fell rage,
Some beauty peep'd through lattice of sear'd age.
A Lover's Complaint, 12

Though I look old, yet I am strong and lusty;
For in my youth I never did apply
Hot and rebellious liquors in my blood,
Nor did not with unbashful forehead woo
The means of weakness and debility;
Therefore my age is as a lusty winter,
Frosty, but kindly.
ADAM, As You Like It, II.III.47

Though now this grained face of mine be hid
In sap-consuming winter's drizzled snow,
And all the conduits of my blood froze up,
Yet hath my night of life some memory,
My wasting lamps some fading glimmer left,
My dull deaf ears a little use to hear.
EGEON, The Comedy of Errors, V.I.312

Aged honor cites a virtuous youth.
HELENA, All's Well That Ends Well, I.III.210

I myself will lead a private life,
And in devotion spend my latter days,
To sin's rebuke and my Creator's praise.
KING HENRY, 3 Henry VI, IV.VI.42

We are old, and on our quick'st decrees
Th' inaudible and noiseless foot of time
Steals ere we can effect them.
KING OF FRANCE, All's Well That Ends Well, V.III.40

You see me here, you gods, a poor old man,
As full of grief as age, wretched in both.
LEAR, King Lear, II.IV.272

I speak not like a dotard nor a fool,
As under privilege of age to brag
What I have done being young, or what would do
Were I not old.

LEONATO, Much Ado About Nothing, V.i.59

Have you not a moist eye, a
dry hand, a yellow cheek, a white bread, a decreasing
leg, an increasing belly? Is not your voice broken,
your wind short, your chin double, your wit single,
and every part of about you blasted with antiquity?
and will you yet call yourself young?

LORD CHIEF JUSTICE, 2 Henry IV, I.ii.180

O sir, you are old,
Nature in you stands on the very verge
Of his confine.

REGAN, King Lear, II.iv.147

An old man is twice a child.

ROSENCRANTZ, Hamlet, II.ii.385

If to be old and merry be a sin, then
many an old host I know is damn'd.

SIR JOHN FALSTAFF, 1 Henry IV, II.iv.471

Why, my skin hangs about me like an old lady's loose
gown; I am wither'd like an old apple-john.

SIR JOHN FALSTAFF, 1 Henry IV, III.iii.3

Thou hast not youth nor age,
But as it were an after-dinner's sleep,
Dreaming on both, for all thy blessèd youth
Becomes as agèd, and doth beg the alms
Of palsied eld; and when thou art old and rich,
Thou hast neither heat, affection, limb, nor beauty,
To make thy riches pleasant.

VINCENTIO, DUKE OF VIENNA, Measure for Measure, III.i.32

OPINION
see also CRITICISM; JUDGMENT

What's the matter, you dissentious rogues,
That rubbing the poor itch of your opinion
Make yourselves scabs?

CAIUS MARTIUS, Coriolanus, I.i.164

You are a great deal abus'd in too bold a persuasion,
and I doubt not you sustain what y'are
worthy of by your attempt.

POSTHUMUS, Cymbeline, I.iv.114

Opinion's but a fool, that makes us scan
The outward habit by the inward man.

SIMONIDES, *Pericles*, II.ii.56

I do now let
loose my opinion, hold it no longer.

TRINCULO, *The Tempest*, II.ii.34

If I, my lord, for my opinion bleed,
Opinion shall be surgeon to my hurt,
And keep me on the side where still I am.

VERNON, *1 Henry VI*, II.iv.52

OPPORTUNITY
see also RISK

O, too much folly is it, well I wot,
To hazard all our lives in one small boat!

LORD TALBOT, *1 Henry VI*, IV.vi.32

Who seeks, and will not take when once 'tis offer'd,
Shall never find it more.

MENAS, *Antony and Cleopatra*, II.vii.83

Why then the world's my oyster,
Which I with sword will open.

PISTOL, *The Merry Wives of Windsor*, II.ii.3

OPTIMISM
see also HOPE

A little gale will soon disperse that cloud,
And blow it to the source from whence it came;
Thy very beams will dry those vapors up,
For every cloud engenders not a storm.

CLARENCE, *3 Henry VI*, V.iii.10

Till when, be cheerful
And think of each thing well.

PROSPERO, *The Tempest*, V.i.250

ORDER
see also DISCIPLINE; NEATNESS

So work the honey-bees,
Creatures that by a rule in nature teach
The act of order to a peopled kingdom.

CANTERBURY, *Henry V*, I.ii.187

But then are we in order when we are most
out of order.

JACK CADE, *2 Henry VI*, IV.ii.189

This is a happier and more comely time
Than when these fellows ran about the streets,
Crying confusion.

SICINIUS VELUTUS, Coriolanus, IV.VI.27

The heavens themselves, the planets, and this center
Observe degree, priority, and place,
Insisture, course, proportion, season, form,
Office, and custom, in all line of order;
And therefore is the glorious planet Sol
In noble eminence enthron'd and spher'd
Amidst the other; whose med'cinable eye
Corrects the ill aspects of planets evil,
And posts like the commandment of a king,
Sans check, to good and bad.

ULYSSES, Troilus and Cressida, I.III.85

PAIN
see also INJURY; MISERY; SUFFERING

Pain pays the income of each precious thing.

The Rape of Lucrece, 334

'Tis good for men to love their present pains
Upon example; so the spirit is eased;
And when the mind is quick'ned, out of doubt,
The organs, though defunct and dead before,
Break up their drowsy grave, and newly move
With casted slough and fresh legerity.

KING HENRY, Henry V, IV.I.18

Thou best know'st
What torment I did find thee in; thy groans
Did make wolves howl, and penetrate the breast
Of ever-angry bears.

PROSPERO, The Tempest, I.II.286

PAINTING
see also ART

Mine eye hath play'd the painter and hath stell'd
The beauty's form in table of my heart;
My body is the frame wherein 'tis held,
And perspective it is best painter's art.

SONNET 24, 1–4

The sleeping and the dead
Are but pictures; 'tis the eye of childhood
That fears a painted devil.

LADY MACBETH, Macbeth, II.II.50

A thousand moral paintings I can show
That shall demonstrate these quick blows of Fortune's
More pregnantly than words.

PAINTER, Timon of Athens, I.I.90

I will say of it,
It tutors nature. Artificial strife
Lives in these touches, livelier than life.

POET, Timon of Athens, I.I.37

Dost thou love pictures? We will fetch thee straight
Adonis painted by a running brook,
And Cytherea all in sedges hid,
Which seem to move and wanton with her breath,
Even as the waving sedges play the wind.

SERVANT, The Taming of the Shrew, IND.II.49

Painting is welcome.
The painting is almost the natural man;
For since dishonor traffics with man's nature,
He is but outside; these pencill'd figures are
Even such as they give out.

TIMON, Timon of Athens, I.I.157

PARANOIA
see also ILLUSION; MADNESS AND MENTAL ILLNESS; SUSPICION

These eyes, that now are dimm'd with death's black veil,
Have been as piercing as the midday sun
To search the secret treasons of the world.

EARL OF WARWICK, 3 Henry VI, V.II.16

To fly the boar before the boar pursues
Were to incense the boar to follow us,
And make pursuit where he did mean no chase.

LORD HASTINGS, Richard III, III.II.28

I am cabin'd, cribb'd, confin'd, bound in
To saucy doubts and fears.

MACBETH, Macbeth, III.IV.23

Present fears
Are less than horrible imaginings:
My thought, whose murder yet is but fantastical,
Shakes so my single state of man that function
Is smother'd in surmise, and nothing is
But what is not.

MACBETH, Macbeth, I.III.137

PARTIES
see also CELEBRATION

> Show a fair presence and put off these frowns,
> An ill-seeming semblance for a feast.
>
> CAPULET, *Romeo and Juliet*, I.v.73

> We did sleep day out of countenance, and made the night
> light with drinking.
>
> ENOBARBUS, *Antony and Cleopatra*, II.II.177

> Have you a ruffian that will swear, drink, dance,
> Revel the night, rob, murder, and commit
> The oldest sins the newest kinds of ways?
>
> KING HENRY IV, *2 Henry IV*, IV.v.124

> Revel it as bravely as the best,
> With silken coats and caps, and golden rings,
> With ruffs and cuffs, and fardingales, and things,
> With scarfs and fans, and double change of brav'ry,
> With amber bracelets, beads, and all this knavery.
>
> PETRUCHIO, *The Taming of the Shrew*, IV.III.54

> I am a fellow o' the strangest mind i' th' world; I delight
> in masques and revels sometimes altogether.
>
> SIR ANDREW AGUECHEEK, *Twelfth Night*, I.III.112

PARTING
see also EULOGY; EXILE

> Farewell, thou art too dear for my possessing,
> And like enough thou know'st thy estimate;
> The charter of thy worth gives thee releasing;
> My bonds in thee are all determinate.
>
> SONNET 87, 1–4

> Our separation so abides and flies,
> That thou residing here, goes yet with me;
> And I hence fleeting, here remain with thee.
>
> ANTONY, *Antony and Cleopatra*, I.III.102

> Therefore our everlasting farewell take:
> For ever, and for ever, farewell, Cassius!
> If we do meet again, why, we shall smile;
> If not, why then this parting was well made.
>
> BRUTUS, *Julius Caesar*, V.I.115

> Then let us take a ceremonious leave
> And loving farewell of our several friends.
>
> BULLINGBROOK, *Richard II*, I.III.50

And so farewell, and fair be all thy hopes,
And prosperous be thy life in peace and war!

> EDMUND MORTIMER, *1 Henry VI*, II.v.113

My tongue is weary, when my legs are too, I will bid
you good night.

> DANCER, *2 Henry IV*, EPI. 33

Sweets to the sweet, farewell!

> GERTRUDE, *Hamlet*, V.i.243

Good night, sweet prince,
And flights of angels sing thee to thy rest!

> HORATIO, *Hamlet*, V.ii.359

I would have broke mine eye-strings, crack'd them, but
To look upon him, till the diminution
Of space had pointed him sharp as my needle;
Nay, followed him till he had melted from
The smallness of a gnat to air, and then
Have turn'd mine eye and wept.

> IMOGEN, *Cymbeline*, I.iii.17

I shall short my word
By length'ning my return.

> JACHIMO, *Cymbeline*, I.vi.200

Good night, good night! Parting is such sweet sorrow,
That I shall say good night till it be morrow.

> JULIET, *Romeo and Juliet*, II.ii.184

Farewell:
We'll no more meet, no more see one another.
But yet thou are my flesh, my blood.

> LEAR, *King Lear*, II.iv.119

"Farewell!"
And for my heart disdainèd that my tongue
Should so profane the word, that taught me craft
To counterfeit oppression of such grief
That words seem'd buried in my sorrow's grave.

> DUKE OF AUMERLE, *Richard II*, I.iv.11

We are time's subjects, and time bids be
gone.

> LORD HASTINGS, *2 Henry IV*, I.iii.109

Por. Fare you well till we shall meet again.
Lor. Fair thoughts and happy hours attend on you!

> LORENZO, PORTIA, *The Merchant of Venice*, III.iii.40

Then thus I turn me from my country's light,
To dwell in solemn shades of endless night.

MOWBRAY, *Richard II*, I.III.176

Little Helen, farewell. If I can remember thee, I will
think of thee at court.

PAROLLES, *All's Well That Ends Well*, I.I.188

Should we be taking leave
As long a term as yet we have to live,
The loathness to depart would grow. Adieu!

POSTHUMUS, *Cymbeline*, I.I.107

Even thus two friends condemn'd
Embrace, and kiss, and take ten thousand leaves,
Loather a hundred times to part than to die.
Yet now farewell, and farewell life with thee!

QUEEN MARGARET, *2 Henry VI*, III.II.353

But that a joy past joy calls out on me,
It were a grief, so brief to part with thee.
Farewell.

ROMEO, *Romeo and Juliet*, III.III.173

Jul. A thousand times good night!
Rom. A thousand times the worse, to want thy light.

ROMEO, JULIET, *Romeo and Juliet*, II.II.154

Farewell! the leisure and the fearful time
Cuts off the ceremonious vows of love
And ample interchange of sweet discourse
Which so long sund'red friends should dwell upon.

STANLEY, *Richard III*, V.III.97

Since that our themes is haste,
I stamp this kiss upon thy currant lip.
Sweet, keep it as my token. Set you forward,
For I will see you gone.

THESEUS, *The Two Noble Kinsmen*, I.I.215

Welcome ever smiles,
And farewell goes out sighing.

ULYSSES, *Troilus and Cressida*, III.III.168

PASSION
see also DEVOTION; LOVE—GENERAL

This aid, impatience chokes her pleading tongue,
And swelling passion doth provoke a pause.

Venus and Adonis, 217

Passion, I see, is catching, for mine eyes,
Seeing those beads of sorrow stand in thine,
Began to water.

ANTONY, Julius Caesar, III.1.283

'Tis your passion
That thus mistakes, the which to you being enemy,
Cannot to me be kind.

ARCITE, The Two Noble Kinsmen, III.1.48

Some bloody passion shakes your very frame.

DESDEMONA, Othello, V.1.44

His passions move me so
That hardly can I check my eyes from tears.

EARL OF NORTHUMBERLAND, 3 Henry VI, I.IV.150

O, what a rogue and peasant slave am I!
Is it not monstrous that this player here,
But in a fiction, in a dream of passion,
Could force his soul so to his own conceit
That from her working all his visage wann'd,
Tears in his eyes, distraction in his aspect,
A broken voice, an' his whole function suiting
With forms to his conceit? And all for nothing,
For Hecuba!
What's Hecuba to him, or he to Hecuba,
That he should weep for her? What would he do
Had he the motive and the cue for passion
That I have? He would drown the stage with tears,
And cleave the general ear with horrid speech,
Make mad the guilty, and appall the free,
Confound the ignorant, and amaze indeed
The very faculties of eyes and ears.
Yet I, a dull and muddy-mettled rascal, peak
Like John-a-dreams, unpregnant of my cause,
And can say nothing; no, not for a king,
Upon whose property and most dear life
A damn'd defeat was made.

HAMLET, Hamlet, II.II.550

Give me that man
That is not passion's slave, and I will wear him
In my heart's core.

HAMLET, Hamlet, III.II.71

A noble temper dost thou show in this,

And great affections wrestling in thy bosom
Doth make an earthquake of nobility.

LEWIS, *King John*, V.II.40

What to ourselves in passion we propose,
The passion ending, doth the purpose lose.

PLAYER KING, *Hamlet*, III.II.194

I was too hot to do somebody good
That is too cold in thinking of it now.

RICHARD, DUKE OF GLOUCESTER, *Richard III*, I.III.310

The color of the King doth come and go
Between his purpose and his conscience,
Like heralds 'twixt two dreadful battles set:
His passion is so ripe, it needs must break.

SALISBURY, *King John*, IV.II.76

PAST

see also HISTORY; MEMORY; TIME

What's past and what's to come is strew'd with husks
And formless ruin of oblivion.

AGAMEMNON, *Troilus and Cressida*, IV.5.166

What's past is prologue; what to come
In yours and my discharge.

ANTONIO, *The Tempest*, II.I.253

Things that are past are done with me.

ANTONY, *Antony and Cleopatra*, I.II.97

O, call back yesterday, bid time return.

EARL OF SALISBURY, *Richard II*, III.II.69

Things without all remedy
Should be without regard: what's done, is done.

LADY MACBETH, *Macbeth*, III.II.11

What's gone and what's past help
Should be past grief.

PAULINA, *The Winter's Tale*, III.II.222

What seest thou else
In the dark backward and abysm of time?

PROSPERO, *The Tempest*, I.II.49

PATIENCE

I do oppose
My patience to his fury, and am arm'd

To suffer, with a quietness of spirit,
The very tyranny and rage of his.

> ANTONIO, *The Merchant of Venice*, IV.I.10

I do think they have patience to make my
adversity asham'd.

> DAUGHTER, *The Two Noble Kinsmen*, II.I.23

I pray thee sort thy heart to patience,
These few days' wonder will be quickly worn.

> DUKE OF GLOUCESTER, *2 Henry VI*, II.IV.69

What cannot be preserv'd when Fortune takes,
Patience her injury a mock'ry makes.

> DUKE OF VENICE, *Othello*, I.III.206

Upon the heat and flame of thy distemper
Sprinkle cool patience.

> GERTRUDE, *Hamlet*, III.IV.123

How poor are they that have not patience!
What wound did ever heal but by degrees?

> IAGO, *Othello*, II.III.370

I shall unfold equal discourtesy
To your best kindness; one of your great knowing
Should learn, being taught, forbearance.

> IMOGEN, *Cymbeline*, II.III.96

I will be the pattern of all patience,
I will say nothing.

> LEAR, *King Lear*, III.II.37

Patience is for poltroons, such as he.

> LORD CLIFFORD, *3 Henry VI*, I.I.62

Yet thou doth look
Like Patience gazing on kings' graves, and smiling
Extremity out of act.

> PERICLES, *Pericles*, V.I.137

Since you will buckle Fortune on my back,
To bear her burden whe'er I will or no,
I must have patience to endure the load.

> RICHARD, DUKE OF GLOUCESTER, *Richard III*, III.VII.228

PATRIOTISM
see also COUNTRY

Who is here so vile that will not love his country?

> BRUTUS, *Julius Caesar*, III.II.32

As for your spiteful false objections,
Prove them, and I lie open to the law;
But God in mercy so deal with my soul
As I in duty love my king and country!
                    DUKE OF GLOUCESTER, *2 Henry VI*, I.III.155

I'll yield myself to prison willingly,
Or unto death, to do my country good.
                    DUKE OF SOMERSET, *2 Henry VI*, IV.VIII.42

These present wars shall find I love my country.
                    PISANIO, *Cymbeline*, IV.III.44

To the love and favor of my country
I commit myself, my person, and the cause.
                    SATURNINUS, *Titus Andronicus*, I.I.58

Hear me profess sincerely: Had I dozen sons, each in my love
alike, and none less dear than thine and my good
Martius, I had rather had eleven die nobly for their
country than one voluptuously surfeit out of action.
                    VOLUMNIA, *Coriolanus*, I.III.21

PEACE
see also DIPLOMACY

The time of universal peace is near.
                    CAESAR (OCTAVIUS), *Antony and Cleopatra*, IV.VI.4

Is all our travail turn'd to this effect?
After the slaughter of so many peers,
So many captains, gentlemen, and soldiers,
That in this quarrel have been overthrown
And sold their bodies for their country's benefit,
Shall we at last conclude effeminate peace?
                    DUKE OF YORK, *1 Henry VI*, V.IV.102

You, Lord Archbishop,
Whose see is by a civil peace maintain'd,
Whose beard the silver hand of peace hath touch'd,
Whose learning and good letters peace hath tutor'd,
Whose white investments figure innocence,
The dove, and very blessèd spirit of peace,
Wherefore do you so ill translate yourself
Out of the speech of peace that bears such grace,
Into the harsh and boist'rous tongue of war?
                    EARL OF WESTMERLAND, *2 Henry IV*, IV.I.41

And more in peace my soul shall part to heaven,
Since I have made my friends at peace on earth.
                    KING EDWARD, *Richard III*, II.I.5

I prithee peace,
Good queen, and whet not on these furious peers,
For blessed are the peacemakers on earth.

KING HENRY, 2 Henry VI, II.i.33

At last, though long, our jarring notes agree,
And time it is, when raging war is done,
To smile at scapes and perils overblown.

LUCENTIO, The Taming of the Shrew, V.ii.1

I bring no overture of war, no taxation of homage; I hold
the olive in my hand; my words are as full of peace as
matter.

OLIVIA, Twelfth Night, I.v.208

The fingers of the pow'rs above do tune
The harmony of this peace.

PHILHARMONUS, Cymbeline, V.v.466

Let them not live to taste this land's increase
That would with treason wound this fair land's peace!
Now civil wounds are stopp'd, peace lives again;
That she may long live here, God say amen!

RICHMOND, Richard III, V.v.38

Why then we shall have a stirring world
again. This peace is nothing but to rust iron, increase
tailors, and breed ballad-makers.

SERVANT, Coriolanus, IV.v.218

Again uncurse their souls, their peace is made
With heads, and not with hands.

SIR STEPHEN SCROOP, Richard II, III.ii.137

PERFECTION
see also UTOPIA

Everything that grows
Holds in perfection but a little moment.

SONNET 15, 1–2

But no perfection is so absolute,
That some impurity doth not pollute.

The Rape of Lucrece, 853

I saw her once
Hop forty paces through the public street;
And having lost her breath, she spoke, and panted,
That she did make defect perfection,
And breathless, pow'r breathe forth.

ENOBARBUS, Antony and Cleopatra, II.ii.228

Her words doth show her wit incomparable,
All her perfections challenge sovereignty.

KING EDWARD, 3 Henry VI, III.II.85

PERSUASION
see also DIPLOMACY; INFLUENCE; POLITICS AND POWER; TEMPTATION

You cram these words into mine ears against
the stomach of my sense.

ALONSO, The Tempest, II.I.107

Look to it, lords, let not his smoothing words
Bewitch your hearts.

CARDINAL BEAUFORD, 2 Henry VI, I.I.156

His form and cause conjoin'd, preaching to stones,
Would make them capable.

HAMLET, Hamlet, III.IV.126

By this face,
This seeming brow of justice, did he win
The hearts of all that he did angle for.

HOTSPUR, 1 Henry IV, IV.III.82

Arm, arm with speed! and, fellows, soldiers, friends,
Better consider what you have to do
Than I, that have not well the gift of tongue,
Can lift your blood up with persuasion.

HOTSPUR, 1 Henry IV, V.II.75

Since we are well persuaded
We carry not a heart with us from hence
That grows not in a fair consent with ours.

KING HENRY, Henry V, II.II.20

Well, God give thee the spirit of persuasion
and him the ears of profiting, that what thou speakest
may move and what he hears may be believ'd.

SIR JOHN FALSTAFF, 1 Henry IV, I.II.152

PHILOSOPHY
see also MIND; THOUGHT

Of your philosophy you make no use,
If you give place to accidental evils.

CASSIUS, Julius Caesar, IV.III.145

I do not always follow lover, elder brother,
and woman; sometime the philosopher.

FOOL, Timon of Athens, II.II.121

I pray thee peace. I will be flesh and blood,
For there was never yet philosopher

That could endure the toothache patiently,
However they have writ the style of gods,
And made a push at chance and sufferance.

LEONATO, *Much Ado About Nothing*, V.I.34

I fear he will prove the weeping philosopher when he grows
old, being so full of unmannerly sadness in his youth.

PORTIA, *The Merchant of Venice*, I.II.48

Rom. O, thou wilt speak again of banishment.
Fri. L. I'll give thee armor to keep off that word:
Adversity's sweet milk, philosophy,
To comfort thee though thou art banished.
Rom. Yet "banished?" Hang up philosophy!
Unless philosophy can make a Juliet,
Displant a town, reverse a prince's doom,
It helps not, it prevails not.

ROMEO, FRIAR LAWRENCE, *Romeo and Juliet*, III.III.53

PHYSICIANS
see also DRUGS AND MEDICATION; HEALING; NATURAL MEDICINE; RECOVERY; SICKNESS

He will be the physician that should be the patient.

AGAMEMNON, *Troilus and Cressida*, II.III.213

Who worse than a physician
Would this report become? But I consider,
By med'cine life may be prolong'd, yet death
Will seize the doctor too.

CYMBELINE, *Cymbeline*, V.V.27

Kill thy physician, and the fee bestow
Upon the foul disease.

EARL OF KENT, *King Lear*, I.I.163

Thou speak'st like a physician, Helicanus,
That ministers a potion unto me
That thou wouldst tremble to receive thyself.

PERICLES, *Pericles*, I.II.67

His friends, like physicians,
Thrive, give him over; must I take th' cure upon me?

SEMPRONIUS, *Timon of Athens*, III.III.11

For the love of God, a surgeon!

SIR ANDREW AGUECHEEK, *Twelfth Night*, V.I.172

PITY
see also COMPASSION; EMPATHY

Pity the world, or else this glutton be,

To eat the world's due, by the grave and thee.

SONNET 1, 13–14

Pity me then, dear friend, and I assure ye,
Even that your pity is enough to cure me.

SONNET 111, 13–14

Root pity in thy heart, that when it grows,
Thy pity may deserve to pitied be.

SONNET 142, 11–12

Her pity-pleading eyes are sadly fixed
In the remorseless wrinkles of his face.

The Rape of Lucrece, 561

For pity is the virtue of the law,
And none but tyrants use it cruelly.

ALCIBIADES, *Timon of Athens*, III.v.8

The people
Deserve such pity of him as the wolf
Does of the shepherds.

COMINIUS, *Coriolanus*, IV.vi.109

For I should melt at an offender's tears,
And lowly words were ransom for their fault.

DUKE OF GLOUCESTER, *2 Henry VI*, III.i.126

Is there no pity sitting in the clouds,
That sees into the bottom of my grief?

JULIET, *Romeo and Juliet*, III.v.196

O heavens, can you hear a good man groan
And not relent, or not compassion him?

MARCUS, *Titus Andronicus*, IV.i.123

Yes, I pity
Decays where e'er I find them, but such most
That sweating in an honorable toil
Are paid with ice to cool 'em.

PALAMON, *The Two Noble Kinsmen*, I.ii.31

PLASTIC SURGERY
see also BEAUTY; COSMETICS

God hath given you one face, and you make yourselves another.

HAMLET, *Hamlet*, III.i.143

Youth is bought more oft than begg'd or borrow'd.

OLIVIA, *Twelfth Night*, III.iv.3

Do thou amend thy face, and I'll amend my life.

SIR JOHN FALSTAFF, *1 Henry IV*, III.iii.24

PLEASURE

see also ENTERTAINMENT; HAPPINESS; JOY; SATISFACTION

> For the love of Love, and her soft hours,
> Let's not confound the time with conference harsh;
> There's not a minute of our lives should stretch
> Without some pleasure now.
>
> ANTONY, *Antony and Cleopatra*, I.I.44

> His delights
> Were dolphin-like, they show'd his back above
> The element they liv'd in.
>
> CLEOPATRA, *Antony and Cleopatra*, V.II.88

> There be some sports are painful, and their labor
> Delight in them sets off.
>
> FERDINAND, *The Tempest*, III.I.1

> Pleasure will be paid, one time or another.
>
> FESTE, *Twelfth Night*, II.IV.70

> A lover may bestride the gossamers
> That idles in the wanton summer air,
> And yet not fall; so light is vanity.
>
> FRIAR LAWRENCE, *Romeo and Juliet*, II.VI.18

> Pleasure and revenge
> Have ears more deaf than adders to the voice
> Of any true decision.
>
> HECTOR, *Troilus and Cressida*, II.II.171

> Pleasure and action make the hours seem short.
>
> IAGO, *Othello*, II.III.379

> That sport best pleases that doth least know how.
>
> PRINCESS OF FRANCE, *Love's Labor's Lost*, V.II.516

POETRY

see also ART; WORDS; WRITING

> If I could write the beauty of your eyes,
> And in fresh numbers number all your graces,
> The age to come would say, "This poet lies,
> Such heavenly touches ne'er touch'd earthly faces."
>
> SONNET 17, 5–8

> Not marble nor the gilded monuments
> Of princes shall outlive this pow'rful rhyme.
>
> SONNET 55, 1–2

> So oft have I invok'd thee for my Muse,
> And found such fair assistance in my verse,

As every alien pen hath got my use,
And under thee their poesy disperse.

SONNET 78, 1–4

Assist me, some extempural god of rhyme, for I am sure I
shall turn sonnet. Devise, wit, write, pen, for I am for
whole volumes in folio.

ARMADO, *Love's Labor's Lost*, I.II.183

I cannot show it in rhyme; I have tried. I can find out no
rhyme to "lady" but "baby," an innocent rhyme; for "scorn,"
"horn," a hard rhyme; for "school," "fool," a babbling
rhyme: very ominous endings. No, I was not born under a rhyming
planet.

BENEDICK, *Much Ado About Nothing*, V.II.36

Never durst poet touch a pen to write
Until his ink were temp'red with Love's sighs:
O then his lines would ravish savage ears
And plant in tyrants mild humility.

BEROWNE, *Love's Labor's Lost*, IV.III.343

Words sweetly plac'd and modestly directed.

EARL OF SUFFOLK, *1 Henry VI*, V.III.179

Only I carried wingèd time
Post on the lame feet of my rhyme,
Which never could I so convey,
Unless your thoughts went on my way.

GOWER, *Pericles*, IV.CHO.47

I had rather be a kitten and cry mew
Than one of these same meter ballet-mongers.
I had rather hear a brazen canstick turn'd,
Or a dry wheel grate on the axle-tree,
And that would set my teeth nothing an edge,
Nothing so much as mincing poetry.

HOTSPUR, *1 Henry IV*, III.I.127

Where words are scarce, they are seldom spent in vain,
For they breathe truth that breath their words in pain.

JOHN OF GAUNT, *Richard II*, II.I.7

Orpheus' lute was strung with poets' sinews,
Whose golden touch could soften steel and stones,
Make tigers tame, and huge leviathans
Forsake unsounded deeps to dance on sands.

PROTEUS, *The Two Gentlemen of Verona*, III.II.77

Cel. Didst thou hear these verses?
Ros. O yes, I heard them all, and more too,
For some of them had in them more feet than the
verses would bear.
Cel. That's no matter; the feet might bear the verses.
Ros. Ay, but the feet were lame, and could not bear
themselves without the verse, and therefore stood
lamely in the verse.

ROSALIND, CELIA, *As You Like It*, III.II.163

Why, thy verse swells with stuff so fine and smooth
That thou art even natural in thine art.

TIMON, *Timon of Athens*, V.I.84

Touch. Truly,
I would the gods had made thee poetical.
Aud. I do not know what "poetical" is. Is it
honest in deed and word? Is it a true thing?
Touch. No, truly; for the truest poetry is the
most feigning, and lovers are given to poetry;
and what they swear in poetry may be said as lovers
they do feign.

TOUCHSTONE, AUDREY, *As You Like It*, III.III.15

POLITICS AND POWER
see also AMBITION; AUTHORITY; CORRUPTION; INFLUENCE; OFFICE POLITICS; PER-
SUASION; PUBLIC OPINION; ROYALTY

Equality of two domestic powers
Breed scrupulous faction.

ANTONY, *Antony and Cleopatra*, I.III.47

Th' abuse of greatness is when it disjoins
Remorse from power.

BRUTUS, *Julius Caesar*, II.I.18

He doth bestride the narrow world
Like a Colussus, and we petty men
Walk under his huge legs, and peep about
To find ourselves dishonorable graves.

CASSIUS, *Julius Caesar*, I.II.135

So much fear'd abroad
That with his name the mothers still their babes?

COUNTESS OF AUVERGNE, *1 Henry VI*, II.III.16

And two men ride of a horse, one must ride behind.

DOGBERRY, *Much Ado About Nothing*, III.V.36

My father hath a power, inquire of him,
And learn to make a body of a limb.

DUKE OF AUMERLE, *Richard II*, III.II.186

All men's honors
Lie like one lump before him, to be fashion's
into what pitch he please.

DUKE OF NORFOLK, Henry VIII, II.ii.47

Get you hence instantly, and tell those friends
They have chose a consul that will from them take
Their liberties, make them of no more voice
Than dogs, that are as often beat for barking
As therefore kept to do so.

JUNIUS BRUTUS, Coriolanus, II.iii.213

His promises were, as he then was, mighty;
But his performance, as his is now, nothing.

KATHERINE, Henry VIII, IV.ii.41

Be it thy course to busy giddy minds
With foreign quarrels, that action, hence borne out,
May waste the memory of the former days.

KING HENRY IV, 2 Henry IV, IV.v.212

Ourself and Bushy, Bagot here and Green,
Observ'd this courtship to the common people,
How he did seem to dive into their hearts
With humble and familiar courtesy,
What reverence he did throw away on slaves,
Wooing poor craftsmen with the craft of smiles
And patient underbearing of his fortune.

KING RICHARD, Richard II, I.iv.23

Get thee glass eyes,
And like a scurvy politician, seem
To see the things thou dost not.

LEAR, King Lear, IV.vi.170

The want is but to put those pow'rs in motion
That long to move.

LORD, Cymbeline, IV.iii.31

Be these juggling fiends no more believ'd,
That palter with us in a double sense,
That keep the word of promise to our ear,
And break it to our hope.

MACBETH, Macbeth, V.viii.19

He wants nothing of a god but
eternity and a heaven to throne in.

MENENIUS AGRIPPA, Coriolanus, V.iv.23

Your heart
Is cramm'd with arrogancy, spleen, and pride.

You have, by fortune and his Highness' favors,
Gone slightly o'er low steps and now are mounted
Where pow'rs are your retainer, and your words
(Domestics to you) serve your will as't please
Yourself pronounce their office.

QUEEN KATHERINE, *Henry VIII*, II.IV.109

The eagle suffers little birds to sing,
And is not careful what they mean thereby,
Knowing that with the shadow of his wings
He can at pleasure stint their melody.

TAMORA, *Titus Andronicus*, IV.IV.83

So our virtues
Lie in th' interpretation of the time,
And power, unto itself most commendable,
Hath not a tomb so evident as a chair
T'extol what it hath done.

TULLUS AUFIDIUS, *Coriolanus*, IV.VI.49

POMP

O, God's will, much better
She ne'er had known pomp!

ANNE BULLEN, *Henry VIII*, II.III.13

Vain pomp and glory of this world, I hate ye!

CARDINAL WOLSEY, *Henry VIII*, III.II.365

Men might say
Till this time pomp was single, but now married
To one above itself.

DUKE OF NORFOLK, *Henry VIII*, I.I.14

POSSESSION
see also BORROWING

Things won are done, joy's soul lies in the doing.
That she belov'd knows nought that knows not this:
Men prize the thing ungain'd more than it is.

CRESSIDA, *Troilus and Cressida*, I.II.287

I, that first saw her; I, that took possession
First with mine eye of all those beauties in her
Reveal'd to mankind. If thou lov'st her,
Or entertain'st a hope to blast my wishes,
Thou art a traitor, Arcite, and a fellow
False as thy title to her. Friendship, blood,
And all the ties between us, I disclaim
If thou once think upon her.

PALAMON, *The Two Noble Kinsmen*, II.II.167

You have among you many a purchas'd slave,
Which like your asses, and your dogs and mules,
You use in abject and in slavish parts,
Because you bought them. Shall I say to you,
"Let them be free! Marry them to your heirs!
Why sweat they under burdens? Let their beds
Be made as soft as yours, and let their palates
Be season'd with such viands?" You will answer,
"The slaves are ours." So do I answer you:
The pound of flesh which I demand of him
Is dearly bought as mine, and I will have it.

SHYLOCK, *The Merchant of Venice*, IV.I.90

POSTERITY
see also FAME; FUTURE

As fast as thou shalt wane, so fast thou grow'st,
In one of thine, from that which thou departest,
And that fresh blood which youngly thou bestow'st
Thou mayst call thine, when thou from youth convertest.

SONNET 11, 1–4

The evil that men do lives after them,
The good is oft interred with their bones.

ANTONY, *Julius Caesar*, III.II.75

If a man do not erect in this age his own tomb ere he dies,
he shall live no longer in monument than the bell rings and
the widow weeps.

BENEDICK, *Much Ado About Nothing*, V.II.77

POVERTY
see also BANKRUPTCY; DOWNFALL; HOMELESSNESS; HUNGER; SUFFERING

Herein Fortune shows herself more kind
Than is her custom. It is still her use
To let the wretched man outlive his wealth
To view with hollow eye and wrinkled brow
An age of poverty; from which ling'ring penance
Of such misery doth she cut me off.

ANTONIO, *The Merchant of Venice*, IV.I.267

All poverty was scorn'd, and pride so great,
The name of help grew odious to repeat.

CLEON, *Pericles*, I.IV.30

Nay, put out all you hands. Not one word more:
Thus part we rich in sorrow, parting poor.

FLAVIUS, *Timon of Athens*, IV.II.28

Fairest Cordelia, that art most rich being poor.

KING OF FRANCE, King Lear, I.I.250

'Tis deepest winter in Lord Timon's purse;
That is, one may reach deep enough and yet
Find little.

LUCIUS' SERVANT, Timon of Athens, III.IV.14

Famine is in thy cheeks,
Need and oppression starveth in thy eyes,
Contempt and beggary hangs upon thy back;
The world is not thy friend, nor the world's law,
The world affords no law to make thee rich;
Then be not poor, but break it, and take this.

ROMEO, Romeo and Juliet, V.I.69

Your lordship may minister the potion of imprisonment
to me in respect of poverty, but how I
should be your patient to follow your prescriptions,
the wise may make some dram of a scruple, or indeed
a scruple itself.

SIR JOHN FALSTAFF, 2 Henry IV, I.II.126

A man I am cross'd with adversity;
My riches are these poor habiliments,
Of which if you should here disfurnish me,
You take the sum and substance that I have.

VALENTINE, The Two Gentlemen of Verona, IV.I.12

PRAISE
see also FLATTERY; HONOR; PRIDE

The worthiness of praise distains his worth,
If that the prais'd himself bring the praise forth.
But what the repining enemy commends,
That breath fame blows, that praise, sole pure, transcends.

AENEAS, Troilus and Cressida, I.III.241

She hath herself not only well defended
But taken and impounded as a stray
The King of Scots; whom she did send to France
To fill King Edward's fame with prisoner kings,
And make her chronicle as rich with praise
As is the ooze and bottom of the sea
With sunken wrack and sumless treasuries.

CANTERBURY, Henry V, I.II.159

The chief perfections of that lovely dame
(Had I sufficient skill to utter them)
Would make a volume of enticing lines,
Able to ravish any dull conceit.

EARL OF SUFFOLK, 1 Henry VI, V.V.12

I will praise any man that will praise me.

ENOBARBUS, *Antony and Cleopatra*, II.VI.88

Ah, when the means are gone that buy this praise,
The breath is gone whereof this praise is made.

FLAVIUS, *Timon of Athens*, II.II.169

One good deed dying tongueless
Slaughters a thousand waiting upon that.
Our praises are our wages.

HERMIONE, *The Winter's Tale*, I.II.92

When no friends are by, men praise themselves.

LUCIUS, *Titus Andronicus*, V.III.118

Do not smile at me that I boast her off,
For thou shalt find she will outstrip all praise
And make it halt behind her.

PROSPERO, *The Tempest*, IV.I.9

He gave you all the duties of a man,
Trimm'd up your praises with a princely tongue,
Spoke your deservings like a chronicle,
Making you ever better than his praise
By still dispraising praise valued with you,
And which became him like a prince indeed.

SIR RICHARD VERNON, *1 Henry IV*, V.II.55

I know no man
Can justly praise but what he does affect.

TIMON, *Timon of Athens*, I.II.214

I prithee now, sweet son, as thou hast said
My praises made thee first a soldier, so,
To have my praise for this, perform a part
Thou hast not done before.

VOLUMNIA, *Coriolanus*, III.II.108

PRAYER
see also BLESSING; HIGHER POWER; SPIRITUALITY AND RELIGION

But yet like prayers divine,
I must each day say o'er the very same,
Counting no old thing old, thou mine, I thine,
Even as when first I hallowed thy fair name.

SONNET 108, 5–8

He is not lulling on a lewd love-bed,
But on his knees at meditation;
Not dallying with a brace of courtesans,
But meditating with two deep divines;

Not sleeping, to engross his idle body,
But praying, to enrich his watchful soul.

BUCKINGHAM, *Richard III*, III.VII.72

He is within, with two right reverend fathers,
Divinely bent to meditation,
And in no worldly suits would he be mov'd,
To draw him from his holy exercise.

CATESBY, *Richard III*, II.VII.61

My words fly up, my thoughts remain below:
Words without thoughts never to heaven go.

CLAUDIUS, *Hamlet*, III.III.97

O, upon my knee
Made hard with kneeling, I do pray to thee.

CONSTANCE, *King John*, III.I.309

Pray, but be not tedious, for
The gods are quick of ear.

LEONINE, *Pericles*, IV.I.68

Wherefore could not I pronounce "Amen?"
I had most need of blessing, and "Amen"
Stuck in my throat.

MACBETH, *Macbeth*, II.II.29

We, ignorant of ourselves,
Beg often our own harms, which the wise pow'rs
Deny us for our good; so find we profit
By losing of our prayers.

MENECRATES, *Antony and Cleopatra*, II.I.5

A thousand knees,
Ten thousand years together, naked, fasting,
Upon a barren mountain, and still winter
In storm perpetual, could not move the gods
To look that way thou wert.

PAULINA, *The Winter's Tale*, III.II.210

If my wind were but long enough to say my prayers, I would
repent.

SIR JOHN FALSTAFF, *The Merry Wives of Windsor*, IV.V.102

PREGNANCY
see also BABIES; BIRTH; FATHERHOOD; MOTHERHOOD

The world must be peopled.

BENEDICK, *Much Ado About Nothing*, II.III.242

The pleasing punishment that women bear.

EGEON, *The Comedy of Errors*, I.I.46

In your daughter's womb I bury them;
Where in that nest of spicery they will breed
Selves of themselves, to your recomforture.

KING RICHARD, *Richard III*, IV.IV.423

La. Cap. So shall you share all he doth possess,
by having him, making yourself no less.
Nurse. No less! nay, bigger: women grow by men.

NURSE, LADY CAPULET, *Romeo and Juliet*, I.III.93

We have laugh'd to see the sails conceive
And grow big-bellied with the wanton wind;
Which she, with pretty and with swimming gait,
Following (her womb then rich with my young squire)
Would imitate, and sail upon the land.

TITANIA, *A Midsummer Night's Dream*, II.I.128

PRESENCE
see also APPEARANCE

O Queen Emilia,
Fresher than May, sweeter
Than her gold buttons on the boughs, or all
Th' enamell'd knacks o' th' mead or garden! yea
(We challenge too) the bank of any nymph,
That makes the stream seem flowers! thou, O jewel
O' th' wood, o' th' world, hast likewise blest a place
With thy sole presence.

ARCITE, *The Two Noble Kinsmen*, III.I.4

O, sir, your presence is too bold and peremptory,
And majesty might never yet endure
The moody frontier of a servant brow.

KING HENRY, *1 Henry IV*, I.III.17

Thus did I keep my person fresh and new,
My presence, like a robe pontifical,
Ne'er seen but wond'red at, and so my state,
Seldom but sumptuous, show'd like a feast,
and wan by rareness such solemnity.

KING HENRY, *1 Henry IV*, III.II.55

Your presence makes us rich.

LORD ROSS, *Richard II*, II.III.63

PRIDE
see also ARROGANCE; CONFIDENCE; HONOR; SELF-RESPECT

He that is proud eats up himself. Pride is his own glass,
his own trumpet, his own chronicle, and whatever praises
itself but in the deed, devours the deed in the praise.

AGAMEMNON, *Troilus and Cressida*, II.III.154

Stand I condemn'd for pride and scorn so much?
Contempt, farewell, and maiden pride, adieu!
No glory lives behind the back of such.
                    BEATRICE, *Much Ado About Nothing*, III.i.108

Small things make base men proud.
                    EARL OF SUFFOLK, *2 Henry VI*, IV.i.106

High-stomach'd are they both and full of ire,
In rage, deaf as the sea, hasty as fire.
                    KING RICHARD, *Richard II*, I.i.18

And for we think the eagle-winged pride
Of sky-aspiring and ambitious thoughts,
With rival-hating envy, set on you
To wake our peace, which in our country's cradle
Draws the sweet infant breath of gentle sleep.
                    KING RICHARD, *Richard II*, I.iii.129

Would he not stumble? Would he not fall down,
Since pride must have a fall, and break the neck
Of that proud man that did usurp his back?
                    KING RICHARD, *Richard II*, V.v.87

Let pride, which she calls plainness, marry her.
                    LEAR, *King Lear*, I.i.129

I am too high-born to be propertied,
To be a secondary at control,
Or useful servingman and instrument
To any sovereign state throughout the world.
                    LEWIS, *King John*, V.ii.79

I can see his pride
Peep through each part of him.
                    LORD ABURGAVENNY, *Henry VIII*, I.i.68

If thou wilt fight, fight by thy father's side,
And commendable prov'd, let's die in pride.
                    LORD TALBOT, *1 Henry VI*, IV.vi.56

My pride fell with my fortunes.
                    ROSALIND, *As You Like It*, I.ii.252

PROCRASTINATION
see also LAZINESS; TIME; WASTE

Take up thy master;
If thou shouldst dally half an hour, his life,
With thine and all offer to defend him,
Stand in assurèd loss.
                    EARL OF GLOUCESTER, *King Lear*, III.vi.92

That we would do,
We should do when we would; for this "would" changes,
And hath abatements and delays as many
As there are tongues, are hands, are accidents,
And then this "should" is like a spendthrift's sigh,
That hurts by easing.

GHOST, Hamlet, IV.VII.118

I wasted time, and now doth time waste me;
For now hath time made me his numb'ring clock.

KING RICHARD, Richard II, V.V.49

I feel me much to blame
So idly to profane the precious time.

PRINCE HENRY, 2 Henry IV, II.IV.361

Look thou be true; do not give dalliance
Too much the rein.

PROSPERO, The Tempest, IV.I.51

Defer no time, delays have dangerous ends.

REIGNER, 1 Henry VI, III.II.33

One inch of delay more is a South-sea of discovery.

ROSALIND, As You Like It, III.II.196

Come, gentlemen, we sit too long on trifles,
And waste the time, which looks for other revels.

SIMONIDES, Pericles, II.III.92

PROMISES
see also OATHS; VOWS

The King is kind, and well we know the King
Knows at what time to promise, when to pay.

HOTSPUR, 1 Henry IV, IV.III.52

These promises are fair, the parties sure,
And our induction full of prosperous hope.

LORD MORTIMER, 1 Henry IV, III.I.1

Promising is the very air o' th' time;
It opens the eyes of expectation.
Performance is ever the duller for his act,
And but in the plainer and simpler kind of people
The deed of saying is quite out of use.
To promise is most courtly and fashionable;
Performance is a kind of will or testament
Which argues a great sickness in his judgment
That makes it.

PAINTER, Timon of Athens, V.I.22

PROPHECY
see also FUTURE

> Woe to the hand that shed this costly blood!
> Over thy wounds now do I prophesy
> (which like dumb mouths do open their ruby lips
> To beg the voice and utterance of my tongue)
> A curse shall light upon the limbs of men;
> Domestic fury and fierce civil strife
> Shall cumber all the parts of Italy;
> Blood and destruction shall be so in use,
> And dreadful objects so familiar,
> That mothers shall but smile when they behold
> Their infants quartered with the hands of war;
> All pity chok'd with custom of fell deeds;
> And Caesar's spirit, ranging for revenge,
> With Atè by his side come hot from hell,
> Shall in these confines with a monarch's voice
> Cry "Havoc!" and let slip the dogs of war,
> That this foul deed shall smell above the earth
> With carrion men, groaning for burial.
>
> ANTONY, *Julius Caesar*, III.I.258

> Our reasons are not prophets
> When oft our fancies are.
>
> EMILIA, *The Two Noble Kinsmen*, V.III.102

> This thy have promised, to show your Highness
> A spirit rais'd from depth of under ground,
> That shall make answer to such questions
> As by your Grace shall be propounded him.
>
> JOHN HUME, *2 Henry VI*, I.II.78

> Beware the ides of March.
>
> SOOTHSAYER, *Julius Caesar*, I.II.18

> In nature's infinite book of secrecy
> A little I can read.
>
> SOOTHSAYER, *Antony and Cleopatra*, I.II.10

PROSPERITY
see also WEALTH

> O, let those cities that of plenty's cup
> And her prosperities so largely taste,
> With their superfluous riots, hear these tears!
>
> CLEON, *Pericles*, I.IV.52

> God in thy good cause make thee prosperous!
>
> JOHN OF GAUNT, *Richard II*, I.III.78

Come, come; for thou shalt thrust thy hand as deep
Into the purse of rich prosperity.

LEWIS, *King John*, V.II.60

PROSTITUTION
see also EXPLOITATION

Let not the creaking of shoes
nor the rustling of silks betray thy poor heart to
woman. Keep thy foot out of brothels, thy hand out of
plackets, thy pen from lenders' books, and defy the
foul fiend.

EDGAR, *King Lear*, III.IV.94

Women? Help heaven! men their creation mar
In profiting by them.

ISABELLA, *Measure for Measure*, II.IV.127

Why, the house you swell in proclaims you
to be a creature of sale.

LYSIMACHUS, *Pericles*, IV.VI.77

O traders and bawds, how earnestly are you set a-work, and
how ill requited! Why should our endeavor be so lov'd and
the performance so loath'd?

PANDARUS, *Troilus and Cressida*, V.X.37

They love thee not that use thee;
Give them diseases, leaving with thee their lust.

TIMON, *Timon of Athens*, IV.III.84

PUBLIC OPINION
see also INFLUENCE; PERSUASION; POLITICS AND POWER

Why does my blood thus muster to my heart,
Making both it unable for itself,
And dispossessing all my other parts
Of necessary fitness?
So play the foolish throngs with one that swounds,
Come all to help him, and so stop the air
By which he should revive; and even so
The general subject to a well-wish'd king
Quit their own part, and in obsequious fondness
Crowd to his presence, where their untaught love
And I will do it without fear or doubt,
To live an unstain'd wife to my sweet love.

ANGELO, *Measure for Measure*, II.IV.20

Our slippery people,
Whose love is never link'd to the deserver
Till his deserts are past.

ANTONY, *Antony and Cleopatra*, I.II.185

This common body,
Like to a vagabond flag upon the stream,
Goes to and back, lackeying the varying tide,
To rot itself with motion.
                        CAESAR (OCTAVIUS), *Antony and Cleopatra*, I.IV.44

He sits high in all the people's hearts;
And that which would appear offense in us,
His countenance, like richest alchymy,
Will change to virtue and to worthiness.
                        CASCA, *Julius Caesar*, I.III.157

Was ever feather so lightly blown
to and fro as this multitude?
                        JACK CADE, *2 Henry VI*, IV.VIII.55

The fool multitude that choose by show,
Not learning more than the fond eye doth teach,
Which pries not to th' interior, but like the martlet
Builds in the weather on the outward wall,
Even in the force and road of casualty.
                        PRINCE OF ARRAGON, *The Merchant of Venice*, II.IX.26

PUNCTUALITY
see also SPEED; TIME

You come most carefully upon your hour.
                        FRANCISCO, *Hamlet*, I.I.6

I have obsev'd thee always for a towardly
prompt spirit—give thee thy due—and one that
knows what belongs to reason; and canst use the time
well, if the time use thee well.
                        LUCULLUS, *Timon of Athens*, III.I.34

PUNISHMENT
see also JUSTICE; LAW; MURDER AND EXECUTION

Whip him, fellows,
Till like a boy you see him cringe his face,
And whine aloud for mercy.
                        ANTONY, *Antony and Cleopatra*, III.XIII.99

King. Sir, I will pronounce your sentence: you
shall fast a week with bran and water.
Cost. I had rather pray a month with mutton and
porridge.
                        COSTARD, KING, *Love's Labor's Lost*, I.I.300

Though well we may not pass upon his life
Without the form of justice, yet our power

Shall do a court'sy to our wrath, which men
May blame, but not control.
DUKE OF CORNWALL, King Lear, III.VII.24

Alas, I look'd when some of you should say
I was too strict to make mine own away.
JOHN OF GAUNT, Richard II, I.III.243

Besides, the King hath wasted all his rods
On late offenders, that he now doth lack
The very instruments of chastisement,
So that his power, like to a fangless lion,
May offer, but not hold.
LORD HASTINGS, 2 Henry IV, IV.i.213

To punish me for what you make me do
Seems much unequal.
MESSENGER, Antony and Cleopatra, II.V.100

If thou neglect'st, or dost unwillingly
What I command, I'll rack thee with old cramps,
Fill all thy bones with aches, make thee roar
That beasts shall tremble at thy din.
PROSPERO, The Tempest, I.II.368

Shy. Most learned judge, a sentence! Come prepare!
Por. Tarry a little, there is something else.
This bond doth give thee here no jot of blood;
The words expressly are "a pound of flesh."
SHYLOCK, PORTIA, The Merchant of Venice, IV.i.304

PURITY
see also GOOD; INNOCENCE

She wakes her heart by beating on her breast,
And bids it leap from thence, where it may find
Some purer chest to close so pure a mind.
The Rape of Lucrece, 759

What stronger breastplate than a heart untainted!
KING HENRY, 2 Henry VI, III.II.232

For we will hear, note, and believe in heart,
That what you speak is in your conscience wash'd
As pure as sin with baptism.
KING HENRY, Henry V, I.II.30

Dost think I am so muddy, so unsettled,
To appoint myself in this vexation, sully
The purity and whiteness of my sheets?
LEONTES, The Winter's Tale, I.II.325

PURPOSE
see also INTENTIONS; WILL

> Many things, having full reference
> To one consent, may work contrariously,
> As many arrows loosèd several ways
> Come to one mark; as many ways meet in one town;
> As many fresh streams meet in one salt sea;
> As many lines close in the dial's center;
> So may a thousand actions, once afoot,
> End in one purpose.
>
> CANTERBURY, *Henry V*, I.II.205

> Purpose is but the slave to memory,
> Of violent birth, but poor validity,
> Which now, the fruit unripe, sticks on the tree,
> But fall unshaken when they mellow be.
> Most necessary 'tis that we forget
> To pay ourselves what to ourselves is debt.
> What to ourselves in passion we propose,
> The passion ending, doth the purpose lose.
>
> PLAYER KING, *Hamlet*, III.II.188

QUARRELS
see also ARGUMENT

> In a false quarrel there is no true valor.
>
> BENEDICK, *Much Ado About Nothing*, V.I.120

> In the managing of quarrels you may say he is wise, for
> either he avoids them with great discretion, or undertakes
> them with a most Christian-like fear.
>
> DON PEDRO, *Much Ado About Nothing*, II.III.189

> And being seated, and domestic broils
> Clean overblown, themselves, the conquerors
> Make war upon themselves, brother to brother,
> Blood to blood, self against self.
>
> DUCHESS OF YORK, *Richard III*, II.IV.60

> And the best quarrels, in the heat, are curs'd
> By those that feel their sharpness.
>
> EDMUND, *King Lear*, V.III.56

> Besides that he's a fool, he's a great quarreler; and but
> that he hath the gift of a coward to allay the gust he hath
> in quarreling, 'tis thought among the gift of a grave.
>
> MARIA, *Twelfth Night*, I.III.29

> Thou wilt quarrel with a man that hath a hair more or a hair
> less in his beard than thou hast. Thou wilt quarrel with a

man for cracking nuts, having no other reason but because
thou hast hazel eyes. What eye but such an eye would spy
out such a quarrel? Thy head is as full of quarrels as an
egg is as full of meat, and yet thy head hath been beaten
as addle as an egg for quarreling. Thou hast quarrel'd with
a man for coughing in the street, because he hath waken'd
thy dog that hath lain asleep in the sun. Didst thou not
fall out with a tailor for wearing his new doublet before
before Easter? with another for tying his new shoes with
old riband? and yet thou wilt tutor me from quarreling!
MERCUTIO, Romeo and Juliet, III.I.17

I warrant you, I dare draw as soon as another man, if I see
occasion in a good quarrel, and the law on my side.
PETER, Romeo and Juliet, II.IV.158

Beware
Of entrance to a quarrel, but being in,
Bear't that th' opposed may beware of thee.
POLONIUS, Hamlet, I.III.65

The venom of such looks we fairly hope
Have lost their quality, and that this day
Shall change all griefs and quarrels into love.
QUEEN ISABEL, Henry V, V.II.18

Come, let us four to dinner. I dare say
This quarrel will drink blood another day.
RICHARD PLANTAGENET, 1 Henry VI, II.IV.132

Your words have took such pains as if they labor'd
To bring manslaughter into form, and set quarreling
Upon the head of valor.
FIRST SENATOR, Timon of Athens, III.V.26

We quarrel in print, by the book; as you have books for good
manners. I will name you the degrees. The first, the
Retort Courteous; the second, the Quip Modest; the third,
the Reply Churlish, the fourth, the Reproof Valiant; the
fifth, the Countercheck Quarrelsome; the sixt, the Lie with
Circumstance; the seventh, the Lie Direct. All these you
may avoid but the Lie Direct; and you may avoid that too,
with an If. I knew when seven justices could not take up a
quarrel, but when the parties were met themselves, one of
them thought but of an If, as "If you said so, then I said
so"; and they shook hands and swore brothers. Your If is
the only peacemaker. Much virtue in If.
TOUCHSTONE, As You Like It, V.IV.90

RASHNESS

see also HASTE

> The middle of humanity thou never knewest
> but the extremity of both ends.
>> APEMANTUS, *Timon of Athens*, IV.III.300

> And then we shall repent each drop of blood
> That hot rash haste so indirectly shed.
>> CONSTANCE, *King John*, II.I.48

> Reserve thy state,
> And in thy best consideration check
> This hideous rashness.
>> EARL OF KENT, *King Lear*, I.I.149

> O my lord,
> You only speak from your distracted soul;
> There's not so much left to furnish out
> A moderate table.
>> FLAVIUS, *Timon of Athens*, III.IV.113

> His rash fierce blaze of riot cannot last,
> For violent fires soon burn out themselves;
> Small show'rs last long, but sudden storms are short.
>> JOHN OF GAUNT, *Richard II*, II.I.33

> His heart's his mouth;
> What his breast forges, that his tongue must vent,
> And, being angry, does forget that ever
> He heard the name of death.
> Here's goodly work!
>> MENENIUS AGRIPPA, *Coriolanus*, III.I.256

> But alas,
> Our hands advanc'd before our hearts, what will
> The fall o' th' stroke do damage?
>> PALAMON, *The Two Noble Kinsmen*, I.II.111

READING

see also BOOKS; LITERACY; WORDS; WRITING

> Light, seeking light, doth light of light beguile;
> So ere you find where light in darkness lies,
> Your light grows dark by losing of your eyes.
>> BEROWNE, *Love's Labor's Lost*, I.I.77

> Pol. What do you read, my lord?
> Ham. Words, words, words.
>> HAMLET, POLONIUS, *Hamlet*, II.II.191

> Serv. I pray, sir, can you read?
> Rom. Ay, mine own fortune in my misery.

Serv. Perhaps you have learn'd it without book.
But I pray, can you read any thing you see?
Rom. Ay, if I know the letters and the language.

ROMEO, CLOWN, *Romeo and Juliet*, I.II.57

REAL ESTATE

Sell when you can, you are not for all markets.

ROSALIND, *As You Like It*, III.v.60

You may buy land now
As cheap as stinking mack'rel.

SIR JOHN FALSTAFF, *1 Henry IV*, II.IV.359

REASON

see also MIND; THOUGHT

My reason, the physician to my love,
Angry that this prescriptions are not kept,
Hath left me, and I desperate now approve
Desire is death.

SONNET 147, 5–8

Reason and love keep little company together nowadays.

BOTTOM, *A Midsummer Night's Dream*, III.I.144

You came in arms to spill mine enemies' blood
But now in arms you strengthen it with yours.

CONSTANCE, *King John*, III.I.102

Every why hath a wherefore.

DROMIO OF SYRACUSE, *The Comedy of Errors*, II.II.43

And let your reason with your choler question
What 'tis you go about: to climb steep hills
Requires slow pace at first.

DUKE OF NORFOLK, *Henry VIII*, I.I.130

When valor preys on reason,
It eats the sword it fights with.

ENOBARBUS, *Antony and Cleopatra*, III.XIII.198

If my reason
Will thereto be obedient, I have reason;
If not, my senses, better pleas'd with madness,
Do bid it welcome.

FLORIZEL, *The Winter's Tale*, IV.IV.482

I would you would make use of your good wisdom
(Whereof I know you are fraught) and put away
These dispositions which of late transport you
From what you rightly are.

GONERIL, *King Lear*, I.IV.219

Reason panders will.

HAMLET, Hamlet, III.IV.88

But we have reason to cool our raging motions, our
carnal stings, or unbitted lusts; whereof I take this
that you call love to be a sect or scion.

IAGO, Othello, I.III.329

Wrath-kindled gentlemen, be rul'd by me,
Let's purge this choler without letting blood.

KING RICHARD, Richard II, I.I.152

Much more, in this great work
(Which is, almost, to pluck a kingdom down
And set another up), should we survey
The plot of situation and the model,
Consent upon a sure foundation,
Question surveyors, know our own estate,
How able such a work to undergo,
To weigh against his opposite.

LORD BARDOLPH, 2 Henry IV, I.III.48

Who will not change a raven for a dove?
The will of man is by his reason sway'd;
And reason says you are the worthier maid.
Things growing are not ripe until their season,
So I, being young, till now ripe not to reason;
And touching now the point of human skill,
Reason becomes the marshal to my will,
And leads me to your eyes, where I o'erlook
Love's stories written in Love's richest book.

LYSANDER, A Midsummer Night's Dream, II.II.114

Manhood and honor
Should have hare hearts, would they but fat their thoughts
With this cramm'd reason; reason and respect
Make livers pale and lustihood deject.

TROILUS, Troilus and Cressida, II.II.47

REBELLION

see also ANARCHY AND CHAOS; CIVIL DISOBEDIENCE; CONSPIRACY; HERESY; TREA-
SON

Rebellion in this land shall lose his sway,
Meeting the check of such another day,
And since this business so fair is done,
Let us not leave till all our own be won.

KING HENRY, 1 Henry IV, V.V.41

Cover your heads, and mock not flesh and blood
With solemn reverence, throw away respect,

Tradition, form, and ceremonious duty.

KING RICHARD, *Richard II*, III.II.171

Unthread the rude eye of rebellion,
And welcome home again discarded faith.

MELUNE, *King John*, V.IV.11

For that same word, rebellion, did divide
The action of their bodies from their souls,
And they did fight with queasiness, constrain'd
As men drink potions, that their weapons only
Seem'd on our side.

MORTON, *2 Henry IV*, I.I.194

This word, rebellion, it had froze them up,
As fish are in a pond.

MORTON, *2 Henry IV*, I.I.199

Ten the hearts
Of all his people shall revolt from him,
And kiss the lips of unacquainted change,
And pick strong matter of revolt and wrath
Out of the bloody fingers' ends of John.

PANDULPH, *King John*, III.IV.164

The main blaze of it is past, but a small thing
would make it flame again; for the nobles receive so to
heart the banishment of that worthy Coriolanus, that
they are in a ripe aptness to take all power from the
people, and to pluck from them their tribunes for ever.

ROMAN, *Coriolanus*, IV.III.20

RECONCILIATION

O, a kiss
Long as my exile, sweet as my revenge!

CORIOLANUS, *Coriolanus*, V.III.44

She lifted the Princess from the earth, and so
locks her in embracing, as if she would pin her to her
heart, that she might no more be in danger of losing.

GENTLEMEN, *The Winter's Tale*, V.II.76

Discharge your powers unto their several counties,
As we will ours, and here between the armies
Let's drink together friendly and embrace,
That all their eyes may bear those tokens home
of our restored love and amity.

PRINCE JOHN, *2 Henry IV*, IV.II.61

If any here
By false intelligence or wrong surmise

Hold me a foe—
If I unwittingly, or in my rage,
Have aught committed that is hardly borne
By any in this presence, I desire
To reconcile me to his friendly peace.
'Tis death to me to be an enmity;
I hate it, and desire all good men's love.

RICHARD, DUKE OF GLOUCESTER, *Richard III*, II.I.54

RECOVERY
see also HEALING; REST

It is but as a body yet distempered,
Which to his former strength may be restored
With good advice and little medicine.

EARL OF WARWICK, *2 Henry IV*, III.I.41

Mend when thou canst, be better at thy leisure,
I can be patient.

LEAR, *King Lear*, II.IV.229

My long sickness
Of health and living now begins to mend,
And nothing brings me all things.

TIMON, *Timon of Athens*, V.I.186

REDEMPTION
see also REPENTANCE

For in my death I murder shameful scorn
My shame so dead, mine honor is new born.

The Rape of Lucrece, 1189

Sir, you have done enough, and have perform'd
A saint-like sorrow. No fault could you make
Which you have not redeem'd; indeed paid down
More penitence than done trespass.

CLEOMINES, *The Winter's Tale*, V.I.1

No, yet time serves wherein you may redeem
Your banish'd honors and restore yourselves
Into the good thoughts of the world again.

HOTSPUR, *1 Henry IV*, I.III.180

By heaven, methinks it were an easy leap,
To pluck bright honor from the pale-fac'd moon,
Or dive into the bottom of the deep,
Where fadom-line could never touch the ground,
And pluck up drowned honor by the locks,
So he that doth redeem her thence might wear

Without corrival all her dignities;
But out upon this half-fac'd fellowship!

HOTSPUR, 1 Henry IV, I.III.201

Stay and breathe a while.
Thou hast redeem'd thy lost opinion,
And show'd thou mak'st some tender of my life
In this fair rescue thou hast brought to me.

KING HENRY, 1 Henry IV, V.IV.47

REFORM
see also CHANGE

Any thing that's mended is but patch'd; virtue that
transgresses is but patch'd with sin, and sin that amends is
but patch'd with virtue.

FESTE, Twelfth Night, I.V.47

REJECTION

Since that my beauty cannot please his eye,
I'll weep what's left away, and weeping die.

ADRIANA, The Comedy of Errors, II.I.114

Foul words is but foul wind, and foul wind is but foul
breath, and foul breath is noisome; therefore I will depart
unkiss'd.

BEATRICE, Much Ado About Nothing, V.II.52

This world I do renounce, and in your sights
Shake patiently my great affliction off.
If I could bear it longer, and not fall
To quarrel with your great opposeless will,
My snuff and loathèd part of nature should
Burn itself out.

EARL OF GLOUCESTER, King Lear, IV.VI.35

Here I disclaim all my paternal care,
Propinquity and property of blood,
And as a stranger to my heart and me
Hold thee from this for ever.

LEAR, King Lear, I.I.113

REPENTANCE
see also SIN

May one be pardon'd and retain the offense?

CLAUDIUS, Hamlet, III.III.56

Men shall deal unadvisedly sometimes,
Which after-hours gives leisure to repent.

KING RICHARD, Richard III, IV.IV.292

I cannot make you what amends I would,
Therefore accept such kindness as I can.

KING RICHARD, *Richard III*, IV.IV.309

Our purposes God justly hath discover'd,
And I repent my fault more than my death,
Which I beseech your Highness to forgive,
Although my body pay the price of it.

LORD SCROOP, *Henry V*, II.II.151

Who by repentance is not satisfied
Is nor of heaven nor earth, for these are pleas'd;
By pentinence th' Eternal's wrath's appeas'd.

VALENTINE, *The Two Gentlemen of Verona*, V.IV.79

REPUTATION
see also HONOR

Seeing his reputation touch'd to death,
He did oppose his foe;
And with such sober and unnoted passion
He did behoove his anger, ere 'twas spent,
As if he had but prov'd an argument.

ALCIBIADES, *Timon of Athens*, III.V.19

Read not my blemishes in the world's report.

ANTONY, *Antony and Cleopatra*, II.III.5

I have offended reputation,
A most unnoble swerving.

ANTONY, *Antony and Cleopatra*, II.XI.48

Reputation, reputation, reputation! O, I have
lost my reputation! I have lost the immortal part of
myself, and what remains is bestial. My reputation,
Iago, my reputation!

CASSIO, *Othello*, II.III.262

Reputation is an idle and most false
imposition; oft got without merit, and lost without
deserving. You have lost no reputation at all,
unless you repute yourself such a loser.

IAGO, *Othello*, II.III.268

Had I so lavish of my presence been,
So common-hackney'd in the eyes of men,
So stale and cheap to vulgar company,
Opinion, that did help me to the crown,
Had still kept loyal to possession,
And left me in reputeless banishment,
A fellow of no mark nor likelihood.

KING HENRY, *1 Henry IV*, III.II.39

The purest treasure mortal times afford
Is spotless reputation; that away,
Men are but gilded loam or painted clay.

MOWBRAY, Richard II, I.I.177

O then, my best blood turn
To an infected jelly, and my name
Be yok'd with his that did betray the Best!
Turn then my freshest reputation to
A savor that may strike the dullest nostril
Where I arrive, and my approach be shunn'd,
Nay, hated too, worse than the great'st infection
That e'er was heard or read.

POLIXENES, The Winter's Tale, I.II.417

Though my estate be fall'n, I was well born,
Nothing acquainted with these businesses
And would not put my reputation now
In any staining act.

WIDOW, All's Well That Ends Well, III.VII.4

RESIGNATION
see also RETIREMENT; SURRENDER

Ay, no, no, ay; for I must nothing be;
Therefore no no, for I resign to thee,
Now mark me how I will undo myself:
I give this heavy weight from off my head,
And this unwieldy scepter from my hand,
The pride of kingly sway from out my heart;
With mine own tears I wash away my balm,
With mine own hands I give away my crown,
With mine own tongue deny my sacred state,
With mine own breath release all duteous oaths;
All pomp and majesty I do forswear;
My manors, rents, revenues I forgo;
My acts, decrees, and statutes I deny;
God pardon all oaths that are broke to me,
God keep all vows unbroke are made to thee!
Make me, that nothing have, with nothing griev'd,
And thou with all pleas'd, that hast all achiev'd!
Long mayst thou live in Richard's seat to sit,
And soon lie Richard in an earthy pit!
God save King Henry, unking'd Richard says,
And send him many years of sunshine days!
What more remains?

KING RICHARD, Richard II, IV.I.201

RESPONSIBILITY
see also DUTY; LOYALTY; SERVICE

> She that her fame so to herself contrives,
> The scars of battle 'scapeth by the flight,
> And makes her absence valiant, not her might.
>
> A Lover's Complaint, 243

> And this fell tempest shall not cease to rage
> Until the golden circuit on my head,
> Like to the glorious sun's transparent beams,
> Do calm the fury of this mad-bred flaw.
>
> DUKE OF YORK, 2 Henry VI, III.i.351

> 'Tis his own blame hath put himself from rest,
> And must needs taste his folly.
>
> GONERIL, King Lear, II.iv.290

> The time is out of joint—O cursèd sprite,
> That I ever was born to set it right!
>
> HAMLET, Hamlet, I.v.188

REST
see also RECOVERY; SLEEP

> There is means, madam.
> Our foster-nurse of nature is repose,
> The which he lacks.
>
> DOCTOR, King Lear, IV.iii.11

> Oppressèd nature sleeps.
> The rest might yet have balm'd thy broken sinews,
> Which, if convenience will not allow,
> Stand in hard cure.
>
> EARL OF KENT, King Lear, III.vi.97

> My old bones aches. Here's a maze trod indeed
> Through forth-rights and meanders! By your patience,
> I needs must rest me.
>
> GONZALO, The Tempest, III.iii.2

> The crickets sing, and man's o'erlabor'd sense
> Repairs itself by rest.
>
> JACHIMO, Cymbeline, II.ii.11

> If ye will needs say I am an old
> man, you should give me rest. I would to God my
> name were not so terrible to the enemy as it is. I were
> better to be eaten to death with a rust than to be
> scour'd to nothing with perpetual motion.
>
> LORD CHIEF JUSTICE, 2 Henry IV, I.ii.216

Alas, now pray you
Work not so hard. I would the lightning had
Burnt up those logs that you are enjoin'd to pile!

MIRANDA, The Tempest, III.i.16

Most heavenly music!
It nips me unto listening, and thick slumber
Hangs upon mine eyes. Let me rest.

PERICLES, Pericles, V.i.233

Here let us rest, if this rebellious earth
Have any resting for her true king's queen.

QUEEN, Richard II, V.i.5

RESTITUTION
see also DEBTS

He hath eaten me out of house and home, he
hath put all my substance into that fat belly of his,
but I will have some of it out again, or I will ride thee
a' nights like the mare.

HOSTESS QUICKLY, 2 Henry IV, II.i.74

Pay her the debt you
owe her, and unpay the villainy you have done with
her. The one you may do with sterling money, and
the other with current repentance.

LORD CHIEF JUSTICE, 2 Henry IV, II.i.118

Many do keep their chambers are not sick;
And if it be so far beyond his health,
Methinks he should the sooner pay his debts,
And make a clear way to the gods.

LUCIUS' SERVANT, Timon of Athens, III.iv.73

That of all things upon the earth he hated
Your person most; that he would pawn his fortunes
To hopeless restitution, so he might
Be call'd your vanquisher.

TITUS LARTIUS, Coriolanus, III.i.14

RETIREMENT
see also RESIGNATION

For mine own part, I could be well content
To entertain the lag end of my life
With quiet hours.

EARL OF WORCESTER, 1 Henry IV, V.i.23

Upon thy sight
My worldly business makes a period.

KING HENRY IV, 2 Henry IV, IV.v.229

'Tis our fast intent
To shake all care and business from our age,
Conferring with them on younger strengths, while we
Unburthen'd crawl toward death.

LEAR, *King Lear*, I.i.38

But this rough magic
I here abjure; and when I have requir'd
Some heavenly music (which even now I do)
To work mine end upon their senses that
This airy charm is for, I'll break my staff,
Bury it certain fadoms in the earth,
And deeper than did ever plummet sound
I'll drown my book.

PROSPERO, *The Tempest*, V.i.50

REVENGE
see also ANGER; CURSES; THREATS

Vengeance is in my heart, death in my hand,
Blood and revenge are hammering in my head.

AARON, *Titus Andronicus*, II.iii.38

She hath despis'd me
rejoicingly, and I'll be merry in my revenge.

CLOTEN, *Cymbeline*, III.v.44

I should kick, being kick'd, and being at that pass,
You would keep from my heels, and beware of an ass.

DROMIO OF EPHESUS, *The Comedy of Errors*, III.i.17

You know his nature,
That he's revengeful; and I know his sword
Hath a sharp edge; it's long, and 't may be said
It reaches far, and where 'twill not extend,
Thither he darts it.

DUKE OF NORFOLK, *Henry VIII*, I.i.108

Heat not a furnace for your foe so hot
That it do singe yourself. We may outrun
By violent swiftness that which we run at,
And lose by overrunning.

DUKE OF NORFOLK, *Henry VIII*, I.i.140

That lie shall lie so heavy on my sword,
That it shall render vengeance and revenge
Till thou the lie-giver and that lie do lie
In earth as quiet as thy father's skull.

DUKE OF SURREY, *Richard II*, IV.i.66

My ashes, as the phoenix, may bring forth
A bird that will revenge upon you all.

DUKE OF YORK, *3 Henry VI*, I.iv.35

O, may diseases only work upon't!
And when he's sick to death, let not that part of nature
Which my lord paid for, be of any power
To expel sickness, but prolong his hour!

FLAMINIUS, *Timon of Athens*, III.i.60

How all occasions do inform against me,
And spur my dull revenge!

HAMLET, *Hamlet*, IV.iv.32

The reasons you allege do more conduce
To the hot passion of distemp'red blood
Than to make up a free determination
'Twixt right and wrong; for pleasure and revenge
Have ears more deaf than adders to the voice
Of any true decision.

HECTOR, *Troilus and Cressida*, II.ii.68

Then lead me hence; with whom I leave my curse:
May never glorious sun reflex his beams
Upon the country where you make abode;
But darkness and the gloomy shade of death
Environ you, till mischief and despair
Drive you to break your necks or hang yourselves!

JOAN DE PUCELLE, *1 Henry VI*, V.iv.86

I am burn'd up with inflaming wrath,
A rage whose heat hath this condition,
That nothing can allay, nothing but blood.

KING JOHN, *King John*, III.i.340

Time hath not yet so dried this blood of mine,
Nor age so eat up my invention,
Nor fortune made such havoc of my means,
Nor my bad life reft me so much of friends,
But they shall find, awak'd in such a kind,
Both strength of limb, and policy of mind,
Ability in means, and choice of friends,
To quit me of them throughly.

LEONATO, *Much Ado About Nothing*, IV.i.193

How shall I be reveng'd on him? for reveng'd I will be!
as sure as his guts are made of puddings.

MISTRESS PAGE, *The Merry Wives of Windsor*, II.i.30

Can vengeance be pursued further than death?

PARIS, *Romeo and Juliet*, V.iii.55

Sal. Why, I am sure if he forfeit thou wilt not take his
flesh. What's that good for?
Shy. To bait fish withal—if it will feed nothing else, it
will feed my revenge.
SHYLOCK, SALERIO, The Merchant of Venice, III.I.51

Strike a free march. To Troy with comfort go;
Hope of revenge shall hide our inward woe.
TROILUS, Troilus and Cressida, V.x.30

REVERENCE

Though mean and mighty, rotting
Together, have one dust, yet reverence
(That angel of the world) doth make distinction
Of place 'tween high and low.
BELARIUS, Cymbeline, IV.II.246

That I shall clear myself,
Lay all the weight ye can upon my patience,
I make as little doubt as you do conscience
In doing daily wrongs. I could say more,
But reverence to your calling makes me modest.
CRANMER, Henry VIII, V.II.100

A father, and a gracious agèd man,
Whose reverence even the head-lugg'd bear would lick,
Most barbarous, most degenerate, have you madded.
DUKE OF ALBANY, King Lear, IV.II.41

O fairest beauty, do not fear nor fly,
For I will touch thee but with reverend hands.
EARL OF SUFFOLK, 1 Henry VI, V.III.84

O Helicanus,
Down on thy knees, thank the holy gods as loud
As thunder threatens us.
PERICLES, Pericles, V.I.197

Had princes sit like stars about his throne,
And he the sun for them to reverence.
PERICLES, Pericles, II.III.39

RIOT
see also ANARCHY AND CHAOS

3. Pleb. Your name, sir, truly.
Cin. Truly, my name is Cinna.
1. Pleb. Tear him to pieces, he's a conspirator.
Cin. I am Cinna the poet, I am Cinna the poet.
4. Pleb. Tear him for his bad verses, tear him for his
bad verses.

Cin. I am not Cinna the conspirator.
4. Pleb. It is no matter, his name's Cinna. Pluck
but his name out of his heart, and turn him going.
3. Pleb. Tear him, tear him!

CINNA, PLEBEIANS, *Julius Caesar*, III.III.26

When that my care could not withhold thy riots,
What wilt thou do when riot is thy care?

KING HENRY IV, *2 Henry IV*, IV.v.134

RISK
see also DANGER; OPPORTUNITY

The wall is high, and yet will I leap down.
Good ground, be pitiful and hurt me not!
There's few or none do know me; if they did,
This ship-boy's semblance hath disguis'd me quite.
I am afraid, and yet I'll venture it.

ARTHUR, *King John*, IV.III.1

No, lord ambassador, I'll rather keep
That which I have than, coveting for more,
Be cast from possibility of all.

CARDINAL, *1 Henry VI*, V.IV.144

We all that are engaged to this loss
Knew that we ventured on such dangerous seas
That if we wrought out life 'twas ten to one,
And yet we ventur'd for the gain propos'd,
Chok'd the respect of likely peril fear'd.

LORD BARDOLPH, *2 Henry IV*, I.I.180

What dangerous action, stood it next to death,
Would I not undergo for one calm look?

PROTEUS, *The Two Gentlemen of Verona*, V.IV.41

ROYALTY
see also GREATNESS; LEADERSHIP; NOBILITY

When beggars die there are no comets seen;
The heavens themselves blaze forth the death of princes.

CALPHURNIA, *Julius Caesar*, II.II.30

There's such divinity doth hedge a king
That treason can but peep to what it would,
Acts little of his will.

CLAUDIUS, *Hamlet*, IV.v.124

Majesty, to keep decorum, must
No less beg than a kingdom.

CLEOPATRA, *Antony and Cleopatra*, V.II.17

The presence of a king engenders love
Amongst his subjects and his loyal friends,
As it disanimates his enemies.

DUKE OF GLOUCESTER, *1 Henry VI*, III.I.180

Yet looks he like a king! Behold, his eye,
As bright as is the eagle's, lightens forth
Controlling majesty.

DUKE OF YORK, *Richard II*, III.III.68

And what have kings, that privates have not too,
Save ceremony, save general ceremony?
And what art thou, thou idol Ceremony?
What kind of God art thou, that suffer'st more
Of mortal griefs than do thy worshippers?
What are thy rents? what are thy comings-in?
O Ceremony, show me thy worth!
What is thy soul of adoration?
Art thou aught else but place, degree, and form,
Creating awe and fear in other men?

KING HENRY, *Henry V*, IV.I.238

Uneasy lies the head that wears a crown.

KING HENRY IV, *2 Henry IV*, III.I.31

My crown is in my heart, not on my head;
Not deck'd with diamonds and Indian stones,
Nor to be seen. My crown is call'd content,
A crown it is that seldom kings enjoy.

KING HENRY, *3 Henry VI*, III.I.62

What must the King do now? Must he submit?
The King shall do it. Must he be depos'd?
The King shall be contented. Must he lose
The name of king? a' God's name let it go.
I'll give my jewels for a set of beads,
My gorgeous palace for a hermitage,
My gay apparel for an almsman's gown,
My figur'd goblets for a dish of wood,
My scepter for a palmer's walking-staff,
My subjects for a pair of carvèd saints,
And my large kingdom for a little grave,
A little, little grave, an obscure grave—
or I'll be buried in the king's highway,
Some way of common trade, where subjects' feet
May hourly trample on their sovereign's head;
For on my heart they tread now whilst I live,
And buried once, why not upon my head?

KING RICHARD, *Richard II*, III.III.144

Is not the king's name twenty thousand names?
> KING RICHARD, *Richard II*, III.II.85

Not all the water in the rough rude sea
Can wash the balm off from an anointed king.
> KING RICHARD, *Richard II*, III.II.54

The king-becoming graces,
As justice, verity, temp'rance, stableness,
Bounty, perseverance, mercy, lowliness,
Devotion, patience, courage, fortitude.
> MALCOLM, *Macbeth*, IV.III.91

There was a lady once ('tis an old story)
That would not be a queen, that would she not,
For all the mud in Egypt.
> OLD LADY, *Henry VIII*, II.III.90

The cess of majesty
Dies not alone, but like a gulf doth draw
What's near with it. Or it is a massy wheel
Fix'd on the summit of the highest mount,
To whose huge spokes ten thousand lesser things
Are mortis'd and adjoin'd, which when it falls,
Each small annexment, petty consequence,
Attends the boist'rous ruin. Never alone
Did the King sigh, but with a general groan.
> ROSENCRANTZ, *Hamlet*, III.III.15

Weigh you the worth and honor of a king
So great as our dread father's in a scale
Of common ounces? Will you with computers sum
The past-proportion of his infinite,
And buckle in a waist most fathomless
With spans and inches so diminutive
As fears and reasons?
> TROILUS, *Troilus and Cressida*, II.II.26

RUDENESS
see also INGRATITUDE; UNKINDNESS

O, to what purpose dost thou hoard thy words,
That thou returnest no greeting to thy friends?
> JOHN OF GAUNT, *Richard II*, I.III.253

You are retired,
As if you were a feasted one and not
The hostess of the meeting. Pray you bid
These unknown friends to 's welcome, for it is
A way to make us better friends, more known.
> SHEPHERD, *The Winter's Tale*, IV.IV.62

Thou art not noble,
For all th' accomodations that thou bear'st
Are nurs'd by baseness.

VINCENTIO, DUKE OF VIENNA, Measure for Measure, II.I.13

RUMORS
see also GOSSIP; SCANDAL

Rumor doth double, like the voice and echo,
The numbers of the feared.

EARL OF WARWICK, 2 Henry IV, III.I.97

But as I travelled hither through the land,
I find the people strangely fantasied,
Possess'd with rumors, full of idle dreams,
Not knowing what they fear, but full of fear.

PHILIP THE BASTARD, King John, IV.II.144

By holy Paul, they love his Grave but lightly
That fill his ears with such dissentious rumors.

RICHARD, DUKE OF GLOUCESTER, Richard III, I.III.45

Rumor is a pipe
Blown by surmises, jealousies, conjectures,
And of so easy and so plain a stop
That the blunt monster with uncounted heads,
The still-discordant wav'ring multitude,
Can play upon it.

RUMOR, 2 Henry IV, I.IND.15

RUNNING

Run
Swifter than wind upon a field of corn,
Curling the wealthy ears.

ARCITE, The Two Noble Kinsmen, II.II.76

We may outrun,
By violent swiftness, that which we run at,
And lose by over-running.

DUKE OF NORFOLK, Henry VIII, I.I.141

SACRIFICE
see also LOSS; MARTYRDOM

Emily,
To buy you I have lost what's dearest to me
Save what is bought, and yet I purchase cheaply,
As I do rate your value.

ARCITE, *The Two Noble Kinsmen*, V.III.112

What would you have me do? Go to the
wars, would you? where a man may serve seven years
for the loss of a leg, and have not money enough in the
end to buy him a wooden one?

BOULT, *Pericles*, IV.VI.170

O, the sacrifice!
How ceremonious, solemn, and unearthly
It was i' th' off'ring!

DION, *The Winter's Tale*, III.I.6

Who told me, when we both lay in the field
Frozen (almost) to death, how he did lap me
Even in his own garments, and did give himself
(All thin and naked) to the numb cold night?

KING EDWARD, *Richard III*, II.I.115

I'll die
For thee, O Imogen, even for whom my life
Is every breath a death; and thus, unknown,
Pitied nor hated, to the face of peril
Myself I'll dedicate.

POSTHUMUS, *Cymbeline*, V.I.25

The back is sacrifice to th' load.

QUEEN KATHERINE, *Henry VIII*, I.II.50

SADNESS
see also CRYING AND TEARS; DEPRESSION; GRIEF; MOURNING; SORROW

For mirth doth search the bottom of annoy,
Sad souls are slain in merry company.

The Rape of Lucrece, 1109

To see sad sights moves more than hear them told,
For then the eye interprets to the ear
The heavy motion that it doth behold,
When every part a part of woe doth bear.

The Rape of Lucrece, 1324

In sooth, I know not why I am so sad;
It wearies me, you say it wearies you;
But how I caught it, found it, or came by it,

What stuff 'tis made of, whereof it is born,
I am to learn;
And such a want-wit sadness makes of me,
That I have much ado to know myself.

ANTONIO, The Merchant of Venice, I.I.1

The King's son have I landed by himself,
Whom I left cooling of the air with sighs,
In an odd angle of the isle, and sitting,
His arms in this sad knot.

ARIEL, The Tempest, I.II.221

Arm. Boy, what sign is it when a man of great spirit grows
melancholy?
Moth. A great sign, sir, that he will look sad.

ARMADO, MOTH, Love's Labor's Lost, I.II.1

In one little body
Thou counterfeits a bark, a sea, a wind:
For still thy eyes, which I may call the sea,
Do ebb and flow with tears; the bark thy body is,
Sailing in this salt flood; the winds, thy sighs,
Who, raging with thy tears, and they with them,
Without a sudden calm, will overset
Thy tempest-tossed body.

CAPULET, Romeo and Juliet, III.V.130

But Palamon's sadness is a kind of mirth,
So mingled as if mirth did make him sad,
And sadness merry; those darker humors that
Stick misbecomingly on others on him
Live in fair dwelling.

EMILIA, The Two Noble Kinsmen, V.III.51

Why then be sad,
But entertain no more of it, good brothers,
Than a joint burden laid upon us all.

PRINCE JOHN, 2 Henry IV, V.II.54

I cannot but be sad; so heavy sad,
As, though on thinking on no thought I think,
Makes me with heavy nothing faint and shrink.

QUEEN, Richard II, II.II.30

SAILING AND SHIPS
see also SEA

He is gone
aboard a new ship to purge melancholy and air himself.

AUTOLYCUS, The Winter's Tale, IV.IV.762

Play with your fancies: and in them behold
Upon the hempen tackle ship-boys climbing;
Hear the shrill whistle which doth order give
To sounds confus'd; behold the threaden sails,
Borne with th' invisible and creeping wind,
Draw the huge bottoms through the furrowed sea,
Breasting the lofty surge.

CHORUS, *Henry V*, III.CHO.7

The barge she sat in, like a burnish'd throne,
Burnt on the water. The poop was beaten gold,
Purple the sails, and so perfumèd that
The winds were love-sick with them; the oars were silver,
Which to the tune of flutes kept stroke, and made
The water which they beat to follow faster,
As amorous of their strokes.

ENOBARBUS, *Antony and Cleopatra*, II.II.191

Good; speak to th' mariners. Fall to't,
yarely, or we run ourselves aground. Bestir, bestir.

MASTER OF A SHIP, *The Tempest*, I.I.3

I'll deliver all,
And promise you calm seas, auspicious gales,
And sail so expeditious, that shall catch
Your royal fleet far off.

PROSPERO, *The Tempest*, V.I.314

With shame
(The first that ever touch'd him) he was carried
From off our coast, twice beaten; and his shipping
(Poor ignorant baubles!) on our terrible seas,
Like egg-shells mov'd upon their surges, crack'd
As easily 'gainst our rocks.

QUEEN, *Cymbeline*, III.I.24

My wind cooling my broth
Would blow me to an ague when I thought
What harm a wind too great might do at sea.
I should not see the sandy hour-glass run
But I should think of shallows and of flats,
And see my wealthy Andrew dock'd in sand,
Vailing her high top lower than her ribs
To kiss her burial. Should I go to church
And see the holy edifice of stone,
And not bethink me straight of dangerous rocks,
Which touching but my gentle vessel's side
Would scatter all her spices on the stream,
Enrobe the roaring waters with my silks,

And in a word, but even now worth this,
And now worth nothing?

SALERIO, *The Merchant of Venice*, I.1.23

SATISFACTION
see also HAPPINESS; JOY; PLEASURE

When we have stuff'd
These pipes and these conveyances of our blood
With wine and feeding, we have suppler souls
Than in our priest-like fasts.

MENENIUS AGRIPPA, *Coriolanus*, V.1.53

He is well paid that is well satisfied.

PORTIA, *The Merchant of Venice*, IV.1.415

Happy thou art not,
For what thou hast not, still thou striv'st to get,
And what thou hast, forget'st.

VINCENTIO, DUKE OF VIENNA, *Measure for Measure*, III.1.21

SCANDAL
see also GOSSIP; RUMORS

Yea, though I die, the scandal will survive,
And be an eye-sore in my golden coat.

The Rape of Lucrece, 204

For greatest scandal waits on greatest state.

The Rape of Lucrece, 1006

Ah, would the scandal vanish with my life,
How happy then were my ensuing death!

JOHN OF GAUNT, *Richard II*, II.1.67

I heard a bustling rumor, like a fray,
And the wind brings it from the Capitol.

PORTIA, *Julius Caesar*, II.IV.18

SEA
see also SAILING AND SHIPS

Though the seas threaten, they are merciful;
I have curs'd them without cause.

FERDINAND, *The Tempest*, V.1.177

I'll warrant him for drowning, though the
ship were no stronger than a nutshell, and as leaky as
an unstanch'd wench.

GONZALO, *The Tempest*, I.1.46

He, doing so, put forth to seas,
Where when men been, there's seldom ease,

For now the wind begins to blow;
Thunder above, and deeps below,
Makes such unquiet, that the ship
Should house him safe is wrack'd and split,
And he, good prince, having all lost,
By waves from coast to coast is toss'd.

GOWER, Pericles, II.CHO.27

The very place puts toys of desperation,
Without more motive, into every brain
That looks so many fadoms to the sea
And hears it roar beneath.

HORATIO, Hamlet, I.IV.75

Let us be back'd with God, and with the seas,
Which he hath giv'n for fence impregnable,
And with their helps only defend ourselves:
In them, and in ourselves, our safety lies.

LORD HASTINGS, 3 Henry VI, IV.I.43

Methinks the wind hath spoke aloud at land,
A fuller blast ne'er shook our battlements.
If it hath ruffian'd so upon the sea,
What ribs of oak, when mountains melt on them,
Can hold the mortise?

MONTANO, Othello, II.I.5

Alas, the seas hath cast me on the rocks,
Wash'd me from shore to shore, and left me breath
Nothing to think on but ensuing death.

PERICLES, Pericles, II.I.5

If the winds rage, doth not the sea wax mad,
Threat'ning the welkin with his big-swoll'n face?

TITUS, Titus Andronicus, III.I.222

SEASONS
see also AUTUMN; SPRING; SUMMER; WINTER

Three winters cold
Have from the forests shook three summers' pride,
Three beauteous springs to yellow autumn turn'd
In process of the seasons have I seen,
Three April perfumes in three hot Junes burn'd,
Since first I saw you fresh, which yet are green.

SONNET 104, 3–8

Why should proud summer boast
Before the birds have any cause to sing?
Why should I joy in any abortive birth?
At Christmas I no more desire a rose

Than wish a snow in May's new-fangled shows;
But like of each thing that in season grows.

> BEROWNE, *Love's Labor's Lost*, I.I.102

Thus sometimes hath the brightest day a cloud,
And after summer evermore succeeds
Barren winter, with his wrathful nipping cold;
So cares and joys abound, as seasons fleet.

> DUKE OF GLOUCESTER, *2 Henry VI*, II.IV.1

The seasons change their manners, as the year
Had found some months asleep and leapt them over.

> DUKE OF GLOUCESTER, *2 Henry IV*, IV.IV.123

Sir, the year growing ancient,
Not yet on summer's death, nor on the birth
Of trembling winter, the fairest flow'rs o' th' season
Are our carnations and streak'd gillyvors
(Which some call Nature's bastards).

> PERDITA, *The Winter's Tale*, IV.IV.79

SECRETS
see also TRUST

Two may keep counsel when the third's away.

> AARON, *Titus Andronicus*, IV.II.144

I'll have this secret from thy heart, or rip
Thy heart to find it.

> CLOTEN, *Cymbeline*, III.v.86

All blest secrets,
All you unpublish'd virtues of the earth.

> CORDELIA, *King Lear*, IV.III.15

Watch thou, and wake when others be asleep,
To pry into the secrets of the state.

> DUKE OF YORK, *2 Henry VI*, I.I.249

The quality of nothing
hath not such need to hide itself.

> EARL OF GLOUCESTER, *King Lear*, I.II.33

This secret is so weighty, 'twill require
A strong faith to conceal it.

> SECOND GENTLEMAN, *Henry VIII*, II.I.144

The players cannot keep counsel, they'll tell all.

> HAMLET, *Hamlet*, III.II.141

Seal up your lips, and give no words but mum;
The business asketh silent secrecy.

> JOHN HUME, *2 Henry VI*, I.II.89

He, his own affections' counselor,
Is to himself (I will not say how true)
But to himself so secret and so close,
So far from sounding and discovery,
As is the bud bit with an envious worm,
Ere he can spread his sweet leaves to the air.

MONTAGUE, *Romeo and Juliet*, I.i.147

Tell me your counsels, I will not disclose 'em.
I have made strong proof of my constancy,
Giving myself a voluntary wound
Here, in the thigh; can I bear that with patience,
And not my husband's secrets?

PORTIA, *Julius Caesar*, II.i.298

What I am, and what I would, are as secret as maidenhead.

VIOLA, *Twelfth Night*, I.v.215

SECURITY
see also CARE AND CONCERN

We have locks to safeguard necessaries,
And pretty traps to catch the petty thieves.

DUKE OF EXETER, *Henry V*, I.ii.176

To be thus is nothing,
But to be safely thus.

MACBETH, *Macbeth*, III.i.47

Well, he may sleep in security,
for he hath the horn of abundance, and the lightness of
his wife shines through it.

SIR JOHN FALSTAFF, *2 Henry IV*, I.ii.45

SELF-DELUSION

To know my deed, 'twere best not to know myself.

MACBETH, *Macbeth*, II.ii.70

SELF-IMPROVEMENT

For competence of life I will allow you,
That lack of means enforce you not to evils,
And as we hear you do reform yourselves,
We will according to your strengths and qualities,
Give you advancement.

KING HENRY V, *2 Henry IV*, V.v.66

SELF-KNOWLEDGE
see also IDENTITY

Before I know myself, seek not to know me.

Venus and Adonis, 525

I know myself now, and I feel within me
A peace above all earthly dignities,
A still and quiet conscience.

> CARDINAL WOLSEY, *Henry VIII*, III.II.378

A wisp of straw were worth a thousand crowns
To make this shameless callet know herself.

> PRINCE EDWARD, *3 Henry VI*, II.II.144

O no! Alas, I rather hate myself
For hateful deeds committed by myself.
I am villain; yet I lie, I am not.
Fool of thyself speak well; fool, do not flatter:
My conscience hath a thousand several tongues,
And every tongue brings in a several tale,
And every tale condemns me for a villain.

> KING RICHARD, *Richard III*, V.III.189

O that you would
turn your eyes toward the napes of your necks and
make but an interior survey of your good selves!

> MENENIUS AGRIPPA, *Coriolanus*, II.I.37

For he's no man on whom perfections wait
That, knowing sin within, will touch the gate.

> PERICLES, *Pericles*, I.I.79

This above all: to thine own self be true.

> POLONIUS, *Hamlet*, I.III.78

Cruel are the times when we are traitors,
And do not know ourselves.

> ROSSE, *Macbeth*, IV.II.18

SELF-PITY

To move wild laughter in the throat of death?
It cannot be, it is impossible:
Mirth cannot move a soul in agony.

> BEROWNE, *Love's Labor's Lost*, V.II.855

Alack, alack, that heaven should practice stratagems
Upon so soft a subject as myself!

> JULIET, *Romeo and Juliet*, III.V.209

It is I
That all th' abhorred things o' th' earth amend
By being worse than they.

> POSTHUMUS, *Cymbeline*, V.V.215

SELF-PROMOTION
see also FAME

> Then shall our names,
> Familiar in his mouth as household words. . .
> Be in their flowing cups freshly rememb'red.
>
> KING HENRY, *Henry V*, IV.III.51

> Simply the thing I am
> Shall make me live.
>
> PAROLLES, *All's Well That Ends Well*, IV.III.333

SELF-RESPECT
see also PRIDE

> Self-love, my liege, is not so vile a sin
> As self-neglecting.
>
> DOLPHIN, *Henry V*, II.IV.73

> Be to yourself
> As you would to your friend.
>
> DUKE OF NORFOLK, *Henry VIII*, I.I.135

> Put forth thy hand, reach at the glorious gold.
> What, is't too short? I'll lengthen it with mine,
> And having both together heav'd it up,
> We'll both together lift our heads to heaven,
> And never more abase our sight so low
> As to vouchsafe one glance unto the ground.
>
> ELEANOR, *2 Henry VI*, I.II.11

> My blood hath been too cold and temperate,
> Unapt to stir at these indignities,
> And you have found me, for accordingly
> You tread upon my patience; but to be sure
> I will from henceforth, rather be myself,
> Mighty and to be fear'd, than my condition,
> Which hath been smooth as oil, soft as young down,
> And therefore lost that title of respect
> Which the proud soul ne'er pays but to the proud.
>
> KING HENRY, *1 Henry IV*, I.III.1

> He that is truly dedicate to war
> Hath no self-love; nor he that loves himself
> Hath not essentially but by circumstance
> The name of valor.
>
> YOUNG CLIFFORD, *2 Henry VI*, V.II.37

SELF-RESTRAINT
see also ABSTINENCE; CHASTITY; TEMPERANCE

I am sure,
Though you can guess what temperance should be,
You know not what it is.

BY RIGHT *ANTONY, Antony and Cleopatra,* III.XIII.120

Great men should drink with harness on their throats.

APEMANTUS, *Timon of Athens,* I.II.52

Would God that any in this noble presence
Were enough noble to be upright judge
Of noble Richard! Then true noblesse would
Learn him forbearance from so foul a wrong.

BISHOP OF CARLISLE, *Richard II,* IV.I.117

Keep yourself within yourself.

CHARMIAN, *Antony and Cleopatra,* II.V.75

Give your dispositions the reins and be
angry at your pleasures.

MENENIUS AGRIPPA, *Coriolanus,* II.I.30

Here pleasures court mine eyes, and mine eyes shun them.

PERICLES, *Pericles,* I.II.6

O vengeance, vengeance!
Me of my lawful pleasure she restrain'd,
And pray'd me oft forbearance; did it with
A pudency so rosy the sweet view on't
Might well have warm'd old Saturn; that I thought her
As chaste as unsunn'd snow.

POSTHUMUS, *Cymbeline,* II.V.8

SELF-RIGHTEOUSNESS

Dost thou think because thou art virtuous there shall be no
more cakes and ale?

SIR TOBY, *Twelfth Night,* II.III.114

SENSUALITY
see also BLINDNESS; EYES AND SIGHT

In faith, I do not love thee with mine eyes,
For they in thee a thousand errors note,
But 'tis my heart that loves what they despise,
Who in despite of view is pleas'd to dote;
Nor are mine ears with thy tongue's tune delighted,
Nor tender feeling to base touches prone,
Nor taste, nor smell, desire to be invited
To any sensual feast with thee alone.

SONNET 141, 1–8

Th' ear,
Taste, touch, all, pleas'd from thy table rise;
They only now come but to feast thine eyes.

CUPID, *Timon of Athens*, I.II.125

Why then your other senses grow imperfect
By your eyes' anguish.

EDGAR, *King Lear*, IV.VI.5

Who cannot feel nor see the rain, being in't,
Knows neither wet nor dry.

EMILIA, *The Two Noble Kinsmen*, I.I.120

My love, give me thy lips.
Look to my chattels and my moveables.
Let senses rule.

PISTOL, *Henry V*, II.III.47

SEPARATION

Even for this, let us divided live,
And our dear love lose name of single one.
That by this separation I may give
That due to thee which thou deserv'st alone.

SONNET 39, 5–8

Since their more mature dignities and royal necessities
made separation of their society, their encounters
(though not personal) hath been royally attorney'd
with interchange of gifts, letters, loving embassies,
that they have seem'd to be together, though absent;
shook hands, as over a vast; and embrac'd as it
were from the ends of oppos'd winds. The heavens
continue their loves!

CAMILLO, *The Winter's Tale*, I.I.24

You never shall, so help you truth and God,
Embrace each other's love in banishment,
Nor never look upon each other's face,
Nor never write, regret, nor reconcile
This low-ring tempest of your home-bred hate,
Nor never by advisèd purpose meet
To plot, contrive, or complot any ill
'Gainst us, our state, our subjects, or our land.

KING RICHARD, *Richard II*, I.III.183

Born in a tempest when my mother died,
This world to me is a lasting storm,
Whirring me from my friends.

MARINA, *Pericles*, IV.I.18

For there will be a world of water shed
Upon the parting of your wives and you.
OWEN GLENDOWER, 1 Henry IV, III.I.93

Large lengths of seas and shores
Between my father and my mother lay,
As I have heard my father speak himself,
When this same lusty gentleman was got.
ROBERT FAULCONRIDGE, King John, I.I.105

This seven years did not Talbot see his son,
And now they meet where both their lives are done.
SIR WILLIAM LUCY, 1 Henry VI, IV.III.37

SERIOUSNESS

There's business in these faces.
CYMBELINE, Cymbeline, V.V.24

The blood of youth burns not with such excess
As gravity's revolt to wantonness.
ROSALINE, Love's Labor's Lost, V.II.73

SERVICE
see also DUTY; OBEDIENCE; SLAVERY

Remember I have done thee worthy service,
Told thee no lies, made thee no mistakings, serv'd
Without or grudge or grumblings.
ARIEL, The Tempest, I.II.246

My gracious lord, I tender you my service,
Such as it is, being tender, raw, and young,
Which elder days shall ripen and confirm
To more approved service and desert.
PERCY, Richard II, II.III.41

Service is no heritage.
LAVATCH, All's Well That Ends Well, I.III.23

The service that I truly did his life
Hath left me open to all injuries.
LORD CHIEF JUSTICE, 2 Henry IV, V.II.7

So service shall with steeled sinews toil,
And labor shall refresh itself with hope
To do your Grace incessant services.
LORD SCROOP, Henry V, II.II.36

O good old man, how well in thee appears
The constant service of the antique world,
When service sweat for duty, not for meed!

Thou art not for the fashion of these times,
Where none will sweat but for promotion,
And having that do choke their service up
Even with the having.

ORLANDO, As You Like It, II.III.56

SEX
see also ATTRACTION; DESIRE; LUST; PROSTITUTION

These blushes of hers must be quench'd with some
present practice.

BOULT, Pericles, IV.II.124

Inch-thick, knee-deep, o'er head and ears a fork'd one!
Go play, boy, play. Thy mother plays, and I
Play too, but so disgrac'd a part, whose issue
Will hiss me to my grave: contempt and clamor
Will be my knell. Go play, boy, play. There have been
(Or I am much deceiv'd) cuckolds ere now,
And many a man there is (even at this present,
Now, while I speak this) holds his wife by th' arm.

LEONTES, The Winter's Tale, I.II.186

My heart unto yours is knit,
So that but one heart we can make of it.
Two bosoms interchainèd with an oath,
So then two bosoms and a single troth.
Then by your side no bed-room me deny;
For lying so, Hermia, I do not lie.

LYSANDER, A Midsummer Night's Dream, II.II.47

Bless me, what a
fry of fornication is at door!

PORTER, Henry VIII, V.IV.35

It pleaseth me so well that I will see you wed,
And then with what haste you can, get you to bed.

SIMONIDES, Pericles, II.V.92

This is the monstruosity in love, lady, that the will is
infinite and the execution confin'd, that the desire is
boundless and the act a slave to limit.

TROILUS, Troilus and Cressida, III.II.81

SHAME
see also GUILT

How sweet and lovely dost thou make the shame
Which, like a canker in the fragrant rose,
Doth spot the beauty of thy budding name!

SONNET 95, 1–3

He burns with bashful shame, she with her tears
Doth quench the maiden burning of his cheeks.

Venus and Adonis, 49

The eye of heaven is out, and misty night
Covers the shame that follows sweet delight.

The Rape of Lucrece, 356

Bloody thou art, bloody will be thy end;
Shame serves thy life and doth thy death attend.

DUCHESS OF YORK, *Richard III*, IV.IV.195

Hast thou not worldly pleasure at command
Above the reach or compass of thy thought?
And wilt thou still be hammering treachery,
To tumble down thy husband and thyself
From top of honor to disgrace's feet?

DUKE OF GLOUCESTER, *2 Henry VI*, I.II.45

Mine honor lives when his dishonor dies,
Or my sham'd life in his dishonor lies.

DUKE OF YORK, *Richard II*, V.III.70

O shame, where is thy blush?

HAMLET, *Hamlet*, III.IV.81

And shall it in more shame be further spoken,
That you are fool'd, discarded, and shook off
By him for whom these shames ye underwent?

HOTSPUR, *1 Henry IV*, I.III.177

Must I hold a candle to my shames?

JESSICA, *The Merchant of Venice*, II.VI.41

Shame hath a bastard fame, well managèd;
Ill deeds is doubled with an evil word.

LUCIANA, *The Comedy of Errors*, III.II.19

My charity is outrage, life my shame,
And in that shame still live my sorrow's rage!

QUEEN MARGARET, *Richard III*, I.III.276

SIBLINGS
see also TWINS

Methinks you are my glass, and not my brother:
I see by you I am a sweet-fac'd youth.

DROMIO OF EPHESUS, *The Comedy of Errors*, V.I.418

You call'd me brother,
When I was but your sister, I you brothers,
When we were so indeed.

IMOGEN, *Cymbeline*, V.V.376

Better it were a brother died at once,
Than that a sister, by redeeming him,
Should die forever.

ISABELLA, Measure for Measure, II.IV.106

Learn this, Thomas,
And thou shalt prove a shelter to thy friends,
A hoop of gold to bind thy brothers in,
That the united vessel of their blood,
Mingled with venom of suggestion
(As, force perforce, the age will pout it in),
Shall never leak, though it do work as strong
As aconitum or rash gunpowder.

KING HENRY IV, 2 Henry IV, IV.IV.41

SICKNESS

see also DRUGS AND MEDICATION; HEALING; MADNESS AND MENTAL ILLNESS; PHYSI-
CIANS; RECOVERY

As testy sick men, when their deaths be near,
No news but health from their physicians know.

SONNET 140, 7–8

Aches contract and starve your supple joints!

APEMANTUS, Timon of Athens, I.i.248

There is a sickness
Which puts some of us in distemper, but
I cannot name the disease and it is caught
Of you that yet are well.

CAMILLO, The Winter's Tale, I.II.384

Being sick, have (in some measure) made me well.

EARL OF NORTHUMBERLAND, 2 Henry IV, I.i.136

'Zounds! how has he the leisure to be sick
In such a justling time?

HOTSPUR, 1 Henry IV, IV.i.17

Sick to death!
My legs like loaden branches bow to th' earth,
Willings to leave their burden.

KATHERINE, Henry VIII, IV.II.2

But health, alack, with youthful wings is flown
From this bare wither'd trunk.

KING HENRY IV, 2 Henry IV, IV.v.228

Is Brutus sick? and is it physical
To walk unbracèd and suck up the humors
Of the dank morning? What, is Brutus sick?

And will he steal out of his wholesome bed
To dare the vile contagion of the night,
And tempt the rheumy and unpurgèd air
To add unto his sickness?

PORTIA, Julius Caesar, II.I.261

O vanity of sickness! fierce extremes
In their continuance will not feel themselves.
Death, having prey'd upon the outward parts,
Leaves them invisible, and his siege is now
Against the mind, the which he pricks and wounds
With many legions of strange fantasies,
Which in their throng and press to that last hold,
Confound themselves.

PRINCE HENRY, King John, V.III.13

Prithee do not turn me about, my stomach is
not constant.

STEPHANO, The Tempest, II.II.114

SILENCE
see also SPEECHLESSNESS

Pray you tread softly, that the blind mole may not
Hear a foot fall.

CALIBAN, The Tempest, IV.I.194

Silence is the perfectest herald of joy; I were but little
happy, if I could say how much!

CLAUDIO, Much Ado About Nothing, II.I.306

So many miseries have craz'd my voice
That my woe-wearied tongue is still and mute.

DUCHESS OF YORK, Richard III, IV.IV.17

His tongue is now a stringless instrument,
words, life and all, old Lancaster hath spent.

EARL OF NORTHUMBERLAND, Richard II, II.I.149

His purse is empty already: all's golden words are spent.

HAMLET, Hamlet, V.II.130

My heart is great, but it must break with silence,
Ere't be disburdened with a liberal tongue.

LORD ROSS, Richard II, II.I.228

I think the best grace of wit will shortly turn into
silence, and discourse grow commendable in none but only
parrots.

LORENZO, The Merchant of Venice, III.V.43

Silence that dreadful bell, it frights the isle
From her propriety.

OTHELLO, Othello, II.III.175

I like your silence, it the more shows off
Your wonder.

PAULINA, The Winter's Tale, V.III.21

Give every man thy ear, but few thy voice.

POLONIUS, Hamlet, I.III.68

SIMPLICITY

Beauty, Truth, and Rarity,
Grace in all simplicity,
Here enclos'd, in cinder lie.

The Phoenix and Turtle, 53

More matter with less art.

GERTRUDE, Hamlet, II.II.95

Happ'ly this life is best,
If quiet life be best.

GUIDERIUS, Cymbeline, III.III.29

Love, therefore, and tongue-tied simplicity
In least speak most.

THESEUS, A Midsummer Night's Dream, V.I.104

Whiles others fish with craft for great opinion,
I with great truth catch mere simplicity;
Whilst some with cunning gild their copper crowns,
With truth and plainness I do wear mine bare.
Fear not my truth: the moral of my wit
Is "plain and true"; there's all the reach of it.

TROILUS, Troilus and Cressida, IV.IV.103

SIN
see also EVIL; REPENTANCE; TEMPTATION; VICE

And in thy shady cell, where none may spy him,
Sits Sin, to seize the souls that wander by him.

The Rape of Lucrece, 881

Why should the private pleasure of some one
Become the public plague of many more?
Let sin, alone committed, light alone
Upon his head that hath transgressed so.

The Rape of Lucrece, 1478

It is great sin to swear unto a sin,
But greater sin to keep a sinful oath.

EARL OF SALISBURY, 2 Henry VI, V.I.182

Some rise by sin, and some by virtue fall;
Some run from brakes of ice and answer none,
And some condemnèd for a fault alone.

ESCALUS, *Measure for Measure*, II.I.38

Then is sin struck down like an ox, and
iniquity's throat cut like a calf.

GEORGE BEVIS, *2 Henry VI*, IV.II.26

To my sick soul, as sin's true nature is,
Each toy seems prologue to some great amiss,
So full of artless jealousy is guilt,
It spills itself in fearing to be spilt.

GERTRUDE, *Hamlet*, IV.V.17

Divinity of hell!
When devils will the blackest sins put on,
They do suggest at first with heavenly shows,
As I do now.

IAGO, *Othello*, II.III.350

Thy sin's not accidental, but a trade.

ISABELLA, *Measure for Measure*, II.I.38

But I am in
So far in blood that sin will pluck on sin.

KING RICHARD, *Richard III*, IV.II.63

Few love to hear the sins they love to act.

PERICLES, *Pericles*, I.I.91

Some sins do bear their privilege on earth,
And do doth yours: your fault was not your folly.

PHILIP THE BASTARD, *King John*, I.I.261

Why, thou globe of sinful continents, what
a life dost thou lead?

PRINCE HENRY, *2 Henry IV*, II.IV.285

If heaven have any grievous plague in store
Exceeding those that I can wish upon thee,
O let them keep it till thy sins be ripe,
And then hurl down their indignation
On thee, the troubler of the poor world's peace!

QUEEN MARGARET, *Richard III*, I.III.216

SINGLEHOOD
see also MARRIAGE

That a woman conceiv'd me, I thank her; that she brought me
up, I likewise give her most humble thanks; but that I will
have a rechate winded in my forehead, or hang my bugle in an

invisible baldrick, all women shall pardon me. Because I
will not do them the wrong to mistrust any, I will do myself
the right to trust none; and the fine is (for the which I
may go the finer), I will live a bachelor.

> BENEDICK, *Much Ado About Nothing*, I.I.238

When I said I would die a bachelor, I did not think I should
live till I were married.

> BENEDICK, *Much Ado About Nothing*, II.III.242

As from a bear a man would run for life,
So fly I from her that would be my wife.

> DROMIO OF SYRACUSE, *The Comedy of Errors*, III.I.154

A married man! that's most intolerable.

> EARL OF WARWICK, *1 Henry VI*, V.IV.79

This precious book of love, this unbound lover,
To beautify him, only lacks a cover.

> LADY CAPULET, *Romeo and Juliet*, I.III.81

Cin. Wisely, I say, I am a bachelor.
2. Pleb. That's as much as to say, they are fools
that marry.

> SECOND PLEBEIAN, CINNA, *Julius Caesar*, III.III.16

A maiden hath no tongue but thought.

> PORTIA, *The Merchant of Venice*, III.II.8

SLANDER
see also LIES

So thou be good, slander doth but approve
Thy worth the greater, being woo'd of time,
For canker vice the sweetest buds doth love,
And thou present'st a pure unstainèd prime.

> SONNET 70, 5–8

My blood shall wash the slander of mine ill;
My live's foul deed, my life's fair end shall free it.

> *The Rape of Lucrece*, 1207

Slander lives upon succession,
For ever hous'd where it gets possession.

> BALTHAZAR, *The Comedy of Errors*, III.I.105

With other vile and ignominious terms:
In confutation of which rude reproach,
And in defense of my lord's worthiness,
I crave the benefit of law of arms.

> BASSET, *1 Henry VI*, IV.I.97

There's none stands under more calumnious tongues
Than I myself, poor man.

CRANMER, Henry VIII, V.I.112

Be thou as chaste as ice, as pure as snow, thou shalt not
escape calumny.

HAMLET, Hamlet, III.I.135

Virtue itself scapes not calumnious strokes.

LAERTES, Hamlet, I.III.38

O, he's the captain of compliments. He fights as you sing
prick-songs, keeps time, distance, and proportion; he rests
his minim rests, one, two, and the third in your bosom: the
very butcher of a silk button, a duelist, a duelist; a
gentleman of the very first house, of the first and second
cause. Ah, the immortal *passado*, the *punto reverso*, the hay!

MERCUTIO (ABOUT TYBALT), Romeo and Juliet, II.IV.19

I am disgrac'd, impeach'd, and baffled here,
Pierc'd to the soul with slander's venom'd spear,
The which no balm can cure but his heart-blood
Which breath'd this poison.

MOWBRAY, Richard II, I.I.170

For he
The sacred honor of himself, his queen's,
His hopeful son's, his babe's, betrays to slander,
Whose sting is sharper than the sword's, and will not
(For as the case now stands, it is a curse
He cannot be compell'd to't) once remove
The root of his opinion, which is rotten
As ever oak or stone was sound.

PAULINA, The Winter's Tale, II.III.84

What shall I need to draw my sword, the paper
Hath cut her throat already! No, 'tis slander,
Whose edge is sharper than the sword, whose tongue
Outvenoms all the worms of Nile, whose breath
Rides on the posting winds and doth belie
All corners of the world.

PISANIO, Cymbeline, III.IV.32

Open your ears; for which of you will stop
The vent of hearing when loud Rumor speaks?
I, from the orient to the drooping west
(Making the wind my post-horse), still unfold
The acts commencèd on this ball of earth.
Upon my tongues continual slander ride,
The which in every language I pronounce,
Stuffing the ears of men with false reports.

RUMOR, 2 Henry IV, I.IND.1

No might nor greatness in mortality
Can censure scape; back-wounding calumny
The whitest virtue strikes.
> VINCENTIO, DUKE OF VIENNA, *Measure for Measure*, III.II.185

SLAVERY
see also SERVICE; SUBMISSION

Being your slave, what should I do but tend
Upon the hours and times of your desire?
I have no precious time at all to spend,
Nor services to do, till you require.
> SONNET 57, 1–4

That god forbid that made me first your slave
I should in thought control your times of pleasure,
Or at your hand th' account of hours to crave,
Being your vassal bound to stay your leisure.
> SONNET 58, 1–4

Why, madam, if I were your father's dog,
You should not use me so.
> EARL OF KENT, *King Lear*, II.II.136

But you are all recreants and dastards,
and delight to live in slavery to the nobility. Let them
break your backs with burdens, take your houses
over your heads, ravish your wives and daughters
before your faces. For me, I will make shift for one;
and so God's curse light upon you all!
> JACK CADE, *2 Henry VI*, IV.VIII.27

Thou most lying slave,
Whom stripes may move, not kindness! I have us'd thee
(Filth as thou art) with human care, and lodg'd thee
In mine own cell, till thou didst seek to violate
The honor of my child.
> PROSPERO, *The Tempest*, I.II.344

SLEEP
see also DREAMS; INSOMNIA; RECOVERY; REST; SNORING

Now stole upon the time the dead of night,
When heavy sleep had clos'd up mortal eyes.
> *The Rape of Lucrece*, 162

I wish mine eyes
Would, with themselves, shut up my thoughts. I find
They are inclin'd to do so.
> ALONSO, *The Tempest*, II.I.191

Boy! Lucius! Fast asleep? It is no matter,
Enjoy the honey-heavy dew of slumber.

Thou hast no figures nor no fantasies,
Which busy care draws into the brains of men;
Therefore thou sleep'st so sound.

BRUTUS, *Julius Caesar*, II.I.229

Young son, it argues a distemperèd head
So soon to bid good morrow to thy bed.
Care keeps his watch in every old man's eye,
And where care lodges, sleep will never lie;
But where unbruisèd youth with unstuff'd brain
Doth couch his limbs, there golden sleep doth reign.

FRIAR LAWRENCE, *Romeo and Juliet*, II.III.33

Sleep, that sometimes shuts up sorrow's eye,
Steal me a while from mine own company.

HELENA, *A Midsummer Night's Dream*, III.II.435

How many thousand of my poorest subjects
Are at this hour asleep! O sleep! O gentle sleep!
Nature's soft nurse, how have I frighted thee,
That thou no more wilt weigh my eyelids downs,
And steep my senses in forgetfulness?
Why rather, sleep, liest thou in smoky cribs,
Upon uneasy pallets stretching thee,
And hush'd with bussing night-flies to thy slumber,
Than in the perfum'd chambers of the great,
Under the canopies of costly state,
And lull'd with sound of sweetest melody?
O thou dull god, why li'st thou with the vile
In loathsome beds, and leavest the kingly couch
A watch-case or a common 'larum-bell?
Wilt thou upon the high and giddy mast
Seal up the ship-boy's eyes, and rock his brains
In cradle of the rude imperious surge,
And in the visitation of the winds,
Who take the ruffian billows by the top,
Curling their monstrous heads and hanging them
With deafing clamor in the slippery clouds,
That with the hurly death itself awakes?
Canst thou, O partial sleep, give then repose
To the wet sea-boy in an hour so rude,
And in the calmest and most stillest night,
With all appliances and means to boot,
Deny it to a king? Then (happy) low, lie down!
Uneasy lies the head that wears a crown.

KING HENRY IV, *2 Henry IV*, III.I.4

The innocent sleep,
Sleep that knits up the revell'd sleave of care,
The death of each day's life, sore labor's bath,
Balm of hurt minds, great second nature's course,
Chief nourisher in life's feast.

MACBETH, *Macbeth*, II.II.33

She bids you on the wanton rushes lay you down,
And rest your gentle head upon her lap,
and she will sing the song that pleaseth you,
And on your eyelids crown the god of sleep,
Charming your blood with pleasing heaviness,
Making such difference 'twixt wake and sleep
As is the difference betwixt day and night
The hour before the heavenly-harness'd team
Begins his golden progress in the east.

OWEN GLENDOWER, *1 Henry IV*, III.I.211

The sweetest sleep and fairest-boding dreams
That ever ent'red in a drowsy head.

RICHMOND, *Richard III*, V.III.227

I'll strive with troubled thoughts to take a nap,
Lest laden slumber peise me down to-morrow.

RICHMOND, *Richard III*, V.III.104

Sleep dwell upon thine eyes, peace in thy breast!
Would I were sleep and peace, so sweet to rest!

ROMEO, *Romeo and Juliet*, II.II.186

Do not omit the heavy offer of it.
It seldom visits sorrow; when it doth,
It is a comforter.

SEBASTIAN, *The Tempest*, II.I.194

Speed. She doth talk in her sleep.
Launce. It's no matter for that, so she sleep not
in her talk.

SPEED, LAUNCE, *The Two Gentlemen of Verona*, III.I.329

SMILE
see also HUMOR

A smile recures the wounding of a frown.

Venus and Adonis, 465

Nobly he yokes
A smiling with a sign, as if the sign
Was that it was for not being such a smile;
The smile mocking the sigh, that it would fly

From so divine a temple to commix
With winds that sailors rail at.
ARVIRAGUS, Cymbeline, IV.II.52

Thus smiling, as some fly had tickled slumber,
Not as Death's dart being laugh'd at; his right cheek
Reposing on a cushion.
ARVIRAGUS, Cymbeline, IV.II.210

Some that smile have in their hearts, I fear,
Millions of mischiefs.
CAESAR (OCTAVIUS), Julius Caesar, IV.I.50

There is, betwixt that smile we would aspire to,
That sweet aspect of princes, and their ruin,
More pangs and fears than wars or women have.
CARDINAL WOLSEY, Henry VIII, II.II.368

Not to a rage, patience and sorrow strove
Who should express her goodliest. You have seen
Sunshine and rain at once; her smiles and tears
Were like a better way: those happy smilets
That play'd on her ripe lip seem'd not to know
That guests were in her eyes, which, parted thence,
As pearls from diamonds dropp'd. In brief,
Sorrow would be a rarity most belovèd,
If all could so become it.
GENTLEMAN, King Lear, IV.III.16

Her. I frown upon him, yet he loves me still.
Hel. O that your frowns would teach my smiles such skill!
HELENA, HERMIA, A Midsummer Night's Dream, I.I.194

SNORING
see also SLEEP

Fast asleep behind the arras, and
snorting like a horse.
PETO, 1 Henry IV, II.IV.528

Yet not so sound, and half so deeply sweet,
As he whose brow with homely biggen bound
Snores out the watch of night.
PRINCE HENRY, 2 Henry IV, IV.V.26

Hark how hard he fetches breath.
PRINCE HENRY, 1 Henry IV, II.IV.530

Thou dost snore distinctly,
There's meaning in thy snores.
SEBASTIAN, The Tempest, II.I.217

SOLDIERS
see also BATTLE; WAR

> There's not a soldier of us all, that in the thanksgiving
> before meat, do relish the petition well that prays for
> peace.
>
> FIRST GENTLEMAN, Measure for Measure, I.II.14

> Come, Desdemona, 'tis the soldiers' life
> To have their balmy slumbers wak'd with strife.
>
> IAGO, Othello, II.III.257

> I am a soldier,
> A name that in my thoughts become me best,
> If I begin the batt'ry once again,
> I will not leave the half-achieved Harfleur
> Till in her ashes she lies buried.
> The gates of mercy shall be all shut up,
> And the flesh'd soldier, rough and hard of heart,
> In liberty of bloody hand, shall range,
> With conscience wide as hell, mowing like grass
> Your fresh fair virgins and your flow'ring infants.
>
> KING HENRY, Henry V, III.III.5

> My lord, our army is dispers'd already:
> Like youthful steers unyok'd, they take their courses
> East, west, north, south, or, like a school broke up,
> Each hurries toward his home and sporting-place.
>
> LORD HASTINGS, 2 Henry IV, IV.II.102

> I am a soldier, and unapt to weep,
> Or to exclaim on fortune's fickleness.
>
> REIGNER, 1 Henry VI, V.III.133

> All furnish'd, all in arms;
> All plum'd like estridges, that with the wind
> Bated like eagles having lately bath'd,
> Glittering in golden coats like images,
> As full of spirit as the month of May,
> And gorgeous as the sun at midsummer:
> Wanton as youthful goats, wild as young bulls.
>
> SIR RICHARD VERNON, 1 Henry IV, IV.I.98

SOLITUDE
see also ALIENATION

> I, measuring his affections by my own,
> Which then most sought where most might not be found,
> Being one too many by my weary self,

Pursued my humor by not pursuing his,
And gladly shunn'd who gladly fled from me.

BENVOLIO, *Romeo and Juliet*, I.I.126

It is vain that you would speak with Timon;
For he is set so only to himself,
That nothing but himself which looks like man
Is friendly with him.

FLAVIUS, *Timon of Athens*, V.I.116

Society is no comfort
To one not sociable.

IMOGEN, *Cymbeline*, IV.II.12

I thank you for your company, but, good faith, I had as
lief have myself been alone.

JAQUES, *As You Like It*, III.II.253

Leave me alone,
For I must think of that which company
Would not be friendly to.

KING HENRY, *Henry VIII*, V.I.74

Choose out some secret place, some reverent room,
More than thou hast, and with it joy thy life.
So as thou liv'st in peace, die free from strife.

BULLINGBROOK, *Richard II*, V.VI.25

I myself am best
When least in company.

ORSINO, DUKE OF ILLYRIA, *Twelfth Night*, I.IV.37

Go,
Let him have a table by himself,
For he does neither affect company,
Nor is he fit for't indeed.

TIMON, *Timon of Athens*, I.II.29

This shadowy desert, unfrequented by woods,
I better brook than flourishing peopled towns:
Here I can sit alone, unseen of any,
And to the nightingale's complaining notes
Tune my distresses and record my woes.

VALENTINE, *The Two Gentlemen of Verona*, V.IV.2

Ay, but give me worship and quietness,
I like it better than a dangerous honor.

WATCHMAN, *3 Henry VI*, IV.III.16

SONGS AND SINGING
see also MUSIC

O my good lord, tax not so bad a voice

To slander music any more than once.
BALTHASAR, *Much Ado About Nothing*, II.III.44

She sings like one immortal, and she dances
As goddess-like to her admired lays.
GOWER, *Pericles*, V.CHO.3

I can suck the melancholy out of a song, as a weasel sucks eggs.
JAQUES, *As You Like It*, II.V.12

Then should you be nothing but musical, for you are
altogether govern'd by humors. Lie still, ye thief, and
hear the lady sing in Welsh.
LADY PERCY, *1 Henry IV*, III.I.232

That piece of song,
That old and antique song we heard last night;
Methought it did relieve my passion much,
More than light airs and recollected terms
Of these most brisk and giddy-paced times.
ORSINO, DUKE OF ILLYRIA, *Twelfth Night*, II.IV.2

Where being but young I framed to the harp
Many an English ditty lovely well,
And gave the tongue a helpful ornament,
A virtue that was never seen in you.
OWEN GLENDOWER, *1 Henry IV*, III.I.121

Take thy lute, wench, my soul grows sad with troubles,
Sing and disperse 'em if thou canst.
QUEEN KATHERINE, *Henry VIII*, III.I.1

He sings
several tunes faster than you'll tell money; he utters
them as he had eaten ballads and all men's ears grew
to his tunes.
SERVANT, *The Winter's Tale*, IV.IV.184

SONS

see also BABIES; CHILDREN; CHILDREN OF UNMARRIED PARENTS; FATHERHOOD; MOTHERHOOD

O wonderful son, that can so stonish a mother!
HAMLET, *Hamlet*, III.II.328

O, twice my father, twice am I thy son!
The life thou gav'st me first was lost and done,
Till with thy warlike sword, despite of fate,
To my determin'd time thou gav'st new date.
JOHN TALBOT, *1 Henry VI*, IV.V.38

A son who is the theme of honor's tongue,
Amongst a grove the very straightest plant,
Who is sweet Fortune's minion and her pride.

KING HENRY, *1 Henry IV*, I.i.81

If I chance to talk a little wild, forgive me;
I had it from my father.

LORD CHAMBERLAIN, *Henry VIII*, I.iv.26

Be now the father and propose a son,
Hear your own dignity so much profan'd,
See your most dreadful laws so loosely slighted,
Behold yourself so by a son disdained;
And then imagine me taking your part,
And in your power soft silencing your son.

LORD CHIEF JUSTICE, *2 Henry IV*, V.ii.92

The heavens have blest you with a goodly son
To be your comforter when he is gone.

LORD GREY, *Richard III*, I.iii.9

Methinks 'tis prize enough to be his son.

RICHARD, DUKE OF GLOUCESTER, *3 Henry VI*, II.i.20

Thy mother's son! like enough, and thy father's shadow.
So the son of the female is the shadow of the
male. It is often so indeed, but much of the
father's substance!

SIR JOHN FALSTAFF, *2 Henry IV*, III.ii.128

If my son were my husband, I should
freelier rejoice in that absence
wherein he won honor than in the embracements of his
bed where he would show most love. When yet he
was but tender-bodied and the only son of my womb;
when youth with comeliness pluck'd all gaze his way;
when for a day of kings' entreaties a mother should not
sell him an hour from her beholding; I, considering
how honor would become such a person, that it
was not better than picture-like to hang by th' wall, if
renown made it not stir, was pleas'd to let him seek
danger where he was like to find fame.

VOLUMNIA, *Coriolanus*, I.iii.2

SORROW

see also CRYING AND TEARS; DEPRESSION; GRIEF; LOSS; MOURNING; SADNESS

So she, deep drenched in a sea of care,

Holds disputation with each thing she views,
And to herself all sorrow doth compare.

The Rape of Lucrece, 1100

For sorrow, like a heavy hanging bell,
Once set on ringing, with his own weight goes.

The Rape of Lucrece, 1493

Not age, but sorrow, over me hath power;
I might as yet have been a spreading flower,
Fresh to myself, if I had self-applied
Love to myself, and to no love beside.

A Lover's Complaint, 74

Sorrow breaks seasons and reposing hours,
Makes the night morning and the noontide night.

BRAKENBURY, *Richard III*, I.IV.76

Fell Sorrow's tooth doth never rankle more
Than when he bites, but lanceth not the sore.

BULLINGBROOK, *Richard II*, I.III.302

My lord, your sorrow was too sore laid on,
Which sixteen winters cannot blow away,
So many summers dry. Scarce any joy
Did ever so long live; no sorrow
But kill'd itself much sooner.

CAMILLO, *The Winter's Tale*, V.III.49

When sorrows come, they come not in single spies,
But in battalions.

CLAUDIUS, *Hamlet*, IV.v.78

All strange and terrible events are welcome,
But comforts we despise; our size of sorrow,
Proportion'd to our cause, must be as great
As that which makes it.

CLEOPATRA, *Antony and Cleopatra*, IV.xv.3

O, if thou teach me to believe this sorrow,
Teach thou this sorrow how to make me die,
And let belief and life encounter so
As doth the fury of two desperate men,
Which in the very meeting fall, and die.

CONSTANCE, *King John*, III.I.29

I take my leave before I have begun,
For sorrow ends not when it seemeth done.

DUCHESS OF GLOUCESTER, *Richard II*, I.II.60

Sorrow and grief have vanquish'd all my powers.
                    DUKE OF GLOUCESTER, *2 Henry VI*, II.i.183

Jul. Either my eyesight fails, or thou lookest pale.
Rom. And trust me, love, in my eye so do you;
Dry sorrow drinks our blood.
                    JULIET, ROMEO, *Romeo and Juliet*, III.v.57

To show an unfelt sorrow is an office
Which the false man does easy.
                    MALCOLM, *Macbeth*, II.III.136

Sorrow concealed, like an oven stopp'd,
Doth burn the heart to cinders where it is.
                    MARCUS, *Titus Andronicus*, III.i.244

Could we but learn from whence his sorrows grow,
We would as willingly give cure as know.
                    MONTAGUE, *Romeo and Juliet*, I.i.154

O, my petition was
Set down in ice, which by hot grief uncandied
Melts into drops; so sorrow wanting form
Is press'd with deeper matter.
                    QUEEN, *The Two Noble Kinsmen*, I.i.107

Sorrow that is couch'd in seeming gladness
Is like that mirth fate turns to sudden sadness.
                    TROILUS, *Troilus and Cressida*, I.i.39

SOUL
see also HIGHER POWER; SPIRITUALITY AND RELIGION
          The earth can have but earth, which is his due,
          My spirit is thine, the better part of me.
                              SONNET 74, 7–8

          Then, soul, live thou upon thy servant's loss,
          And let that pine to aggravate thy store;
          Buy terms divine in selling hours of dross;
          Within be fed, without be rich no more.
                              SONNET 146, 9–12

There be souls must be saved, and there be souls must not
be saved.
                    CASSIO, *Othello*, II.III.104

Every subject's
duty is the King's, but every subject's soul is his own.
                    KING HENRY, *Henry V*, IV.i.176

Hang there like fruit, my soul,
Till the tree die!

                    POSTHUMUS, *Cymbeline*, V.v.263

SPEAKING AND SPEECH

see also ACTORS AND ACTING; CONVERSATION; VERBOSITY; WORDS

I have neither wit, nor words, nor worth,
Action, nor utterance, nor the power of speech
To stir men's blood; I only speak right on.

ANTONY, *Julius Caesar*, III.II.221

He has a tongue will tame tempests,
And make the wild rocks wanton.

ARCITE, *The Two Noble Kinsmen*, II.III.16

She speaks poniards, and every word stabs.

BENEDICK, *Much Ado About Nothing*, II.I.247

For what I speak
My body shall make good upon this earth,
Or my divine soul answer it in heaven.

BULLINGBROOK, *Richard II*, I.I.36

When he speaks,
The air, a charter'd libertine, is still,
And the mute wonder lurketh in men's ears
To steal his sweet and honeyed sentences.

CANTERBURY, *Henry V*, I.I.47

But for your words, they rob the Hybla bees,
And leave them honeyless.

CASSIUS, *Julius Caesar*, V.I. 34

He hath a heart as sound as a bell, and his tongue is the
clapper, for what his heart thinks, his tongue speaks.

DON PEDRO, *Much Ado About Nothing*, III.II.12

Then, York, unloose thy long-imprisoned thoughts,
And let thy tongue be equal with thy heart.

DUKE OF YORK, *2 Henry VI*, V.I.88

I will speak daggers to her, but use none.
My tongue and soul in this be hypocrites—
How in my words somever she be shent,
To give them seals never, my soul, consent!

HAMLET, *Hamlet*, III.II.396

It oft falls out,
To have what we would have, we speak not what we mean.

ISABELLA, *Measure for Measure*, II.IV.117

How silver-sweet sound lovers' tongues by night,
Like softest music to attending ears!

ROMEO, *Romeo and Juliet*, II.II.165

Harry, now I do
not speak to thee in drink, but in tears; not in pleasure,
but in passion; not in words only, but in woes.

SIR JOHN FALSTAFF, 1 Henry IV, II.IV.414

Speaking is for beggars; he wears his tongue in's arms.

THERSITES, Troilus and Cressida, III.III.269

SPEECHLESSNESS
see also SILENCE

Ay; beauty's princely majesty is such,
'Confounds the tongue and makes the senses rough.

EARL OF SUFFOLK, 1 Henry VI, V.III.70

What my tongue dares not, that my heart shall say.

GROOM, Richard II, V.v.97

He has strangled
His language in his tears.

KING HENRY, Henry VIII, V.I.156

Though thy speech doth fail,
One eye thou hast to look to heaven for grace.

LORD TALBOT, 1 Henry VI, I.IV.82

What passion hangs these weights upon my tongue?

ORLANDO, As You Like It, I.II.257

SPEED
see also HASTE; PUNCTUALITY

Celerity is never more admir'd
Than by the negligent.

CLEOPATRA, Antony and Cleopatra, III.VII.24

This tiger-footed rage, when it shall find
The harm of unscann'd swiftness, will (too late)
Tie leaden pounds to 's heels.

MENENIUS AGRIPPA, Coriolanus, III.I.310

And as the thing that's heavy in itself
Upon enforcement flies with greatest speed,
So did our men, heavy in Hotspur's loss,
Lend to this weight such lightness with their fear
That arrows fled not swifter toward their aim
Than did our soldiers, aiming at their safety,
Fly from the field.

MORTON, 2 Henry IV, I.I.119

The spirit of the time shall teach me speed.

PHILIP THE BASTARD, King John, IV.II.176

The swiftest harts have posted you by land,
And winds of all the corners kiss'd your sails,
To make your vessel nimble.

POSTHUMUS, *Cymbeline*, II.IV.28

He that rides at high speed and with his
pistol kills a sparrow flying.

PRINCE HENRY, *1 Henry IV*, II.IV.345

SPIRITUALITY AND RELIGION

see also BLESSING; CLERGY; FAITH; HEAVEN; HELL; HERESY; HIGHER POWER;
PRAYER; SOUL

O, pardon me, in that my boast is true:
The accident which brought me to her eye
Upon the moment did her force subdue,
And now she would the caged cloister fly:
Religious love put out religion's eye.

A Lover's Complaint, 246

In religion,
What damnèd error but some sober brow
Will bless it, and approve it with a text,
Hiding the grossness with fair ornament?

BASSANIO, *The Merchant of Venice*, III.II.77

Sweet religion makes
A rhapsody of words.

HAMLET, *Hamlet*, III.IV.47

'Tis mad idolatry
To make the service greater than the god.

HECTOR, *Troilus and Cressida*, II.II.56

I see you have some religion in you, that you fear.

JACHIMO, *Cymbeline*, I.IV.136

If we did think
His contemplation were above the earth,
And fix'd on spiritual object, he should still
Dwell in his musings, but I am afraid
His thinkings are below the moon, not worth
His serious considering.

KING HENRY, *Henry VIII*, III.II.130

You are full of heavenly stuff, and bear the inventory
Of your best graces in your mind; the which
You were now running o'er. You have scarce time
To steal from spiritual leisure a brief span
To keep your earthly audit.

KING HENRY, *Henry VIII*, III.II.136

They say miracles are past, and we have our philosophical
persons, to make modern and familiar, things supernatural
and causeless. Hence it is that we make trifles of terrors,
ensconcing ourselves into seeming knowledge, when we should
submit ourselves to an unknown fear.

LAFEW, *All's Well That Ends Well*, II.III.1

It is religion that doth make vows kept,
But thou hast sworn against religion,
By what thou swear'st against the thing thou swear'st,
And mak'st an oath the surety for thy truth
Against an oath; the truth thou art unsure
To swear, swears only not be forsworn,
Else what a mockery should it be to swear!
But thou dost swear only to be forsworn,
And most forsworn, to keep what thou dost swear
Therefore thy later vows, against thy first,
Is in thyself rebellion to thyself.

PANDULPH, *King John*, III.I.279

SPRING
see also SEASONS

From you have I been absent in the spring
When proud-pied April (dress'd in all his trim)
Hath put a spirit of youth in every thing.

SONNET 98, 1–3

Well-apparell'd April on the heel
Of limping winter treads.

CAPULET, *Romeo and Juliet*, I.II.27

O, how this spring of love resembleth
The uncertain glory of an April day,
Which now shows all the beauty of the sun,
And by and by a cloud takes all away.

PROTEUS, *The Two Gentlemen of Verona*, I.III.84

STARS
see also MOON; NIGHT

Not from the stars do I my judgment pluck,
And yet methinks I have astronomy.

SONNET 14, 1–2

The benediction of these covering heavens
Fall on their heads like dew! for they are worthy
To inlay heaven with stars.

BELARIUS, *Cymbeline*, V.V.350

Swear his thought over
By each particular star in heaven, and
By all their influences, you may as well
Forbid the sea for to obey the moon.
CAMILLO, The Winter's Tale, V.I.68

At my poor house look to behold this night
Earth-treading stars that make dark heaven light.
CAPULET, Romeo and Juliet, I.II.24

It is the stars,
The stars above us, govern our conditions.
EARL OF KENT, King Lear, IV.III.35

The stars, I see, will kiss the valleys first;
The odds for high and low's alike.
FLORIZEL, The Winter's Tale, V.I.206

Stars, stars,
And all eyes else dead coals!
LEONTES, The Winter's Tale, V.I.68

STOICISM
see also TEMPERANCE

Happy is your Grace,
That can translate the stubbornness of fortune
Into so quiet and so sweet a style.
AMIENS, As You Like It, II.I.18

Content and anger
In me have but one face.
ARCITE, The Two Noble Kinsmen, III.I.107

What we know must be, and is as common
As any most vulgar thing to sense,
Why should we in our peevish opposition
Take it to heart?
CLAUDIUS, Hamlet, I.II.98

It is no little thing to make
Mine eyes to sweat compassion.
CORIOLANUS, Coriolanus, V.III.194

Things without all remedy
Should be without regard: what's done, is done.
LADY MACBETH, Macbeth, III.II.11

We cannot weep
When our friends don their helms, or put to sea,
Or tell of babes broach's on the lance, or women

That have sod their infants in (and after eat them)
The brine they wept at killing 'em.
                                    PIRITHOUS, *The Two Noble Kinsmen*, I.III.17

What, hath thy fiery heart so parch'd thin entrails
That not a tear can fall for Rutland's death?
                                    QUEEN MARGARET, *3 Henry VI*, I.IV.87

STORMS
see also ELEMENTS

Love's lightning, the precursors
O' th' dreadful thunder-claps, more momentary
And sight-outrunning were not; the fire and cracks ·
Of sulfurous roaring the most mighty Neptune
Seem to besiege, and make his bold waves tremble,
Yea, his dread trident shake.
                                    ARIEL, *The Tempest*, I.II.201

Are you not mov'd, when all the sway of the earth
Shakes like a thing unfirm? O Cicero,
I have seen tempests when the scolding winds
Have riv'd the knotty oaks, and I have seen
Th' ambitious ocean swell, and rage, and foam,
To be exalted with the threat'ning clouds;
But never till to-night, never till now,
Did I go through a tempest dropping fire.
Either there is a civil strife in heaven,
Or else the world, too saucy with the gods,
Incenses them to send destruction.
                                    CASCA, *Julius Caesar*, I.III.3

Blow wind, swell billow, and swim bark!
The storm is up, and all is on the hazard.
                                    CASSIUS, *Julius Caesar*, V.I.67

Untimely storms makes men expect a dearth.
                                    CITIZEN, *Richard III*, II.III.35

The wrathful skies
Gallow the very wanderers of the dark,
And make them keep their caves. Since I was man,
Such sheets of fire, such bursts of horrid thunder,
Such groans of roaring wind and rain, I never
Remember to have heard. Man's nature cannot carry
Th' affliction nor the fear.
                                    EARL OF KENT, *King Lear*, III.II.43

Now would I give a thousand furlongs of sea
for an acre of barren ground, long heath, brown furze,

any thing. The wills above be done! but I would fain
die a dry death.

GONZALO, *The Tempest*, I.I.65

Blow, winds, and crack your cheeks! rage, blow!
Your cataracts and hurricanoes, spout
Till you have drench'd our steeples, drown'd the cocks!
You sulf'rous and thought-executing fires,
Vaunt-couriers of oak-cleaving thunderbolts,
Singe my white head! And thou, all-shaking thunder,
Strike flat the thick rotundity o' th' world!
Crack nature's molds, all germains spill at once
That makes ingrateful man!

LEAR, *King Lear*, III.II.I

If after every tempest come such calms,
May the winds low till they have waken'd death!
And let the laboring bark climb hills of seas
Olympus-high, and duck again as low
As hell's from heaven!

OTHELLO, *Othello*, II.I.185

Yet cease your ire, you angry stars of heaven!
Wind, rain, and thunder, remember earthly man
Is but a substance that must yield to you.

PERICLES, *Pericles*, II.I.I

The winds, piping to us in vain,
As in revenge, have suck'd up from the sea
Contagious fogs; which, falling in the land,
Hath every pelting river made so proud
That they have overborne their continents.

TITANIA, *A Midsummer Night's Dream*, II.I.88

Yond same black cloud, yond
huge one, looks like a foul bumbard that would shed
his liquor. If it should thunder as it did before, I know
not where to hide my head. Yond same cloud cannot
choose but fall by pailfuls.

TRINCULO, *The Tempest*, II.II.20

STORYTELLING

see also BOOKS; HISTORY; IMAGINATION; WRITING

Thus far, with rough and all-unable pen,
Our bending author hath pursu'd the story,
In little room confining mighty men,
Mangling by starts the full course of their glory.

CHORUS, *Henry V*, EPI.I

Then give me leave that I may turn the key,
That no man enter till my tale be done.

> DUKE OF AUMERLE, *Richard II*, V.III.36

Ah, kill me with thy weapon, not with words!
My breast can better brook thy dagger's point
Than can my ears that tragic history.

> KING HENRY, *3 Henry VI*, V.VI.26

In winter's tedious nights sit by the fire
With good old folks and let them tell thee tales
Of woeful ages long ago betid;
And ere thou bid good night, to quite their griefs,
Tell thou the lamentable tale of me,
And send the hearers weeping to their beds.

> KING RICHARD, *Richard II*, V.I.40

What need'st thou run so many miles about,
When thou mayest tell thy tale the nearest way?

> KING RICHARD, *Richard III*, IV.IV.460

The strangeness of your story put
Heaviness in me.

> MIRANDA, *The Tempest*, I.II.306

Your tale, sir, would cure deafness.

> MIRANDA, *The Tempest*, I.II.106

An honest tale speeds best being plainly told.

> QUEEN ELIZABETH, *Richard III*, IV.IV.358

If the tale we have told
(For 'tis no other) any way content ye
(For to that honest purpose it was meant ye),
We have our end; and ye shall have ere long
I dare say many a better, to prolong
Your old loves to us.

> THESEUS, *The Two Noble Kinsmen*, EPI.12

STRENGTH
see also COURAGE; DETERMINATION

I am able now, methinks
(Out of a fortitude of soul I feel),
To endure more miseries and greater far
Than my weak-hearted enemies dare offer.

> CARDINAL WOLSEY, *Henry VIII*, III.II.387

It cannot be this weak and writhled shrimp
Should strike such terror to his enemies.

> COUNTESS OF AUVERGNE, *1 Henry VI*, II.III.23

And as the wretch whose fever-weak'ned joints,
Like strengthless hinges, buckle under life,
Impatient of his fit, breaks like a fire
Out of his keeper's arms, even so my limbs,
Weak'ned with grief, being now enrag'd with grief,
Are thrice themselves.
EARL OF NORTHUMBERLAND, 2 Henry IV, I.I.140

It is excellent
To have a giant's strength; but it is tyrannous
To use it like a giant.
ISABELLA, Measure for Measure, II.II.107

STUBBORNNESS

The Queen is obstinate,
Stubborn to justice, apt to accuse it, and
Disdainful to be tried by't: 'tis not well
She's going away.
CARDINAL CAMPEIUS, Henry VIII, II.IV.122

I'll not budge an inch, boy; let him come and kindly.
CHRISTOPHER SLY, The Taming of the Shrew, IND.I.14

I am sorry for thee, friend, 'tis the Duke's pleasure,
Whose disposition, all world well knows,
Will not be rubb'd nor stopp'd.
EARL OF GLOUCESTER, King Lear, II.II.152

You know the fiery quality of the Duke,
How unremovable and fix'd he is
In his own course.
EARL OF GLOUCESTER, King Lear, II.IV.92

Now
beshrew my father's ambition! he was thinking of
civil wars when he got me; therefore was I created
with a stubborn outside, with an aspect of iron, that
when I come to woo ladies, I fright them.
KING HENRY, Henry V, V.II.224

To wisdom he's a fool that will not yield.
LORD, Pericles, II.IV.54

I am as peremptory as she proud-minded;
And where two raging fires meet together,
They do consume the thing that feeds their fury.
Though little fire grows great with little wind,
Yet extreme gusts will blow out fire and all;

So I to her, and so she yields to me,
For I am rough, and woo not like a babe.

> PETRUCHIO, *The Taming of the Shrew*, II.I.131

O sir, to willful men,
The injuries that they themselves procure
Must be their schoolmasters.

> REGAN, *King Lear*, II.IV.302

STUPIDITY
see also IGNORANCE

Ajax. And all men were of my mind—
Ulyss. Wit would be out of fashion.

> AJAX, ULYSSES, *Troilus and Cressida*, II.III.215

What a pretty thing man is when he goes in his doublet and
hose and leaves off his wit!

> DON PEDRO, *Much Ado About Nothing*, V.I.199

There's many a man hath more hair than wit.

> DROMIO OF SYRACUSE, *The Comedy of Errors*, II.II.82

Not Hercules
Could have knock'd out his brains, for he had none.

> GUIDERIUS, *Cymbeline*, IV.II.114

SUBMISSION
see also OBEDIENCE; SLAVERY

For ever may my knees grow to the earth.

> DUKE OF AUMERLE, *Richard II*, V.III.30

I'll either make thee stoop and bend thy knee,
Or sack this country with a mutiny.

> HENRY BEAUFORD, *1 Henry VI*, V.I.61

I hardly yet have learn'd
To insinuate, flatter, bow, and bend my knee.
Give sorrow leave a while to tutor me
To this submission.

> KING RICHARD, *Richard II*, IV.I.164

Myself I throw, dread sovereign, at thy foot,
My life thou shalt command, but not my shame.

> MOWBRAY, *Richard II*, I.I.165

To whom with all submission, on my knee,
I do bequeath my faithful services
And true subjection everlastingly.

> PHILIP THE BASTARD, *King John*, V.VIII.103

SUCCESS
see also ACHIEVEMENT

> Her joy with heav'd-up hand she doth express,
> And wordless so greets heaven for his success.
>> *The Rape of Lucrece*, 111

> 'Tis won as towns with fire—so won, so lost.
>> BEROWNE, *Love's Labor's Lost*, I.i.146

> 'Tis a common proof
> That lowliness is young ambition's ladder,
> Whereto the climber-upward turns his face;
> But when he once attains the upmost round,
> He then unto the ladder turns his back,
> Looks in the clouds, scorning the base degrees
> By which he did ascend.
>> BRUTUS, *Julius Caesar*, II.i.21

> Upon your sword
> Sit laurel victory, and smooth success
> Be strew'd before your feet!
>> CLEOPATRA, *Antony and Cleopatra*, I.iii.99

> 'Tis with my mind
> As with the tide swell'd up unto his height,
> That makes a still-stand, running neither way.
>> EARL OF NORTHUMBERLAND, *2 Henry IV*, II.iii.62

> I know he will be glad of our success;
> We are the Jasons, we have won the fleece.
>> GRATIANO, *The Merchant of Venice*, III.ii.240

> Screw your courage to the sticking place,
> And we'll not fail.
>> LADY MACBETH, *Macbeth*, I.vii.60

> O, such a day!
> So fought, so followed, and so fairly won,
> Came not till now to dignify the times,
> Since Caesar's fortunes.
>> LORD BARDOLPH, *2 Henry IV*, I.i.20

> Such a nature,
> Tickled with good success, disdains the shadow
> Which he treads on at noon.
>> SICINIUS VELUTUS, *Coriolanus*, I.i.259

SUFFERING
see also MISERY; PAIN

> And the ass more captain than the lion, the fellow

Loaden with irons wiser than the judge,
If wisdom be in suffering.

ALCIBIADES, Timon of Athens, III.V.49

One fire burns out anothers' burning,
One pain is less'ned by another's anguish;
Turn giddy, and be holp by backward turning;
One desperate grief cures with anothers' languish:
Take thou some new infection to the eye,
And the rank poison of the old will die.

BENVOLIO, Romeo and Juliet, I.II.45

I think afflictions may subdue the cheek,
But not take in the mind.

CAMILLO, The Winter's Tale, IV.IV.576

Sweet are the uses of adversity,
Which, like the toad, ugly and venomous,
Wears yet a precious jewel in his head;
And this our life, exempt from public haunt,
Finds tongues in trees, books in the running brooks,
Sermons in stones, and good in every thing.

DUKE SENIOR, As You Like It, II.I.12

When we our betters see bearing our woes,
We scarcely think our miseries our foes.
Who alone suffers, suffers most i' th' mind,
Leaving free things and happy shows behind,
But then the mind much sufferance doth o'erskip,
When grief hath mates, and bearing fellowship.
How light and portable my pain seems now,
When that which makes me bend makes the King bow.

EDGAR, King Lear, III.VI.102

The poor beetle that we tread upon
In corporal sufferance finds a pang as great
As when a giant dies.

ISABELLA, Measure for Measure, III.I.78

There is so hot a summer in my bosom
That all my bowels crumble up to dust.
I am scribbled form, drawn with a pen
Upon a parchment, and against this fire
Do I shrink up.

KING JOHN, King John, V.VII.30

He jests at scars that never felt a wound.

ROMEO, Romeo and Juliet, II.II.1

SUICIDE
see also DEATH; EUTHANASIA

> I do find it cowardly and vile,
> For fear of what might fall, so to prevent
> The time of life.
>
> BRUTUS, *Julius Caesar*, V.I.103

> Is it sin
> To rush into the secret house of death
> Ere death dare come to us?
>
> CLEOPATRA, *Antony and Cleopatra*, IV.xv.80

> She's tickled now; her fume needs no spurs,
> She'll gallop far enough to her destruction.
>
> DUKE OF BUCKINGHAM, *2 Henry VI*, I.III.150

> Why railest thou on thy birth? the heaven and earth?
> Since birth, and heaven, and earth, all three do meet
> In thee at once, which thou at once wouldst lose.
>
> FRIAR LAWRENCE, *Romeo and Juliet*, III.III.119

> To be, or not to be, that is the the question:
> Whether 'tis nobler in the mind to suffer
> The slings and arrows of outrageous fortune,
> Or to take arms against a sea of troubles,
> And by opposing, end them. To die, to sleep—
> No more, and by a sleep to say we end
> The heart-ache and the thousand natural shocks
> That flesh is heir to; 'tis a consummation
> Devoutly to be wish'd. To die, to sleep—
> To sleep, perchance to dream—ay, there's the rub,
> For in that sleep of death what dreams may come,
> When we have shuffled off this mortal coil,
> Must give us pause; there's the respect
> That makes calamity of so long life:
> For who would bear the whips and scorns of time,
> Th' oppressor's wrong, the proud man's contumely,
> The pangs of despis'd love, the law's delay,
> The insolence of office, and the spurns
> That patient merit of th' unworthy takes,
> When he himself might his quietus make
> With a bare bodkin; who would fardels bear,
> To grunt and sweat under a weary life,
> But that the dread of something after death,
> The undiscover'd country, from whose bourn
> No traveler returns, puzzles the will,
> And makes us rather bear those ills we have,

Than fly to others that we know not of?
Thus conscience does make cowards of us all,
And thus the native hue of resolution
Is sicklied o'er with the pale cast of thought,
And enterprises of great pitch and moment
With this regard their currents turn awry,
And lose the name of action.

HAMLET, Hamlet, III.I.55

O that this too sallied flesh would melt,
Thaw, and resolve itself into a dew!
Or that the Everlasting had nor fix'd
His canon 'gainst self-slaughter!

HAMLET, Hamlet, I.II.129

Look
I draw the sword myself, take it, and hit
The innocent mansion of my love, my heart.
Fear not, 'tis empty of all things but grief.

IMOGEN, Cymbeline, III.IV.66

Against self-slaughter
There is a prohibition so divine
That cravens my weak hand.

IMOGEN, Cymbeline, III.IV.76

He that hath a will to die by
himself fears it not from another.

MENENIUS AGRIPPA, Coriolanus, V.II.104

If thou didst but consent
To this most cruel act, do but despair,
And if thou want'st a cord, the smallest thread
That ever spider twisted from her womb
Will serve to strangle thee; a rush will be a beam
To hang thee on; or wouldst thou drown thyself,
Put but a little water in a spoon,
And it shall be as all the ocean,
Enough to stifle such a villain up.

PHILIP THE BASTARD, King John, IV.III.125

Graves only be men's works, and death their gain!
Sun, hide thy beams, Timon hath done his reign.

TIMON, Timon of Athens, V.I.222

SUMMER
see also SEASONS

A summer's day will seem an hour but short,
Being wasted in such time-beguiling sport.

Venus and Adonis, 23

As call it winter, which being full of care,
Makes summer's welcome thrice more wish'd, more rare.

SONNET 56, 13–14

Shall I compare thee to a summer's day?
Thou art more lovely and more temperate:
Rough winds do shake the darling buds of May,
And summer's lease hath all too short a date.

SONNET 18, 1–4

Then let not winter's ragged hand deface
In thee thy summer ere thou be distill'd:
Make sweet some vial; treasure thou some place
With beauty's treasure ere it be self-kill'd.

SONNET 6, 1–4

SUN

see also DAY; SUNRISE; SUNSET

Look as the fair and fiery-pointed sun,
Rushing from forth a cloud, bereaves our sight
Even so the curtain drawn, his eyes begun
To wink, being blinded with a greater light.

The Rape of Lucrece, 372

The golden sun salutes the morn
And having gilt the ocean with his beams,
Gallops the zodiac in his glistering coach,
And overlooks the highest-peering hills.

AARON, *Titus Andronicus*, II.I.5

King. How is it that the clouds still hang on you?
Ham. Not so, my lord, I am too much in the sun.

HAMLET, CLAUDIUS, *Hamlet*, I.II.66

The sun with one eye vieweth all the world.

LORD TALBOT, *1 Henry VI*, I.IV.84

Yet herein will I imitate the sun,
Who doth permit the base contagious clouds
To smother up his beauty from the world,
Than when he please again to be himself,
Being wanted, he may be more wond'red at
By breaking through the foul and ugly mists
Of vapors that did seem to strangle him.

PRINCE HENRY, *1 Henry IV*, I.II.197

The weary sun hath made a golden set,
And by the bright tract of his fiery car
Gives token of goodly day to-morrow.

RICHMOND, *Richard III*, V.III.19

As whence the sun 'gins his reflection
Shipwracking storms and direful thunders break,
So from that spring whence comfort seem'd to come
Discomfort swells.

SERGEANT, *Macbeth*, I.II.25

SUNRISE
see also MORNING; SUN

Even as the sun with purple-color'd face
Had ta'en his last leave of the weeping morn,
Rose-cheek'd Adonis hied him to the chase.

Venus and Adonis, 1

The day begins to break, and night is fled,
Whose pitchy mantle overveil'd the earth.

DUKE OF BEDFORD, *1 Henry VI*, II.II.1

How bloodily the sun begins to peer
Above yon bulky hill!

KING HENRY, *1 Henry IV*, V.I.1

This battle fares like to the morning's war,
When dying clouds contend with growing light,
What time the shepherd, blowing of his nails,
Can neither call is perfect day nor night.

KING HENRY, *3 Henry VI*, II.v.1

The silent hours steal on,
And flaky darkness breaks within the east.

STANLEY, *2 Henry VI*, V.III.85

SUNSET
see also NIGHT; SUN

In me thou seest the twilight of such day
As after sunset fadeth in the west,
Which by and by black night doth take away,
Death's second self, that seals up all in rest.

SONNET 73, 5–8

The sun's o'ercast with blood; fair day, adieu!

BLANCH OF SPAIN, *King John*, III.I.325

Thy sun sets weeping in the lowly west,
Witnessing storms to come, woe, and unrest.

EARL OF SALISBURY, *Richard II*, II.IV.21

SUPERNATURAL
see also AFTERLIFE; FAIRIES; GHOSTS

These are not natural events, they strengthen
From strange to stranger.

ALONSO, *The Tempest*, V.I.228

Caesar, I never stood on ceremonies,
Yet now they fright me. There is one within,
Besides the things that we have heard and seen,
Recounts most horrid sights seen by the watch.
A lioness hath whelpèd the streets,
And graves have yawn'd and yielded up their dead;
Fierce fiery warriors fight upon the clouds
In ranks and squadrons and right form of war,
Which drizzled blood upon the Capitol;
The noise of battle hurtled in the air;
Horses did neigh, and dying men did groan,
And ghosts did shriek and squeal about the streets.

CALPHURNIA, Julius Caesar, II.II.13

'Tis now the very witching time of night,
When churchyards yawn and hell itself breathes out
Contagion to this world. Now could I drink hot blood,
And do such bitter business as the day
Would quake to look on.

HAMLET, Hamlet, III.II.388

There are more things in heaven and earth, Horatio,
Than are dreamt of in your philosophy.

HAMLET, Hamlet, I.V.166

O, learn'd indeed were that astronomer
That knew the stars as I his characters;
He'ld lay the future open.

IMOGEN, Cymbeline, III.II.27

I must not yield to any rites of love,
For my profession's sacred from above.
When I have chased all thy foes from hence,
Then will I think upon a recompense.

JOAN DE PUCELLE, 1 Henry VI, I.II.113

This supernatural soliciting
Cannot be ill; cannot be good. If ill,
Why hath it given me earnest of success,
Commencing in a truth? I am Thane of Cawdor.
If good, why do I yield to that suggestion
Whose horrid image doth unfix my hair
And make my seated heart knock at my ribs,
Against the use of nature?

MACBETH, Macbeth, I.III.130

His mother was a witch, and one so strong
That could control the moon, make flows and ebbs,
And deal in her command without her power.

PROSPERO, The Tempest, V.I.269

Patience, good lady, wizards know their times.
Deep night, dark night, the silent of the night,
The time of night when Troy was set on fire,
The time when screech-owls cry and ban-dogs howl,
And spirits walk, and ghosts break up their graves.

ROGER BULLINGBROOK, *2 Henry VI*, I.IV.15

The bay-trees in our country are all wither'd,
And meteors fright the fixèd stars of heaven,
The pale-fac'd moon looks bloody on the earth,
And lean-look'd prophets whisper fearful change,
Rich men look sad, and ruffians dance and leap,
The one in fear to lose what they enjoy,
The other to enjoy by rage and war.
These signs forerun the death or fall of kings.

WELSH CAPTAIN, *Richard II*, II.IV.8

By the pricking of my thumbs,
Something wicked this way comes.

SECOND WITCH, *Macbeth*, IV.I.44

SURPRISE

We may surprise and take him at our pleasure?
Our scouts have found the adventure very easy;
That as Ulysses and stout Diomede
With sleight and manhood stole to Rhesus' tents
And brought from thence the Thracian fatal steeds,
So we, well cover'd with the night's black mantle,
At unawares may beat down Edward's guard.

EARL OF WARWICK, *3 Henry VI*, IV.II.17

Wherefore gaze this goodly company,
As if they saw some wondrous monument,
Some comet or unusual prodigy?

PETRUCHIO, *The Taming of the Shrew*, III.II.94

Having found the back door open
Of the unguarded hearts, heavens, how they wound
Some slain before, some dying, some their friends
O'erborne i' th' former wave.

POSTHUMUS, *Cymbeline*, V.III.45

Those things do best please me
That befall prepost'rously.

PUCK, *A Midsummer Night's Dream*, III.II.120

SURRENDER
see also RESIGNATION

And were I strong, I would not shun their fury,

The sands are numb'red that makes up my life,
Here must I stay, and here my life must end.

DUKE OF YORK, 3 Henry VI, I.iv.24

Therefore, great King,
We yield our town and lives to thy soft mercy.
Enter our gates, dispose of us and ours,
For we no longer are defensible.

GOVERNOR, Henry V, III.iii.47

SUSPICION

see also PARANOIA

See what a ready tongue suspicion hath!
He that but fears the thing he would not know
Hath by instinct knowledge from others' eyes
That what he fear'd is chanced.

EARL OF NORTHUMBERLAND, 2 Henry IV, I.i.84

Who finds the heifer dead and bleeding fresh,
And sees fast by a butcher with an axe,
But will suspect 'twas he that made the slaughter?

EARL OF WARWICK, 2 Henry VI, III.ii.188

He will suspect us still, and find a time
To punish this offense in other faults.

EARL OF WORCESTER, 1 Henry IV, V.ii.6

You should have fear'd false times when you did feast:
Suspect still comes where an estate is least.

FLAVIUS, Timon of Athens, IV.iii.513

The lady doth protest too much, methinks.

GERTRUDE, Hamlet, III.ii.230

Both your pardons,
That e'er I put between your holy looks
My ill suspicion.

LEONTES, The Winter's Tale, V.iii.147

My lord, you do me shameful injury
Falsely to draw me in these vile suspects.

QUEEN ELIZABETH, Richard III, I.iii.87

Suspicion always haunts the guilty mind;
The thief doth fear each bush an officer.

RICHARD, DUKE OF GLOUCESTER, 3 Henry VI, V.vi.11

I smell a device.

SIR TOBY, Twelfth Night, II.iii.162

SWIMMING
see also DROWNING

'Tis a naughty
night to swim in. Now a little fire in a wild field were
like an old lecher's heart, a small spark, all the rest
on 's body cold.

FOOL, *King Lear*, III.IV.110

Though thou canst swim like a duck, thou art made like
a goose.

STEPHANO, *The Tempest*, II.II.131

TALENT

Proclaim that I can sing, weave, sew, and dance,
With other virtues, which I'll keep from boast,
And will undertake all these to teach.

MARINA, *Pericles*, IV.VI.183

Wherefore are these things hid? Wherefore have these gifts
a curtain before 'em? Are they like to take dust, like
Mistress Mall's picture? Why dost thou not go to church in
a galliard, and come home in a coranto? My very walk should
be a jig. I would not so much as make water but in a
sink-a-pace. What dost thou mean? Is it a world to hide
virtues in?

SIR TOBY, *Twelfth Night*, I.III.125

TASTE
see also DISCRETION

Some men there are love not a gaping pig;
Some that are mad if they behold a cat;
And others, when the bagpipe sings i' th' nose,
Cannot contain their urine: for affection,
Master of passion, sways it to the mood
Of what it likes or loathes.

SHYLOCK, *The Merchant of Venice*, IV.I.47

TAXES

Upon these taxations,
The clothiers all, not able to maintain
The many to them 'longing, have put off
The spinsters, carders, fullers, weavers, who,
Unfit for other life, compell'd by hunger
And lack of other means, in desperate manner
Daring th' event to th' teeth, are all in uproar,
And danger serves among them.

DUKE OF NORFOLK, *Henry VIII*, I.II.30

The commons hath he pill'd with grievous taxes,
And quite lost their hearts.

LORD ROSS, Richard II, II.1.246

TEACHERS
see also EDUCATION

Those that do teach young babes
Do it with gentle means and easy tasks.

DESDEMONA, Othello, IV.II.111

His breeding, sir, hath been at my charge.
I have so often blush'd to acknowledge him, that now
I am braz'd to't.

EARL OF GLOUCESTER, King Lear, I.I.9

Thy schoolmaster, made thee more profit
Than other princess' can, that have more time
For vainer hours, and tutors not so careful.

PROSPERO, The Tempest, I.II.172

TEMPERANCE
see also SELF-RESTRAINT; STOICISM

Being once chaf'd, he cannot
Be rein'd again to temperance; then he speaks
What's in his heart, and that is there which looks
With us to break his neck.

JUNIUS BRUTUS, Coriolanus, III.III.27

But come yourself with speed to us again
For more is to be said and to be done
Than out of anger can be uttered.

KING HENRY, 1 Henry IV, I.I.105

My blood hath been too cold and temperate,
Unapt to stir at these indignities.

KING HENRY, 1 Henry IV, I.III.1

Peace, lady, pause, or be more temperate.
It ill beseems this presence to cry aim
To these ill-tuned repetitions.

KING PHILIP, King John, II.1.195

TEMPTATION
see also PERSUASION; SIN; VICE

Those pretty wrongs that liberty commits
When I am sometime absent from thy heart,
Thy beauty and thy years full well befits,
For still temptation follows where thou art.

SONNET 41, 1–4

'Tis one thing to be tempted, Escalus,
Another thing to fall.

> ANGELO, *Measure for Measure*, II.i.17

Most dangerous
Is that temptation that doth goad us on
To sin in loving virtue.

> ANGELO, *Measure for Measure*, II.ii.180

O cunning enemy, that to catch a saint,
With saints bait thy hook.

> ANGELO, *Measure for Measure*, II.ii.179

They'll take suggestion as a cat laps milk;
They'll tell the clock to any business that
We say befits the hour.

> ANTONIO, *The Tempest*, II.i.288

Devils soonest tempt, resembling spirits of light.

> BEROWNE, *Love's Labor's Lost*, IV.iii.253

Gold were as good as twenty orators,
And will, no doubt, tempt him to anything.

> PAGE, *Richard III*, IV.ii.38

O my most sacred lady,
Temptations have since then been born to 's: for
In those unfledg'd days was my wife a girl;
Your precious self had then not cross'd the eyes
Of my young playfellow.

> POLIXENES, *The Winter's Tale*, I.ii.77

TENNIS

His present and your pains we thank you for.
When we have match'd our rackets to these balls,
We will in France, by God's grace, play a set
Shall strike his father's crown into the hazard.
Tell him he hath made a match with such a wrangler
That all the courts of France will be disturb'd
With chaces.

> KING HENRY, *Henry V*, I.ii.260

They must either
(For so run the conditions) leave those remnants
Of fool and feather that they got in France,
With all their honorable points of ignorance
Pertaining thereunto, as fights and fireworks,
Abusing better men than they can be
Out of a foreign wisdom, renouncing clean
The faith they have in tennis and tall stockings,

Short blist'red breeches, and those types of travel,
And understand again like honest men,
Or pack to their old playfellows.

SIR THOMAS LOVELL, *Henry VIII*, I.III.24

THEATER
see also ACTORS AND ACTING; ART

Ber. Our wooing doth not end like an old play:
Jack hath not Jill. These ladies' courtesy
Might well have made our sport a comedy.
King. Come, sir, it wants a twelvemonth an' a day,
And then 'twill end.
Ber. That's too long for a play.

BEROWNE, FERDINAND, *Love's Labor's Lost*, V.II.874

If this were play'd upon a stage now, I could condemn it as
an improbable fiction.

FABIAN, *Twelfth Night*, III.IV.127

The play's the thing
Wherein I'll catch the conscience of the King.

HAMLET, *Hamlet*, II.II.604

The purpose of playing, whose end, both at the first and
now, was and is, to hold as 'twere the mirror up to nature:
show virtue her feature, scorn her own image, and the very
age and body of the time his form and pressure.

HAMLET, *Hamlet*, III.II.20

They thought it good you hear a play,
And frame your mind to mirth and merriment,
Which bars a thousand harms and lengthens life.

MESSENGER, *The Taming of the Shrew*, IND.II.134

A play there is, my lord, some ten words long,
Which is as brief as I have known a play;
But by ten words, my lord, it is too long,
Which makes it tedious, for in all the play
There is not one word apt, one player fitted.

PHILOSTRATE, *A Midsummer Night's Dream*, V.I.61

New plays and maidenheads are near akin—
Much follow'd both, for both much money gi'en,
If they stand sound and well; and a good play
(Whose modest scenes blush on his marriage-day,
And shake to lose his honor) is like her
That after holy tie and first night's stir,
Yet still is modesty, and still retains
More of the maid to sight than husband's pains.

PROLOGUE, *The Two Noble Kinsmen*, PRO.1

You shall hear
Scenes, though below his art, may yet appear
Worth two hours' travail. To his bones sweet sleep!
Content to you! If this play do not keep
A little dull time from us, we perceive
Our losses fall so thick we must needs leave.

    PROLOGUE, *The Two Noble Kinsmen*, PRO.27

Those that come to see
Only a show or two, and so agree
The play may pass, if they be still and willing,
I'll undertake may see away their shilling
Richly in two short hours.

    PROLOGUE, *Henry VIII*, PRO.9

It is not the fashion to see the lady the epilogue; but it
is not more unhandsome than to see the lord the prologue.
If it be true that good wine needs no bush, 'tis true that
a good play needs no epilogue. Yet to good wine they do
use good bushes; and good plays prove the better by the
help of good epilogues.

    ROSALIND, *As You Like It*, EPI.1

No epilogue, I pray you; for your play needs no excuse.
Never excuse; for when the players are all dead, there need
none to be blam'd.

    THESEUS, *A Midsummer Night's Dream*, V.I.355

THEFT

see also CRIME; POSSESSION

At his own shadow let the thief run mad,
Himself, himself seek every hour to kill.

    The Rape of Lucrece, 997

Thieves for their robbery have authority
When judges steal themselves.

    ANGELO, *Measure for Measure*, II.II.175

Easy it is
Of a cut to steal a shive.

    DEMETRIUS, *Titus Andronicus*, II.I.86

If you meet a thief, you may suspect him, by
virtue of your office, to be no true man; and for
such kind of men, the less you meddle or make
with them, why, the more is for your honesty.

    DOGBERRY, *Much Ado About Nothing*, III.III.50

Let us be Diana's
foresters, gentlemen of the shade, minions of the moon,
and let me say we be men of good government, being

govern'd, as the sea is, by our noble and chaste mistress
the moon, under whose countenance we steal.

SIR JOHN FALSTAFF, 1 Henry IV, I.II.25

Like workmen, I'll example you with thievery:
The sun's a thief, and with his great attraction
Robs the vast sea; the moon's an arrant thief,
And her pale fire she snatches from the sun;
The sea's a thief, whose liquid surge resolves
The moon into salt tears; the earth's a thief,
That feeds and breed by a composture stol'n
From gen'ral excrement; each thing's a thief.
The laws, your curb and whip, in their rough power
Has uncheck'd theft.

TIMON, Timon of Athens, IV.III.435

THOUGHT
see also CONSCIENCE; MIND; REASON

I think good thoughts whilst other write good words.

SONNET 85, 5

Thoughts are but dreams till their effects be tried.

The Rape of Lucrece, 353

Let me have men about me that are fat,
Sleek-headed men and such as sleep a-nights.
Yond Cassius has a lean and hungry look;
He thinks too much: such men are dangerous.

CAESAR, Julius Caesar, I.II.192

Make not your thoughts your prisons.

CAESAR (OCTAVIUS), Antony and Cleopatra, V.II.185

My thoughts were like unbridled children grown
Too headstrong for their mother.

CRESSIDA, Troilus and Cressida, III.II.122

I am far better born than is the King;
More like a king, more kingly in my thoughts.

DUKE OF YORK, 2 Henry VI, V.I.28

There is nothing either good or bad, but thinking makes it
so.

HAMLET, Hamlet, II.II.249

The native hue of resolution
Is sicklied o'er with the pale cast of thought.

HAMLET, Hamlet, III.1.83

O, from this time forth,
My thoughts be bloody, or be nothing worth!

HAMLET, Hamlet, IV.IV.65

But thoughts, the slaves of life, and life, time's fool,
And time, that takes survey of all the world,
Must have a stop.

HOTSPUR, *1 Henry IV*, V.IV.81

My thought, whose murder yet is but fantastical,
Shakes so my single state of man that function
Is smother'd in surmise, and nothing is
But what is not.

MACBETH, *Macbeth*, I.III.139

Thought is free.

MARIA, *Twelfth Night*, I.III.69

In lie whereof, I pray you bear me hence
From forth the noise and rumor of the field,
Where I may think the remnant of my thoughts
In peace, and part this body and my soul
With contemplation and devout desires.

MELUNE, *King John*, V.IV.44

For him, I think not on him. For his thoughts,
Would they were blanks, rather than fill'd with me.

OLIVIA, *Twelfth Night*, III.I.103

Give thy thoughts no tongue,
Nor any unproportion'd thought his act.

POLONIUS, *Hamlet*, I.III.59

THREATS
see also CURSES; DANGER

And then against my heart he set his sword,
Swearing, unless I took all patiently,
I should not live to speak another word.

The Rape of Lucrece, 1640

He hath a killing tongue and a quiet sword;
by the means whereof 's breaks words, and keeps
whole weapons.

BOY, *Henry V*, III.II.34

By gar, I vill cut all his two stones; by gar, he shall not
have a stone to throw at his dog.

DOCTOR CAIUS, *The Merry Wives of Windsor*, I.IV.111

If it appear not plain and prove untrue,
Deadly divorce step between me and you!

HELENA, *All's Well That Ends Well*, V.III.317

Pet. Come, come, you wasp, i' faith you are too angry.
Kate. If I be waspish, best beware my sting.

> PETRUCHIO, KATE, *The Taming of the Shrew*, II.I.209

In faith, I'll break thy little finger, Harry,
And if thou wilt not tell me all thing true.

> LADY PERCY, *1 Henry IV*, II.III.87

Tyb. What wouldst thou have with me?
Mer. Good King of Cats, nothing but one of your nine lives;
that I mean to make bold withal, and as you shall use
me hereafter, dry-beat the rest of eight.

> MERCUTIO, TYBALT, *Romeo and Juliet*, III.I.76

If thou more murmur'st, I will rend an oak
And peg thee in his knotty entrails till
Thou hast howl'd away twelve winters.

> PROSPERO, *The Tempest*, I.II.294

But if thou, jealous, does not return to pry
In what I farther shall intend to do,
By heaven, I will tear thee joint by joint,
And strew this hungry churchyard with thy limbs.

> ROMEO, *Romeo and Juliet*, V.III.33

Thou call'dst me dog before thou hadst a cause,
But since I am a dog, beware my fangs.

> SHYLOCK, *The Merchant of Venice*, III.III.6

Therefore, you clown, abandon—which is in the vulgar leave
—the society—which in the boorish is company—of this female
—which in the common is woman: which together is, abandon
the society of this female, or, clown, thou perishest; or to
thy better understanding, diest; or (to wit) I kill thee,
make thee away, translate thy life into death, thy liberty
into bondage. I will deal in poison with thee, or in
bastinado, or in steel; I will bandy with thee in faction; I
will o'errun thee with policy; I will kill thee a hundred
and fifty ways: therefore tremble and depart.

> TOUCHSTONE, *As You Like It*, V.I.47

THRIFT

Thrift, thrift, Horatio, the funeral bak'd-meats
Did coldly furnish forth the marriage tables.

> HAMLET, *Hamlet*, I.II.179

Thrift is blessing, if men steal it not.

> SHYLOCK, *The Merchant of Venice*, I.III.90

TIME
see also CHANGE; FUTURE; HISTORY; PAST; PROCRASTINATION; PUNCTUALITY

But wherefore do not you a mightier way
Make war upon this bloody tyrant Time?

SONNET 16, 1–2

Make glad and sorry seasons as thou fleet'st,
And do what e'er thou wilt, swift-footed Time,
To the wide world and all her fading sweets.

SONNET 19, 5–7

Like as the waves make towards the pebbled shore,
So do our minutes hasten to their end,
Each changing place with that which goes before.

SONNET 60, 1–3

Misshapen Time, copesmate of ugly Night,
Swift subtle post, carrier of grisly care,
Eater of youth, false slave to false delight,
Base watch of woes, sin's pack-horse, virtue's snare!
Thou nursest all, and murth'rest all that are.

The Rape of Lucrece, 925

What's past and what's to come is strew'd with husks
And formless ruin of oblivion.

AGAMEMNON, *Troilus and Cressida*, IV.v.166

We see which way the stream of time doth run,
And are enforc'd from our most quiet there
By the rough torrent of occasion.

ARCHBISHOP, *2 Henry IV*, IV.i.70

Time goes on crutches till love have all his rites.

CLAUDIO, *Much Ado About Nothing*, II.i.357

I play the noble huswife with the time,
To entertain it so merrily with a fool.

COUNTESS OF ROSSILLION, *All's Well That Ends Well*, II.ii.60

Time is a very bankrout and owes more than he's worth to season.
Nay, he's a thief too: have you not heard men say,
That Time comes stealing on by night and day?

DROMIO OF SYRACUSE, *The Comedy of Errors*, IV.ii.58

Every time
Serves for the matter that is then born in't.

ENOBARBUS, *Antony and Cleopatra*, II.i.9

Thus the whirligig of time brings in his revenges.

FESTE, *Twelfth Night*, V.i.376

And then he drew a dial from his poke,
And looking on it, with lack-luster eye,
Says very wisely, "It is ten a' clock.
Thus we may see," quoth he, "how the world wags.
'Tis but an hour ago since it was nine,
And after one hour more 'twill be eleven,
And so, from hour to hour, we ripe and ripe,
And then from hour to hour, we rot and rot;
And thereby hangs a tale."

JAQUES, *As You Like It*, II.VII.20

In a minute there are many days.

JULIET, *Romeo and Juliet*, II.v.45

Come what come may,
Time and the hour runs through the roughest day.

MACBETH, *Macbeth*, I.III.146

Whereby I see that Time's the king of men.

PERICLES, *Pericles*, II.III.45

What a devil hast thou to do with the time of day?
Unless hours were cups of sack, and minutes capons,
and clocks the tongues of bawds, and dials the signs of
leaping-houses, and the blessed sun himself a fair hot
wench in flame color'd taffeta.

PRINCE HENRY, *1 Henry IV*, I.II.6

Time is the nurse and breeder of all good.

PROTEUS, *The Two Gentlemen of Verona*, III.I.245

Ros. Time travels in divers
paces with divers persons. I'll tell you who Time
ambles withal, who Time trots withal, who Time
gallops withal, and who he stands still withal.
Orl. I prithee, who doth he trot withal?
Ros. Marry, he trots hard with a young maid
between the contract of marriage and the day
it is solemniz'd. If the interim be but a se'nnight,
Time's pace is so hard that it seems the length of
seven year.
Orl. Who ambles Time withal?
Ros. With a priest that lacks Latin, and a rich
man that hath not the gout; for the one sleeps easily
because he cannot study, and the other lives merrily
because he feels no pain; the one lacking the
burden of lean and wasteful learning, the other
knowing no burden of heavy tedious penury. These

Time ambles withal.
Orl. Who doth he gallop withal?
Ros. With a thief to the gallows; for though he
go as softly as foot can fall, he thinks himself too
soon there.
Orl. Who stays it still withal?
Ros. With lawyers in the vacation; for they sleep
between term and term, and then they perceive not
how Time moves.

ROSALIND, ORLANDO, *As You Like It*, III.II.308

Time hath, my lord, a wallet at his back,
Wherein he puts alms for oblivion,
A great-siz'd monster of ingratitudes.
Those scraps are good deeds past, which are devour'd
As fast as they are made, forgot as soon
As done.

ULYSSES, *Troilus and Cressida*, III.III.145

Let not virtue seek
Remuneration for the thing it was;
For beauty, wit,
High birth, vigor of bone, desert in service,
Love, friendship, charity, are subjects all
To envious and calumniating Time.

ULYSSES, *Troilus and Cressida*, III.III.169

TOASTS

Come, gentlemen, I hope we shall drink down all unkindness.

PAGE, *The Merry Wives of Windsor*, I.I.196

Make the coming hour o'erflow with joy
And pleasure drown the brim.

PAROLLES, *All's Well That Ends Well*, II.IV.46

Therefore to make his entrance more sweet,
Here, say we drink this standing-bowl of wine to him.

SIMONIDES, *Pericles*, II.III.64

Mar. He's drunk nightly in your company.
Sir To. With drinking healths to my niece. I'll drink to
her as long as there is a passage in my throat, and drink in
Illyria. He's a coward and a coistrel that will not drink
to my niece till his brains turn o' th' toe like a
parish-top.

SIR TOBY, MARIA, *Twelfth Night*, I.III.36

TRANSIENCE
see also INCONSTANCY; UNCERTAINTY

This weak impress of love is as a figure

Trenched in ice, which with an hour's heat
Dissolves to water, and doth lose his form.

DUKE, The Two Gentlemen of Verona, III.II.6

I see things may serve long, but not serve ever.

LAVATCH, All's Well That Ends Well, II.II.58

There's a daisy. I would give you some violets, but they
wither'd all when my father died.

OPHELIA, Hamlet, IV.I.184

TRAVEL

Weary with toil, I haste me to my bed,
The dear repose for limbs with travel tired,
But then begins a journey in my head
To work my mind, when body's work's expired.

SONNET 27, 1–4

How heavy do I journey on the way,
When what I seek (my weary travel's end)
Doth teach that ease and that repose to say,
"Thus far the miles are measur'd from thy friend."

SONNET 50, 1–4

That is my home of love; if I have rang'd,
Like him that travels I return again,
Just to the time, not with the time exchanged,
So that myself bring water for my stain.

SONNET 109, 5–8

Men are merriest when they are from home.

KING HENRY, Henry V, I.II.272

Safe mayst thou wander, safe return again!

PISANIO, Cymbeline, III.V.104

I'll put a girdle round about the earth
In forty minutes.

PUCK, A Midsummer Night's Dream, II.I.175

A traveler! By my faith, you have great reason to be sad.
I fear you have sold your own lands to see other men's; then to
have seen much, and to have nothing, is to have rich eyes
and poor hands.

ROSALIND, As You Like It, IV.I.21

When I was at home, I was in a better place, but travelers
must be content.

TOUCHSTONE, As You Like It, II.IV.17

Home-keeping youth have ever homely wits.
Were't not affection chains thy tender days
To the sweet glances of thy honor'd love,

> I rather would entreat thy company
> To see the wonders of the world abroad,
> Than (living dully sluggardized at home)
> Wear out thy youth with shapeless idleness.
>
> VALENTINE, *The Two Gentlemen of Verona*, I.I.2

TREASON
see also BETRAYAL; CONSPIRACY; ENEMY

> Even at the base of Pompey's statue
> (Which all the while blood ran) great Caesar fell.
> O, what a fall was there, my countrymen!
> Then I, and you, and all of us fell down,
> Whilst bloody treason flourish'd over us.
>
> ANTONY, *Julius Caesar*, III.II.188

> Thou art a traitor and miscreant,
> Too good to be so, and too bad to live,
> Since the more fair and crystal is the sky,
> The uglier seem the clouds that in it fly.
>
> BULLINGBROOK, *Richard II*, I.I.39

> Et tu, Brute?
>
> CAESAR, *Julius Caesar*, III.I.77

> Never was there queen
> So mightily betrayed! yet at the first
> I saw the treasons planted.
>
> CLEOPATRA, *Antony and Cleopatra*, I.III.24

> Traitors have never other company.
>
> DUKE OF BURGUNDY, *1 Henry VI*, II.I.19

> Alack,
> You are transported by calamity
> Thither where more attends you, and you slander
> The helms o' th' state, who care for you like fathers,
> When you curse them as enemies.
>
> MENENIUS AGRIPPA, *Coriolanus*, I.I.74

> Treason's true bed and yielder-up of breath.
>
> PRINCE JOHN, *2 Henry IV*, IV.II.123

> Thy friends suspect for traitors while thou liv'st,
> And take deep traitors for thy dearest friends!
>
> QUEEN MARGARET, *Richard III*, I.III.222

TRUST
see also SECRETS

> O, love's best habit is in seeming trust,
> And age in love loves not t' have years told.
>
> SONNET 138, 11–12

What trust is in these times?
They that, when Richard liv'd, would have him die,
Are not become enamor'd on his grave.

ARCHBISHOP, *2 Henry IV*, I.ii.100

I do not greatly care to be deceiv'd,
That have no use for trusting.

CLEOPATRA, *Antony and Cleopatra*, V.ii.14

Mine eyes
Were not in fault, for she was beautiful;
Mine ears, that heard her flattery, nor my heart,
That thought her like her seeming. It had been vicious
To have mistrusted her; yet, O my daughter,
That it was folly in me, thou mayst say,
And prove it in thy feeling.

CYMBELINE, *Cymbeline*, V.v.63

Natures of such deep trust we shall much need;
You we first seize on.

DUKE OF CORNWALL, *King Lear*, II.i.115

Trust not him that hath once broken faith.

QUEEN ELIZABETH, *3 Henry VI*, IV.iv.30

Who should be trusted, when one's right hand
Is perjured to the bosom?

VALENTINE, *The Two Gentlemen of Verona*, V.iv.67

TRUTH
see also HONESTY

O truant Muse, what shall be thy amends
For thy neglect of truth in beauty dy'd?
Both truth and beauty on my love depends.

SONNET 101, 1–3

Truth may seem, but cannot be,
Beauty brag, but 'tis not she,
Truth and Beauty buried be.

The Phoenix and Turtle, 62

Can the devil speak true?

BANQUO, *Macbeth*, I.iii.107

Truth hath a quiet breast.

BULLINGBROOK, *Richard II*, I.iii.96

The truth you speak doth lack some gentleness,
And time to speak it in. You rub the sore,
When you should bring the plaster.

GONZALO, *The Tempest*, II.i.138

And I can teach thee, coz, to shame the devil
By telling truth: tell truth and shame the devil.

HOTSPUR, *1 Henry IV*, III.I.57

Truth is truth
To th' end of reck'ning.

ISABELLA, *Measure for Measure*, V.I.45

'Tis so strange,
That, though the truth of it stands off as gross
As black and white, my eye will scarcely see it.

KING HENRY, *Henry V*, II.II.102

What in the world should make me now deceive,
Since I must lose the use of all deceit?
Why should I then be false, since it is true
That I must die here and live hence by truth?

MELUNE, *King John*, V.IV.26

If circumstances lead me, I will find
Where truth is hid, though it were hid indeed
Within the center.

POLONIUS, *Hamlet*, II.II.157

Methinks the truth should live from age to age,
As 'twere retail'd to all posterity.

PRINCE EDWARD, *Richard III*, III.I.76

Truth hath better deeds than words to grace it.

PROTEUS, *The Two Gentlemen of Verona*, II.III.17

He that will all the treasure know o' th' earth
Must know the center too; he that will fish
For my least minnow, let him lead his line
To catch one at my heart.

QUEEN, *The Two Noble Kinsmen*, I.I.114

Truth loves open dealing.

QUEEN KATHERINE, *Henry VIII*, III.I.40

The truth appears so naked on my side
That any purblind eye may find it out.

RICHARD PLANTAGENET, *1 Henry VI*, II.IV.20

There is enough scarce truth alive to make societies secure,
but security enough to make fellowships accurs'd. Much upon
this riddle runs the wisdom of the world.

VINCENTIO, DUKE OF VIENNA, *Measure for Measure*, III.II.226

TWINS
see also SIBLINGS

We are two lions litter'd in one day,

And I the elder and more terrible.

> CAESAR, *Julius Caesar*, II.II.44

Twinn'd brothers of one womb,
Whose procreation, residence, and birth
Scarce is dividant, touch them with several fortunes,
The greater scorns the lesser.

> TIMON, *Timon of Athens*, IV.III.3

TYRANNY
see also CORRUPTION; INJUSTICE

And I will chain these legs and arms of thine,
That hast by tyranny these many years
Wasted our country, slain our citizens,
And sent our sons and husbands captivate.

> COUNTESS OF AUVERGNE, *1 Henry VI*, II.III.39

Thou ominous and fearful own of death,
Our nation's terror and their bloody scourge!
The period of thy tyranny approacheth.

> GENERAL, *1 Henry VI*, IV.II.15

The people cry you mock'd them; and of late,
When corn was given them gratis, you repin'd,
Scandall'd the suppliants for the people, call'd them
Time-pleasers, flatterers, foes to nobleness.

> JUNIUS BRUTUS, *Coriolanus*, III.I.42

Upon thy eyeballs murderous tyranny
Sits in grim majesty, to fright the world.

> KING HENRY, *2 Henry VI*, III.II.49

Great tyranny, lay thou thy basis sure,
For goodness dare not cheek thee; wear thou thy wrongs,
The title is affeer'd.

> MACDUFF, *Macbeth*, IV.III.32

I knew him tyrannous, and tyrants' fears
Decrease not, but grow faster than the years.

> PERICLES, *Pericles*, I.II.84

For how can tyrants safely govern home,
Unless abroad they purchase great alliance?

> QUEEN MARGARET, *3 Henry VI*, III.III.69

I will show myself a tyrant: when I have fought with the
men, I will be civil with the maids; I will cut off their
heads.

> SAMPSON, *Romeo and Juliet*, I.I.21

UGLINESS

With unattainted eye
Compare her face with some that I shall show,
And I will make thee think thy swan a crow.

BENVOLIO, *Romeo and Juliet*, I.II.85

I am as ugly as a bear;
For beasts that meet me run away for fear.

HELENA, *A Midsummer Night's Dream*, II.II.94

His face is the worst thing about him.

POMPEY, *Measure for Measure*, II.I.155

UNCERTAINTY
see also INCONSTANCY; TRANSIENCE

Until I know this sure uncertainty,
I'll entertain the offered fallacy.

ADRIANA, *The Comedy of Errors*, II.II.85

I do not like "but yet," it does allay
The good precedence; fie upon "But yet"!
"But yet" is as a jailer to bring forth
Some monstrous malefactor.

CLEOPATRA, *Antony and Cleopatra*, II.V.54

We know what we are, but know not what we may be.

OPHELIA, *Hamlet*, IV.V.43

Thou are not certain,
For thy complexion shifts to strange effects,
After the moon.

VINCENTIO, DUKE OF VIENNA, *Measure for Measure*, III.I.23

UNDERSTANDING
see also MATURITY; WISDOM

I speak as my understanding in-
structs me, and as mine honesty puts it to utterance.

ARCHIDAMUS, *The Winter's Tale*, I.I.19

Thus do we of wisdom and of reach,
With windlasses and with assays of bias,
By indirections find directions out.

POLONIUS, *Hamlet*, II.I.61

Their understanding
Begins to swell, and the approaching tide
Will shortly fill the reasonable shores
That now lie foul and muddy.

PROSPERO, *The Tempest*, V.I.79

The mutual conference that my mind hath had,
By day, by night, waking and in my dreams,
In courtly company, or at my beads,
With you, mine alder-liefest sovereign,
Makes me the bolder to salute my king
With ruder terms, such as my wit affords
And overjoy of heart doth minister.

QUEEN MARGARET, *2 Henry VI*, I.I.25

When a man's verses cannot be understood, nor a man's good
wit seconded with the forward child, understanding, it
strikes a man more dead than a great reckoning in a little
room.

TOUCHSTONE, *As You Like It*, III.III.12

UNITY
see also MARRIAGE

So they loved as love in twain
Had the essence but in one,
Two distincts, division none.

The Phoenix and Turtle, 25

The broken rancor of your high-swoll'n hates,
But lately splinter'd, knit, and join'd together,
Must gently be preserv'd, cherish'd, and kept.

BUCKINGHAM, *Richard III*, II.II.117

Then you love us, we you, and we'll clasp hands:
When peers thus knit, a kingdom ever stands.

HELICANUS, *Pericles*, II.IV.57

UNKINDNESS
see also RUDENESS

That you were once unkind befriends me now,
And for that sorrow which I then did feel
Needs must I under my transgression bow,
Unless my nerves were brass or hammered steel.

SONNET 120, 1–4

O, call not me to justify the wrong
That thy unkindness lays upon my heart.

SONNET 139, 1–2

In nature there's no blemish but the mind;
None can be call'd deform'd but the unkind.

ANTONIO, *Twelfth Night*, III.IV.367

Give me a bowl of wine.
In this I bury all unkindness.

BRUTUS, *Julius Caesar*, IV.III.158

Unkindness may do much,
And his unkindnesss may defeat my life,
But never taint my love.

DESDEMONA, Othello, IV.II.159

Tut, tut, thou art all ice, thy kindness freezes.

KING RICHARD, Richard III, IV.II.22

She hath tied
Sharp-tooth'd unkindness, like a vulture, here.

LEAR, King Lear, II.IV.134

Rich gifts wax poor when givers prove unkind.

OPHELIA, Hamlet, III.I.100

They have all been touch'd and found base metal,
For they have all denied him.

SERVANT, Timon of Athens, III.III.6

That nature being sick of man's unkindness
Should yet be hungry!

TIMON, Timon of Athens, IV.III.176

UTOPIA
see also PERFECTION

Let me live here ever,
So rare a wond'red father and a wise
Make this place Paradise.

FERDINAND, The Tempest, IV.I.123

I' th' commonwealth I would, by contraries,
Execute all things; for no kind of traffic
Would I admit; no name of magistrate;
Letters should not be known; riches, poverty,
And use of service none; contract, succession,
Bourn, bound of land, tilth, vineyard, none;
No use of metal, corn, or wine, or oil;
No occupation, all men idle, all;
And women too, but innocent and pure;
No sovereignty.

GONZALO, The Tempest, II.I.148

VEGETARIANISM
see also FOOD

If you can mock a leek, you can eat a leek.

FLUELLEN, Henry V, V.I.37

And I think this word "sallet" was born to do me
good; for many a time, but for a sallet, by brain-pan
had been cleft with a brown bill; and many a time,

when I have been dry and bravely marching, it hath
serv'd me instead of a quart pot to drink in; and now
the word "sallet" must serve me to feed on.

JACK CADE, 2 Henry VI, IV.x.10

I am a great eater of beef, and I believe that does harm to
my wit.

SIR ANDREW AGUECHEEK, Twelfth Night, I.III.85

We cannot live on grass, on berries, water,
As beasts and birds and fishes.

TIMON, Timon of Athens, IV.III.422

VERBOSITY

see also CONVERSATION; SPEAKING AND SPEECH

Fie, what a spendthrift is he of his tongue!

ANTONIO, The Tempest, II.1.24

I spoke it tender juvenal as a congruent epitheton
appertaining to thy young days, which we may nominate
tender.

ARMADO, Love's Labor's Lost, I.II.13

Taffeta phrases, silken terms precise,
Three-pil'd hyperboles, spruce affectation,
Figures pendantical—these summer flies
Have blown me full of maggot ostentation.

BEROWNE, Love's Labor's Lost, V.II.406

He draweth out the thread of his verbosity finer than the
staple of his argument. I abhor such fanatical
phantasimes, such insociable and point-devise companions,
such rackers of orthography, as to speak "dout," fine, when he
should say "doubt"; "det," when he should pronounce "debt"—
    d,e,b,t
not d,e,t: he clepeth a calf, "cauf"; half, "hauf"; neighbor
vocatur "nebor"; neigh abbreviated "ne." This is
abhominable—which he would call "abominable."

HOLOFERNES, Love's Labor's Lost, V.I.16

Par. I love not many words.
2. Lord. No more than a fish loves water.

PAROLLES, SECOND LORD, All's Well That Ends Well, III.VI.84

Silence! one word more
Shall make me chide thee, if not hate thee.

PROSPERO, The Tempest, I.II.476

Nurse. I pray you, sir, what saucy merchant was this,
that was so full of his ropery?

Rom. A gentleman, nurse, that loves to hear himself talk,
and will speak more in a minute than he will stand to in a month.
ROMEO, NURSE, *Romeo and Juliet*, II.IV.145

VICE
see also SIN; TEMPTATION

There is no vice so simple but assumes
Some mark of virtue on his outward parts.
BASSANIO, *The Merchant of Venice*, III.II.76

The world's a huge thing; it is a great price
For a small vice.
EMILIA, *Othello*, IV.III.69

In the fatness of these pursy times
Virtue itself of vice must pardon beg,
Yea, curb and woo for leave to do him good.
HAMLET, *Hamlet*, III.IV.153

Be not thy tongue thy own shame's orator:
Look sweet, speak fair, become disloyalty:
Apparel vice like virtue's harbinger;
Bear a fair presence, though your heart be tainted;
Teach sin the carriage of a holy saint.
LUCIANA, *The Comedy of Errors*, III.II.10

Who has a book of all that monarchs do,
He's more secure to keep it shut than shown,
For vice repeated is like the wand'ring wind,
Blows dust in other's eyes, to spread itself.
PERICLES, *Pericles*, I.I.94

Twice treble shame on Angelo,
To weed my vice, and let his grow!
VINCENTIO, DUKE OF VIENNA, *Measure for Measure*, III.II.269

VIOLENCE
see also WAR

Great men have reaching hands; oft have I struck
Those that I never saw, and struck them dead.
LORD SAY, *2 Henry VI*, IV.VII.81

It will have blood, they say; blood will have blood.
MACBETH, *Macbeth*, III.IV.121

VIRGINITY
see also CHASTITY; PURITY

The tender spring upon thy tempting lip
Show thee unripe; yet mayst thou well be tasted.
Venus and Adonis, 127

You do impeach your modesty too much,
To leave the city and commit yourself
Into the hands of one that loves you not;
To trust the opportunity of night,
And the ill counsel of a desert place,
With the rich worth of your virginity.

DEMETRIUS, A Midsummer Night's Dream, II.I.214

If you would conjure in her, you
must make a circle; if conjure up Love in her in his
true likeness, he must appear naked and blind. Can
you blame her then, being a maid yet ros'd over
with the virgin crimson of modesty, if she deny the
appearance of a naked blind boy in her naked seeing
self?

DUKE OF BURGUNDY, Henry V, V.II.292

Your house, but for this virgin that doth prop it,
Would sink and overwhelm you.

LYSIMACHUS, Pericles, IV.VI.119

It is not politic in the commonwealth of nature to preserve
virginity. Loss of virginity is rational increase, and
there was never virgin got till virginity was first lost.
That you were made of is metal to make virgins. Virginity,
by being once lost, may be ten times found; by being ever
kept, it is ever lost. 'Tis too cold a companion; away
with't!

PAROLLES, All's Well That Ends Well, I.I.126

Earthlier happy is the rose distill'd,
Than that which withering on the virgin thorn
Grows, lives, and dies in single blessedness.

THESEUS, A Midsummer Night's Dream, I.I.76

VIRTUE
see also GOOD; HONESTY; HONOR; LOYALTY; TRUTH

Know you not, master, to some kind of men
Their graces serve them but as enemies?
No more do yours. Your virtues, gentle master,
Are sanctified and holy traitors to you.

ADAM, As You Like It, II.III.10

Virtue is beauty, but the beauteous evil
Are empty trunks o'erflourish'd by the devil.

ANTONIO, Twelfth Night, III.IV.369

And had I twenty times so many foes,
And each of them had twenty times their power,

All these could not procure me any scathe
So long as I am loyal, true, and crimeless.
DUKE OF GLOUCESTER, 2 Henry VI, II.IV.59

'Tis virtue that doth make them most admir'd,
The contrary doth make thee wond'red at.
DUKE OF YORK, 3 Henry VI, I.IV.130

As I hope
For quiet days, fair issue, and long life,
With such love as 'tis now, the murkiest den,
The most opportune place, the strong'est suggestion
Our worser genius can, shall never melt
Mine honor into lust.
FERDINAND, The Tempest, IV.I.24

Assume a virtue, if you have it not.
HAMLET, Hamlet, III.IV.160

Her virtues, gracèd with external gifts,
Do breed love's settled passions in my heart,
And like a rigor of tempestuous gusts
Provokes the mightiest hulk against the tide.
KING HENRY, 1 Henry VI, V.V.1

What thou wouldst highly,
That wouldst thou holily.
LADY MACBETH, Macbeth, I.V.20

His virtues
Will plead like angels, trumpet-tongu'd, against
The deep damnation of his taking-off.
MACBETH, Macbeth, I.VII.18

Mark how his virtue, like a hidden sun,
Breaks through his baser garments.
PIRITHOUS, The Two Noble Kinsmen, II.V.23

How far that little candle throws his beams!
So shines a good deed in a naughty world.
PORTIA, The Merchant of Venice, V.I.90

The rarer action is
In virtue than in vengeance.
PROSPERO, The Tempest, V.I.27

Virtue is of so little regard in these
costermongers' times that true valor is turn'd berrord;
pregnancy is made a tapster.
SIR JOHN FALSTAFF, 2 Henry IV, I.II.168

Virtue is bold, and goodness never fearful.
VINCENTIO, DUKE OF VIENNA, Measure for Measure, III.I.208

VOWS
see also OATHS; PROMISES

> Riotous madness,
> To be entangled with those mouth-made vows,
> Which break themselves in swearing!
>
> CLEOPATRA, *Antony and Cleopatra*, I.III.29

> 'Tis not the many oaths that make the truth,
> But the plain single vow that is vow'd true.
>
> DIANA, *All's Well That Ends Well*, IV.II.21

> O Warwick, I do bend my knee with thine,
> And in this vow do chain my soul to thine!
>
> PRINCE EDWARD, *3 Henry VI*, II.III.33

> The end of life cancels all bands,
> And I will die a hundred thousand deaths
> Ere break the smallest parcel of this vow.
>
> KING HENRY, *1 Henry IV*, III.II.157

> This royal hand and mine are newly knit,
> And the conjunction of our inward souls
> Married in league, coupled, and link'd together
> With all religious strength of sacred vows.
>
> KING PHILIP, *King John*, III.I.226

> I do know,
> When the blood burns, how prodigal the soul
> Lends the tongue vows. These blazes, daughter,
> Giving more light than heat, extinct in both
> Even in their promise, as it is a-making,
> You must not take for fire.
>
> POLONIUS, *Hamlet*, I.III.115

VULNERABILITY
see also WEAKNESS

> Marry, my lord, lest by a multitude
> The new-heal'd wound of malice should break out,
> Which would be so much the more dangerous,
> By how much the estate is green and yet ungovern'd.
>
> BUCKINGHAM, *Richard III*, II.II.124

> Let me wring your heart, for so I shall
> If it be made of penetrable stuff,
> If damnèd custom have not brass'd it so
> That it be proof and bulwark against sense.
>
> HAMLET, *Hamlet*, III.IV.35

> You would play upon me, you would seem to know my stops, you
> would pluck out the heart of my mystery, you would sound me

from my lowest note to the top of my compass; and there is
much music, excellent voice, in this little organ, yet
cannot you make it speak. 'Sblood, do you think I am easier
to be play'd on than a pipe? Call me what instrument you
will, though you fret me, yet you cannot play upon me.

HAMLET, Hamlet, III.ii.364

I will wear my heart upon my sleeve
For daws to peck at.

IAGO, Othello, I.i.64

Who builds his hope in air of your good looks
Lives like a drunken sailor on a mast,
Ready with every nod to tumble down
Into the fatal bowels of the deep.

LORD HASTINGS, Richard III, III.iv.98

I have supp'd full with horrors;
Direness, familiar to my slaughterous thoughts,
Cannot once start me.

MACBETH, Macbeth, V.v.13

Their sense thus weak, lost with their fears thus strong,
Made senseless things begin to do them wrong,
For briers and thorns at their apparel snatch;
Some sleeves, some hats, from yielders all things catch.

PUCK, A Midsummer Night's Dream, III.ii.27

Free lords, cold snow melts with the sun's hot beams:
Henry my lord is cold in great affairs,
Too full of foolish pity; and Gloucester's show
Beguiles him as the mournful crocodile
With sorrow snares relenting passengers;
Or as the snake roll'd in a flow'ring bank,
With shining checker'd slough, doth sting a child
That for the beauty thinks it excellent.

QUEEN MARGARET, 2 Henry VI, III.i.223

Call them again, I am not made of stones,
But penetrable to your kind entreaties,
Albeit against my conscience and my soul.

RICHARD, DUKE OF GLOUCESTER, Richard III, III.vii.223

WALKING

Go, I pray you,
Walk, and be cheerful once again, reserve
That excellent complexion, which did steal
The eyes of young and old.

DIONYZA, Pericles, IV.i.38

A turn or two I'll walk
To still my beating mind.

PROSPERO, *The Tempest*, IV.I.162

Thus far into the bowels of the land
Have we march'd on without impediment.

RICHMOND, *Richard III*, V.II.3

WAR
see also BATTLE; ENEMY; SOLDIERS; VIOLENCE; WEAPONS

Make war breed peace, make peace stint war, make each
Prescribe to other as each other's leech.

ALCIBIADES, *Timon of Athens*, V.IV.82

Cry "Havoc!" and let slip the dogs of war.

ANTONY, *Julius Caesar*, III.I.273

Comets prewarn, whose havoc in vast field
Unearthèd skulls proclaim, whose breath blows down
The teeming Ceres' foison, who dost pluck
With hand armipotent from forth blue clouds
The mason'd turrets, that both mak'st and break'st
The stony girths of cities: me thy pupil
Youngest follower of thy drum, instruct this day
With military skill, that to thy laud
I may advance my streamer, and by thee
Be styl'd the lord o' the' day. Give me, great Mars
Some token of thy pleasure.

ARCITE, *The Two Noble Kinsmen*, V.I.49

Disorder, horror, fear, and mutiny
Shall here inhabit, and this land be call'd
The field of Golgotha and dead men's skulls.

BISHOP OF CARLISLE, *Richard II*, IV.I.142

We go to gain a little patch of ground
That hath in it no profit but the name.

CAPTAIN, *Hamlet*, IV.IV.18

Deliver up the crown, and to take mercy
On the poor souls for whom this hungry war
Opens his vasty jaws; and on your head
Turning the widows' tears, the orphans' cries,
The dead men's blood, the privy maidens' groans,
For husbands, fathers, and betrothèd lovers,
That shall be swallowed in this controversy.

DUKE OF EXETER, *Henry V*, II.IV.102

Now for our consciences, the arms are fair
When the intent of bearing them is just.

HOTSPUR, *1 Henry IV*, V.II.87

March on, join bravely, let us to it pell-mell;
If not to heaven, then hand in hand to hell.

KING RICHARD, *Richard III*, V.III.312

A victory is twice itself when the achiever brings home
full numbers.

LEONATO, *Much Ado About Nothing*, I.I.8

Wars 'twixt you twain would be
As if the world should cleave, and that slain men
Should solder up the rift.

OCTAVIA, *Antony and Cleopatra*, III.IV.30

If you do fight against your country's foes,
Your country's fat shall pay your pains the hire.

RICHMOND, *Richard III*, V.III.257

In God's name cheery on, courageous friends,
To reap the harvest of perpetual peace
By this one bloody trial of sharp war.

RICHMOND, *Richard III*, V.II.14

Thou know'st, great son,
The end of war's uncertain; but this certain,
That, if thou conquer Rome, the benefit
Which thou shalt thereby reap is such a name
Whose repetition will be dogg'd with curses.

VOLUMNIA, *Coriolanus*, V.III.140

WASTE

More water glideth by the mill
Than wots the miller of.

DEMETRIUS, *Titus Andronicus*, II.I.85

Fie, fie, thou shamest thy shape, thy love, thy wit,
Which like a usurer abound'st in all,
And usest none in that true use indeed
Which should bedeck thy shape, thy love, thy wit.

FRIAR LAWRENCE, *Romeo and Juliet*, III.III.122

Our rash faults
Make trivial price of serious things we have,
Not knowing them until we know their grave.
Oft our displeasures, to ourselves unjust,
Destroy our friends, and after weep their dust;

Our own love waking cries to see what's done,
While shameful hate sleeps out the afternoon.
            KING OF FRANCE, *All's Well That Ends Well*, V.III.57

To expostulate
What majesty should be, what duty is,
Why day is day, night night, and time is time,
Were nothing but to waste night, day, and time.
                              POLONIUS, *Hamlet*, II.II.86

The greater cantle of the world is lost
With very ignorance, we have kiss'd away
Kingdoms and provinces.
                    SCARUS, *Antony and Cleopatra*, III.x.6

WEAKNESS
see also VULNERABILITY

To fear the foe, since fear oppresseth strength,
Gives in your weakness strength unto your foe,
And so your follies fight against yourself.
              BISHOP OF CARLISLE, *Richard II*, III.II.180

Palamon
Is but his foil, to him, a mere dull shadow;
He's swarth and meager, of an eye as heavy
As if he had lost his mother; a still temper,
No stirring in him, no alacrity,
Of all this sprightly sharpness, not a smile.
Yet these that we count errors may become him.
            EMILIA, *The Two Noble Kinsmen*, IV.II.25

He plies her hard, and much rain wears the marble.
          RICHARD, DUKE OF GLOUCESTER, *3 Henry VI*, III.II.49

Can you think to blow out the intended
fire your city is ready to flame in, with such weak
breath as this?
                        WATCH, *Coriolanus*, V.II.45

WEALTH
see also EXCESS; GREED; MONEY; PROSPERITY

Honor for wealth, and oft that wealth doth cost
The death of all, and all together lost.
                              The Rape of Lucrece, 146

Who would not wish to be from wealth exempt,
Since riches point to misery and contempt?
                    FLAVIUS, *Timon of Athens*, IV.II.31

Poor and content is rich, and rich enough,
But riches fineless is as poor as winter
To him that ever fears he shall be poor.

IAGO, *Othello*, III.III.172

They are but beggars that can count their worth,
But my true love is grown to such excess
I cannot sum up sum of half my wealth.

JULIET, *Romeo and Juliet*, II.VI.32

The learned pate
Ducks to the golden fool.

TIMON, *Timon of Athens*, IV.III.17

WEAPONS
see also BATTLE; SOLDIERS; WAR

Cap. What noise is this? Give me my long sword, ho!
La. Cap. A crutch, a crutch! why call you for a sword?

CAPULET, LADY CAPULET, *Romeo and Juliet*, I.I.75

His brandish'd sword did blind men with his beams;
His arms spread wider than a dragon's wings;
His sparkling eyes, replete with wrathful fire,
More dazzled and drove back his enemies
Than midday sun fierce bent against their faces.

DUKE OF GLOUCESTER, *1 Henry VI*, I.I.10

Conscience is but a word that cowards use,
Devis'd at first to keep the strong in awe:
Our strong arms be our conscience, swords our law!

KING RICHARD, *Richard III*, V.III.309

Behold, I have a weapon;
A better never did itself sustain
Upon a soldier's thigh. I have seen the day
That with this little arm, and this good sword,
I have made my way through more impediments
Than twenty times your stop.

OTHELLO, *Othello*, V.II.259

WIDOWHOOD
see also GRIEF; HUSBANDS; LOSS; MARRIAGE; MOURNING; WIVES

It is for fear to wet a widow's eye
That thou consum'st thyself in single life?
Ah! if thou issueless shalt hap to die,
The world will wail thee like a makeless wife,
The world will be thy widow and still weep,
That thou no form of thee hast left behind,

When every private widow well may keep,
By children's eyes, her husband's shape in mind.

SONNET 9, 1–8

A beauty-waning and distressèd widow,
Even in the afternoon of her best days,
Made prize and purchase of his wanton eye.

BUCKINGHAM, *Richard III*, III.VII.185

A widow cries; be husband to me, heavens!

CONSTANCE, *King John*, III.I.108

Thou art a widow; yet thou art a mother,
And hast the comfort of thy children left;
But death hath snatch'd my husband from mine arms,
And pluck'd two crutches from my feeble hands.

DUCHESS OF YORK, *Richard III*, II.II.55

So came I a widow,
And never shall have length of life enough
To rain upon remembrance with mine eyes.

LADY PERCY, *2 Henry IV*, II.III.57

WILL
see also DESIRE; INTENTIONS; PURPOSE

Kings are earth's gods; in vice their law's their will.

PERICLES, *Pericles*, I.I.103

It's come to pass
This tractable obedience is a slave
To each incensèd will.

QUEEN KATHERINE, *Henry VIII*, I.II.63

But still, where danger was, still there I met him,
And like rich hangings in a homely house,
So was his will in his old feeble body.

RICHARD, *2 Henry VI*, I.II.11

WINTER
see also SEASONS

When forty winters shall besiege thy brow,
And dig deep trenches in thy beauty's field,
Thy youth's proud livery, so gaz'd on now,
Will be a totter'd weed of small worth held.

SONNET 2, 1–4

For never-resting time leads summer on
To hideous winter and confounds him there,
Sap check'd with frost and lusty leaves quite gone,
Beauty o'ersnow'd and bareness everywhere.

SONNET 5, 5–8

When great leaves fall, then winter is at hand;
When the sun sets, who doth not look for night?

CITIZEN, Richard III, II.III.33

We'll set thee to school to an ant, to
teach thee there's no laboring i' th' winter.

FOOL, King Lear, II.IV.67

Winter's not gone yet, if the wild geese fly
that way.

FOOL, King Lear, II.IV.46

Abide the change of time.
Quake in the present winter's state, and wish
That warmer days would come.

POSTHUMUS, Cymbeline, II.IV.4

Now is the winter of our discontent
Made glorious summer by this sun of York;
And all the clouds that low'r'd upon our house
In the deep bosom of the ocean buried.

RICHARD, DUKE OF GLOUCESTER, Richard III, I.I.1

WISDOM

see also EXPERIENCE; KNOWLEDGE; MATURITY; UNDERSTANDING

My lord, wise men ne'er sit and wail their woes,
But presently prevent the ways to wail.

BISHOP OF CARLISLE, Richard II, III.II.179

I never knew so young a body with so old a head.

DUKE OF VENICE, The Merchant of Venice, IV.I.163

Your Grace hath still been fam'd for virtuous,
And now may seem as wise as virtuous
By spying and avoiding Fortune's malice,
For new men rightly temper with the stars.

EARL OF WARWICK, 3 Henry VI, IV.VI.26

All places that the eye of heaven visits
Are to a wise man ports and happy havens.

JOHN OF GAUNT, Richard II, I.III.275

So what you will, your wisdom be your guide.

LADY NORTHUMBERLAND, 2 Henry IV, II.III.6

Sweet Earl, divorce nor wisdom from your honor,
The lives of all your loving complices
Lean on your health, the which, if you give o'er
To stormy passion, must perforce decay.

MORTON, 2 Henry IV, I.I.162

For wisdom cries out in
the streets, and no man regards it.

> PRINCE HENRY, *1 Henry IV*, I.II.88

So wise so young, they say do never live long.

> RICHARD, DUKE OF GLOUCESTER, *Richard III*, III.I.79

WISHES
see also HOPE

The sweets we wish for turn to loathèd sours
Even in the moment that we call them ours.

> *The Rape of Lucrece*, 867

Wishers were ever fools.

> CLEOPATRA, *Antony and Cleopatra*, IV.XV.37

Our wishes on the way
May prove effects.

> GONERIL, *King Lear*, IV.II.14

I wish but for the thing I have.

> JULIET, *Romeo and Juliet*, II.II.132

Thy wish was father, Harry, to that thought.

> KING HENRY IV, *2 Henry IV*, IV.V.92

WIT AND WITTINESS

Bene. Thy wit is as quick as the greyhound's mouth, it
catches.
Marg. And yours as blunt as the fencer's foils, which hit,
but hurt not.

> BENEDICK, MARGARET, *Much Ado About Nothing*, V.II.11

Always the dullness of the fool is the whetstone of the
wits.

> CELIA, *As You Like It*, I.II.54

Those wits that think they have thee do very oft prove
fools; and I that am sure I lack thee, may pass for a wise
man. For what says Quinapalus? "Better a witty fool than
a foolish wit."

> FESTE, *Twelfth Night*, I.V.33

Brevity is the soul of wit.

> POLONIUS, *Hamlet*, II.II.90

A good wit will make use
of any thing. I will turn diseases to commodity.

> SIR JOHN FALSTAFF, *2 Henry IV*, I.II.247

His wit's as thick as Tewksbury mustard, there's
no more conceit in him than is in a mallet.

SIR JOHN FALSTAFF, *2 Henry IV*, II.IV.240

I would you had the wit, 'twere better than
your dukedom.

SIR JOHN FALSTAFF, *2 Henry IV*, IV.III.86

Wit shall not go unrewarded while I am king of
this country.

STEPHANO, *The Tempest*, IV.I.242

I shall ne'er be ware of mine own wit till I break my shins
against it.

TOUCHSTONE, *As You Like It*, II.IV.58

WIVES
see also HUSBANDS; MARRIAGE; WIDOWHOOD; WOMEN

You are my true and honorable wife,
As dear to me as are the ruddy drops
That visit my sad heart.

BRUTUS, *Julius Caesar*, II.I.288

Would we all had such wives, that the men might go to wars
with the women.

ENOBARBUS, *Antony and Cleopatra*, II.II.65

Such duty as the subject owes the prince,
Even such a woman oweth to her husband;
And when she is froward, peevish, sullen, sour,
And not obedient to his honest will,
What is she but a foul contending rebel,
And graceless traitor to her loving lord?
I am asham'd that women are so simple
To offer war where they should kneel for peace,
Or seek for rule, supremacy, and sway,
When they are bound to serve, love, and obey.
Is dearly bought as mine, and I will have it.

KATE, *The Taming of the Shrew*, V.II.155

Within the bond of marriage, tell me, Brutus,
Is it excepted I should know no secrets
That appertain to you? Am I yourself
But, as it were, in sort or limitation.
To keep with you at meals, comfort your bed,
And talk to you sometimes? Dwell I but in the suburbs
Of your good pleasure? If it be no more,
Portia is Brutus' harlot, not his wife.

PORTIA, *Julius Caesar*, II.I.280

Let me give light, but let me not be light.
For a light wife doth make a heavy husband.
                    PORTIA, *The Merchant of Venice*, V.I.129

Have I liv'd thus long (let me speak myself,
Since virtue finds no friends) a wife, a true one?
A woman (I dare say without vainglory)
Never yet branded with suspicion?
Have I with all my full affections
Still met the King? Lov'd him next heav'n? Obey'd him?
Been, out of fondness, superstitious to him?
Almost forgot my pray'rs to content him?
And am I thus rewarded?
                    QUEEN KATHARINE, *Henry VIII*, III.I.125

O, that women that cannot make her fault her husband's
occasion, let her never nurse her child herself, for she
will breed it like a fool!
                    ROSALIND, *As You Like It*, IV.I.173

WOMEN

see also DAUGHTERS; FEMINISM; GENDER; MISOGYNY; MOTHERHOOD; WIDOWHOOD

From women's eyes this doctrine I derive:
They are the ground, the books, the academes,
From whence doth spring the true Promethean fire.
                    BEROWNE, *Love's Labor's Lost*, IV.III.298

A woman is a dish for the gods, if the devil dress her not.
                    CLOWN, *Antony and Cleopatra*, V.II.274

Kindness in women, not their beauteous looks,
Shall win my love.
                    HORTENSIO, *The Taming of the Shrew*, IV.II.41

All the expected good w'are like to hear
For this play at this time, is only in
The merciful construction of good women.
                    KING HENRY, *Henry VIII*, EPI.8

Ne'er trust me then; for when a world of men
Could not prevail with all their oratory,
Yet hath a woman's kindness overrul'd.
                    LORD TALBOT, *1 Henry VI*, II.II.48

Women will love her, that she is a woman
More worth than any man; men, that she is
The rarest of all women.
                    SERVANT, *The Winter's Tale*, V.I.110

WONDER
see also BEWILDERMENT

> For we which now behold these present days
> Have eyes to wonder, but lack tongues to praise.
>
> SONNET 106, 13–14

> Such a deal of
> wonder is broken out within this hour that ballad-
> makers cannot be able to express it.
>
> GENTLEMEN, *The Winter's Tale*, V.II.23

WORDS
see also POETRY; SPEAKING AND SPEECH; WRITING

> So of concealed sorrow may be said,
> Free vent of words love's fire doth assuage.
>
> *Venus and Adonis*, 333

> Or like the deadly bullet of a gun,
> His meaning struck her ere his words begun.
>
> *Venus and Adonis*, 462

> This helpless smoke of words doth me no right.
>
> *The Rape of Lucrece*, 1027

> Sweet smoke of rhetoric!
>
> ARMADO, *Love's Labor's Lost*, III.I.62

> Beat. Will you not eat your word?
> Bene. With no sauce that can be devis'd to it.
>
> BENEDICK, BEATRICE, *Much Ado About Nothing*, IV.I.278

> Good words are better than bad strokes.
>
> BRUTUS, *Julius Caesar*, V.I.29

> How long a time lies in one little word!
>
> BULLINGBROOK, *Richard II*, I.III.213

> My words fly up, my thoughts remain below:
> Words without thoughts never to heaven go.
>
> CLAUDIUS, *Hamlet*, III.III.97

> Words are but wind.
>
> DROMIO OF EPHESUS, *The Comedy of Errors*, III.I.75

> These haughty words of hers
> Have batt'red me like roaring cannon-shot,
> And made me almost yield upon my knees.
>
> DUKE OF BURGUNDY, *1 Henry VI*, III.III.78

> These words will cost ten thousand lives this day.
>
> PRINCE EDWARD, *3 Henry VI*, I.II.177

Words to the heat of deeds too cold breath gives.

MACBETH, *Macbeth*, II.1.61

When thou didst not, savage,
Know thine own meaning, but wouldst gabble like
A thing most brutish, I endow'd thy purposes
With words that made them known.

MIRANDA, *The Tempest*, I.II.355

Moth. They have been at a great feast of languages, and
stol'n the scraps.
Cost. O, they have liv'd long on the alms-basket of words.
I marvel thy master hath not eaten thee for a word,
for thou art not so long by the head as
honorificabilitudinitatibus: thou art easier swallow'd
than a flap-dragon.

MOTH, COSTARD, *Love's Labor's Lost*, V.1.36

He speaks plain cannon-fire, and smoke, and bounce,
He gives the bastinado with his tongue;
Our ears are cudgell'd—not a word of his
But buffets better than a fist of France.
'Zounds, I was never so bethump'd with words
Since I first call'd my brother's father dad.

PHILIP THE BASTARD, *King John*, II.1.462

Pol. What do you read, my lord?
Ham. Words, words, words.

POLONIUS, HAMLET, *Hamlet*, II.II.191

Words, words, mere words, no matter from the heart.

TROILUS, *Troilus and Cressida*, V.III.108

Thu. Sir, if you spend word for word with me, I shall make
your wit bankrupt.
Val. I know it well, sir; you have an exchequer of words
and, I think, no other treasure to give your followers;
for it appears by their bare liveries that they live by
your bare words.

VALENTINE, THURIO, *The Two Gentlemen of Verona*, II.IV.41

They that dally nicely with words may quickly make them
wanton.

VIOLA, *Twelfth Night*, III.1.13

WORK
see also BUSINESS; OFFICE POLITICS

To business that we love we rise betime,
And go to't with delight.

ANTONY, *Antony and Cleopatra*, IV.IV.20

The sweat of industry would dry and die,
But for the end it works to.

BELARIUS, *Cymbeline*, III.VI.31

I cannot draw a cart, nor eat dried oats,
If it be man's work, I'll do't.

CAPTAIN, *King Lear*, V.III.38

Sir, I am a true laborer: I earn that I eat, get that I
wear, owe no man hate, envy no man's happiness, glad of
other men's good, content with my harm, and the greatest of
my pride is to see my ewes graze and my lambs suck.

CORIN, *As You Like It*, III.II.73

My sweet mistress
Weeps when she sees me work, and says such baseness
Had never like executor. I forget;
But these sweet thoughts do even refresh my labors,
Most busiest when I do it.

FERDINAND, *The Tempest*, III.I.11

Many a man's tongue shakes out his master's undoing.

LAVATCH, *All's Well That Ends Well*, II.IV.23

The labor we delight in physics pain.

MACBETH, *Macbeth*, II.III.50

How well this honest mirth becomes their labor!

PERICLES, *Pericles*, II.1.95

If all the year were playing holidays,
To sport would be as tedious as to work.

PRINCE HENRY, *1 Henry IV*, I.II.204

You take my house when you do take the prop
That doth sustain my house; you take my life
When you do take the means whereby I live.

SHYLOCK, *The Merchant of Venice*, IV.1.375

Methinks thou art more honest now than wise,
For, by oppressing and betraying me,
Thou might'st have sooner got another service;
For many so arrive at second masters,
Upon their first lord's neck.

TIMON, *Timon of Athens*, IV.III.502

WORLD

It is a reeling world indeed, my lord,
And I believe will never stand upright.

CATESBY, *Richard III*, III.II.38

The little O, th' earth.

CLEOPATRA, *Antony and Cleopatra*, V.II.81

O my good lord, the world is but a word;
Were it all yours to give it in a breath,
How quickly were it gone!

FLAVIUS, *Timon of Athens*, II.II.152

This goodly frame, the earth, seems to me a sterile
promontory; this most excellent canopy, the air, look you,
this brave o'erhanging firmament, this majestical roof
fretted with golden fire, why, it appeareth nothing to me
but a foul and pestilent congregation of vapors.

HAMLET, *Hamlet*, II.II.298

This is no world
To play with mammets and to tilt with lips.
We must have bloody noses and crak'd crowns,
And pass them current too.

HOTSPUR, *1 Henry IV*, II.III.91

Bad is the world, and all will come to nought,
When such ill dealing must be seen in thought.

SCRIVENER, *Richard III*, III.VI.13

WORRY
see also CARE AND CONCERN; FEAR

Her eyes, though sod in tears, look'd red and raw,
Her lively color kill'd with deadly cares.

The Rape of Lucrece, 1592

Cheer your heart,
Be you not troubled with the time, which drives
O'er your content these strong necessities,
But let determin'd things to destiny
Hold unbewail'd their way.

CAESAR (OCTAVIUS), *Antony and Cleopatra*, III.VI.81

Why doth the great Duke Humphrey knit his brows,
As frowning at the favors of the world?

ELEANOR, *2 Henry VI*, I.II.3

You have too much respect upon the world.
They lose it that do buy it with much care.

GRATIANO, *The Merchant of Venice*, I.I.74

Tell me, sweet lord, what is't that takes from thee
Thy stomach, pleasure, and thy golden sleep?
Why dost thou bend thine eyes upon the earth,
And start so often when thou sit'st alone?

Why hast thou lost the fresh blood in thy cheeks,
And given my treasures and my rights of thee
To thick-ey'd musing and curst melancholy?

LADY PERCY, *1 Henry IV*, II.III.40

Drew sleep out of mine eyes, blood from my cheeks,
Musings into my mind, with thousand doubts
How I might stop this tempest ere it came,
And finding little comfort to relieve them,
I thought it princely charity to grieve for them.

PERICLES, *Pericles*, I.II.96

Cease to lament for that thou canst not help,
And study help for that which thou lament'st.

PROTEUS, *The Two Gentlemen of Verona*, III.I.243

WRITING
see also ART; BOOKS; LETTERS; LITERACY; POETRY; STORYTELLING; WORDS

O, let me, true in love, but truly write,
And then believe me, my love is as fair
As any mother's child, though not so bright
As those gold candles fix'd in heaven's air.

SONNET 21, 9–12

O, know, sweet love, I always write to you,
And you and love are still my argument;
So all my best is dressing old words new,
Spending again what is already spent.

SONNET 76, 9–12

O, blame me not if I no more can write!
Look in your glass, and there appears a face
That overgoes my blunt invention quite,
Dulling my lines, and doing me disgrace.

SONNET 103, 5–8

This must crave
(And if this be at all) a most strange story.

ALONSO, *The Tempest*, V.I.116

Think not, although in writing I preferr'd
The manner of thy vile outrageous crimes,
That therefore I have forg'd, or am not able
Verbatim to rehearse the method of my pen.

DUKE OF GLOUCESTER, *1 Henry VI*, III.I.10

I'll call for pen and ink, and write my mind.

EARL OF SUFFOLK, *1 Henry VI*, V.III.66

'Tis most sweet
When in one line two crafts directly meet.

HAMLET, *Hamlet*, III.IV.210

These trees shall be my books,
And in their barks my thoughts I'll character,
That every eye which in this forest looks
Shall see thy virtue witness'd every where.

ORLANDO, As You Like It, III.II.5

Who cannot be crush'd with a plot?

PAROLLES, All's Well That Ends Well, IV.III.325

One vice but a minute old, for one
Not half so old as that. I'll write against them,
Detest them, curse them; yet 'tis greater skill
In a true hate, to pray they have their will:
The very devils cannot plague them better.

POSTHUMUS, Cymbeline, II.V.31

YOUTH
see also BABIES; CHILDREN; GROWING UP

Some say thy fault is youth, some wantonness,
Some say thy grace is youth and gentle sport;
Both grace and faults are lov'd of more and less:
Thou mak'st faults graces that to thee resort.

SONNET 96, 1–4

The colt that's back'd and burden'd being young,
Loseth his pride, and never waxeth strong.

Venus and Adonis, 419

A man loves the meat in his youth that he cannot endure in
his age.

BENEDICK, Much Ado About Nothing, II.III.238

Young blood doth not obey an old decree.

BEROWNE, Love's Labor's Lost, IV.III.213

My salad days,
When I was green in judgment.

CLEOPATRA, Antony and Cleopatra, I.V.73

Deal mildly with his youth,
for young hot colts being rag'd do rage the more.

DUKE OF YORK, Richard II, II.I.69

Rouse up thy youthful blood, be valiant and live.

JOHN OF GAUNT, Richard II, I.III.83

What? can so young a thorn begin to prick?

KING EDWARD, 3 Henry VI, V.V.13

O foolish youth,
Thou seek'st the greatness that will overwhelm thee.

KING HENRY IV, 2 Henry IV, IV.V.96

The canker galls the infants of the spring
Too oft before their buttons be disclos'd,
And in the morn and liquid dew of youth
Contagious blastments are most imminent.

LAERTES, *Hamlet*, I.III.39

She is young and apt.
Our own precedent passions do instruct us
What levity's in youth.

OLD ATHENIAN, *Timon of Athens*, I.I.132

Such a hare is madness the youth to skip o'er the
meshes of good counsel the cripple.

PORTIA, *The Merchant of Venice*, I.II.19

See how the morning opes her golden gates,
And takes her farewell of the glorious sun!
How well resembles it the prime of youth,
Trimm'd like a younker prancing to his love!

RICHARD, DUKE OF GLOUCESTER, *3 Henry VI*, II.I.21

Yet youth, the more it is wasted, the
sooner it wears.

SIR JOHN FALSTAFF, *1 Henry IV*, II.IV.401

You that are old
consider not the capacities of us that are young, you do
measure the heat of our livers with the bitterness
of your galls; and we that are in the vaward of our
youth, I must confess, are wags too.

SIR JOHN FALSTAFF, *2 Henry IV*, I.II.173

❧ GLOSSARY

This glossary offers definitions of idiomatic, archaic, and obscure words, expressions, and phrases that appear in quotations throughout this book.

Abram: reddish-brown
Accomodations: comforts
Aconitum: a poison
Adamant: lodestone, magnet
Additions swell's: titles inflate us
Adoption: allegiance
Adoption tried: proven friendship
Advanc'd: roused
Advertise: advise
Affected: inclined
Affection: desire, passion; character;
    instinctual feeling
Affections of delight: pastimes, plea-
    sures
Affiance: confidence
Against: expecting
Alarums: calls to arms
Alchymy: alchemy
Alder-liefest: most dear
Almsman's gown: poor person's
    clothes
Aloes: bitterness
Ambassage: message
Ambuscadoes: attacks
Ancientry: tradition
An end: on end
Anticly: wildly dressed

Antique: quaint
Apprehension: imagination
Apprehensive: intelligent
Approve: prove
Apricock: apricot
Araise: resurrect
Argument: main concern
Armipotent: well armed
Arrouse: gently sprinkle upon
Artificial: creative
Artless jealousy: wild suspicion
Assay: attempt
Assays of bias: indirect attempt
Ate: goddess of discord
At my beads: praying with my rosary
Atomi: tiny beings
Attax'd: blamed
Bald: stupid; trivial
Baldrick: sling
Ballet-mongers: ballad
Balls: eyes
Ban-dogs: dogs that are chained and
    confined
Banes: announcement of intention to
    be married
Bankrout: bankrupt
Barbed: armored

Barnes: children
Baseless fabric: structure lacking a
    physical dimension
Bate: dull; deduct
Bawcock: fine fellow
Beads: religious beads
Become disloyalty: make infidelity
    seem becoming
Before: ahead
Be gladded in't: be satisfied by pro-
    ducing an heir
Beguile the time: deceive the world
Behavior: proper manners
Beldame: old woman
Berrord: one who leads bears
Bett'ring: magnifying
Big compare: comparison to objects of
    grandeur
Biggen: nightcap
Bird-bolts: blunt-headed arrow used
    for bird-hunting
Black: dark complexioned
Blench: turn aside
Bodlein: dagger
Boist'rous: violent
Bonneted: removed their hats
Bosky: shrubbed, wooded
Bourn: place, region; boundary
Bravely: splendidly dressed
Braz'd: desensitized
Brazen: brass
Breather: living person
Breeching scholar: young pupil
Brook: endure
Brotherhoods: trade unions
Brown bill: rusty axelike weapon
Brow of Egypt: face of a gypsy
Bumbard: leather jug
Butt: tub
Buttons: buds
By lottery: by chance
Ça: that one
Cadent: falling
Callet: strumpet, scold
Candle-wasters: moralists, philoso-
    phers
Canker: canker-worm; wild rose

Canon: law
Canstick: candlestick
Cantle: portion
Capable of: susceptible to
Cap-and-knee slaves: subservient peo-
    ple who raise their hats and bow
    carelessly: without care
Captivate: to hold one against one's
    will
Carrions: people close to death
Carve: woo civicly
Case: exterior
Casted slough: old skin shed
Casualties: accidents
Cat-a-mountain: wildcat
Cautelous: deceitful
Censure: opinion
Ceres: goddess of agriculture
Certain: stable
Cess: death
Chaces: pursuits
Chafed: irritated
Chapless: jawless
Charnel-house: vault where old bones
    are stored
Charter of: right afforded by
Check: find offense in
Chev'ril: soft and pliable leather
Chez les narines de feu: with fiery nos-
    trils
Childing: fruitful, pregnant
Cinquepace: lively dance
Civet: perfume
Claw: flatter
Clear: cheerful, bright
Cleep: embrace
Close: [n] union; [v] heal
Cloyed will: sexual desire
Cockatrice: basilisk, monster
Cockled: possessing a shell
Coign of vantage: advantageous corner
Coil: turmoil
Coistrel: knave
Cold obstruction: utter stillness
Collop: chunk, portion
Compact: made of
Compass'd crest: neck's arched ridge

Complexion: one's physical and mental being

Con: memorize

Conceit: imagination

Condole: arouse pity

Confine: outer limit

Confined doom: limited duration

Confound: waste; lose

Confounding: destroying

Congreeing: agreeing

Congruent epitheton: appropriate adjective

Continents: bounds

Copesmate: companion

Coranto: quick running dance

Cormorant: ravenous

Corrival: partner

Costermongers: people involved in commerce

Couchings: bows

Coulter: knife

Countenance: approval

Countervail: equal

Cozen: dishonesty

Cozening: treacherous

Crafts: plots

Craves: demands

Cressets: meteors

Crisped: curled

Crudy: curded

Cry: pack of hounds

Cry aim to: urge onward

Cur: dog

Curdied: frozen

Current: real, not counterfeit

Curstness: bad temper

Curtal: dock-tailed

Curvets: hops on back legs

Cytherea: Venus

Dan: sir

Darnel: ryegrass

Dateless: eternal

Dear man: person who is noble

Debosh'd: debased

Deed of saying: promises fulfillment

Degrees: rank

Deliverly: nimbly

Demi-cannon: large cannon

Derancinate: root up

Descant: comment

Desert: unpeopled

Determinate: [v] conclude; [adj] no longer valid

Determines: allots to

Dew-lapp'd: with skin hanging from neck

Dial: sundial; watch

Displant: transplant

Disposed: is inwardly like

Disputation: exchange

Dissension of a doit: argument over trivial matter

Distains: tarnishes

Distemperatures: maladies

Distinction: discrimination

Division: variation on melody

Doublet: coat

Dress: prepare food

Dropsied: unhealthily swollen

Dry-beat: thrash without spilling blood

Dudgeon: wooden handle

Dunnest: darkest

Dying fall: slowing cadence

Ean: birth

Ear-bussing: whispered

Earthly godfathers: astronomers

Ecstasy: agitation

Egall: equal

Eglantine: sweet-brier, a variety of rose

Eld: old age

Emulation: envy

Enforced: violated

Engross: fatten

Engrossed: accumulated

Engrossing: all-encompassing

Enseamed: soaked in sweat

Ercles: Hercules

Erebus: dark realm between Earth and Hades

Erring: wandering

Estates: status

Estridge: a powerful ostrich

Even-pleach'd: neatly landscaped and interwoven

Example you: teach you through examples

Excess: interest

Excrement: physical appearance

Exercises: athletic activity

Express: exact

Exsufflicate: exaggerated

Extemporal: impromptu

Extenuate: made moderate; thinned

Eye wink at: be blind to

Fadom: fathom

Fairer eye: object of affection

Faithless error: treacherous lie

Fall: cadence

Fallow leas: unplanted fields

Fanatical phantasimes: people with wild imaginations

Fanes: temples

Fantastical: imaginary

Fardels: burdens

Fardingdales: hooped skirts of petticoats

Fashion in a carriage: fake a behavior

Fashion-monging: faddish in dress

Feater: elegantly

Featur'd: attractive

Fee: worth

Feel deeds: cruel acts

Feelingly: through the senses

Fee-simple: in control of oneself

Feigning: created by the imagination

Fell: cruel; violent; fierce

Femetary: fumitory (a weed)

Fetches: vetch (foddering plant)

Figur'd: ornate

Figures: conjured images

Fillop: strike

Find: understand

Fine: refined

Fineless: unlimited

Firstlings: first-born

Fitted: cast appropriately

Fixture: established position

Flag: iris

Flaw: brief windstorm

Fleckled: spotted

Flesh'd: fierce

Flew'd: hanging cheeks

Foison: plenty

Fond: foolish

Forked heads: two-pronged hunting arrows

Form: propriety

Forth: out

Fortune's star: nature's blemish

Forward: precocious

Four elements: earth, water, fire and air

Fracted dates: missed payments

Framing: creating

Freely: of its own accord

Frenzy: madness

Fresh numbers: new verses

Friends: family

Frisk: hop, leap

From prevention: being held back

Froward: obstinate, uncooperative

Fulsome: detestable

Furze: gorse (a plant)

Fust: grow moldy

Gall: injure

Gall of hazard: bitterness of fortune

General filths: prostitutes

Germane to: relative of

Gins: traps

Gins his reflection: begins to turn back

Girths: boundaries, walls

Glass: mirror

Glassy essence: a person's rational soul

Globe: head

God buy you: goodbye

Golden circuit: crown

Goose-quills: pens

Gossamers: spider webs

Got: begotten

Gouts: large drops

Graciously: by God's grave

Grant: gift

Graveness: dignity

Greatly: nobly

Great reckoning: large bill
Great'st: pharaoh
Green: fresh and growing
Greener: younger
Grin: bare teeth
Gripe: grasp
Grise: a level or step
Grudging stomachs: hostile tempers
Guerdon: martyrdom
Guiled: dangerous
Gust: gusto
Gyves: fetters
Habit: demeanor
Half-blown: half-opened
Hallowmas: All Saint's Day
Hare: timid
Harshness: disobedience
Hart: deer; heart
"Havoc!": war cry signaling destruction and looting
Hay: home thrust
Heart: spirit
Heath: heather
Heat-oppressed: feverish, crazed
Heavy: sorrowful
Heavy summons: sleepiness
Hedge: cheat
Heed: protection
Helpful ornament: beautiful lyrics
Heps: rosehips
Hesperides: garden of golden apples
Hest: directive, command
Hideousness: threatening
Hie: rush; quicken
Hiems: god of winter
High-sighted: arrogant
High top: topmost
Hind: female deer
Holds a trencher: waits tables
Holp: cured
Homely: plain, simple
Honest: honorable
Honorificabilitudinitatibus: Latin tongue-twister
Hoxes: hamstrings
Hulling: drifting
Humble: courteous

Humorous: moody
Humors: dampness
Hurricanoes: water spouts
Husbandry: thrift
Hushering: ushering
I am out: I've lost my place
Idly: indifferently
Imbecility: weakness
Immanity: horrible cruelty
Imperial charge: under King's pressure
Imp of fame: one of noble stock
Impress: impression
Incapable: unknowing of
Incarnadine: turn red
Incontinent: immediately
Incorporate: united
Incorrect: unsubmissive
Indian: dark-skinned
Indifferently: impartially
Indirection: dishonesty
Inductions: initial preparations
Inhoop'd: fighting in an enclosed space
Inly: inward
In power: capability
In project of: hoping for
Insisture: steadiness
Insuppressive: unquenchable
Intestate: dead without a will
Intrinse: intricate
Invention: ability to scheme
Jade: tired or inferior horse
Jets: struts
John-a-dreams: lethargic person
Juggler: sorcerer
Justling: turbulent
Jutty: projection of a building
Juvenal: youth
Kecksies: parsley plants
Kind manage: superior discipline
Knacks: ornaments
Kneaded clod: common mass
Knolls: rings, reverberates
Knot-grass: weed thought to be a growth-inhibitor
Lamps: eyes
Lank'd: grew thin, emaciated

Lapse in fullness: lie when rich
Large-handed: boundless, unrestrained
Lauds: hymns
Lave: wash
Law of children: changed at whim
Lays: songs
Leas: fertile land
Lease: term
Le cheval volant: the flying horse
    (Pegasus)
Leech: doctor
Lees: drags
Legerity: nimbleness, agility
Lethe: stream of death
Lethe: obliviousness
Letters: learning
Lettice: lattice
Leviathans: whales
Lichas: Hercules' servant
Light: wanton
Limed: trapped with bird lime
Lisp: speak with affectation
Little room: mediocre accomodations
Livers pale: sign of cowardice
Lodestars: guiding stars
Lowliness: humility
Lowly courtesies: low bows
Lowly feigning: pretended humility
Lurch: pilfer
Lust-dieted: indulgent
Luxurious: lecherous
Makeless: without a partner
Make the doors: shut the doors
Mandragora: an opiate
Mannerly-modest: moderate in tempo
Manners: character
Mansionary: nest
Market: profit
Martlet: martin; a swallow
Mast: acorns
Mates: suppresses, checkmates
Maw: stomach
Mealy: delicate; made of powder
Mean: in the middle
Measures: dances
Med'cinable: healing, correcting
Meed: reward

Mere anatomy: skeleton
Merely: completely
Meshes: nets
Mew'd up: caged
Mewling: crying
Mickle: wondrous; much
Minute-jacks: opportunistic people
Misthought: misjudged
Modern ecstasy: workaday feeling
Modern instances: clichéd illustrations
Moe: more
Monster'd: treated as if one were larger
    than life
Moody frontier: disdain expressed in
    one's forehead
Moody-mad: furious
Mop'd: dazed
Mortis'd: fixed
Mortise: joints
Motives: causes
Mountebank: quack
Muddy-mettled: drab
Muss: scramble
Mutton: slang for prostitute
Native: hereditary
Near aim: probability
Neglection: neglect
Nestor: grave Trojan hero
Nether: earthly
Nicely: meticulously
Noble carelessness: nobility's disinter-
    est
Noisome: foul-smelling
Nonage: minority
Not prizing: ignoring
Numbers: verses
Nurture: education
O'er-crows: defeats (from cockfight-
    ing)
O'er-leavens: corrupts
Obbraidings: upbraidings
Oblivious: causing forgetfulness
Obsequies: acts performed for the dead
Occurents: occurrences
One of thine: your child
On the hazard: at stake
Oppugnancy: opposition

Ordnance: cannon
Or ere: before
Ostent: appearance
Outfacing: insolent
Overblown: blown over
Overborne their continents: overflown
 their banks
Ovid: Latin poet of love
Ow'dst: had, owned
Owe: own
Oxlips: flowering plant resembling
 the cowslip
Pack: leave
Paint: flatter
Painted: artificial
Pale: park; enclosure
Pale cast: pallor
Palfreys: saddle horses
Pall: envelop
Palmer: pilgrim
Palter: lie, deceive
Pantaloon: doddering old person
Pard: leopard
Partialize: make prejudiced
Pass: thrust
Passado: forward thrust
Passion: grief
Path: continue onward
Pattern: draw precedent to
Peak: sulk
Peise: weigh
Pell-mell: with great vigor
Pensioners: royal bodyguards
Peregrinate: foreign
Peremptory: overbearing
Physical: good for one's health
Physics pain: cures discomfort
Picked: refined
Pick-thanks: noisy person
Plausive: pleasing
Play the wantons: frolic
Play truant: shift from serious matters
Poined and twilled: undercut by water
 and contained by branches
Point-devise: very precise
Pole-clipt: pruned
Police: pocket

Poltroons: cowards
Poor malice: feeble enmity
Porpentine: porcupine
Portcullis'd: grating blocking gateway
 of a castle
Pow'rs: people with influence
Precious instance: profound token
Prefer: present
Pregnancy: intellect
Pregnant: promising good fortune
Pregnant enemy: devil
Pregnantly: succinctly
Prepost'rously: out of natural order
Presence strow'd: royal presence-
 chamber strewn with rushes
President: model
Pressure: exact image
Prodigious: ominous
Promethean fire: heavenly fire
Proof: of proven strength
Propinquity: kinship
Propose: pretend, imagine
Provand: provisions
Puddings: sausages
Pudency: modesty
Punto reverso: backward thrust
Purblind: totally blind
Purge: seek a cure
Pursy: bloated
Put a strange face: not to admit
Quaintly: meticulously
Quern: tool used for grinding grain by
 hand
Questant: seeker
Quicken: give life to
Quietus: full discharge (legal term)
Quillets: nuances
Quit: revenge
Rack: stretch
Range: rank, live amongst
Rash: strike violently
Ravening: eating voraciously
Ravin: devour
Raz'd: scraped out, erased
Rechate: notes played on a hunting
 horn
Reck: pay attention to

Recoil: give way
Rectorship: rule
Rede: advice
Red-lattice phrases: alehouse slang
Redoubted: feared
Reek: sweat; unhealthy mist, fog
Reeky: damp, foul
Refuge their shame: protect them-
    selves from shame
Regreet: greet
Rent: tear
Rents: revenues
Repin'd: showed regret
Repining: begrudging
Replication: echo
Reproof: rebuff; disproof
Rere-mice: bats
Resolv'd correction: punishment pre-
    vented
Respect: consideration
Resting: unwavering
Revoultion lowering: sinking in our
    assessment
Rhapsody: hodge-podge
Rheumy: dank
Rich proud cost: magnificent monu-
    ments
Right form: normal military forma-
    tion
Rigor: tyranny
Ripe: immediate
Ripeness: readiness, maturity
Rive: explode; rend
Rooky: full of rooks
Ropery: knavery
Rough-hew: block them out
Round: plain
Roundel: dance
Round hose: breeches
Rub: obstacle, impediment
Runagate: fugitive
Sallet: raw vegetable
Sallied: sullied; solid
Sanded: sandy color
Sate: sat; waited
Saucy: insolent; arrogant
Savors: perfumes

Saws: aphorisms
Scandall'd: slandered; disgraced
Scanted: gave a little of
Scapes: escapes
Scathe: harm
Scorch'd: slashed, wounded
Scrambling: brawling
Scruple: very small unit of weight
Scutcheon: painted shield with noble's
    coat of arms exhibited at
Se'nnight: week
Season: preserve
Sedge: grass-like plant
Seek prevention: try to anticipate or
    second-guess
Seeling: blinding
Seely: simple, crude
Seem: dissemble
Self-breath: said by oneself
Self-mettle: natural vigor
Sells pardon from: damns
Sentence: aphorism
Serious in mortality: worthwhile in
    life
Set me light: devalue me
Shadowed livery: dark noble uniform
Shaping fantasies: active imaginations
Sheeds: sheds
Sheep's guts: violin strings
Shent: rebuked
Sherris-sack: sherry
Shive: slice
Shot: fee
Shows: appearances
Shuffle: act underhandedly
Silly: helpless
Silly-ducking observants: overly-duti-
    ful attendants
Simpleness: sincerity
Simples: components
Sinews: nerves
Single star: weak
Sixt: sixth
Slightly: readily
Slubber: do slovenly
Smoky cribs: hovels lacking chimneys
Sol: the sun

Soliciting: temptation
Sop: pulp
Sorteth: mingles
Sot: fool
Soul of adoration: admiration's secret
Sounding: being fully known, understood
Speed me: let me prosper
Speeds: wins
Spices: samples, examples
Spills: destroys
Spinners: spiders
Spitting: transfixing
Splenitive: impetuous
Sprite: ghost
Square: formulate
Stain: cover, hide
Stale: urine
Stanchless: insatiable
Starv'd: empty, trivial
Stell'd: fixed, painted
Sticking place: notch holding bowstring of crossbow
Stick'st not: hesitate
Sting: lust
Stint: halt
Stir: rigorous efforts
Stockish: wooden, unfeeling
Stocks: sticks, pieces of wood
Stomach: desire, taste
Stomachs: resentment
Stonish: astonish
Stood on ceremonies: cared about omens
Stover: winter hay
Strain: trait
Strave: eat away, paralyze
Streamer: banner
Strond: shore
Strooken: struck
Study help: learn to fix
Submission: confession
Suggestion: temptation
Sum up sum: calculate
Surfeit: grief, induced sickness
Surmise: imagined action
Swain: shepherd

Sway: order
Sweet mouth: sweet tooth
'Swounds: by Christ's wounds
Swounds: faints
Table: writing tablet
Take in: subdue
Taste: any trace
Taxation of homage: demand for tribute
Tear a cat: rant
Teem: to have children
Tell money: count
Tenures: real estate titles
Term: session
Terminations: words
Tetchy: cranky
Thought-executing: acting impulsively
Thrasonical: boastful
Threaden: made of thread
Thrift: profit
Thwart disnatur'd: obscenely unnatural
Tilth: agriculture
Timeless: untimely
Timely-parted: dead of natural causes
Time's flies: insects that only appear in good weather
Tithe-pig: pig paid as church dues
Told: counted
To season: at any one moment
Toy: trifle
Toys: whims
Traducement: slander
Traffic: trade
Trenched: cut
Trots hard: rides uncomfortably
True: trustworthy
True birth: innate goodness
Turtles: turtledoves
Unattained: objective
Unback'd: never ridden
Undergoing: courageous
Uneasy pallets: uncomfortable beds
Ungalled: unhurt
Unkind: not natural
Unpay: erase; repair

Unpregnant of: not motivated by
Unproportion'd: unfitting
Unpurged: unpurified
Unrespective sieve: garbage basket
Use: interest; custom; practice
Utt'red: put up for sale
Validity: ability to last
Valure: valor
Vanities forespent: past antics
Vanity: earthly pleasure
Vaulty: arched; tomb-like
Vaunt-couriers: heralds, precursors
Vaward: edge, outer boundary
Venom of suggestion: ill-natured gossip
Videlect: namely
Viewless: unseeable
Vild: base
Vizard-like: masklike
Vocatur: is called
Voluble: animated
Wag: dismiss
Wags: keeps on going
Wanton: [n] spoiled child; [v] sway amorously
Wants similes: lack comparisons
Waste: spend
Watch: stay up

Water-colors: flimsy excuses
Wave-worn basis bowed: cliff carved by ocean
Weeps: showers in dew
Well-favor'd: handsome
Whirligig: spinning top
Whitest: most pure
Wimpled: blindfolded
Windlasses: circular methods
Windy suspiration: panting
Wink: glimpse
Winks: blinds oneself to it
Without all: beyond any possibility
Without-door: outward
Witness'd usurpation: noticeable destruction
Wonted liveries: accustomed apparel
Woodbine: honeysuckle
Wordly: worldly
Worser genius: evil spirit
Wot: know
Wrack: destruction
Wrangler: opponent
Wreakful: vengeful
Wrest: subject forcibly
Writhled: wrinkled
Yare: quick
Younker: young man

❧ BY-WORK INDEX

*БBY-SPEAKER INDEX